BROADCASTING FOR WALES

BROADCASTING FOR WALES

THE EARLY YEARS OF S4C

ELAIN PRICE

UNIVERSITY OF WALES PRESS
2022

www.uwp.co.uk

British Library Cataloguing-in-Publication Data
A catalogue record for this book is available from the British Library.

ISBN 978-1-78683-964-0
eISBN 978-1-78683-965-7

Typeset by Marie Doherty
Printed by CPI Antony Rowe, Melksham, United Kingdom

Contents

List of Illustrations

List of Acronyms

ABS	Association of Broadcasting Staffs
ACTT	Association of Cinematograph, Television and Allied Technicians
AGB	Audits of Great Britain
BARB	Broadcasters' Audience Research Board
BBC	British Broadcasting Corporation
BBFC	British Board of Film Classification
BECTU	Broadcasting, Entertainment, Cinematograph and Theatre Union
C4	Channel 4
C4UK	Channel 4 UK
CBI	Confederation of British Industry
DCMS	Department for Digital, Culture, Media and Sport
ETB	Euskal Telebista
GTHPC	Dr Glyn Tegai Hughes Private Collection
HTV	Harlech Television
IBA	Independent Broadcasting Authority
IMG	International Management Group
IPA	Institute of Practitioners in Advertising
ITA	Independent Television Authority
ITCA	Independent Television Companies Association
ITN	Independent Television News
ITP	Independent Television Publications
ITV	Independent Television
JMPC	Dr Jamie Medhurst Private Collection
LWT	London Weekend Television
MIP TV	Marché International des Programmes de Television
NAR	Net Advertising Revenue
NSSAW	National Screen and Sound Archive of Wales
NUJ	National Union of Journalists
OBA	Open Broadcasting Authority
PACT	Producers Alliance for Cinema and Television

PMM	Peat, Marwick and Mitchell
RPI	Retail Price Index
RTÉ	Raidió Teilifís Éireann
RTS	Royal Television Society
S4C	Sianel Pedwar Cymru
S4CC	S4C Collection
SVOD	Subscription Video On Demand
TAC	Teledwyr Annibynnol Cymru
TG4	TG Ceathair
TVG	Televisión de Galicia
TWI	Trans World International
TWW	Television Wales and West
WAC	Written Archives Centre (BBC)
WASC	Welsh Affairs Select Committee
WCC	Welsh Consumer Council
WFCA	Welsh Fourth Channel Authority

Acknowledgements

I would like to thank a number of people for their support and assistance as I conducted this research. Firstly, I wish to thank the staff at S4C, past and present, who were especially helpful in assisting this research. In particular, I would like to thank Nia Ebenezer, Carys Evans, Iona Jones, John Walter Jones, Lynette Morris, Kathryn Morris, Jen Pappas, Gwyn Williams and Phil Williams for their help and support. I also wish to thank many of BBC Cymru Wales's staff, past and present for responding so helpfully to my queries, Siôn Brynach, Karl Davies, Edith Hughes, Keith Jones, Yvonne Nicholson and Menna Richards. I would like to thank James Codd at the BBC Written Archive Centre for his help and guidance during my visits to Caversham. Thanks also to Phil Henfrey, Shone Hughes, Elin Llŷr, Owain Meredith, Siôn Clwyd Roberts and Huw Rossiter at ITV Cymru / Wales for their help. I also wish to acknowledge the invaluable advice and support I received from staff at the National Library of Wales, National Screen and Sound Archive of Wales, the ITA/IBA/Cable Authority Archive in Bournemouth University and the Parliamentary Archives in Westminster.

I was very fortunate to meet and interview a number of individuals who were key to the Welsh broadcasting sector throughout the 1970s and early 1980s. I would wish to sincerely thank Wil Aaron, Huw H. Davies, Chris Grace, the late Dr Glyn Tegai Hughes, Sir Jeremy Isaacs, the late Geraint Stanley Jones, Eleri Wynne Jones, Huw Jones, Robin Lyons, Mair Owen, the late Rev. Dr. Alwyn Roberts and the late Euryn Ogwen Williams for sharing their time, memories and anecdotes and their generous support throughout. I also received invaluable help from the late Owen Edwards, who gave kindly of his time despite his ill health. Thanks are also due to the experts in the field who were also invaluably helpful, Ifan Gwynfil Evans, the late John Hefin, Dr Martin Johnes and Kevin Williams and a special thanks to Dr Jamie Medhurst for his continued guidance and for sharing and lending materials.

I'm indebted to the Centre for Welsh Medium Higher Education (now Y Coleg Cymraeg Cenedlaethol) for the funding to complete the PhD which is the basis of this monograph. I wish to thank all of the staff for their support both financial and otherwise during the research. Thanks too to the HEFCW Wales Studies Publication Fund, Swansea University for funding the publication of this monograph, to Gerwyn Wiliams for all his support and guidance with the original Welsh version of this volume, to Elin Lewis for her expert eye for detail in the proof reading of this volume and to all of the staff at the University of Wales Press for their enthusiasm and unstinting support during the publishing process.

I am always grateful to my colleagues in the Media and Communication team at Swansea University for their support, friendship and good humour. Thanks are also due to Dr Gwenno Ffrancon for all her guidance and patience as my PhD supervisor. Her friendship and support was key as I undertook this research.

Finally, I would like to thank my close friends and family, especially Mam, Dad, Elfyn, Guto, Branwen and Caio. But most of all I am beyond grateful to my husband Nick, and sons Gruff and Deian – there are no words which can fully express how thankful I am for their love, encouragement, patience and for inspiring me to continue with this work. *Diolch o waelod calon i chi'ch tri am bopeth.*

Dr Elain Price
Cardiff
February 2022

For Nick, Gruff and Deian

Introduction

Since its launch nearly forty years ago, Sianel Pedwar Cymru (S4C) has transformed broadcasting in Wales and entertained, educated and informed generations of viewers young and old. S4C is no ordinary channel: it was established due to a combination of political, social, cultural and linguistic reasons, and therefore its contribution must be considered in those complex terms and not solely on its appeal to the audience and its viewing statistics. No period in the channel's history illustrates this better than the trial period given to it between 1981 and 1985. The channel broadcasting today is very different to the one launched in 1982, but the struggle is the same as it ever was, namely the ongoing effort to ensure fair terms and a secure future for broadcasting Welsh language programmes on one designated channel. As government finances continue to be stretched, and with the prospect of significant change, not least due to the threats to the very existence of public service broadcasting, it is vital to look back at the channel's early foundational years in order to evaluate its successes and failures, and remember how and why these green shoots grew into a comprehensive service of programmes for the Welsh audience.

This volume, therefore, intends to analyse and interpret the history of establishing S4C as a new channel in the Welsh broadcasting landscape and the circumstances of forming a third broadcasting authority for Britain. It will look at the channel's probationary period in detail, taking into account the challenges faced by the new authority, and by channel officials and their staff as they designed and delivered a comprehensive Welsh language television service, formulated policies, and forged effective relationships with broadcasters and other programme producers. The volume will also reflect on the audience's reaction to the service and programmes by examining viewing figures and viewers' letters, and it will also consider how the Home Office reviewed the channel at the end of its 1985 trial period.

Nature of the volume

This volume is an institutional history and is therefore based on comprehensive empirical research which examined a combination of primary and secondary sources, press articles and interviews with key individuals. The volume is structured around a variety of previously unstudied documents in the form of the Welsh Fourth Channel Authority (WFCA) minutes and papers from 1981 to 1986, the correspondence of the chairman of the authority, Sir Goronwy Daniel, and that of the director, Owen Edwards. The minutes of the Independent Broadcasting Authority's (IBA) Welsh Committee and the BBC's Broadcasting Council for Wales, in addition to the joint meetings of these organisations with the S4C Authority were examined to ensure as comprehensive and multifaceted a picture as possible of the channel's achievements during the period under review.[1] In order to strengthen and augment the portrait of these early years, interviews were held with a number of individuals who were instrumental to S4C's development in its early years. Interviews were conducted with members of the authority, some of the channel's early officials and with individuals who were instrumental in implementing the channel's partnerships with the BBC, HTV, the independent producers and Channel 4 (C4),[2] thus seeking to ensure a fair representation of the organisations that were key to the initiative, and a range of perspectives to form a balanced portrayal of those events.

It is not, therefore, a study of the programmes broadcast on S4C, and any discussion of specific programmes depends on references to them in minutes, reports or correspondence. The channel's programmes merit an equally detailed study to consider the nature of productions during the early 1980s and the portrayal of Wales and the Welsh seen during that period. Neither is there an analysis of the provision of Welsh language programmes made in the days before S4C, nor very detailed analysis of the struggle to secure a Welsh language channel, but there is enough discussion to remind the reader of the context of its establishment. This is due to the fact that many writers, politicians, protesters, broadcasters and historians have already provided a comprehensive analysis of the many twists and turns of the campaign.[3] Rather, the greatest attention is given to the channel's activities after the protests came to an end, compensating, hopefully, for the lack of attention given to the activities of the channel's authority and officials in previous publications.

This volume, therefore, seeks to ensure that public understanding of S4C's early history is rooted in the study of primary sources, and that a detailed picture of the channel's successes and failures is discussed in all their complexity. It is entirely appropriate that a comprehensive study of

S4C be drawn up before stories and anecdotes become cemented as facts, and it is timely – given the upcoming fortieth anniversary of the channel and the recent debates surrounding its budget and the independence of the channel – for a study to be published on its formative years. This study also has an important role to play in ensuring that the memories, impressions and interpretations of some of the key individuals who were instrumental in building the foundations of the channel are preserved, providing significant context to newspaper reports and anecdotal evidence.

Structure

The opening chapter explores the context of the establishment of the channel, discusses the campaign by the protestors, the parliamentary debates in the form of the Crawford, Siberry, Annan and Trevelyan/Littler committee reports before moving on to a detailed analysis of the amendments introduced to the Broadcasting Act 1981 in order to incorporate William Whitelaw's U-turn to create the WFCA. The second chapter analyses what was achieved after the campaign, and considers the formation of the authority and its numerous activities during the months of preparatory work before broadcasting began in November 1982. It therefore includes a detailed discussion of the key decisions undertaken in forming the channel, analyses the crucial discussions with programme providers and C4, and the need to secure fair funding from the IBA to make the initiative a reality.

Chapter three focuses on the opening night and the first weeks of broadcasts, and considers the press's and audience's reaction to the output. It also discusses how the enthusiasm waned after the first few weeks of audience curiosity and the efforts of S4C staff to retain and attract more viewers. Chapter four looks at the constant struggle to secure suitable funding from the IBA to sustain the service and the other financial activities that the channel undertook through its Mentrau subsidiary. The volume concludes with an analysis of the opinion polls conducted during the probationary period and the most important appraisal of them all, the Home Office review in 1985 that would determine whether there was a future for Welsh language programming on one channel.

Minority-language broadcasting

Elin Haf Gruffydd Jones has described S4C as a 'trailblazer' of minority-language television broadcasting, which is undisputed since it stole the march on the launch of other European minority-language television stations.[4] S4C began broadcasting a whole two months before the launch of Euskal Telebista (ETB), the Basque television channel now known as ETB1, which launched on 31 December 1982 and started broadcasting regularly from 16 February 1983. The Catalan television channel TV3 also started broadcasting in 1983 and was soon followed by the Galician TVG in 1985.[5] Other Celtic language broadcasters, such as TG4, the Irish language broadcaster, did not launch until 1996 though RTÉ, in a similar fashion to broadcasting in Wales before S4C, had broadcast some Irish language programming from the early 1960s. TeleG launched in Scotland in 1999 and broadcast one hour of Gaelic language programmes per day, and was discontinued nearly two years after BBC Alba started broadcasting initially only on satellite; but when it was confirmed that BBC Alba would be available on Freeview in 2011 it took on the mantle of broadcasting in Gaelic.[6] TV Breizh launched in 2000 and broadcast a small amount of Breton language programmes, but these programmes had almost disappeared entirely by 2010. Further afield Māori Television did not launch until March 2004, but conversations were taking place nearly twenty years earlier between S4C and representatives of the New Zealand Māori Council, who were attempting to establish a television channel to broadcast Māori language and cultural programmes as early as 1985.[7]

Even though S4C was a pioneer and seen as an example that could be emulated, Jones has stated that S4C was very different from its fellow broadcasters who also launched in the early and mid-1980s. These channels were set up by the new parliaments of the autonomous communities in Spain, while S4C had been established by the UK Government even though Wales had rejected devolution in 1979. In Catalunya, Galicia and the Basque Country: 'regional autonomy and its broadcasting corporations mapped onto each other in a neat and corresponding pattern', while S4C developed to fit into the established British patterns of broadcasting.[8] There are other significant differences between S4C and the other pioneers, in that in the nearly four decades since they launched, several of the other minority-language broadcasters have introduced a range of other channels in their languages to serve the various interests of their audiences with specific news, sports and children's channels: for example, ETB has four channels broadcasting in both Basque and Spanish, and TV3 has six channels broadcasting in Catalan and some Spanish. While in Wales, apart from the short-lived S4C2 (1999–2010), growth has not progressed at the same pace.

S4C today

Whilst initially writing this study as a doctoral dissertation back in 2010, at the height of the channel's *annus horribilis*, the future of the channel was precarious because of the fundamental changes to the level and source of its funding. In the years leading up to 2010 the channel had received around £100 million annually from the government's Department for Digital, Culture, Media and Sport (DCMS), an amount linked to the retail price index (RPI) and thus grew steadily. But after the Conservative and Liberal Democrat coalition government's spending review, and what is now acknowledged as an eleventh-hour deal between the BBC and the government, without any consultation whatsoever with S4C, it was decided that from 2013 onwards the DCMS's funding of S4C would be cut by around 93 per cent.[9] The rest of the funding for the channel would come from the TV licence and the BBC would manage that contribution. But the money would not match the levels seen until 2010, and by 2020–1 S4C's funding was £74.5 million from the licence fee and £6.851 million from the DCMS.[10] This situation will change once again in 2022 with the DCMS contribution ending entirely and all of S4C's funding, apart from the income the channel generates from commercial ventures, coming entirely from the licence fee. At the time of writing the licence fee has been frozen until 2024, and even though S4C have been awarded an extra £7.5 million per annum towards digital output development, taking their annual income from the licence fee to £88.8 million, the future remains uncertain with the licence fee's future remaining precarious.[11] The desire by some in government to eliminate the licence fee has been described by Professor Richard Wyn Jones as an 'existential threat' to the Welsh language, since its demise threatens not only the funding of S4C, but also the £20 million the BBC spends on producing programmes for broadcast on S4C which would significantly impact the channel.[12] It also threatens the future funding of BBC Radio Cymru and since 'about 70% of all Welsh language media consumed are broadcast by BBC Radio Cymru' the demise of the licence fee could be disastrous for the language.[13]

Since the BBC now provides the lion's share of S4C's budget, the partnership between the two organisations has changed significantly, mainly because S4C is now accountable to the BBC for licence fee expenditure, sending the corporation a 'Financial Assurance Report' twice a year.[14] Fundamental questions were raised about S4C's independence after these changes were announced, with real concerns that the corporation would unduly influence S4C's editorial procedures and decisions. These fears were intensified by the fact that, initially, the BBC's national trustee for Wales, Professor Elan Closs Stephens, sat on the S4C Authority; however, that requirement came to an end in 2017 as the S4C governance structures were changed from an authority to a unitary board model.[15] Asking other broadcasters to fund S4C is not an original or revolutionary principle. In its early years S4C was funded by the ITV network and this was the pattern of funding throughout the 1980s. However, the channel remained independent and did not report to ITV companies since that money was distributed through the IBA. Neither did the funding come with any expectations that an ITV network member should be included on the S4C Authority, nor requirements for the channel to discuss its plans with that network's companies or seek permission before implementing specific policies.[16] The influence of the ITV network therefore did not weigh heavily on the channel's activities and S4C could set its priorities and create its own distinctive character.[17] Nor are partnerships a new notion for the channel: the history of the channel's probationary period shows that partnerships were key to that early success; however, the channel was not in partnership with one organisation, but several. Just as the IBA and ITV network were not able to influence the channel, neither could the other partners, the BBC and C4, unduly influence the channel as their representation on the authority did not allow them to dominate discussions. Such partnerships can be beneficial to S4C; what was understandably worrying, however, was that one organisation – the BBC – because of its status and size, may have dominated the authority and the channel's activities because of its role as a financier. In order to guard against this and protect S4C's editorial, managerial and operational independence, a formal operating agreement was published in January 2013 and revised in 2017.[18] By 2021 that partnership has grown and now also encompasses programme co-production, with *Y Gwyll/Hinterland* (Fiction Factory, 2013–16), *Un Bore Mercher/Keeping Faith* (Vox Pictures, 2017–21) and *Craith/Hidden* (Severn Screen 2018–) the most prominent examples of successful collaboration to produce back-to-back English and Welsh programmes for both broadcasters. Since late 2014, S4C programmes have also been made available through BBC iPlayer, which means that in addition to its own catch-up service Clic, Welsh language programmes from all of S4C's programme providers have been able to reach potentially larger audiences on the BBC's ubiquitous platform. In addition, from 27 January 2021, S4C's presentation was broadcast from the BBC's new headquarters in Central Square, Cardiff, following an agreement to share technical broadcast services to secure efficiencies and savings.[19]

The sharp cuts to the channel's budget since 2010 have led to other significant savings in staffing and the money spent on programmes. By 2015 the channel had lost the equivalent of 37.75 full-time staff and cut its overheads to 3.98 per cent of the budget; by 2020–1 that figure was down to 3.7 per cent.[20] In addition, by 2015 the average costs of new programmes commissioned had been cut by 39 per cent from £52,700 per hour to £32,200 per hour.[21] By 2020–1 that cost had increased to £45,562, with an increase in the cost per hour of all programme genres, apart from religious programming. The recent increase reflects the not insignificant impact of COVID-19 on production costs.[22] The number of repeats broadcast have also risen from 50 per cent in 2013 to 57 per cent in 2015 as a decision was made to maintain the number of broadcast hours despite the significant budget cuts.[23] That figure has now risen to 67.6 per cent in the most recent annual review period, a figure that is undoubtedly higher due to the challenges the broadcast sector faced because of the limitations placed on production during the pandemic.[24] The impact of the cuts seen since 2010 can be consequently seen directly on screen, as fewer new programmes are commissioned and the service has become increasingly repetitive.

The impact is also reflected in some of the channel's viewing figures: for example, the weekly reach for Welsh speakers in Wales viewing on a television set has fallen from 187,000 in 2013–14 to 150,000 in 2020–1.[25] There is a similar pattern for all Wales viewers too with a drop from 383,000 in 2013–14 to 321,000 in 2020–1; however, this figure is an increase on the figures for the previous financial year.[26] The picture is more encouraging beyond Wales's borders, where weekly viewing of the channel increased exponentially, from 168,000 in 2013–14 to 502,000 in 2020–1.[27] The picture is even more encouraging given the viewing now taking place online, with 1,881,000 hours viewed on BBC iPlayer, a 20 per cent increase on the previous year, and 819,000 hours viewed on Clic, a 45 per cent increase on the previous year.[28] Online viewing is even more encouraging if the figures for viewing on Facebook and YouTube are taken into account, at 280,300 and 322,800 hours respectively.[29] These figures show that the channel's audience is changing. Welsh speakers are increasingly living in mixed-language households, and the viewing sessions on a traditional family set are diminishing. Watching Welsh language programmes is therefore becoming a much more individual experience as many turn to Clic, BBC iPlayer or other social media and streaming platforms to watch online. It is also apparent that there is a growing demand for Welsh language provision beyond the borders of Wales, as Welsh people in England and beyond are drawn to watching the channel's programmes.

S4C, similarly to all public service broadcasters, is facing the challenge of attempting to appeal to a very mobile and changing audience and the ever-present competition from an increasing range of global streaming services. The channel has so far responded by developing programme strands for specific audiences, such as the online service Hansh, and in 2020–1 it employed its own journalists and launched its own digital news service Newyddion S4C, producing original news stories and re-packaging items from its *Newyddion S4C* TV programme. However, as ever, there are considerable hurdles ahead. As mentioned, securing suitable and adequate funding remains a substantial challenge, especially given the precarious future of the licence fee. In addition to this, the phenomenal growth in available content in the increasingly competitive world of streaming and a revolution in viewing habits has made it tougher for public service broadcasters to compete.[30] In this climate, public service broadcasters are being required to justify their existence in the face of the dominance of global streaming services such as Netflix, services that are very difficult to compete with in terms of scale given that: 'it is estimated that 209 million households now have a Netflix subscription, whilst BBC iPlayer only has a potential domestic reach of some 28.1 million households. To put that another way, BBC iPlayer's audience is only 13.4% the size of Netflix's audience.'[31] With further consolidation of ownership amongst many of the large media conglomerates bringing more viewer data, which drives the personalisation model that is key to the business of Subscription Video On Demand (SVOD) platforms, under the control of the main companies, it makes it close to impossible for the BBC, let alone a small minority-language broadcaster such as S4C, to compete with the viewing experience offered by the SVOD platforms.[32]

However, there are also opportunities afforded by the current media landscape. Public service broadcasters and media are highly valued by their audiences. This is especially true of S4C's core audience, with Welsh viewers awarding the channel an appreciation index score of 82 (out of 100) in comparison with their score of 78 for other public service broadcasting channels in Wales.[33] There are also positives to be found in the audience's belief that S4C is the channel that most accurately reflects what it is like to live in Wales, with 79 per cent of those surveyed agreeing with this statement.[34] In an increasingly global world with a global television offering, this gives S4C an unique opportunity to stand apart and speak to its audience in Wales and beyond about what it is to live in Wales in the twenty-first century. To face these opportunities S4C has a new chief executive, Siân Doyle, who from 1 January 2022 became the eighth to lead the channel through increasingly choppy waters. We are on the brink of change, but how radical those changes will be, only time will tell. The only thing that is absolutely certain is that we are in an equally unpredictable and anxious period as that of the birth of the channel in the early 1980s.

1

The campaign for a Welsh TV channel

The circumstances of S4C's birth were completely unique, since it is a channel won by the voice of the people rather than the wishes of politicians or industry; because of this, close attention has been paid to the campaign by various authors already. The same is also true of the contribution of the BBC, TWW, Teledu Cymru and HTV to Welsh language broadcasting before the arrival of S4C. This chapter is therefore intended to revisit some of the main events of the campaign to establish S4C to remind the reader of the context, focusing on the parliamentary debates held in the form of the Crawford and Annan committees and the Siberry and Trevelyan/Littler working groups, the broadcasters' attitudes to the fourth channel and the events of the years 1979–80, which were a turning point in the campaign. The chapter ends with a detailed analysis of the Broadcasting Act 1981 that would bring Sianel Pedwar Cymru into existence.

The origins of the fourth channel

In the late 1960s and early 1970s there was general awareness amongst the broadcasting industry and the public that a licence for a fourth channel had not been utilised by the UK Government. Maggie Brown noted in her volume on the history of Channel 4 (C4): 'Television sets in the late 1960s came with four buttons ... but the fourth was blank, even though there was capacity for another service. It was known as the empty channel and became a growing source of vexation.'[1] It is possible to trace the possibility of adding a fourth channel to the British broadcasting network back to the 1962 Pilkington Committee report.[2] When the committee reported on the future distribution of wavelengths, despite its harsh criticisms of ITV, it was proposed that the network could secure an additional channel, but only after proving its understanding of the main objectives of broadcasting. For several years following the publication of the report discussions about the future of the fourth channel were pushed to the bottom of the political agenda, first by the Harold Wilson Labour government and then by the Conservative government of Edward Heath. By the time the idea was revived in the early 1970s, a number of other groups were interested in the fourth channel. These groups were lobbying against the idea of creating an ITV2 because they wanted the channel to enrich the broadcasting landscape and provision in the UK, by producing or commissioning programmes that appealed to minority audiences, and ensuring that alternative points of view could be heard.[3] There was growing dissatisfaction amongst members of the industry and parts of the audience, as this statement by Anthony Smith,[4] member of the TV4 Campaign and one of the most prominent voices in favour of breaking the broadcasting duopoly in Britain shows:

> You have to understand the role of the duopoly and why it became a tremendous vexation for thousands of people. The point was that society was no longer homogeneous. There were a great many different interest groups – the 1960s had shown that – but the screens were not catching up . . . we were all made to believe the broadcasting we were getting was very good. I suppose it was by international standards; but it was all in the hands of this rather well-paid, superior civil-service class . . . They couldn't hear, literally and metaphorically, what was going on around them, what demands were really being made – demands that their comfortable duopoly was able to frustrate.[5]

Anthony Smith would go on to outline a plan that would provide the foundations for the new channel, an idea dubbed the National Television Foundation.[6] In an article published in *The Guardian* on 21 April 1972 he proposed radical ideas for the new channel: one of the most important elements of the proposal was that the broadcasting organisation would not produce its own programmes but, instead, commission programmes from outside producers. It would widen the scope of broadcasting in Britain, ensuring that new voices, who were not part of the large organisations of the BBC and ITV, could be heard. That core concept of providing key opportunities for a variety of new voices developed to be the cornerstone of the service eventually created, and also had a significant influence on the fourth channel in Wales, changing the established patterns of broadcasting in the UK.

The debates in Wales concerning the potential opportunities offered by the channel were different. Cymdeithas yr Iaith's (Welsh Language Society) broadcasting campaign started at the end of the 1960s with a call for an increase in hours of Welsh language programming, mainly on the BBC, since HTV had only just started broadcasting.[7] But it wasn't until the early 1970s that their formal policy on broadcasting was created, with the aim of claiming more than just additional Welsh language programming from the networks. At the society's general meeting in 1969 the following policy was agreed: 'That we demand from Government a national channel for Wales for Welsh language television programmes, in addition to the channel for non-Welsh speakers, and a wavelength for Welsh language radio programmes'.[8]

This campaign heralded a much more strategic feel to the society's work, pamphlets were published (many authored by the writer, former lecturer and television drama director, Emyr Humphreys), discussing broadcasting in Wales and suggesting action plans on how broadcasting structures could be adapted to benefit the Welsh language.[9] In addition to the policy and strategy work, there were extended periods of campaigning and direct protests:

> Rallies and protests were held at the broadcasting centres of the BBC and HTV and at the offices of the Independent Broadcasting Authority; members scaled television transmitters and interfered with broadcasts; radio programmes were broadcast on the illegal wavelength 'Y Ceiliog' (The Cockerel); the proceedings of both the House of Commons and the House of Lords were disrupted; and television studios and broadcasting stations in Wales and England were broken into and equipment damaged.[10]

Over the course of the campaign over fifty campaigners were imprisoned for such direct action, with sentences ranging from a night in prison to a year in custody.[11] The most successful and effective element of the campaign was the support given to the call for the people of Wales to refuse to pay their radio and television licences. The campaign drew new members to the society, with teachers, lecturers, ministers of religion and other professionals extending their support in this way.[12] The respectability associated with many of the campaigners' occupations was key to ensuring credibility to the campaign; this was also instrumental in contributing to the impression that the government was rapidly losing the support of 'moderate opinion' in the context of broadcasting in Wales.

Although the campaign succeeded in persuading large numbers of Welsh people that the best conditions for the language would be found by securing a separate channel for Welsh language programmes, not everyone agreed. There was a group of influential and passionate Welsh men and women, that included Professor Jac L. Williams, Jennie Eirian Davies, Sir Alun Talfan Davies and Alun R. Edwards of HTV, who disagreed with the statement that a separate channel would benefit the Welsh language. Jac L. Williams warned that the Welsh language would suffer if programmes were pushed to 'the understairs cupboard of the fourth channel'.[13] It was felt that the Welsh language would lose out if non-Welsh-speaking viewers and Welsh speakers who were not necessarily passionate about the language were isolated from Welsh language programmes completely: a Welsh ghetto would be created to the further detriment of the language.[14] Instead, this group recommended increasing the number of hours of Welsh language programmes broadcast on the popular channels, BBC Wales and HTV Wales, in order to ensure that everyone was exposed to the language. But, with tensions between Welsh speakers and non-Welsh speakers increasing, such a plan was likely to make the situation worse.[15] These individuals were in the minority and the campaign for a separate channel saw support from unexpected factions, such as Labour MPs, like George Thomas and Leo Abse, who were known to be unsupportive of the Welsh language. Some were concerned that preventing the demise of the language was not the motive for these individuals, but rather that they were eager to see the Welsh language pushed aside and disappearing entirely from BBC Wales and HTV schedules. Aneirin Talfan Davies vocalised these worries by stating: 'When I see Mr George Thomas and Mr Leo Abse . . . rushing to embrace Dafydd Iwan, I would suggest that it is only the most naïve of people who would believe that their motives are the same.'[16] Despite these fears, the support of non-Welsh-speaking groups was an integral part of the final decision to set Welsh language programmes on the fourth channel, since they were vociferous in their complaints about network programmes being unavailable for them to view in Wales.

Parliamentary committees

In addition to all of the discussions held amongst broadcasters, politicians and the citizens of Wales during the 1970s, two parliamentary committees and two working groups were established to research and discuss the future of broadcasting in Britain. Although the focus of terms of reference of each was different, every committee had something special to say about broadcasting in Wales and how social tensions could be alleviated. The Crawford Committee was established in 1973, chaired by Sir Stewart Crawford, former deputy undersecretary of state for the Foreign and Commonwealth Office, to mainly consider regionalism and questioned the extent to which the broadcasting services met the needs of viewers in the nations and regions.[17] The committee received evidence from a number of small and large Welsh organisations, showing the genuine concerns felt by many Welsh residents about the state of the broadcasting system and its importance in their lives. They received evidence from both sides of the argument, and though the Crawford Committee considered increasing the number of Welsh language programmes broadcast on the main channels, they concluded that the bulk of the evidence called for Welsh language programmes to be placed on a separate channel.[18] The committee was persuaded by the evidence that the circumstances in Wales were much more critical than in the rest of Britain, especially in terms of the future of the Welsh language. Therefore, they felt that the fourth channel should be released for Welsh language programming as soon as possible:

> We give the highest priority in this field to a solution of the Welsh-language problem by the use in Wales of the Fourth Channel. And recommend that this should be undertaken, without waiting for a decision on its introduction in the rest of the country, and should not be delayed by restrictions on capital expenditure.[19]

The committee also recommended that the BBC and HTV's Welsh language programmes be transferred to the new channel, and that a subsidy be provided to enable an increase in the number of hours produced to 25, from the 13 hours broadcast in 1974. The committee believed that the subsidy would be a worthy investment:

> The cost would represent an investment in domestic, cultural and social harmony in the United Kingdom; the money spent would, in effect, be aimed at supporting within the home the other central

> and local government expenditure which is being incurred to satisfy Welsh aspirations.[20]

The Crawford Committee had begun to understand the nature of the broadcasting problem in Wales, and its members fully understood the importance for any Welsh language service to broadcast programmes of an equal standard to those broadcast in English if it was to attract and retain viewers.[21] Despite Crawford's clear support, the committee's recommendations were both a boost and a hindrance to the campaign for a separate channel for Wales, ironically, because the proposals met many of the campaigners' requirements. Alwyn D. Rees announced in his editorial column in *Barn* that the Welsh had 'Won the Television Battle' and Cymdeithas yr Iaith noted that 'there was little appetite for serious direct action . . . when everyone was under the impression that a big victory had been won'.[22]

As part of the government's commitment to the Crawford Committee's recommendations, a working group was established in January 1975 under the chairmanship of Mr J. W. M. Siberry, a former undersecretary to the Welsh Office, to consider how the establishment of the fourth channel in Wales could be realised. The working group report shows that members continued to consider that programmes for the fourth channel should be produced exclusively through the BBC and HTV. The idea of interweaving the programmes produced by both broadcasters together was rejected, and it was noted that the week should be split in half. It was recommended that HTV should broadcast on Mondays, Wednesdays and Fridays and the BBC on Tuesdays, Thursdays and Saturdays, and Sundays would be split between the two.[23] This pattern was convenient to ensure that advertisements could be placed between HTV programmes without disrupting the BBC's provision; but, ultimately, this was a wasteful solution since it would lead to the duplication of resources on both sides.[24] Despite the obvious divide between providers there was a desire to establish a single presenting approach and a similar pattern of programming throughout the week. There was strong disagreement on this issue from the BBC and HTV, since the BBC wished to programme its output in a block in order to ensure that they were known as the corporation's programmes, while HTV wanted to distribute its output across the schedule, broadcasting programmes for women during the day, reserving late afternoon for children's programmes, and so on.[25] One of Siberry's main recommendations was that 25 hours of Welsh language programming should be broadcast each week, double what was broadcast at the time and exactly the number the campaigners were calling for. Despite the positive report from Siberry, it was published during difficult financial times for the government who were reluctant to spend on new initiatives. In addition, another broadcasting committee, the Annan Committee, chaired by Lord Noel Annan, provost of University College London (1966–78), was already debating the future of British broadcasting and, as a result, the recommendations of the Siberry working group were not actioned.

The issue of the fourth channel in Wales was not discussed in detail by Annan, as John Davies states in his volume: 'As the government had by then accepted the Crawford Report and had established the Siberry working party, the Committee's members assumed that, at least where Wales was concerned, the fourth channel issue had already been settled.'[26] The Annan report recommended that the fourth channel be given to the Open Broadcasting Authority (OBA), a national organisation that would commission programmes from bodies such as the Open University, ITV companies and independent companies meeting the expectations of Anthony Smith and the TV4 campaign.[27] The report recognised that the OBA was unlikely to be ready to start broadcasting until the early 1980s,[28] and therefore in Wales it suggested that the proposals of the Siberry working group should be implemented with the fourth channel being placed in the care of the BBC and HTV before being transferred to the OBA when it was established. In essence Annan reinforced what had been recommended by Crawford in 1974, but it can also be argued that the report weakened the argument by the use of inconclusive language in the report: 'The proposals of the Siberry Working Party for establishing a fourth television channel in Wales broadcasting in the Welsh language *should be implemented as soon as the Government can find the necessary finance*.'[29] This offered the government a course to avoid making a decision at a time of financial difficulty.[30] Many also saw that the transfer of the Welsh language channel into the hands of the OBA when it was operational would be problematic, as it moved further away from the concept of creating a 'Welsh language channel' and a separate broadcasting authority for Wales. It was criticised in Cymdeithas yr Iaith's 'Teledu Cymru i Bobl Cymru' pamphlet in these terms: 'the aim of the Report seemed to be to find a way of keeping Welsh language broadcasting within the grasp of British infrastructure'.[31] Annan was also likely to have been influenced by Professor Jac L. Williams's powerful argument, as the report declared:

> The Siberry Working Party envisaged that there would be no programmes in Welsh on the other television services; but we would regret it if all Welsh language programmes were banished to the fourth channel and we think it would be the worse for the Welsh language and the heritage of Wales.[32]

Annan, therefore, dismantled the consensus that had been created between Crawford and Siberry for the future of broadcasting in Wales. The fragile consensus was further shattered by the next working group, chaired by Dennis Trevelyan, which was created in order to update Siberry's work, as that had become dated due to delays in implementing its recommendations.[33] The government was keen to show that it was taking some action on the issue of a Welsh television channel, despite having concluded, in the 1976 public expenditure review, that such spending could not be justified by the state's financial austerity.[34] Members of the working group included a number of Home Office broadcasting department staff, along with two BBC representatives, Owen Edwards, controller BBC Wales and G. D. Cook, the corporation's head of transmitter engineering, and two representatives of the ITV network, Anthony Pragnell, deputy director general of the Independent Broadcasting Authority (IBA) and Aled Vaughan, HTV's director of programmes for Wales.[35] The era of ambitious principles and ideas was now over, and here was an opportunity for those who knew the ins and outs of the broadcasters' operations to bring a measure of realism to the discussions regarding establishing a Welsh language channel. The working group discussed matters for 14 months and when the report was published, Dr Glyn Tegai Hughes declared that it was nothing more than a diluted version of the Siberry report.[36] Glyn Tegai Hughes was undoubtedly provoked in this regard given that the working group had been discussing 21 hours of Welsh language broadcasting, rather than the 25 hours previously recommended.[37] This was justified by the working group, who stated that it was keen to see the growth in Welsh language broadcasting set on firm foundations: 'the gradual build-up of resources in terms of finance, human resources and studio capacity would enable the respective broadcasting organisations to provide their contributions to the Welsh language service in a smooth and controlled manner'.[38] The implication here is that the Welsh language service could be fettered with unsustainable heavy production requirements, and that, as a result, it would fail. The figure of 25 hours had become symbolic, due to it being a significant increase in Welsh language programming, with the Siberry report stating that there was no point in establishing an independent Welsh language service unless it started from that basis. But to reach that hallowed figure there was desperate need for more studio space, additional technical facilities and the employment of nearly 400 additional staff, developments that could not be actioned overnight.[39] It is also clear that the financial context of the late 1970s had a significant impact on the working group's discussions, since it recommended an initial expenditure that was less than half the investment recommended by Siberry.[40]

John Davies argues that the influence of the working group was significantly diminished by the government publishing their White Paper on broadcasting – and adopting much of Annan's recommendations – on the very same day as the publication of the Trevelyan/Littler report.[41] But in fact a detailed study of the recommendations of the 1978 Broadcasting White Paper shows that the working group's influence on government plans had been significant. The government adopted the working group's approach to gradually developing the number of hours of Welsh language programming to ensure quality rather than quantity. It stated:

> The Government agrees that, in all the circumstances and in view of the need to get the project started, it would be desirable to begin the service at a somewhat lower level than envisaged in the Siberry proposals, adding to it from time to time as appropriate.[42]

The clause that detailed the governance of Welsh language broadcasting also took the government further from Annan's suggestions. It disagreed with Annan's plan to transfer Welsh broadcasting responsibilities on the fourth channel to the British OBA service when that authority was established. Instead, the White Paper stated:

> It would be wrong, moreover, to treat the Welsh language service in isolation from English language programmes originating in Wales, whether these come from the BBC, from the independent system or from the OBA. For these reasons, the Government considers that it would not be appropriate to treat the Welsh language television service of the fourth channel as a service to be provided and supervised exclusively by the OBA: it should be treated as a national service for Wales to which all three broadcasting

> organisations will have an identifiable contribution to make and with the management of which all three broadcasting authorities will need to be associated.[43]

It was the government's intention to form what became known as the Welsh Language Television Council, with members of BBC Wales, the IBA, ITV (which meant HTV) and the OBA sitting on it, with an OBA member acting as chairman.[44] This was a significant step forward for the campaign, as it introduced an organisation that would oversee broadcasting in Wales. It was clear that not all of Annan's recommendations were adopted, and the White Paper offered hope and disappointment to the campaigners at the same time.

Looking back at the contributions of these many committees, it must be emphasised that all, with the exception of the Trevelyan/Littler report, recommended schemes that met the expectations of the campaigners in Wales and had noted the importance of prioritising the requirements in Wales before the rest of Britain. Having said that, none of them provided enough impetus for the government to urgently create a Welsh language channel. They had, at times, made things problematic for the campaigners since they created the impression that the government was listening to the wishes of the Welsh community, making it difficult to persuade people to continue their protests demanding a Welsh channel. However, it could also be argued that they all contributed to the success of the campaign by making the demands and the difficulties faced by the Welsh language due to the shortcomings of the television service in Welsh credible to a broader audience.

The perspective of the broadcasters

The BBC's approach throughout the period of the campaign to establish a Welsh language channel was, almost without exception, to support the principle of transferring Welsh language programmes to one channel seeing as, in the words of Alwyn Roberts, 'the BBC was largely influenced by its perception of the difficulty of satisfying any part of its audience by the existing practice of opting out of network schedules to provide a service for its Welsh viewers'.[45] The failure to meet the needs of the audience was clear to the corporation in Wales, due to the persistent correspondence received from the Welsh-speaking and non-Welsh-speaking audience. The substitution of English language programmes for Welsh language ones provoked exceptionally strong feelings amongst the audience:

> It is not easy for those who did not receive this kind of correspondence to believe the rancour and the bitterness which it revealed. It suggested that the question of broadcasting had become a cancer in Welsh life leading not only to the protests and counter protests which marked the period but also to a festering bitterness in the minds of many individuals and for every one who wrote, there were probably a hundred who shared the view and the resentment.[46]

The BBC, therefore, had to be careful when trying to extend the provision of Welsh language programmes. It also appears that the BBC held back with developments for Welsh-medium audiences to avoid further annoyance to the non-Welsh-speaking audience:

> In 1975, the corporation was producing nearly seven hours in Welsh a week; it acknowledged that it had the resources to produce nine hours, but it had refrained from doing so in order to avoid increasing the antagonism of the English-speaking Welsh.[47]

The interests of the Welsh language were not the BBC's only consideration: the transfer of Welsh language programmes to a new channel would also allow BBC1 to be relaunched in Wales as a channel for non-Welsh speakers in order to attract the thousands of viewers who had turned their aerials to receive broadcasts from over the border.[48]

The BBC did not support the campaigners' calls verbatim, however. The corporation did not, for example, support the establishment of a separate broadcasting authority for Wales, due to the possibility of devolution and the establishment of a Welsh assembly. The rationale behind these arguments – and the same sentiments were discussed in Scotland – was the concern that the parties in power in the devolved nations would seek to influence the broadcasting system of that nation. Since the politics of Scotland and Wales were both dominated in the 1970s by the Labour Party, there was a real likelihood, for some, that one political party would succeed in influencing and controlling the media in addition to the possible new systems of government in those countries.[49]

HTV's approach to utilising the fourth channel for Welsh language programming, on the other hand, could be described as going against mainstream public opinion. Given the ITV network's hierarchy and management systems, it could be claimed that the attitudes of its regulatory body, the IBA, influenced views expressed publicly by HTV. The attitudes of the other ITV network companies also weighed heavily and influenced HTV's approach, without forgetting the different views amongst the company's Welsh board members. The fact that the BBC was able to 'win' an additional channel following the Pilkington report was considered a slight on the ITV network companies and there was a feeling amongst them that the BBC had received favourable treatment by government when they launched BBC2. When the time came to discuss adding a fourth channel to the UK television network during the 1970s, ITV companies thought that this was their chance to be placed on an equal footing with the BBC. The prospect of a new channel on which advertising space could be sold was too tempting to ignore and they saw it as an opportunity to redress this perceived unfairness. ITV companies were keen to expand the nature of the programmes they produced in order to offer more comprehensive coverage and extend the programmes available to minorities.[50] Despite these commendable claims, the programmes that ITV companies had in mind were programmes covering minority interests in music, art, books, golf and industrial affairs, rather than programmes for those who were not catered for, such as ethnic minorities and the gay community. Despite this misconception about the nature of the word 'minority', the attitude of the commercial companies is evident in this statement: 'ITV today takes the field against the BBC with one arm tied behind its back.'[51]

HTV believed that there were additional reasons why the use of the fourth channel was important to the company when broadcasting in Wales. They saw an opportunity to attract viewers back from the other companies that were 'trespassing' on their territory, such as Granada, by moving the Welsh language content off the main ITV channel which was considered to disrupt English language provision for non-Welsh speakers on HTV Wales. To push this argument HTV would claim that these schemes were in the best interests of Wales and the Welsh language, adopting the ghetto argument and highlighting the dangers of installing Welsh language programmes on one channel. They emphasised that there was a need to look beyond the immediate satisfaction that would arise from moving the Welsh language from existing channels. They argued that consideration should be given to the fact that the fourth channel would, in due course, be launched across the UK with English language programmes, which would certainly appeal to some groups in Wales, but those programmes would not be available to watch because of the Welsh content that was broadcast there. Lord Harlech, chairman of HTV, argued:

> It would also be the best solution for Wales ... The alternative solution rising out of the Crawford Committee would mean confining Welsh exclusively to a single channel of its own with damaging consequences for the language while at the same time depriving the English-speaking Welsh of a service which at some state [*sic*] would be available to the whole of the rest of the U.K. I cannot think that this result would promote social harmony in the Principality.[52]

Many prominent Welsh citizens who were members of HTV's Welsh board were also convinced that the two-channel principal was the best solution for the Welsh language. On the board were individuals such as Dame Amy Parry-Williams, Sir Alun Talfan Davies and Alun Llywelyn Williams. But as Geraint Talfan Davies testifies: 'HTV found itself out of step with prevailing opinion.'[53] HTV were also going against the views of the IBA's Welsh committee which supported the idea of a single Welsh channel. The Welsh committee disagreed with the standpoint of the authority's main committee for much of the 1970s, which held the same view as the ITV network companies.[54] This policy led to intense protest against HTV and against prominent individuals associated with the company, especially at the National Eisteddfod, such as in 1980, when the broadcaster's stand was destroyed.[55]

HTV's attitude during this period could be described as changeable, or, perhaps even, opportunistic. The company's main argument was that Welsh language programmes should appear on two channels, but, following the publication of the Crawford, Annan and Siberry reports, HTV set aside these aspirations in order to follow the recommendation that Welsh language programming should be placed on a separate channel. But with all of the delays between the publication of the committee recommendations and their implementation, HTV and the ITV network were given a glimmer of hope that the official view might change, and that ITV2 could be realised after all. HTV was then seen to resurrect their view that sharing Welsh language programming between two channels would be the best solution for Wales:

> The Government's suggestions are in harmony with HTV Wales's views, views that have been company policy since the start of the fourth channel discussions, although it is true to say that HTV has been ready as we should be, to work together to implement the previous Government's plans of transmitting all HTV and BBC Welsh language programmes on one channel. However, the company has never believed that this would be the best course of action. HTV has not 'changed its mind' about the issue.[56]

HTV was therefore being pragmatic in responding to developments in the discussions surrounding the fourth channel. The company pushed its ideas when the door was ajar, but accepted that it was necessary to work within the policy priorities agreed by successive governments in order to remain part of any benefits connected to the broadcasting of Welsh-medium programmes. This attitude was to be expected and is wholly acceptable for any commercial company as it adapts its plans to the changing circumstances of the industry. Had HTV's Welsh board and officials unquestionably accepted the arguments for a separate Welsh language channel, when there was an opportunity to try to secure the fourth channel for ITV's use, the company would have disregarded its responsibilities to its shareholders and its fellow ITV companies. It was also clear that there was considerable scepticism about the principle of establishing a separate channel amongst its ranks for reasons beyond trade and profit.

1979–80

During the 1979 election campaign there was a remarkable consensus on the issue of Welsh language broadcasting. Each political party pledged in their Welsh manifesto their intention, if elected, to secure Welsh language programmes on the fourth channel. Although there was agreement regarding the basic principle, there were some noticeable differences between the proposals. The Conservatives, for example, were keen not to establish a new broadcasting regime and rejected the idea of the OBA advocated by the Annan Committee and also discussed in the Broadcasting White Paper of 1978. Instead, they wanted to relinquish the care of the fourth channel to the IBA. Following the Conservative Party and Margaret Thatcher's victory in the General Election on 4 May 1979, the plans for the fourth channel were outlined by William Whitelaw, the new Home Secretary, in a statement to the Royal Television Society conference at Cambridge on 12 September 1979.[57] Amongst the statements about the funding of the channel, one startling exception was announced to that promoted in the election manifesto: they intended to increase the number of Welsh language programmes, but rather than being broadcast on one channel, as expected, the aim was now to split them between the BBC and the IBA channels. In his memoir, Whitelaw set out the reasoning behind this statement:

> My colleagues in Wales did not consider that the proportion of Welsh speakers could justify delivering the whole new channel in the Welsh language. I therefore proposed safeguards in the Bill requiring the IBA to ensure that at least twelve hours a week of programmes broadcast in Wales should be in Welsh. Taken in common with BBC broadcasts, that would mean up to twenty hours of air time in Welsh. Our aim was to foster the further development of the Welsh language, while not consuming so many hours of air time that many good commercially produced English programmes might never be scheduled in Wales.[58]

This statement was considered as a significant backward step in the broadcasting campaign, as Alwyn Roberts recalled:

> This was a possibility that had never been seriously canvassed since Crawford's rejection of an IBA proposal on these lines. It implied a worsening of the problems of opting-out and a heightening of the feeling of deprivation. Ironically, the non-Welsh speakers would be the main sufferers and the language would become an even more acute cause of resentment.[59]

While the Home Secretary believed that sharing Welsh language programmes across two channels was the best solution, the people of Wales knew that this would be a continuation of the current unacceptable situation, even with an additional channel to share the burden. Although Alwyn Roberts's statement is correct in that non-Welsh speakers would lose out due to the increase in the number of Welsh hours, it was also a bad deal for Welsh speakers. The anger that he mentions, and which had already been strongly expressed to the broadcasters, would ensure that it would be impossible to increase the number of Welsh hours beyond the 20 hours that the Conservatives had recommended. The government scheme guaranteed that Welsh language provision could not evolve and become a comprehensive service that would meet the needs of its diverse audience. This decision, therefore, was a continuation of the situation that already existed, ignoring all the principles and messages of the broadcasting campaign to secure a level playing field for the Welsh language on screen.

Whitelaw's announcement was the necessary impetus for the broadcast campaign, as it had suffered from a lack of momentum due to the government's continued delays during the second half of the 1970s. As Sir Wyn Roberts noted: 'We had handed them [Cymdeithas yr Iaith and Plaid Cymru] a just cause on a plate. We had broken a manifesto promise.'[60] The U-turn rekindled the passion amongst activists, and without the announcement the government's delaying tactic could have buried the idea of a Welsh language channel in protracted negotiations for many years. Whitelaw's statement elicited a furious response from Cymdeithas yr Iaith and Plaid Cymru, with members of Cymdeithas yr Iaith discussing more serious acts of civil disobedience and law breaking,[61] and Plaid Cymru reiterating the call to refuse to pay licences.[62] In spite of these efforts, in reality, the campaign was directionless.[63] In addition, many public figures and former supporters of the campaign turned their backs on the battle to secure a separate channel. Along with Jennie Eirian Davies and HTV, there were now organisations such as a number of county councils and individuals including Tom Ellis, Wrexham Labour MP, Alun R. Edwards and Euryn Ogwen Williams, a former HTV staff member who was now an independent producer, expressing their support for the idea of distributing Welsh language programmes over two channels.[64]

The campaigns of Cymdeithas yr Iaith and Plaid Cymru had not been enough to prevent the government from pushing forward its plans to broadcast Welsh language programmes on two channels. The Broadcasting Bill was published on 6 February 1980 and contained details of a British channel that would broadcast ITV's Welsh language programmes as local opt-outs to the national service in Wales only. The bill suggested that the intention was for Welsh language programmes to be broadcast on the BBC's second channel and the IBA's second channel. Dafydd Wigley insisted that this did not follow the argument of the late Professor Jac L. Williams since it appeared to place the Welsh language in two ghettoes.[65] The publication of this bill was seen as further evidence of government betrayal and a pattern of disregarding the needs and views of the people of Wales.

The measure included, for the first time, the government's intention to legislate on Welsh-medium broadcasting.[66] However, it contained no indication of the number of Welsh language programmes or the number of hours the channel would be expected to broadcast, with the feeble phrase 'a suitable proportion of matter in Welsh' appearing several times.[67] There is one firm recommendation in the measure, namely that money would be set aside to meet the costs of a consultant, to be appointed by the Secretary of State, who would advise the BBC and the IBA on the scheduling of their Welsh language programmes. These costs were expected to be minimal, which suggests that the issue was not given paramount importance.[68] There was strong opposition to this clause of the Broadcasting Bill from Dafydd Elis-Thomas, Plaid Cymru MP for Meirionnydd, who believed that the measure would lead to a 'one-man quango':

> I totally oppose the concept that there should be a person who determines the schedule. It has always been determined by those who make the programmes and by the structures of the broadcasting system, whether the bureaucracy of a commercial company or of the BBC. It has always been the prerogative of those companies to determine scheduling.[69]

In addition, he queried whether it was advisable to allocate the task of appointing a suitable person to such an important rôle to the Home Secretary. Dafydd Elis-Thomas predicted that the Home Secretary was unlikely to have extensive knowledge of Welsh affairs, and that this appointment could be completely ineffective if the views of key parties, such as the Secretary of State for Wales and the broadcasting authorities, were not taken into account when selecting an appropriate individual.[70]

In addition, the bill contained a clause that stated that the BBC and the IBA would have a duty to meet to discuss their strategies for scheduling Welsh language programmes.[71] Although this had not happened at a formal level, as suggested in the bill, BBC Wales and HTV had for several years discussed scheduling issues and had succeeded in ensuring that there were no clashes between the Welsh language programmes broadcast on both networks.[72] It is obvious why the Broadcasting Bill was not popular with campaigners in Wales. It did not contain any form of firm commitment that provided a clear picture of how Welsh audiences would benefit from the new broadcasting pattern, or how the revised structures could be used to increase the number of Welsh language programmes broadcast on the networks.

These completely unsatisfactory developments and the ineffective nature of the campaign weighed heavily on the conscience of one man above all others: Gwynfor Evans, Plaid Cymru's president and former Plaid Cymru MP for Carmarthen. Rhys Evans, in his masterful volume on the life of the politician, suggests that for some months before Whitelaw's announcement, Gwynfor had been planning a shocking act to re-invigorate the national movement.[73] The broadcasting campaign, therefore, proved a convenient hook for Gwynfor Evans to undertake such an act. Although, as a letter written by Gwynfor Evans to Dafydd Williams (one of Plaid Cymru's officials) shows, a separate channel was second in his considerations:

> Although I shall be aiming at the government, the impact on the Welsh people will be far more important. I hope that I can urge nationalists to do more determined work, and that it will restore some backbone to other Welshmen and women and focus their minds. The industrial as well as the cultural crisis will be a backdrop.[74]

The act would be a fast until death, or until the government promised a separate channel for the Welsh language. The fast was inspired by the success of similar actions by Ghandi; nevertheless the morality of the act 'troubled him'.[75] Although he shared the information with a select few in early 1980, Gwynfor Evans did not announce his intention to fast until early May. He first informed the Plaid Cymru executive on 3 May, and then released an official announcement two days later that the fast would start on 5 October 1980, at the start of the new political term.[76]

The statement had an immediate and direct impact. The day following the announcement Cymdeithas yr Iaith had planned for some time for a bus to travel to London to take action on other matters: 'Very few names were down for the bus from Aberystwyth to London, but the night before, after hearing the announcement on television, the list of names for the bus filled up within the hour.'[77] There followed vociferous protests during Mrs Thatcher's visits to Wales, on Anglesey on 18 July and in Swansea two days later.[78] The protests took a nasty turn as explosive devices were installed at the home of the Secretary of State, Nicholas Edwards.[79]

This shocking event shows how close the situation in Wales came to deteriorating further, and emulating elements of the campaigns seen in Northern Ireland and echoing the activities of the Free Wales Army in Wales during the investiture.

It is unnecessary to trace every detail of the communication between the parties, broadcasters, civil servants, campaigners and Gwynfor Evans during the summer of 1980, as the details were comprehensively recorded in Rhys Evans's volume, the autobiography of Sir Wyn Roberts and Alwyn Roberts's lecture to the Cymmrodorion.[80] However, it is necessary to revisit some of the main events of that tempestuous summer to try to understand how and why it was decided that, after all, Welsh language programmes should be placed on one channel.

The government's first public response to Gwynfor Evans's statement came in the form of a concession that the new pattern could be revisited within a year, with the promise that it would be changed if the IBA and the BBC recommended it.[81] Needless to say, Gwynfor Evans rejected this concession since he knew that it would be impossible to change a broadcasting pattern once established. Weeks later, in early July, an emergency meeting was held at the Home Office between MPs William Whitelaw, Nicholas Edwards, Leon Brittan and Wyn Roberts, chairman of the BBC Sir Michael Swann and its director general Ian Trethowan, chairman of the IBA, Dame Bridget Plowden, and the authority's director general, Sir Brian Young, Alwyn Roberts (in his role as chairman of the BBC Broadcasting Council for Wales), Huw Morris-Jones (IBA Welsh representative) and Glyn Tegai Hughes, who had recently been appointed as a Welsh member of the C4 management board, to discuss how the broadcasting problem in Wales could be resolved.[82] It was clear that the government was concerned about Gwynfor Evans's stance, as Whitelaw stated that he was fully aware that Gwynfor Evans could reject any new concession; nevertheless he was convinced that they needed to concede some ground.[83] The Home Office decided to propose the creation of a co-ordinating committee, with representation from the BBC and the IBA, to protect the interests of Welsh language programming within both regimes and ensure a comprehensive service.[84] Some civil servants believed that the main bone of contention was that the idea of a Welsh broadcasting council had been downgraded to one consultant.[85] Civil servants and government ministers felt that the new compromise was very close to an amendment proposed by Dafydd Elis-Thomas to the Broadcasting Bill which had been discussed and rejected in the House of Commons on 24 June 1980.[86] Government officials were therefore fairly confident that their concession would succeed in isolating Gwynfor Evans if he could not be persuaded to stop his fast. But the proposals were not enough to meet the demands of the Welsh delegates, or to convince Gwynfor Evans and the campaigners to end their battle:

> The Welsh representatives were unanimously of the view that, whatever the practical merits of the proposals, they did not in any way meet the conditions laid down by Mr. Evans and would not be seen in Wales to be a proposal which he could not reasonably refuse to accept.[87]

At the beginning of August 1980, the Lliw Valley Eisteddfod became one of the most important events of the campaign. The campaigners protested vociferously and destroyed the HTV and IBA stands, and halted the Secretary of State's car; these protests were not the only feature, as the Eisteddfod Court also appointed a delegation to visit the Home Secretary.[88] Those appointed were Sir Goronwy Daniel, principal of University of Wales College, Aberystwyth until 1979, Archbishop of Wales, G. O. Williams, and Baron Cledwyn of Penrhos, three men who, according to Rhys Evans, 'possessed considerable diplomatic skills'.[89] After discussing their views and tactics in a series of letters, the delegation visited William Whitelaw on 10 September 1980.[90] Their aim was to persuade the government to return to its original promise, because the arguments in favour of broadcasting Welsh programmes on the fourth channel were strong, and as this was the only scheme likely to satisfy Gwynfor Evans.[91] Although Gwynfor Evans's fast was a motivating factor in their visit to Westminster, they were keen not to appear as his ambassadors, and not be 'completely bound by his requirements'.[92] The main weapon in their arsenal was to emphasise the attitude of the common man, and the lack of respect and trust that the people of Wales now had towards government and constitutional methods.[93] All three were fully aware that they faced an 'unusually difficult' task as there was not much room for manoeuvre in trying to find a solution that would be acceptable to Gwynfor Evans but would also enable the government to change its mind without appearing to be giving way to threats.[94] G. O. Williams eloquently outlined the tactic that they should adopt: 'What we ask the Government is not to bend to threats but to acknowledge after weighing all the considerations of the current situation that they have made a mistake. Whoever is brave enough to do so will gain rather than lose dignity.'[95]

It is unnecessary to state that this approach was successful, along with the conclusive solution presented at the meeting by Cledwyn Hughes, but originally proposed by Leopold Kohr, the economist and lecturer in politics from Aberystwyth University, in a letter to *The Times* but which he had also discussed with Gwynfor Evans.[96] The proposal was to turn the Secretary of State's first compromise on its head, and rather than trial the two-channel scheme for a year, trial the Welsh language channel for two years, with the option of returning to the original plan should it not be successful.[97] Although the government adopted the proposal, and extended the trial period to three years, it was not clear to the delegation that their visit had been a success.[98] But, within a week, William Whitelaw and Nicholas Edwards had succeeded in persuading the prime minister and the Treasury that it was necessary to give way. On 17 September 1980, less than a month before the start date of the proposed fast, it was announced that the government would establish a Welsh language channel on the fourth channel in Wales. The delegation's achievement was remarkable, completely overturning the government's opinion, especially considering the memo compiled a day prior to the meeting by the Home Office Broadcasting Department which reported their confidence that William Whitelaw would succeed in persuading reasonable individuals of how unreasonable Gwynfor Evans was behaving. In addition, to coincide with the delegation's meeting, a statement was issued by the Home Office announcing the name of the chair of the new Welsh Language Television Committee, Dafydd Jones-Williams.[99] It was an unrivalled performance by the men who became publicly known as the 'three wise men' since they managed to persuade a stubborn government that had been pushed into a corner. Wyn Roberts was also a key voice in those internal discussions, but Gwynfor Evans's contribution to this victory cannot be ignored, and he undoubtedly deserves the credit for pushing the campaign to its conclusion. Without the threat of a fast, it is easy to imagine that the campaign would have stumbled along directionless. The key fact here is that Gwynfor Evans was the one who was threatening to fast; as Rhys Evans points out, if anyone else had threatened to do so, it is unlikely that they would have elicited the same response or produced the same result.

A number of other factors, mentioned by those who have discussed this chapter in our history, deserve more attention and recognition.

Discussed in Alwyn Roberts's article, and further supported by Rhys Evans's monograph, are the concerns about Northern Ireland that were part of the unofficial, personal discussions between individuals engaged in those official meetings.[100] The Home Secretary appears to have been very concerned about how any decision made about Gwynfor Evans's fast would affect the situation in Northern Ireland. This is a fair conclusion given that William Whitelaw served as Secretary of State for the region between 1972 and 1974 during one of the most turbulent times in its history. It could therefore be argued that Whitelaw's experiences in Northern Ireland encouraged him to surrender to the threat of Gwynfor rather than stand strongly in opposition. In his autobiography, Whitelaw noted that he had experienced how communities could respond to death by political fasting, when members of the IRA at Crumlin Road Prison had fasted to demand political rights.[101] Undoubtedly these experiences greatly influenced Whitelaw, and he foresaw serious difficulties in Wales if Gwynfor Evans were to fast, though he does not refer to them when discussing the issue of the fourth channel in his memoir.

Another forgotten event in the history of S4C is the contribution of a paper written by Geraint Stanley Jones and presented to the Home Office on 29 July 1980 by Sir Michael Swann.[102] The paper explained why it was not technically possible to achieve the government's plans to place Welsh language programmes on BBC2. Alwyn Roberts described it as such: 'It was, to my mind, a demonstration that the two-channel solution was not compatible with any notion of an integrated service.'[103] Geraint Stanley Jones argued that BBC2 was not a suitable platform to create a consistent Welsh language service, due to the need for consistency of timing to create the service. The BBC2 schedule was not designed to receive a consistent series of regional opt-outs as it was designed to be as flexible as possible. It had only one regular programme start time each night, at 9 o'clock in the evening, and as such there was no set hour at which to leave and re-join the BBC2 service easily. Trying to consistently broadcast Welsh language programmes at the same time each night would result in the loss of some of that channel's most popular programmes such as Wimbledon tennis, snooker, golf and cricket.[104] The same would apply to the Welsh language children's programmes which were expected to be broadcast between 16.30 and 17.30, and which would disrupt the sports programmes that were central to the BBC2 schedule.[105] To cut across these programmes to broadcast Welsh language programmes would only continue to antagonise the viewers in Wales:

> It would simply not be possible to create the sort of service envisaged by the Government without totally re-scheduling the BBC-2 early-evening schedules. This in turn would create a degree of deprivation of BBC-2 programmes which we know from hard past experience would be bitterly resented by a substantial and influential section of the community. Any limited degree of flexibility which we have at present would be further eroded by the need to avoid clashing with the service in Welsh on ITV-2. It is simply not possible to carve out a new service of this length across two channels in the way which has been promised.[106]

With one of the key partners insisting that it was not viable to implement the new plans, it would be logical to assume that government officials would have begun to doubt their stubbornness. Instead, there was a fierce reaction criticising the BBC for their unhelpful attitude: 'The BBC are being generally unhelpful about this and they have objected to a number of points which have been put to them about the role of the Welsh Language Television Committee and its composition.'[107] Even though civil servants were dismissive of the BBC's arguments, the contents of the memorandum concerned the Secretary of State for Wales, and he considered the document to be very dangerous if ever published.[108] Nicholas Edwards was, however, persuaded that the problems discussed were not insurmountable, and were, in fact, part of an attempt by the BBC to return to the principle of a separate Welsh language channel. However, the Secretary of State was keen to see a document that refuted the BBC's assertions beyond doubt in case the issue arose when the House of Lords discussed the Broadcasting Bill in the autumn.[109] The memorandum raised doubts, but the discussion that followed demonstrated the disregard within government towards the concept of creating a consistent Welsh language service during peak hours, a service that could enhance the viewing experience for the Welsh public. Officials were remarkably single-minded in their vision, considering any difficulties revealed to them as trivial interference which prevented them from pushing their measure through the House of Commons.

Rumours swirled during August 1980 that the opposition and other MPs would push amendments to the Broadcasting Bill in the House of Lords debate on 8 October. It was believed that several of the lords, including Cledwyn Hughes, Elwyn Jones, Goronwy Roberts and Emlyn Hooson, would propose amendments that would recommend placing all Welsh language broadcasts on the fourth channel, on the basis that the Conservative government's argument about the prohibitive cost of the single channel solution were invalid.[110] Since the discussions in the House of Lords were expected to start two days after the start of Gwynfor Evans's fast, Wyn Roberts was concerned that the government's case would be severely hampered. The financial reasoning was the government's only remaining argument, and in some quarters it was no longer convincing: Lord David Gibson-Watt, the former Welsh secretary of the Heath Conservative government, had indicated that he would not vote with the government in those discussions. Home Office ministers and the Welsh Office were losing the support of their own party, making their position even more difficult to justify.

It could be argued that a combination of events led to the government losing the argument and prompted William Whitelaw's second U-turn. It is undeniable that Gwynfor Evans's action was the most prominent and influential of these events, but the combination of all these factors pushed the government closer to the brink, forcing the Conservatives to overhaul their broadcasting plans for Wales for the second time in just over a year.

The passing of the Broadcasting Act

The first step in establishing the channel was to include it in the Broadcasting Bill which, when William Whitelaw's 'W-turn' took place, was making its way through the House of Commons and the House of Lords.[111] The bill had already left the House of Commons, after two readings and a parliamentary committee debate. In order to bring about the changes and amendments that would ensure that Wales had a separate channel, the passage of the bill through the House of Lords had to be halted. It was fortuitous, therefore, that the government had not rushed to pass the bill, due to the reservations about launching a fourth channel in a time of financial uncertainty.

The amendments to the bill were introduced on 2 October 1980, about three weeks after the second U-turn and following discussions between the Home Secretary, the chancellor and the leader of the House of Commons.[112] Days later, on 8 October 1980, details of the changes were announced in the deliberations of the broadcasting committee, and a month later, on 10 November 1980, a more extensive debate took place on the floor of the House of Commons where the developments were welcomed by members of all parties without exception.[113] Nevertheless, some Conservative members took the opportunity to point out their concerns about the costs of the channel, the amount of talent available in Wales to create the Welsh language programmes and the deprivation Welsh viewers might feel by not being able to view some Channel 4 programmes.[114] Despite these misgivings the amendments were passed, and the bill was transferred back to the House of Lords where on 13 November 1980 it received royal assent. After many years of debate, delay and campaigning, it took just over a month to steer the bill through the House of Commons and House of Lords, and into existence.

The main difference between the original Broadcasting Bill introduced in the House of Commons and the Broadcasting Act which received royal assent was that it required the creation of a new authority to look after Welsh language broadcasting. This was something new and unexpected for those campaigning for a separate channel. Although the establishment of an authority to look after all radio and television broadcasts in Wales had been part of the campaigners' list of demands, this was the first time that any document relating to fourth channel legislation had referred to an independent authority. A Welsh Television Council was suggested in the 1978 White Paper, which would have been a supplementary committee to the OBA to advise on Welsh issues, but not a separate authority for Wales.

These new plans were groundbreaking. It proposed that the authority would have a chair and four members to be appointed by the Home Secretary, but, in practice, that decision would be made in conjunction with the Welsh secretary.[115] The Act did not specify who the members would be, but William Whitelaw stated his intention to secure representation from the BBC and the IBA on the authority:

> I have it in mind, for example, to appoint the BBC governor for Wales and the IBA member for Wales to the new authority. I think that there may also be advantage in appointing somebody from the board of the IBA's fourth channel subsidiary. From the preliminary consultations I have had with the BBC and the IBA, I believe that the broadcasting authorities also see advantage in some cross-membership of this kind.[116]

Not everyone was happy with the proposed membership of the new authority. Dafydd Elis-Thomas noted that some obvious cohorts were missing from the proposed structure:

> I should like the Minister to indicate who will represent the great Welsh public and who will be the representative, if any, of independent producers. It seems to me that there is a danger that the Welsh fourth channel authority will end up perpetuating the duopoly in Welsh broadcasting rather than allowing greater public participation and independent participation in the control of the working of the authority.[117]

But there was no further discussion on the matter during that debate on the floor of the House. Neither did the Home Office minister Leon Brittan respond to this question as he answered the many issues put before him during the debate on the Broadcasting Bill.[118] The Home Office did not wish to discuss further the nature of the new authority since it was a much more contentious issue than it first appeared and there was very little consensus on the matter. Dame Plowden, chair of the IBA, did not want members of the new authority to come from the BBC or the IBA, as she insisted that the independence of the new authority was essential. Following her opposition, the wording of the Act was changed so that the BBC's chair of the Broadcasting Council for Wales and the Welsh member of the IBA would not be *ex officio* members.[119]

The main responsibilities of members of the new authority were to provide high-quality programmes for broadcast on the IBA's fourth channel network in Wales.[120] Programmes would be the main business of the new authority and it would have no wider responsibilities for the network of transmitters in Wales. The authority would therefore be dependent on the IBA's expertise and ability to ensure that the reach of the new channel in Wales was sufficient for its launch. The authority would also have no responsibilities or control over the advertisements broadcast on the channel as it would be the responsibility of the IBA and the independent company in the region to sell the space and collect the advertisements, which reflected a similar division of powers that existed for the fourth channel in the rest of the UK.

In the case of Channel 4 (C4), the Broadcasting Act 1981 was extremely prescriptive and rigorous in its consideration of the types of programmes that should be shown on the new channel. It contained three guidelines that set out exactly the nature of the programmes to be broadcast:

> **11.** – (1) As regards the programmes (other than advertisements) broadcast on the Fourth Channel it shall be the duty of the Authority –
> *(a)* to ensure that the programmes contain a suitable proportion of matter calculated to appeal to tastes and interests not generally catered for by ITV,
> *(b)* without prejudice to so much of section 2(2)(a) as relates to the dissemination of education, to ensure that a suitable proportion of the programmes are of an educational nature,
> *(c)* to encourage innovation and experiment in the form and content of programmes,
> and generally to give the Fourth Channel a distinctive character of its own.[121]

The character and priorities for C4 were clearly outlined in the Act, setting it on a path to provide programmes that were different from what was already seen on the independent broadcasting network. There are no similar restrictions in the sections dealing with the nature of the programmes that would be shown on the fourth channel in Wales. Clause 47 (5) states that the channel should follow the public service broadcasting tradition by showing programmes that would inform, educate and entertain the audience, but goes into no further detail.[122] This is arguably unsurprising given the providers who were expected to create most of the programmes, and the BBC and HTV had developed from the outset with public service broadcasting at the heart of their provision. Undoubtedly politicians also realised that it would be a difficult task to specify the brief for a channel created to provide a service that would appeal to Welsh speakers of all ages and backgrounds. C4, on the other hand, was created to appeal to small, minority and unique groups within society since the other three channels effectively appealed to the general public.

The sections of the Act that dealt with the programme providers for the Welsh fourth channel were much more prescriptive than the section dealing with C4's programme producers. There are clauses setting out the need for the BBC and the IBA contractor in Wales to provide programmes for the new channel. But there is no specific legislation on the number of hours that they are expected to produce. Only the ambiguous phrase that states that the BBC and the independent company are expected to provide programmes that meet the 'reasonable requirements of the Welsh Authority'.[123] In discussing the BBC's responsibilities, it was enacted that the corporation should be expected to provide programmes free of charge to the channel, and to ensure that the number of Welsh language programmes it produced did not fall below the number of hours it would have produced for broadcast on its own channels had the new authority not been created.[124] There are no phrases that bind the independent television company to a minimum number of programmes; it was noted instead that the provision of programmes for the new authority would be on commercial terms, although there is no definition or explanation of what commercial terms constitutes in this context. The Act also makes it clear that these specific clauses do not prevent the new authority from commissioning and broadcasting Welsh language programmes from other sources, thus ensuring that this new channel could offer an unrivalled opportunity for an independent sector to grow and offer different programmes from those produced by the cosy duopoly between BBC and ITV.

The Act also legislated on the importance of the need for the authority to provide and maintain a high-quality service. The purpose of the reference to high standards was undoubtedly to state clearly that the broadcasters needed to raise the quality of the Welsh language programmes currently on offer. This was further reinforced by the discussions held in the House of Commons where the importance of training was mentioned as key so that more variety could be seen in Welsh language programmes rather than the reliance on talking head programmes which dominated the schedules:

> We have often complained about the standard of programmes, and about the continuous talking head programmes in which too many of us have taken part . . . We have often criticised the standard of the programmes and said that the reason for the low standard is lack of funding.[125]

Highlighting the importance of quality showed that the government was aware that Welsh language programming needed to be of a high standard in order to attract viewers from the English language programmes broadcast on the other three channels. By emphasising the quality of the output, the government demonstrated an understanding of a crucial and ever-present problem with the Welsh-speaking audience, namely that it was a bilingual audience and, as a result, had no obligation to watch only Welsh programmes. This clause shows an understanding of how necessary it was for the new channel to provide attractive and high-quality programming, to retain its viewers and to ensure its success and popularity for years to come.

The Act also required that a 'substantial proportion of the programmes included in the programme schedules provided by the Welsh Authority shall be in Welsh'.[126] The government expected that the majority of those Welsh programmes would be broadcast during peak hours – between 18.30 and 22.00 – but as the Act did not specify that all Welsh hours should be during those hours, as originally required by Gwynfor Evans, this offered flexibility, which would enable the channel to broadcast school and children's programmes at appropriate times.[127] There is no reference to the number of hours that the authority would be expected to provide in Welsh and the careful but vague wording clearly indicates that the channel's destiny was not to be a channel where the majority of the programmes would be in Welsh, but rather a channel where more Welsh language content was broadcast on one platform.

On the issue of the relationship between the British fourth channel and the fourth channel in Wales, it included a clause stating what was expected to be broadcast around the Welsh language programming that would dominate its peak hours. Since only around one-third of all the channel's content would be in Welsh, these other programmes would be a significant part of the new channel's provision for its audience. The Act states:

> for any period not allocated to the broadcasting of a programme not in Welsh, the programme broadcast is normally the same as the programme (or one of the programmes) broadcast on the Fourth Channel in that period for reception otherwise than in Wales.[128]

There is a clear recommendation here that the fourth channel in Wales should transmit C4 programmes live when not broadcasting a Welsh language programme. Although the words in brackets suggest that this rule could be modified somewhat, the discussions in the House of Commons reinforced the idea that the government's preferred option was that C4 programmes would be broadcast live, since they were aware of the technical costs and additional rights payments which would be incurred should they be broadcast at different times.[129] Despite its clear preference for this option, the government recognised that the Welsh fourth channel authority would have responsibility for the channel's schedules and therefore various scheduling plans were not rejected by the Act.

The Broadcasting Act gave the new authority a framework that defined the extent of its responsibilities and the pattern of the new service. The comprehensive nature of the new plans detailed in the Act suggests that these were not ideas that were thrown together urgently after the visit of the three wise men.[130] The details about the nature of the providers, the programmes, the schedule and its relationship with C4 suggest – although there is no firm evidence to prove this – that civil servants had been actively developing these principles over a longer period of time than the mere three weeks between the second U-turn and the introduction of the amendments to the bill. Despite all the derision aimed at the Conservatives, in the form of the authority Wales gained a far more influential and powerful institution than any Welsh television committee or council envisaged by the other parliamentary measures and committees. The new authority was given the opportunity to create an independent and unique service for Welsh speakers and, if it so wished, with its own distinctive identity and voice. An exciting new chapter in the history of broadcasting in Wales opened, and significant pressure was placed on the authority and broadcasters in Wales to ensure its success.

2

The early days of the Welsh Fourth Channel Authority

Following all the bustle and tumult of the various campaigns and Gwynfor Evans's threat to fast, the Conservative government's second U-turn and the publication of the Broadcasting Act, the reality of what had been secured and the scale of the task ahead dawned on those who would be charged with the responsibility to establish and manage this long-awaited channel. S4C was an unrivalled enterprise, and one of its unique features was that the programmes broadcast on it would come from a variety of sources. The channel faced a huge undertaking in discussing new programming ideas and the terms of supplying that content with the BBC, HTV and independent producers, and then merging these programmes into one cohesive and unified schedule with Channel 4's (C4) English language output. Given the importance of creating an attractive and entertaining schedule to safeguard the future of the channel, the importance of this task cannot be underestimated. This chapter analyses what was gained after all the campaigning, and discusses the formation of the Welsh Fourth Channel Authority (WFCA) and the various partnerships that would be key to its success.

The Welsh Fourth Channel Authority

In the wake of the Broadcasting Act receiving its royal assent on 13 November 1980, there was no obvious urgency to form the new authority before Christmas that year. The delay was enough to inspire Cymdeithas yr Iaith to threaten to break the law again to ensure that the issue became a top priority and a matter of urgency.[1] One of the most obvious reasons for the delay was the uncertainty surrounding who would receive the franchise to broadcast on the ITV network in Wales until the Independent Broadcasting Authority's (IBA) decision in early 1981.

The Welsh Affairs Select Committee's (WASC) tactics of attacking the BBC and HTV for paying too much attention to Welsh politics and overspending on Welsh language programmes also slowed the process.[2] It was inconsistent to criticise spending on Welsh language programmes in one government committee, while another branch of government proceeded with establishing an authority that would spend more than ever before on such provision. This delay on the part of government, particularly as C4 had long appointed a management board and officials, was seen as further evidence of the government's reluctance to give the Fourth Channel in Wales a fair crack at the whip during its probationary period.

The government finally appointed the authority in January 1981. The chairman selected to steer the authority through the probationary years and to ensure that it fulfilled the aims of the Broadcasting Act was Sir Goronwy Daniel, one of the three wise men who visited William Whitelaw on 10 September 1980. Sir Goronwy Daniel had also presided over the broadcasting conference sponsored by the Lord Mayor of Cardiff and chaired by the archbishop of Wales, G. O. Williams, in July 1973.[3] There was a clear connection therefore between the campaign to secure the Welsh language channel and the task of establishing and developing it. However, Sir Goronwy Daniel did not have a prominent broadcasting background prior to his appointment as chairman of the authority.[4] He had been chief statistician for the Ministry of Fuel and Power (1947–55), had served as a civil servant as the first permanent secretary of the Welsh Office (1964–9), before moving to Aberystwyth as principal of the University of Wales College there (1969–79).[5] Sir Goronwy Daniel may not have been the first choice to lead the Fourth Channel Authority in Wales; an article in *Y Faner* had suggested that Lord Emlyn Hooson was first choice for the post.[6] Choosing Sir Goronwy Daniel as chairman was a fortunate choice, with Rhys Evans describing him as: 'both wise and judicious, giving S4C the best possible start'.[7] In his obituary Meic Stephens described his contribution to the development of S4C in the following terms:

> It [S4C] may be properly considered as a monument not only to the readiness of Gwynfor Evans to sacrifice himself for the sake of a principle but also to the practical skills of Sir Goronwy Daniel, who guided the frail bark through what were then uncharted and choppy waters.[8]

His experience of working with the Welsh Office, and his understanding of the language and clandestine ways of Westminster and Whitehall were crucial as the channel formed relationships with politicians and government departments. His education and background in economics and statistics were also crucial in writing funding applications to the IBA and in deciphering complex and difficult viewing figures.

Although the Act contained no guidance on which individuals or organisations should be represented on the authority, the government had specific ideas as to who should take responsibility for shaping the channel.[9] It was inevitable therefore that Rev. Dr. Alwyn Roberts, the chair of the BBC's Broadcasting Council for Wales,[10] Professor Huw Morris-Jones, the IBA's Welsh member[11] and Dr Glyn Tegai Hughes, Wales's representative on the C4 board, would be appointed to the authority of the new channel.[12] However apparent to a historian that these individuals would be appointed – with the privilege of being able to look back over the discussions on the floor of the House of Commons – to the individuals concerned the invitation appeared less certain. The process of contacting the prospective members was a hasty one that betrayed the government's urgency to show that they were finally making progress after such a long delay. Alwyn Roberts recalls that he received a phone call on a Tuesday afternoon from the Home Office – and that they wished to announce the names in less than two days on the Thursday.[13] One member who did not represent a broadcasting organisation was D. Ken Jones, a former winger for Wales and the Lions, and now a successful managing director of Takiron UK, the first Japanese manufacturing company to establish an operation in Wales.[14]

Not everyone was happy with the appointment of representatives from the BBC, IBA and C4, and the composition of the authority was heavily criticised during WASC discussions. There were suggestions that their involvement created an incestuous relationship between the broadcasting organisations, which would lead to questions of whether members had the fourth channel and the public's best interests at heart or their own organisations. Leo Abse MP exemplified this attitude in his question to Sir Goronwy Daniel:

> Do you not think that, given the conflicts and undercurrents which we have already observed in the course of our evidence, the public interest may not in fact assume the highest degree of priority and that the band of brothers may be too accommodating to

> each other precisely because three of them are representing vested interests?[15]

The allegations were swept aside by the Home Secretary, William Whitelaw, and by Sir Goronwy Daniel as they emphasised that the opposite was true, and that members of the authority put the interests of the Welsh language channel first.[16] The WASC was not persuaded by this argument, and were particularly concerned by the presence of the Welsh member of the IBA, since the financial interests of the ITV network and S4C could not be aligned in the committee's view.[17] The committee therefore recommended that: 'the WFCA should be reconstituted and that cross-membership with the BBC and IBA be discontinued in order that the WFCA can be seen to be carrying out its transactions with other broadcasting bodies on a clear "arm's length" basis'.[18] This statement overlooked the fact that a number of decisions were able to be made quickly due to the presence of these members on the authority, and that help was given without difficulty due to the status, contacts and knowledge of those members. The IBA's Welsh committee in its response to the WASC's recommendations stated:

> the Welsh Fourth Channel Authority had achieved a considerable amount in the short time that it had been in existence. This was largely explained by the fact that three out of the five members of the Welsh Fourth Channel Authority were in some way connected with broadcasting.[19]

It became very clear that collaboration between the broadcasting organisations would be one of the cornerstones of the success or failure of the new channel, but not all parties providing programmes for the new channel were represented on the authority, as there was no representation of independent producers. Although Ken Jones had a business background, he had no obvious links with the independent production sector. During this time, however, there were very few independent producers in Wales, and at the time the sector was not expected to make a significant contribution to the channel.

It could be claimed that another group was not being represented either: the viewing public. This issue was identified and criticised by Dafydd Elis-Thomas in the House of Commons.[20] However, as the members of the authority themselves were also viewers of Welsh language programmes, it is possible to argue that they were indeed representing the audience. But the membership only comprised one or two different social groups; the most noticeable gap was the lack of female members who could bring a female perspective to the channel's programming.[21]

After the delay in appointing the members of the authority, the next few months were characterised by a flurry of activity. In fact Sir Goronwy was described as being: 'ready to take on the job with energy and enthusiasm as well as that wisdom which is so characteristic of him and which will be absolutely necessary during the establishment of the service'.[22] A few days after the announcement, the authority held its first formal meeting in Gregynog on the weekend of 31 January–1 February 1981.[23] This first extended meeting highlighted two things for the members: the enormity of the task which faced them and the great emphasis there would be on collaboration. This emphasis became clear as Eirion Lewis, IBA secretary in Wales, Owen Edwards, controller BBC Wales, Sir Alun Talfan Davies, chairman of the HTV Welsh board and Ron Wordley, HTV's managing director, were invited to take part in the discussions.

The weekend was split into four separate sessions, with the first session being for authority members only to discuss some of the initial details, such as temporary office and staff arrangements. According to the minutes of the meeting the first thing that was discussed and decided upon was the name of the new channel, Sianel Pedwar Cymru, which would be abbreviated to S4C.[24] There is no record of any other names being discussed or considered, and indeed members of the authority remember that the decision was quick and easy.[25] Another early decision was to urgently advertise for a chief executive for the channel, so that they could be part of the key decisions of finding permanent office space and appointing staff. It is possible to infer from this that the authority's aim was to find a chief executive who would put their own stamp on the channel and that they would be in charge of the day-to-day running of the new channel, rather than the authority.[26] The personal qualities that the authority hoped to find in a chief executive were discussed with the WASC, with Sir Goronwy Daniel insisting that the authority be obliged to select a person who would be master of his craft, and who would have the ability to negotiate and reason with the other broadcasters in such a way as to ensure equivalent status for the new channel. It was also imperative to find an individual with brilliant financial skills. The authority was fully aware that there was no guarantee that all the necessary skills could be found in one individual:

> maybe the Archangel will be appointed. My suspicion is that we will, because of the fallibility of human beings, have somebody who is very strong in certain fields of expertise, besides having the general qualities of character which are essential. Then we shall need to complement him in the things in which he happens to be less strong from the expertise point of view.[27]

The second session of the authority's meeting discussed the need for temporary administrative support and the IBA offered a room and administrative support at their offices at Elgin House on St Mary's Street, Cardiff and the BBC offered the services of a typist.[28] Eirion Lewis also took on the responsibility of acting as the authority's temporary secretary, taking care of the minutes.[29] The authority was very reliant on the goodwill of other organisations at the outset, and this shows the enormity of the task before them since they started with no facilities or money to buy or hire offices.

Implicit in the minutes of this first meeting are some of the main themes of the discussions and the authority's priorities as it worked towards making the channel a reality. Unsurprisingly, what dominated the initial discussions was the nature of the channel's programming. Members of the authority also considered their responsibilities under the Broadcasting Act and raised questions about some of the vague details contained within it. Clarification was sought on many aspects from the Home Office, such as whether adverts were counted in the number of hours the authority was expected to broadcast. In a similar fashion to the discussions on the final wording of the Act when it was debated in the House of Commons, clarification was also required on the scheduling and broadcasting of C4 programmes. The authority decided that the 'once around transmitters' principle needed to be discussed with C4 and possibly with the unions.[30] The S4C Authority had considered, from the outset, that re-scheduling C4 programmes at its discretion rather than receiving them live around the Welsh language programmes was key to the success of S4C. It can also be argued that they were prepared to do so knowing that there may be additional costs since the unions could demand that artists receive a repeat payment if their work was shown on S4C at a different time from C4. Receiving further clarification on this issue was essential to the authority in planning their budget and schedules.

Another urgent and pressing issue was finding suitable facilities. Although amenities for producing programmes would not be needed, the new channel would require some form of broadcasting facilities. The authority discussed three different schemes, namely that S4C set up its own facilities, emphasising its position as a new independent broadcaster; that the channel fully embrace the ethos of collaboration and develop facilities at BBC or HTV sites; or that they share facilities with the other broadcasters, with each using their own presenters. The image of the service was the most important consideration, although the risk of duplicating resources – especially in financially constrained times – also weighed heavily. Another issue that was particularly important when considering the facilities was the availability of technical links between S4C, the other broadcasters and BT lines.[31] The authority had received invitations from the councils of Swansea, Aberystwyth, Bangor and Mold to consider establishing the headquarters of the new channel outside Cardiff;[32] the lack of discussion on the issue at the meeting indicates that authority members already knew that establishing the channel's broadcasting headquarters some distance from the other broadcasters and BT switching centres would not be feasible. It was also decided early on that independent facilities were the only solution that offered the channel the necessary freedom to create and manage its own service.[33] The search for suitable facilities was undertaken, and a site at Sophia Close, in the Pontcanna area of Cardiff was selected. The staff relocated there in mid-July 1981, in the midst of intensive building and conversion work to ensure that the building could be used as a broadcasting centre.[34]

With the authority's membership being small, and because expertise was not available in each area, a decision was made to establish a number of working groups, inviting members of the IBA, BBC and HTV to participate in the discussions. These small committees would cover the most important areas for the authority, such as programmes, finance and accounts, administration and engineering, and make recommendations to the authority at the end of their deliberations. This policy emphasises, once again, how dependent the new authority was on the cooperation of the other broadcasters and their willingness to offer advice and staff time while setting aside any selfish agenda. It highlights again the enormity of the task facing the authority: there was no prototype to follow to facilitate and guide their decisions in establishing this unique channel.

One element that is not apparent from reading the minutes but which was emphasised in talks with members of the authority is the protracted nature of these meetings, the tireless drive of Sir Goronwy to continue discussions and his work ethic. Many remember that time meant nothing to him and that he would continue to work until the early hours without much consideration for what hour of the day it was. Glyn Tegai Hughes described the industrious nature of Sir Goronwy Daniel as follows:

> He had very little idea of how other people felt or worked. He would come into the office about half past five, everyone had been working all day, and he would come in and keep going . . . and Goronwy would keep going for hours.[35]

The chairman was a unique personality and often brusque; indeed he was described by Meic Stephens in this way, 'for those who did not know him well his rather forthright way of speaking could be disconcerting'.[36] Some also found that he was not the most disciplined chairman as he would 'discuss all matters hither and thither', but, nevertheless, was described as 'firm', 'single minded', 'wise' and 'determined'.[37] His dedicated and diligent nature meant that the authority's meetings were extraordinary.

One of the authority's priorities was to appoint staff to undertake the urgent work that needed to be done for the channel to develop and move forward. Contrary to expectations, the chief executive was not the first person to be appointed to the channel's staff, but an administrator, Mrs Mair Owen. Very soon after the formation of the authority it became apparent that Eirion Lewis needed help if he was to undertake his work with the IBA as well as acting as the authority's secretary. As a result, Mair Owen, who had worked for the BBC and Mudiad Ysgolion Meithrin (the nursery school movement), was invited to undertake temporary administrative work for the new authority, and began working for the channel on 1 March 1981.[38] Within a month the chief executive had been appointed following advertisements published in the Welsh press and London papers in February seeking applications and nominations. There are no indications in the authority's records of the numbers nominated or who applied. The only information available is a reference to the fact that four were interviewed for the post in Cardiff on 6 March 1981.[39] They appointed Owen Edwards, who had been controller of BBC Wales since June 1974; he had led the corporation through a period of tremendous growth in the number of Welsh and English hours produced by the BBC in Wales, through the launch of Radio Cymru and Radio Wales, and had steered the BBC expertly through the turbulent Welsh fourth channel campaign.[40] Some newspaper reports give the impression that Owen Edwards had not applied of his own volition for the job, but was instead invited to interview after being nominated.[41] Owen Edwards also recalls that he received a call from the chairman of the authority asking him if he was ready to '[g]wasanaethu' ('serve').[42] Sir Goronwy Daniel's use of the term 'gwasanaethu' was highly appropriate, since Owen Edwards would need to consider the position in that context. Leaving a secure job and career with the BBC and joining a new channel without a guaranteed future was a brave decision, especially given that a likely promotion to a job with the corporation in London would await him in the future if he so wished.[43] Owen Edwards was considered a wise and ideal choice for the channel in its formative years. His professional background demonstrated his suitability for the role with his experience as controller of BBC Wales clearly proving his practical experience in dealing with the day-to-day issues of running a broadcasting service. He was also familiar with overseeing and managing a significant increase in provision, a vital element of the work. In addition, Owen Edwards's background and lineage emphasised, especially to Welsh speakers, how suitable he was for the post. It was highly fitting that the son of Sir Ifan ab Owen Edwards, founder of the Urdd, and grandson of Sir O. M. Edwards, chief inspector of schools for the Welsh Board of Education and a great benefactor of the Welsh language and culture – two of the most prominent names of the Welsh establishment and who had been instrumental in modernising the Welsh language and making it a living part of Welsh life – would pioneer the Welsh language television channel which would be a way of ensuring that the language remained modern and relevant.

Following the appointment of the chief executive, who decided to adopt the title of 'director', a small core group of key staff were appointed to steer the channel and its development.[44] There were some concerns that finding staff would be a difficult task since S4C would be in direct competition with the BBC and HTV at a time when all of the broadcasters were busy recruiting due to the projected increase in output required by all of the providers.[45] Applicants could have been concerned about accepting a job with a channel that did not have a secure future, and that it would be wiser to apply for jobs with the BBC or HTV, who were not going through a trial period, but concerns within S4C were misplaced as it proved very attractive to experienced individuals and new entrants to the industry. The next staff member to be appointed, because of the urgency to start negotiating and commissioning programmes, was the programme editor, who would also act as deputy to the director. Euryn Ogwen Williams was appointed to the post, who had an extensive background in broadcasting having worked for TWW, and then HTV, until 1977, where he had been head of the religious and sports programming departments, before leaving to form the independent production company EOS.[46] His appointment also complemented Owen Edwards's skill-set, as he brought awareness and understanding of the commercial side of broadcasting, compared with the director's experience with the BBC. This ensured that S4C had a detailed awareness of how all of its partners were operating.[47]

Independent Broadcasting Authority (IBA)

Another issue at the top of the channel's list of priorities was securing adequate funding, and an application was submitted to the IBA; discussions began shortly after the appointment of the authority and the S4C chairman met Lord Thomson and Sir Brian Young in early February.[48] The channel was informed that there was likely to be a gap between the budget S4C wished to receive and what the IBA could reasonably collect from ITV network companies. Given that the use of public funds was anathema to the new government, in order to fund the fourth channel a system was devised that required ITV network companies to pay the IBA an annual subscription from a portion of their Net Advertising Revenue (NAR) for the right to sell advertisements to be placed on the fourth channel in their broadcast region.[49] This scheme was originally designed to fund only C4, and the government had not yet announced exactly how it would adapt the plan to cope with the funding of the S4C Authority. It was anticipated that there would be some disquiet amongst ITV companies about increasing the subscription to fund a channel that most could not profit from.[50] Indeed, the Independent Television Companies Association (ITCA) announced that it was totally against the concept that the Welsh language channel should be paid for by members of its association.[51] Since S4C was a public service for the benefit of society, the ITCA believed that it should be funded by public money.[52] In their evidence to the WASC they highlighted the intense unease of the companies who served areas where there were other ethnic and linguistic minorities who also demanded increased provision:

> It would be highly damaging to them to be seen to be paying a subscription designed specifically to alleviate the problems in Wales.

> In political terms it could rebound on their operations in their own regions and it has to be said on their behalf that they would not willingly accede to such an arrangement.[53]

The ITCA also felt that the financial circumstances of the ITV network was not sufficiently healthy to sustain funding for an additional channel because of the new franchise agreements which sought to increase the number of hours produced by each company and required higher rental payments to the IBA.[54] Despite the various arguments put forward by the ITCA, its position was undoubtedly influenced by financial considerations above ideological principles. This can be seen clearly by its admission that the companies would be happy if the cost of the two fourth channels remained within the original parameters of £60–80 million.[55] They also alleged that the IBA had misled the companies who had not expected to pay more towards the fourth channel in Wales.

The ITCA's argument was invalid, especially given that the Broadcasting Act and the discussions in the House of Commons had openly stated that the costs of the fourth channel would be higher because of the revised plans in Wales.[56] The notion that the ITV companies would pay for the development of Welsh language programmes was also old news, since it was intended under the two-channel solution to finance the growth in Welsh language programming by means of a hidden subsidy, which all companies except HTV would pay. Each ITV network company, from the smallest to the largest, would have paid higher rental payments to the IBA to offset the reduction in HTV's rental, ensuring that the production of more Welsh language programmes did not become an insurmountable burden on the company.[57]

Although the ITCA's arguments were not completely genuine, the IBA's awareness of the dissatisfaction amongst network companies would weigh heavily on the dialogue surrounding finance with S4C. This was evidenced in their early discussions, as the IBA suggested that they could only raise an additional £10 million from the network companies for S4C.[58] Owen Edwards, following his appointment, set about working closely with the chairman to produce a memorandum that would present the case and justify the need for sufficient funding for the channel. That memorandum was sent to the IBA on the first day of May 1981 and a month later, on 1 June 1981, Owen Edwards and Sir Goronwy Daniel travelled to the IBA offices on Brompton Road, London to discuss their application, which estimated that a total of £20.7 million was necessary to run the channel until the end of March 1983. It was estimated that £19.4 million would need to be spent on programme costs and £1.3 million invested in building and equipment, and to cover administration, marketing, research, etc.[59] The document produced was praised for its quality and clarity, but there was extensive discussion during the meeting about the proposed costs of HTV programmes as they constituted the most significant percentage of the channel's budget. Sir Goronwy Daniel noted that HTV was disappointed by S4C's financial estimates, as the amount allocated in the proposed budget for nine hours of HTV programming a week was significantly lower than the figure presented to S4C by HTV for that number of hours.[60] Despite these concerns, the IBA felt that an application for £20 million could be justified and that the amount was fair. But before setting the final amount and committing to the budget the IBA would need a concrete answer from the Home Office of its intentions to adjust the tax burden on the ITV companies.[61] The IBA found itself in a difficult position, because it was impossible for the Home Secretary to give his opinion on potential budgets as he could be called upon as a referee, under the terms of the Act, should S4C and the IBA fail to come to an agreement. As it was not possible to obtain confirmation that the Home Office agreed to the sum of £20 million, the IBA could not be certain that the tax burden on ITV companies would be adjusted to ensure that the authority could then afford to offer this sum to S4C. The IBA faced a catch-22, trying to secure fair funding for S4C but also wanting to ensure that the amount did not create difficulties or affect the prosperity of the ITV network. To resolve the impasse, the Home Office in conjunction with the Treasury decided to inform the IBA informally that, if the IBA and S4C agreed a sum of £20 million, the government could be relied upon to adjust the tax burden to ensure that ITV companies were not overly penalised.[62] After this informal confirmation, the IBA and S4C were able to reach an agreement, and it was announced on 21 July 1981 that S4C would be funded to the tune of £20 million until the end of March 1983. However, it wasn't until the following day that a statement by William Whitelaw in the House of Commons confirmed exactly how the additional investment was to be funded: the government would increase the proportion of the non-taxable advertising money from £250,000 or 2 per cent (whichever was the greater) to £650,000 or 2.8 per cent (whichever was the greater).[63] Following this announcement, which gave some financial security, S4C began to plan and commission in earnest.

In addition to finance, S4C was totally dependent on the IBA to ensure that Welsh transmitters would be ready to broadcast the channel. Back in 1979 a bill was introduced in the House of Commons which authorised the IBA to build a network of transmitters for the fourth channel, and Wales was given the highest priority.[64] This measure was passed independently of the other broadcasting measures surrounding the fourth channel, since the IBA insisted that it could not undertake the building work until legislation was issued to enable it to do so. Due to the time required by the IBA for the construction work, all the delays were undermining the planned launch dates for the fourth channel in Wales, and concerns were expressed in late 1978 by the Welsh committee of the IBA that it would no longer be possible to broadcast the service until 1983, damaging the plans set out in the White Paper.[65]

After the election of the Thatcher government, and the announcement of its plans to broadcast Welsh language programmes on two channels, the principle of launching the channel in Wales before the rest of the UK, as originally hoped by the IBA's Welsh committee, disappeared. The IBA's national plans now suggested that C4 would be available to 80 per cent of the population for a 'big bang' launch; to achieve this it was anticipated that the reach in Wales would be much lower.[66] Members of the Welsh committee were unhappy with this development as they felt that the Independent Broadcasting Authority Act 1979 had been passed with the principle of giving Welsh transmitters priority. There was further concern that these plans would lead to some rural Welsh communities being deprived of Welsh language broadcasts in their entirety, since the UHF (ultra high frequency) service was not available in Wales as a whole and that the two-channel solution proposed that the Welsh language programmes be moved to BBC2 and C4.[67] The IBA's plans envisaged that the main transmitters at Blaenplwyf, Carmel and Preseli would not be modified in the first phase, depriving large parts of west, mid and north Wales of Welsh language programmes for up to two years.[68] In light of this, the IBA's Welsh committee recommended that Welsh language programming should continue to be broadcast on BBC1 Wales and HTV even after the fourth channel began broadcasting.[69]

The IBA centrally was eventually persuaded that the main transmitters in Wales should be adjusted during the first phase of the scheme. However, it did not anticipate that the reach would match that of UHF by the channel's opening night, and instead expected that around 80 per cent of the population would receive the service.[70] Despite the change in attitude, it would still be impossible for large parts of rural Wales to receive the new fourth channel broadcasts. With the recommendation that Welsh language programmes should continue to be broadcast on ITV until adequate reach could be achieved weighing heavily on their minds, the IBA announced that they intended to secure 90 per cent reach in Wales.[71]

Due to a herculean effort by the IBA, they succeeded in adapting more than initially envisaged, with 95 sub-transmitters and the six main transmitters being adapted to broadcast four channels rather than three.[72] Compared to the adaption works in the rest of the UK for C4, the work and effort in Wales compared very favourably, since it was anticipated that a significant number of the cities and towns of England and Scotland – such as Edinburgh, Bath, Bristol and Sheffield – were unlikely to be able to receive C4 in its opening weeks.[73] However, of the ten sub-transmitters in Wales which had not been adapted, three were in largely Welsh-speaking areas, such as Dolybont, which served villages north of Aberystwyth including Taliesin, Llandre and Dolybont itself; Llanrhaeadr-ym-Mochnant in Powys serving the Tanat Valley and Trefin in Pembrokeshire.[74] Because of this delay, Welsh communities would be completely deprived of Welsh language programmes on television. This, especially in the case of the Trefin and Llanrhaeadr-ym-Mochnant transmitters, was an absurd situation since their UHF transmitters had only been in operation since December 1981 and January 1982. This meant that the residents of these areas had only received Welsh language programmes for 11 months, at the end of which they were deprived of them again.[75] They would be deprived of Welsh language programmes not for weeks but for an extended period of 19 months: the Dolybont and Llanrhaeadr-ym-Mochnant transmitters were not completed until May 1984 and the wait was longer in Trefin because their transmitter was not scheduled to be adapted until 1985.[76] The communities campaigned and petitioned as they faced being deprived of the exciting programming which was advertised in the newspapers, and their protests were supported by Urdd Gobaith Cymru who corresponded and met with the IBA to express its concern about the impact of the situation on the children of these areas.[77]

These gaps in the Welsh transmitter network had serious consequences, but the situation would have been far worse had it not been for the efforts of the IBA engineers. Eirion Lewis, the IBA secretary for Wales, revealed that by July 1984, 33 per cent of English transmitters were broadcasting

C4, 32 per cent in Northern Ireland and 23 per cent in Scotland. In comparison, the 92 per cent of Welsh transmitters able to broadcast S4C was strikingly higher, and a testament to the IBA's effort and commitment.[78] This effort demonstrates the IBA's commitment to ensuring the best conditions for S4C during its probationary period.

Welsh Affairs Select Committee (WASC)

Although the S4C Authority was answerable to the Home Office by the submission of its annual reports, during its first year it also needed to engage with another branch of government by providing evidence to the WASC, chaired by Leo Abse, Labour MP for Pontypool. The committee's remit was 'Broadcasting in the Welsh language and the implications for Welsh and non-Welsh-speaking viewers and listeners'. This was a broad area that gave members the opportunity to consider issues, such as the financial conditions necessary for S4C, political balance on Welsh (not just Welsh language) news programmes and the lack of consideration given to non-Welsh-speaking viewers in Wales. The committee's main priority was to provide a factual basis for the arguments surrounding Welsh language broadcasting: 'For too long, in our opinion, emotion rather than fact has dominated discussions of Welsh-language broadcasting. In this Report, we have set out to establish facts wherever we can and then seek to base our conclusions on them.'[79] The committee was set up in the midst of government discussions with Gwynfor Evans after he announced his intention to fast, and so the threat was one of the main reasons behind the committee turning its gaze towards broadcasting.[80] It was intended to act as an intermediary between the government and groups calling for a separate Welsh language channel, easing the tension through open discussion that would 'help to "ease out" the violence that is now beginning to come from people whom he [Abse] described as "Welsh language fanatics"'.[81] By the time the committee began to receive witness testimony in public on 29 October 1980, that tension had subsided following William Whitelaw's second U-turn on 17 September 1980. Consequently, the committee's main task changed to seeking to establish facts in order to justify the substantial public expenditure on Welsh language broadcasting, and discussing the implications of the new Broadcasting Act and how its recommendations should be interpreted when establishing the Welsh language channel.[82]

Gathering concrete facts was not an easy task since there had not been a consistent pattern of measuring the viewing patterns of the Welsh-speaking audience before S4C's arrival. In their evidence, a number of organisations offered contradictory figures on the proposed costs for S4C, creating confusion about the true cost of moving Welsh language programmes to one channel. The frustration of the chairman Leo Abse could be felt during the S4C Authority's first visit to the committee on 25 February 1981, just one month after the authority's members were appointed. Sir Goronwy Daniel and Dr Glyn Tegai Hughes represented the authority and provided a brief memorandum to the committee detailing some of the authority's key decisions at their first two meetings.[83] The main theme of the questioning was the planned costs of the channel, and Sir Goronwy Daniel gave a masterful performance as he repeatedly refused to disclose details of the channel's budget, despite significant committee pressure throughout the morning and afternoon session.[84] It was early days for the financial negotiations and Sir Goronwy Daniel was obviously keen to keep any budgetary ideas he and his colleagues had been considering confidential, until the relevant information could be gathered and so that the chief executive of the channel – who had not yet been appointed – could put forward their own ideas on a necessary budget. The only comment Sir Goronwy Daniel made on the early figures discussed by the committee was to note his disbelief in some of them.[85] This was a shrewd tactic by Sir Goronwy Daniel, albeit one that annoyed the chairman of the WASC, as it ensured that the authority did not reveal any figures to which the channel could be tied, should further research and discussion indicate the need for a much larger or much smaller budget. During the channel's second appearance on 6 May 1981, it was possible to share many more financial details, since it had now sent its financial memorandum to the IBA.[86] The committee was amazed by what appeared to be a significant difference between the estimated costs of HTV programmes (£30–2 million) and the amount requested by S4C to fund the first months' programmes and its reserve stock (£19.5 million).[87] The WASC was so concerned that a copy of the memorandum sent to the IBA was requested, and a demand for a full explanation of the significant difference between S4C's and HTV's costs.[88]

By the time the WASC report was published in July 1981 the budget had been agreed by the IBA and S4C, and therefore the recommendations made by the committee on finance issues had little or no effect. However, they do reveal the attitude that existed in some factions towards a Welsh language television service. The committee made recommendations that the channel should be given fair funding that would enable it to fulfil its responsibilities under the Act. But at the same time, revealing the true loyalty of some committee members, the following sentence was included: 'we should be strongly opposed to any parsimony in the provision of funds for Welsh-language services rebounding on the quality and range of service available to the English-language viewer'.[89] This statement gives the impression that protecting English language provision was the reasoning behind the call for adequate funding for Welsh language programmes. The committee was concerned that the production of cheap Welsh language programming would lead to a belief that it would be acceptable to meet the needs of non-Welsh-speaking viewers by producing low-quality regional programmes too.

An issue that was briefly discussed at the end of S4C's second visit to the committee, but became one of the main recommendations of the WASC, was whether S4C should commission and fund English language programmes about Wales in order to attract non-Welsh-speaking viewers to the channel.[90] Leo Abse raised the issue, which received a robust response from Owen Edwards who stated that the Broadcasting Act did not place those responsibilities on the channel, and that it was not financially possible within the agreed resources to commission English language programmes. S4C had by this time arranged and agreed its budget with the IBA on the basis of funding 12 hours a week of Welsh language productions (with an additional 10 hours a week being provided free of charge by the BBC): trying to produce English language programmes within the same budget would result in spending the money at the expense of the Welsh language programmes, and would lead to producing cheap programmes for both audiences. Abse was unimpressed by the response from S4C, and tried to convince its representatives of his argument:

> I am rather surprised at your tough rejection or interpretation. I would have thought that it would have been to the benefit of all of us – English and Welsh-speaking Welshmen – if in fact there were also some titbits of great interest to the English-speaking Welshman on that programme, which might induce them to continue to look and indeed, if their Welsh is inadequate, to improve it as a result of looking at the other programmes?[91]

The logic of Leo Abse's suggestion is clear, that English language programmes about Wales should be used to attract non-Welsh-speaking viewers to the channel who would then be tempted to watch some of the Welsh language programmes. Whatever the merits of the suggestion, the recommendation was invalid, as the Act did not allow it. If the channel had responsibility for commissioning English language provision as well as Welsh language programmes, an increase in the budget would be required from the IBA. One issue that was not mentioned in the debate, and which would certainly be a valid reason for not commissioning English language programmes about Wales for S4C, is that the BBC and HTV would be highly unlikely to support the idea of S4C stepping on their toes and responsibilities. In an attempt to calm the waters, Sir Goronwy Daniel proposed that the channel would commission some musical programmes, for example, which would be accessible to non-Welsh speakers. He also promised that the channel's officials would pass on any good ideas for English language programmes about Wales to C4 to be considered for commissioning. Despite Sir Goronwy Daniel's pragmatic solutions, the WASC was not persuaded, and a clause was published in the final report recommending that S4C should commission programmes in English about Wales.

The WASC's second report could be described as unremarkable, the result of a committee that, after the government's second U-turn and the establishment of the S4C Authority, had lost its purpose and focus. There were a number of empty recommendations encouraging activities and approaches already implemented by the broadcasting organisations, such as requiring the BBC, the IBA and HTV to reconsider their requirement for some management posts to have staff who were Welsh speakers and to offer Welsh learning facilities for members of staff.[92] The press response to the report was minimal, and Alwyn Roberts described its appearance as a 'damp squib';[93] it had very little influence on the development and operation of broadcasting systems in Wales, despite its fiery and entertaining discussions.

Channel 4 (C4)

Initially only 22 hours a week of Welsh language programmes were intended to be broadcast on S4C. This equated to just over three hours a day. To fill the remaining schedule hours, it would be necessary to show English language programmes produced for C4. The relationship established between S4C and C4 was therefore of key importance to the channel, as the generosity or ill-humoured nature of that relationship could have an adverse effect on the channel's other activities, especially if C4 decided that it was in direct competition with S4C. The arguments for establishing S4C and C4 were not entirely compatible. C4's *raison d'être* was to provide unique programming for minority audiences with specialist interests, offering viewers a real choice in programmes that differed significantly from those that were broadcast on other networks. In contrast S4C was trying to be a comprehensive popular service that appealed and attracted the largest audiences for Welsh language programming. It was difficult for S4C to justify creating programmes for a small niche audience within an audience that was already a minority, as it would reflect poorly on viewing figures. S4C's responsibility was to please everyone at the same time, and the content of both channels could have been wholly incompatible as S4C faced the challenge of trying to create a joint service for the people of Wales from programmes produced for different purposes.

It was essential to form a unified service from the two schedules, to ensure that the Welsh language was not placed in a ghetto, and thus fulfilling the fears of Professor Jac L. Williams.[94] English language C4 programmes would be responsible for attracting many viewers to the channel, and it was hoped that the appeal of those programmes would attract viewers who were not ardent supporters of the language. There was an anticipation that viewers who chose to view the fourth channel for its English language output would be attracted to watch the Welsh language programmes when those programmes ended, with the inheritance factor giving the channel's audience figures a boost and securing a broader audience. But in order to produce those engaging and entertaining programmes C4 would have to compete with S4C for the relatively small amount of funding available from the IBA. HTV would not be able to collect enough advertising revenue from selling adverts on the fourth channel in Wales to meet S4C's financial needs and therefore it was inevitable that some of the money raised by selling advertising space on C4 would be used to make up the shortfall in the money collected in Wales.[95] Should C4 feel that it was not receiving sufficient funding, the relationship between C4 and S4C could possibly be challenging, with both sides battling to ensure that they received their fair share.

Although there were clear differences between the ethos of the two channels and possible competition between them for resources, some of the likely tensions were eliminated due to the relationship of the two leaders. From their first meeting at the Celtic Film and Television Festival in

Harlech in 1981, where both were scheduled to address the audience, an easy working relationship and friendship was established between Owen Edwards and Jeremy Isaacs. Their relationship was based on the fact that they both began their careers in television in the late 1950s at Granada.[96] Those common experiences formed the basis of a close friendship and one that Glyn Tegai Hughes described as 'critical' for the channel.[97] Several issues between the channels were solved when Owen Edwards would pick up the phone to speak to his colleague in London. Owen Edwards's comments also confirm this: 'I couldn't praise him enough, such a civilised person. Jeremy was a great help to us at the beginning . . . so supportive.'[98] Jeremy Isaacs's recollections reinforce these comments and in his memoir *Storm over 4* he stated that he believed there were clear reasons why C4 and S4C could work together to make the initiative a success:

> Channel 4 and S4C could easily have been at loggerheads from the word go . . . Yet it seemed to me then, and seems to me still, that in our different obligations to service special needs and fulfil distinctive cultural goals there was much, much more to unite us than to divide us.[99]

One of the issues where the two channels could have been at cross purposes were the discussions surrounding the practical arrangements and financial terms of showing C4 programmes on S4C. The exact meaning of the following clause of the Broadcasting Act was widely debated as it was drafted and after it was published:

> for any period not allocated to the broadcasting of a programme not in Welsh, the programme broadcast is normally the same as the programme (or one of the programmes) broadcast on the Fourth Channel in that period for reception otherwise than in Wales.[100]

This clause was included in order to save money on repeat costs, as it was feared that a repeat fee could be demanded if the programme was shown at a different time on S4C to C4.[101] In such a situation S4C would have very little flexibility in its schedule, and there would be severe practical difficulties in its implementation, as Lord Cledwyn noted when discussing the Act in the House of Lords:

> the break might occur in the middle of a programme. Let us assume that a ballet or 'Hamlet' was being performed, which might take two or more hours. You could not cut into the middle of that and insert it into the Welsh Fourth Channel. It seems to me that it would be better if the Welsh Authority could if necessary choose from other suitable Fourth Channel programmes already recorded. At least it would be prudent for the Bill to provide for this to be done.[102]

Since the majority of Welsh hours were intended to be broadcast during peak hours, approximately half of the 35 hours of English language programming per week planned for broadcast by C4 would be completely lost to the Welsh audience. This loss of peak programming would undoubtedly mean that the Welsh audience would be deprived of C4's most attractive programmes. Implementing such a scheme would have resulted in perpetuating the injustice felt amongst the non-Welsh-speaking audience that they were being denied interesting and attractive English language programmes, thus breaking one of S4C's core purposes of alleviating social tensions. Another significant consequence of this plan was that it would have been difficult for S4C to put its own stamp and logo on the channel during the hours taken live from C4, making it more challenging to create an identity for the channel. The original plan proposed by the government was therefore not practical, and attempts were made to find ways in which the new channel could define the clause in a way that would not confine S4C to the C4 schedule.

In response to inquiries from Dafydd Wigley MP and Dafydd Elis-Thomas MP, Leon Brittan, the Home Office minister of state, confirmed that the Act did not prevent the fourth channel from re-scheduling English language C4 programmes, should it wish to do so.[103] However, he noted that the government was convinced that the costs of tapes, staffing and the additional rights payments for performers and artists were too high to justify. It was in the written evidence of the Cymdeithas Darlledwyr Cymraeg (Association of Welsh Broadcasters) to the WASC on 4 February 1981 that a solution was discussed publicly for the first time, and that a pattern of re-scheduling could be implemented at no great cost to the channel:

> he [Lord Belstead] envisages a difficulty in transmitting on the Fourth Channel in Wales any programmes which have been

> broadcast at a different time in the remainder of the United Kingdom. 'It is much more expensive' – he says – 'if you cannot use it simultaneously and have to get a repeat running.'
>
> Not so. Such an arrangement does not constitute a 'repeat' but is regarded as 'non-simultaneous transmission', and as such, incurs no extra costs.[104]

There were no additional costs connected to the 'once around transmitters' principle already used by ITV companies to ensure that regions did not need to pay to show network programmes displaced by local programming and could also be applied to the fourth channel. Assurance would have to be received from C4 officials that this principle was acceptable to them and that it would not create difficulties with the unions. It was envisaged that most, if not all, C4 programmes could be re-scheduled on S4C by opening the service earlier than C4, ensuring the necessary space and flexibility for programmes broadcast during C4's peak hours to be rescheduled.[105]

With C4 and S4C competing against each other for IBA funding, C4 could have chosen to ignore the growing consensus and rather attempted to secure more money for its own coffers by refusing to provide the programmes free of charge. But C4's chief executive was a man who believed that the two channels shared an ethos of serving minorities, albeit in a very different manner, and so S4C was given the freedom to broadcast C4 programmes according to its own schedule rather than be bound by C4's schedule. Isaacs says of that decision:

> Channel 4 made all its programmes available to S4C free of charge. They were free to schedule them as they wished, so our programmes of necessity – even the finest of them – went late or early. And there was not room in their schedule for all of our stuff. But I was always content to respect Owen's sovereignty over what was his, and leave scheduling decisions to him and his colleagues . . . I urged only that, in their discretion, they should not leave out altogether what we were proudest of.[106]

S4C would be able to show C4's most attractive programmes, but at slightly less convenient times. This replaced deprivation with inconvenience for the non-Welsh-speaking audience. Although this was not an ideal solution, it meant that viewers in Wales could watch most C4 programmes. There were some benefits to the scheme as it gave viewers more choice since they did not have to decide between programmes, say on ITV and C4, at 8 o'clock, as the C4 programme could be watched at another time on S4C.

There were a number of advantages to this approach, but it was not entirely straightforward. Although both channels were happy, the Musicians' Union threatened not to accept the principle, although this did not develop into a full dispute.[107] Another problem that arose was that information about the C4 schedule appeared in publications read by Welsh viewers and created confusion: viewers expected to see programmes at the times advertised by C4 but, in reality, they would have to wait a day or two before they were broadcast in Wales, which added to the sense of deprivation that some audience members felt.

Despite these minor difficulties, the decision to ensure that S4C had full control over its schedule was a crucial one, and although this led to more work for the planning team it meant that staff could make the most of the programmes available to them. Not everything was broadcast on S4C: sadly C4's innovative hour-long news programme would not be broadcast in Wales. However, the re-scheduling led to 80 per cent of C4 programmes being shown on S4C, and a loss of 20 per cent was much better than the 50 per cent that would have disappeared completely under the government's original plans.[108] C4's decision not to charge S4C for its programmes was also crucial. S4C's programme budget would certainly have been squeezed with the consequence of more low-cost Welsh language programmes had C4 demanded remuneration: the decision meant that every possible penny could be spent on producing quality Welsh language programmes. The understanding and harmonious relationship forged between S4C and C4 freed the channel's officials, enabling them to focus on forming partnerships with the broadcasters who would produce Welsh language programmes for its service.

S4C and its providers

Despite the attitudes of the broadcasters during the battle for a fourth channel, from the outset the willingness of the BBC and HTV to be involved in the early developments and the authority's readiness to include them in the formative discussions was evident.[109] However, although representatives of both broadcasters were present on the first weekend of the authority's discussions, they were treated in subtly different ways. The BBC was involved in the general discussions on the structure of the new service through the presence of Owen Edwards, the controller of BBC Wales, and the IBA was represented by the IBA secretary for Wales and the west of England, Eirion Lewis.[110] HTV representatives Sir Alun Talfan Davies and Ron Wordley were only invited to a separate session to discuss HTV's likely contribution to the new service.[111] The different approach is attributed to the fact that the authority turned to organisations of the same status for support, and the organisations that supported the campaign for Welsh programmes on the fourth channel. Asking for help from a company with whom it would have to form a commercial relationship in a matter of months would be much more complicated. The authority was also uncertain as to the extent of HTV's responsibility to provide programmes for its service under the new contract with the IBA as the Broadcasting Act was vague. Therefore, before undertaking any assistance or advice offered by HTV, clarification was needed on the requirements of the Act.[112] Attempts were made to remedy the situation, however, by inviting HTV representatives to be part of the specialist working groups that met to produce advisory documents for the authority on programming and engineering.[113]

Following these early meetings, the authority initiated discussions and the drawing up of contracts or memoranda of understanding with its providers. These documents were key in defining and guiding the development of the key relationships between S4C and its programme providers. The context for producing these documents and their finalised details is a key element in the task of assessing and examining the relationship between the BBC, HTV and S4C.

BBC

The first correspondence between the BBC and S4C regarding programmes came in February 1981, with Owen Edwards, then the controller of BBC Wales, sending a letter to the authority outlining the costs of BBC programmes.[114] Due to the substance of the Broadcasting Act, S4C was not obliged to discuss costs with the BBC as the authority would not be required to pay for the programmes provided by the corporation: the corporation had a statutory responsibility to provide a specified number of programmes which corresponded to the Welsh language provision that the BBC would have broadcast on its own channels had the new channel not been created, and to do so free of charge, paying for them from the TV licence.[115] Why, therefore, was this information sent to the authority? Its evidence to the WASC shows that they were discussing the possibility of the

BBC providing an additional hour of programming, in addition to its statutory responsibility, for a fixed charge. This suggests that the authority was not fully confident that they could secure sufficient hours of independent sector programmes to complete the 22 hours. The skill of the independent producers was not the only issue that concerned the authority: some members were worried that HTV would be seeking huge sums of money and that the required number of programmes may not be affordable. Another possible reason, of course, was that the authority wanted to see that the corporation was investing sufficiently in the Welsh language programmes.

With the exception of discussions surrounding news provision for the new channel, discussed later in this chapter, there were no formal talks on the relationship between the BBC and S4C until Euryn Ogwen Williams was appointed programme editor in May 1981. The first formal meeting between the programme editor and the heads of BBC and HTV programmes, Gareth Price and Huw Davies, was held in June that year. They decided that there would be monthly meetings between the three to discuss ways of creating a unified service from the various programme sources while discussions on specific programme genres and content would be held independently with the individual broadcasters.[116] These meetings would also explore issues such as how to avoid overusing the same actors and presenters, to avoid hindering the new channel with the misconception that there was not enough talent working in Welsh to maintain the service.[117] The fact that this was discussed at the first meeting of programme heads shows the prominence of the issue. Indeed, it was discussed in WASC's activities after HTV claimed that only 60–70 Equity members could speak Welsh.[118] Equity sought to reverse that view by providing evidence stating that 198 of its members were Welsh-speaking.[119] One member of the WASC, Dr Roger Thomas MP, doubted the accuracy of that figure, as he could think of no more than seventy-five Welsh actors; the National Association of Theatrical, Television and Kine Employees suggested that not all 198 were fluent enough to work in the language, especially in dramatic productions.[120] These discussions show that there was paranoia about arguments regarding the supposed lack of talent available to work in Welsh. These concerns were valid, however, as director Stephen Bayly stated in *Sight and Sound* magazine:

> There is one nightmarish aspect of directing drama in Welsh – casting. There are only 110 female and 186 male actors listed in

> *Oriel*, the Actors Equity directory of Welsh-speaking 'actors'. Not a huge range from which to cast roles ranging between the ages of 18 and 96, especially given that not all the members listed are actors first and foremost . . . In *Joni Jones* we had to use puppeteers, cabaret artists, opera singers and tap-dancers . . .[121]

Although the number of Welsh Equity members were limited, the union was not happy to see the channel considering encouraging amateur performers to take part in its productions, and the discussions between the channel and the union were characterised by public dispute. Before meeting with S4C officials, Equity had expressed its concerns that programme producers would seek to use amateur actors and performers in order to save on production costs.[122] The union had been provoked into this response by the possibility of the channel taking advantage of the tradition of Welsh choral singing to provide a platform for the many amateur choirs of Wales. S4C hoped for flexibility in the union's policies that would enable it to utilise new actors and local talents as Welsh language drama provision increased significantly. This was anathema to Equity, and since television was a closed shop, the union believed that this would lead to producers using actors who did not already have Equity cards. They feared that this would set a precedent that would lead to independent producers using amateur actors to cut their costs and secure drama productions at the expense of the larger broadcasting corporations that adhered to union rules.[123] Despite the differing views, the negotiations between S4C and Equity started relatively smoothly.[124] But a month later the relationship had deteriorated and Owen Edwards released a press release expressing his disappointment at the union's rigid attitude.[125]At the 1981 Machynlleth Eisteddfod, Owen Edwards set Equity a challenge as he declared his determination to give opportunities to young, new, bright talent, and that Equity's membership card was not the only criterion of quality, talent or professionalism.[126] Angering the union further, he announced that the tenor Trebor Edwards would be appearing in his own programme, despite the fact that Equity had used him as an example of an individual who should not be allowed to perform on television due to his main occupation being farming rather than singing.[127] The dispute illustrates the duality of the channel's ethos: the emphasis on the one hand on the provision of quality content that would compare favourably with the other channels, and on the other hand reflecting Welsh culture, which because of the traditions of the eisteddfod, local drama companies and countless choirs, depended heavily on amateur performers. Equity, it seemed, was trying to impose uniform British rules on a channel that needed to appeal to a Welsh audience who expected to see programmes reflecting the Welsh community and offering a much-awaited platform for talents such as Trebor Edwards. Given that a significant number of Welsh language actors did not hold Equity cards and the proposed substantial increase in drama production, there was a need for the union to relax its rules so that complaints about the same old familiar faces did not become a cacophony. Equity's Welsh-medium members eventually increased and a special licence was agreed with S4C allowing producers to use more amateurs than usual to reflect the diversity of talent in Wales.[128] Equity remained sceptical, and called for a review of the situation in six months' time to ensure that the rules were not being abused by producers.[129] This arrangement meant that many new actors were allowed to secure work, and the drama *Coleg* (HTV) was a key production that showcased new young talents such as Tony Llywelyn, Janet Aethwy, Judith Humphreys and Stifyn Parri. By 1983, the focus of the debate had changed: there was now concern that there was a significant imbalance in the range of actors because of the significant influx of young actors – there were now not enough older actors. The arrival of S4C inspired a tremendous interest in acting and performance amongst young people, and it was envisaged that there would not be enough work for them all after graduating from college.[130] The nature of the pool of Welsh actors was completely transformed, and less than a year after broadcasting began the priority changed from increasing the numbers of Welsh-speaking actors to increasing the standard of their performances.

Following discussions between the programme heads, the new BBC Wales controller, Geraint Stanley Jones, was invited to the authority's July 1981 meeting.[131] There he mentioned a potential conflict between the BBC Charter and the responsibilities of the S4C Authority under the Broadcasting Act.[132] He foresaw tension between the BBC's responsibility to provide programmes for S4C in a way that met the reasonable needs of the authority, and the requirements of the Charter that the BBC's governors, or the broadcasting council in Wales, should oversee all policy and content for corporation programmes.[133] In the event of disagreement between the two parties, for example on the content of programmes, a stalemate could be foreseen as neither the Act nor the Charter gave any guidance as to how it might be resolved. Despite these fears, it was felt that this problem would not arise, since there was a great deal of goodwill within both organisations which was likely to avert any disagreement.[134]

However, it was necessary to be realistic, and it was anticipated that it would be difficult to guarantee that the corporation's output would successfully meet the needs of both parties when considering the quality of the content, the cost and also the nature of the programmes provided. Furthermore, it was predicted that there would be tension between the needs of the channel in terms of programmes and the amount of money available from the licence fee to meet these requirements. Once again, common sense and the goodwill and willingness of both parties to compromise would be key should such a problem arise. As a mark of the BBC's commitment to S4C's success and evidence of the respect that existed within the corporation towards the new venture, the BBC in Wales had agreed to spend £3.5 million on Welsh language programming before receiving confirmation of the increase in funding following the proposed increase in the licence fee.[135] Despite this belief that common sense would prevail should there be any dispute or disagreement, it could be argued that there was an over-reliance in these discussions on the goodwill between the two channels at the start of a new venture. This strategy would not work in the long term as it did not lay solid foundations for collaboration when different personalities, who did not have a friendly personal relationship or a history of working together, would be at the helm.

There were also more practical discussions about the nature of the links between the different channels. It was suggested that bi-monthly meetings be held between members of the S4C Authority and the broadcasting council, to discuss programmes; the heads of S4C, BBC and HTV would be expected to meet on a monthly basis, with meetings of the heads of programmes and heads of planning and presentation following the same pattern. Despite the close and frequent contact for senior members of staff, the BBC did not want to involve other heads of departments in the discussions, and it certainly did not want informal links between S4C staff and BBC production staff. It was thought that such discussions could undermine the authority of the department heads within the corporation's management structure.[136] Similar sentiments were discussed in internal documents circulated amongst some senior BBC executives who wanted a clear editorial relationship between BBC staff and their managers so that staff would not become confused because the programmes were being produced for broadcast on S4C.[137]

Many of the same matters were communicated in the 'statement of intent' document sent by the BBC to S4C in June 1982.[138] The BBC was not statutorily obliged to produce a document that defined its relationship with the new channel, however it was considered that there was value in formalising the relationship by setting guidelines and a framework to which both parties could refer if difficulties arose. The document included a number of clauses that were similar to the previous discussions with Geraint Stanley Jones, with potential conflict between the Charter and Broadcasting Act once again raising its head. Interestingly, echoing those discussions, the document also states that goodwill is key to a flourishing relationship between the two organisations:

> It is clear that the development of a successful working relationship is dependent upon trust and good-will between both organisations. For its part, the BBC re-affirms its commitment to the success of S4C which it regards as essential to meet the needs of the audience in Wales and as the successful outcome of the case for a single channel joint service which the BBC advocated consistently throughout the 1970s.[139]

Despite this, later in the same document the BBC can be seen clearly setting out the expected division between the responsibilities of the two organisations: S4C would have responsibility for the form and balance of its service but that the BBC would retain editorial, technical and financial responsibility for the programmes it produced.[140] Although the document made clear that effective discussion and information-sharing processes were expected to be established, tensions were anticipated due to the division of responsibilities, particularly in terms of programme content. The BBC could, in principle, create a programme that did not please S4C in terms of content, technical standards or financial investment, but as it was the BBC's responsibility to look after those aspects, S4C would have little choice but to broadcast or face a gap in its schedule. This possibility is recognised in the statement of intent when discussing how to resolve any disagreement. Clause 11 of the document states that S4C officials may demand a copy of a script or programme about which they were concerned, but only on completion. If S4C's fears persisted, the BBC would give serious consideration to the changes or recommendations made by the channel's officials. However, the final decision on whether to adapt the programme would rest with the BBC, and if the disagreement continued, even after high-level discussions between the authority and the broadcasting council, then S4C would be free not to broadcast the programme. In such a situation the BBC would not be obliged to provide a replacement programme.[141] There were consequently areas where the relationship between S4C and the BBC could break down, which would result in a detrimental effect on the schedule and service provided to the audience. S4C's right to reject a programme gave it some control over the content produced for it by the BBC, but Euryn Ogwen Williams argued that it was not practical to exercise that right: 'We have a right to reject a programme but this is purely cosmetic as the BBC has no responsibility to replace it.'[142] During the trial period, therefore, no programme produced by the BBC was refused broadcast, but tensions were brewing due to the lack of control that S4C officials felt over the content produced by the corporation.

Some practical details were also explored in the document as the BBC confirms that an average of 10 hours per week would be produced. The number of hours per week would vary depending on the time of year, with flexibility to adjust its provision when major national events such as an eisteddfod or sports were to be broadcast. It was also agreed that not all 10 hours would be original programming as some repeats could be included as part of the total, at levels similar to those on other BBC services.[143] Repeating some past BBC Welsh language programmes would tie the service to the previous provision, ensuring that it would be seen as a natural evolution of the service provided by the BBC, TWW and HTV, rather than an entirely new service. The document also noted the BBC's intention to provide a range of drama, light entertainment, religious programmes, documentaries or features, sports programmes, children's programmes, outside broadcasts of major national events such as the National Eisteddfod and the Royal Welsh, and discussion programmes.[144]

Despite the comprehensive nature of this document, some issues remained unresolved, more than a year after initial discussions. It was noted that a separate statement was required in order to agree where the legal responsibility lay for the BBC's programmes on S4C. The BBC would retain all rights to commercially exploit the content, but there was uncertainty as to who would be responsible if an individual complained of libel.[145] These issues had already been discussed, with the BBC in principle believing that it could take on the legal responsibility, but only for the first broadcast of any programme. If S4C were to repeat a problematic programme, without consideration of the complaints against it, that was a much more complex issue.[146] It was clearly a difficult issue to resolve, because confirmation that the legal responsibility would sit with the BBC was not received until January 1983, more than two months after the channel began broadcasting.[147]

At the end of the document there is a statement showing the duality of the relationship between the BBC and S4C. There was a strong desire to ensure the success and prosperity of the channel, but the corporation also needed to consider its wider needs and responsibilities, and so a clear division of responsibilities between the two organisations was needed at the start of the initiative:

> This letter of intention is of necessity, carefully worded and thus may seem negative in tone. It is, therefore, worth repeating the point made in paragraph 3: the BBC will do all it can to work in a friendly spirit with S4C to ensure the resounding success of this new adventure.[148]

HTV

Unlike the collaborative relationship established between S4C and the BBC, the relationship formed between S4C and HTV was rather different. In the Broadcasting Act only one paragraph lay out the parameters of HTV's relationship with S4C providing guidelines for its discussions:

> The contract between the IBA and the TV programme contractor whose duty it is to provide programmes for broadcasting on ITV for reception in Wales shall contain all such provisions as the IBA think necessary or expedient to ensure that, while the IBA are providing both ITV and the Fourth Channel in Wales, the programme contractor is under a duty to supply to the Welsh Authority (on commercial terms) a reasonable proportion of the television programmes in Welsh which the Welsh Authority need . . . and to do so in a way which meets the reasonable requirements of the Welsh Authority.[149]

This short paragraph does not give much in the way of guidance to either party. It contains a number of ambiguous expressions, for example, 'reasonable needs', which could be interpreted in a variety of ways. The most equivocal of them is 'commercial terms', and these words became the source of many fierce arguments as the relationship between HTV and S4C was forged. Despite the ambiguity there is confirmation of certain conditions that would define the relationship between HTV and S4C. It states that HTV must provide programmes for S4C, that S4C would have to pay for those programmes and that the IBA would ensure that maintaining this provision was part of its agreement with HTV as well as part of a formal agreement between the Welsh language channel and HTV.

One of the first occasions where consideration could be given to how HTV would work with the new channel was the WASC discussions. One of the hotly debated topics, and an area that would define S4C's relationship with HTV, was how much money would be needed to run the channel. Broadcasting organisations had not fully considered the funding required to establish and operate the new channel, particularly a channel expected by statute: 'to ensure that the programmes provided by them [S4C Authority] maintain a high general standard in all respects, and in particular in respect of their content and quality'.[150] It was not logical, therefore, to consider that the channel could be operated on a budget that was significantly smaller than other broadcasters. However, during the WASC's first discussions with HTV Dr Roger Thomas MP for Carmarthen suggested that the channel could be run on £1.5 million a year:

> 243. [Dr Roger Thomas] We have had evidence from one source – I will not reveal the source – that it is possible to run this channel for 22 hours per week for the whole year on £1½ million. Do you think that is feasible or not?
>
> [Mr Wordley, managing director, HTV] One and a half million pounds per hour. I would not argue too much with.
>
> 244. [Dr Roger Thomas] Not £1½ million per year?[151]

These figures clearly caused some surprise to the committee's chairman, who stated after hearing the exchange above: 'Listening to those figures, I am getting a bit terrified as to what the proportion [of the Fourth Channel subscription] is likely to be if you are going to get a full Wales Fourth Channel [*sic*].'[152]

The IBA initially proposed that the Welsh channel's share of the fourth channel's subscription would be between £7 and £9 million, and later in their evidence this was increased to £10.3 million.[153] Evidently, there had been no open discussions between the IBA and HTV about what S4C's likely budget would be, as HTV representatives noted that the company would need to receive £15 million a year in order to provide 10 hours a week of programmes on the current mix. Some necessary genres such as drama and light entertainment were lacking in that current provision and would require higher costs to be added into the mix. Given that the new channel would be expected to commission at least two hours a week from other sources, such as independent companies, the figures proposed by the IBA to provide 12 hours of programming and administrative costs were highly unrealistic. Either the broadcasting authority figures were unworkable or HTV was being greedy, capitalising on a source of funding that could be exploited to continue with its plans to build a new studio at Culverhouse Cross.

The financial discussions that took place between the IBA and S4C show that there is truth to both of these interpretations. The IBA's original estimates were certainly low considering the production costs of the period, due to the pressure exerted by ITV's regional companies to keep the costs of the Welsh language fourth channel low to ensure that the financial burden placed on them was not overwhelming. On the other hand, the costs presented by HTV were higher than the average costs expected of an ITV network company.[154] It could be suggested that, as a commercial company, battling for a healthy budget for the new channel was a tactic devised by self-interest on HTV's behalf which would mean that they could secure favourable financial terms when negotiating programme costs with the new channel. The initial confusion about the true cost of the fourth Welsh language channel could therefore be blamed on both sides.

Towards the end of the WASC negotiations, further figures were received from HTV that suggested that S4C needed £2.3 million an hour as this was the budget available to C4.[155] The company stated that if this was the budget available for English language programmes then that should be the aim for Welsh language programmes as well, and that it should aim for a minimum budget of £27.6 million for programme production alone:

> Welsh-language programmes cost no less to produce than English-language programmes. It follows that the funds required by WFCA to enable it to provide a service comparable in quality to that of 4CUK must logically be in excess of the £2.3 million per annum for each weekly hour to be purchased . . . the total funds

> should therefore exceed £30 million unless a second-class service unable to properly compete for viewers is to result.[156]

This statement suggests that self-interest was not the only motivating factor for HTV as it advocated for a fair budget, but rather because it firmly believed that Welsh language programmes should be created on the same financial terms as English language programmes, if they were to attract and retain viewers. No doubt it was the combination of the two perspectives that motivated the company to fight for fair financial conditions for the channel. Whatever the opinion of HTV's motive, it is clear that their evidence to the WASC ensured that reasonable and fair figures were considered in the discussions about the channel's financial needs. In that task HTV successfully resisted the pressure from its ITV network partners, who were convinced that the necessary funding could not be found to maintain a channel of high-quality Welsh language programming. HTV's evidence to the WASC was instrumental in seeking fair and equitable funding that would enable S4C to create quality and attractive programmes that could compete with other broadcasters' output on relatively equal terms.

The minutes of the first meeting between HTV and the authority during that first weekend of meetings at Gregynog are revealing and give an insight into the difficulties that both sides would face and the complex nature of the relationship that would develop between them. The basis of the meeting was a memorandum of specific questions forwarded to the authority by Ron Wordley. Given that these opening discussions were held at the authority's first meeting, some of the questions were impossible to answer, as it was far too early for the authority to make such critical decisions. Questions such as whether S4C would like HTV to continue providing three and a half hours of children's programming for the new channel, and what changes did the channel want to see in the range of programmes the company already produced.[157] These were difficult questions to discuss as they addressed programme and schedule details that had not yet been considered by the authority. Had the authority responded concretely without fully considering the implications, it would have tied the channel and its staff to decisions that would be difficult to overturn. The needs of the service and the strengths and qualities of all providers had to be considered, and authority members were astute enough not to give replies that would commit the channel too early to decisions that they might come to regret.

HTV could be discussed in light of its public image at this time as a self-interested company, but the company's response during this first meeting offers a more complex picture. Ron Wordley's answers in considering the facilities needed by S4C suggests that HTV representatives also considered what would be best for the new service rather than the benefits for their company alone. Although there was a potential opportunity to secure additional funding for HTV's developments at Culverhouse Cross, the minutes do not show the company representatives offering to share facilities with S4C. Indeed, Ron Wordley's recommendation was that independent facilities would be best, though perhaps more problematic and expensive due to the necessity to arrange and rent audio and image circuits between S4C's presentation location and the British Telecom National Switching Centre in Cardiff.[158] Here we see the duality at the core of HTV's approach to the fourth channel developments. On the one hand the company was keen to provide support for the new channel, but on the other there was an eagerness to safeguard its best interests and those of its shareholders.

Following the first meeting, HTV was invited to provide estimates for an 8-, 9- and 10-hour service, emphasising that the authority would have limited resources.[159] But these conditions were apparently ignored, and HTV returned proposals of costs much higher than those seen in any previous discussions. An hourly cost of more than £50,000 was identified, excluding any profit for HTV.[160] Given the scale of the costs that the company had identified during the discussions before the WASC, this was a huge leap. HTV did not agree with that interpretation, however, and Ron Wordley stated:

> that HTV had provided evidence to the Select Committee on the basis of £1.5m an hour (1979–80 prices and at the current mix). 10 hours of programmes would cost £15m. By including 18% inflation, rentals and payments to the IBA and a change in the mix, the cost would increase to £27m a year – £2.7m an hour. This was completely consistent with the figures and evidence.[161]

These comments raise several pertinent points that should be given full consideration. Britain's economic situation was volatile with a period of high inflation, and as a result the costs of producing programmes could be quite different from one year to the next, causing a large gulf between the figures presented at different times during the debates. In addition, the figures provided to the WASC referred to the cost of producing the programmes broadcast by HTV through the medium of Welsh at the time.[162] However, when providing programmes for S4C, the provision would have to be strengthened by introducing programmes that were more expensive to produce, such as drama and light entertainment. Adding these genres to the mix would push up the hourly average price of programmes.

HTV included a number of additional costs over and above the programme production costs, such as rent and payments to the IBA, in their quotes. Some members of the S4C Authority were sceptical about whether S4C should pay towards part of their tax liabilities and the new HTV broadcasting centre, and expressed their concerns that 'the Company's development costs are being borne by S4C and the Welsh language programmes'.[163] Some of these fears were confirmed by the IBA and they noted that some of the administrative and additional costs were high.[164] Although HTV staff insisted that only the relevant percentage of costs were included, a seed of doubt had been planted in the authority's mind. Despite these obstacles, HTV was keen to finalise an agreement in June 1981, so that the company could proceed with the necessary preparatory work, but the negotiations would rumble on for more than a year.

Discussions with HTV were postponed in April 1981, as they became increasingly complex and intricate. Concern was expressed that the negotiations were futile since S4C was unsure about the range of programmes they would eventually require from HTV, and it was also noted that the sums available to pay HTV for their productions would be highly dependent on the funding available from the IBA.[165] It is important to recall that in April 1981 the authority had only just appointed Owen Edwards and that Euryn Ogwen Williams, the programme editor, had not yet been interviewed. It is possible that the authority conducted these discussions too early, without having the necessary information to be able to have constructive discussions with HTV. On the other hand, however, with pressure to outline costs to the IBA urgently, there was no option but to start discussions even whilst some details were vague or unconfirmed.

Discussions resumed following the appointment of Euryn Ogwen Williams with consideration given to the type of programmes that S4C wanted HTV to produce.[166] It was suggested that HTV could develop a programme that would provide an opportunity for the audience to share their opinions on the channel's output, a show of which Williams had high expectations: 'it should sparkle and provide talking points for the following day'.[167] It was proposed that the popular programme *Siôn a Siân* could be transferred to S4C after a short time off-air to ensure that the audience would not become bored by it, and Williams requested a change of emphasis in the children's programmes suitable for the early evening slot.[168] Williams rejected some ideas put forward by HTV, with weekly situation comedy being considered too risky, though he agreed that some pilots for shorter series could be considered for experimentation without a firm commitment. One of the reasons behind Euryn Ogwen Williams's hesitation to commit to sitcoms, hour dramas and a new soap opera by HTV was concern at the shortage of actors to appear in such programmes, especially in the first year of the channel. He felt that commissioning and producing half-hour dramas would be a wise choice, and using them as a tool to develop new talent in the fields of writing, performing and directing.[169] Although some ideas were confirmed and others rejected, S4C's new programme editor did not want to give HTV a concrete idea of the full range of programmes it wished to receive, because: 'I wish to wait until I have a clearer picture of what the BBC are offering and the balance of the Independent's proposals before making a commitment on your mix.'[170]

Arguably, it was unfair for S4C to use HTV programmes as a way of filling the gaps between the programmes produced by the BBC and independent producers; but, in reality, it was the only reasonable solution for S4C, as the BBC's programmes were provided free of charge, and as such they had very little control over them. There was also no guarantee that the independent producers would be able to produce a very wide range of programmes, and therefore S4C would have taken too much of a gamble by assuming that the independent producers could fulfil the gaps between BBC and HTV programmes. To consider the situation from a different perspective, there is evidence here of the faith that S4C held in HTV, and the ability and experience of the company to turn its hand to any genres and thus to provide programmes that would act as a glue to unify the provision.

By September 1981, HTV had drawn up a first draft of a likely agreement for the programmes. But when that draft was discussed there were three fundamental points of disagreement. The most problematic aspects were that S4C would have no control over the quality of the programmes provided, that the deal remained without review until 1989 and that the cost of the programmes far exceeded the money that was likely to be available for programming.[171] On receipt of this draft the authority decided to appoint specialist consultants from broadcasting management to assist in negotiating the terms of the agreement with HTV, namely Peat, Marwick and Mitchell (PMM).[172]

Negotiations dragged on until the end of 1981, without either side compromising on the main stumbling blocks. This dispute was not surprising, as PMM confirmed that the contract was unique in the broadcasting sector.[173] There was no template to follow, and all aspects had to be considered in detail before signing this one-of-a-kind agreement. After disagreeing on the draft agreement submitted by HTV, S4C offered a new price and an agreement drafted by PMM, but HTV refused to negotiate on those terms as the price submitted was not suitable. HTV required £15.3 million a year, or its equivalent in future years, for the production of 9 hours a week when Culverhouse Cross opened its doors.[174] Of the £15.3 million, £1.25 million was earmarked for the developments at Culverhouse Cross, and in view of this S4C introduced a new approach to try to determine a figure that would be acceptable to the authority, which could also be defended publicly, especially in a time of financial austerity.[175] The suggestion was to keep the costs that would pay for HTV resources separate from the discussions on programme costs and proposed that a separate financial contribution could be offered to HTV towards Culverhouse Cross. Any such contribution would be a commercial investment, with assurances that S4C could make use of the facilities and get a share of the profits if they were sold in the future. It was considered that such a proposal would avoid confusion between the programme and capital costs of both companies.[176] Although such an idea may have guaranteed greater transparency in the programme agreement, some authority members were concerned that such an investment would give the impression that S4C had a vested interest in the commercial success of HTV and could lead to a conflict of interest.[177] The idea was put to Lord Harlech and HTV officials, but it was rejected on the grounds that the company wanted to retain control of the development and investment.[178]

By early 1982 HTV and S4C had adopted new tactics in an attempt to bring the negotiations to a close, with S4C stating that if there was no progress, the channel would refuse to negotiate a deal on 9 hours of programmes a week and negotiate a 7-hour deal instead.[179] Authority members were aware that a contract for 7 hours a week would be insufficient for HTV as their evidence to the WASC indicated that a 10-hour agreement was required to justify the level of investment and maintenance of the new facilities at Culverhouse Cross.[180] S4C was not the only party to use the number of broadcasting hours as a bargaining tool. S4C was offered two options by HTV: it was suggested that a 7-hour contract could be made, but that those programmes would be produced to the standard of the Welsh language programmes currently being broadcast, or a 9-hour agreement that would include a stronger mix of programmes and those at a higher standard. The differences in quality were due to the fact that 7 hours could be provided at the current standard from HTV's Pontcanna facilities, but, in order to achieve more hours, a stronger mix and quality, the new facilities needed to be built, and thus a higher price paid for the output. Although there is a practical truth here, as Ron Wordley explained to the WASC, this was undoubtedly a bargaining tactic to persuade S4C to adopt a scheme that would be more beneficial to HTV:

> One of the major problems is of course that the cost of the development is so high that the price of the programmes must at least cover the investment. It is almost a chicken and egg situation ... But in order to create the facilities to make that possible the programmes have to be sold at a price which makes it possible to create the facilities. It is totally inter-related.[181]

The impression given here is that the new resources were only needed because of the requirement to produce increased hours of Welsh language programmes. It was known, however, that this was not quite the case: Ron Wordley had stated this in his first meeting with the S4C Authority and in the evidence presented to the WASC.

> One cannot say that Culverhouse Cross is entirely because of the Welsh Fourth Channel Authority requirement. It is partly because of that and partly because of the contractual commitment in 1982 which the IBA have proposed to us a condition of our new contract. It is not just the Welsh Fourth Channel.[182]

In addition, in a 1979 pamphlet published by the broadcaster regarding its stance on the fourth channel in Wales, the following was included: 'Our plans are already in hand, with millions of pounds earmarked for the construction of a brand new television centre at Culverhouse Cross, near Cardiff.'[183] This statement gives the impression that the plans for

Culverhouse Cross were well underway, and already fully funded. The claims that Welsh language programmes needed to pay for the new facilities were, therefore, no more than a means to secure more money.

The language used at this time also suggests a marked change in the tone of the discussions. S4C staff members used phrases such as: 'We could win this "battle" and lose the "war" for the success of the channel.'[184] There were also suggestions of concern amongst S4C staff about the ability of HTV to provide a significant amount of programmes: 'There was some concern about the standards of HTV programmes because of the lack of information about what the company had in mind and because of the number of their best staff who had become independent producers.'[185] These comments were unfair, because some S4C staff had been successful in their attempts to persuade the top talent amongst the broadcasters' staff to set up on their own as independent production companies.[186] This was done for several reasons, including trying to strengthen the independent sector, which was in its infancy, to enable it to produce at least two hours a week for S4C. But following the contractual dispute between S4C and HTV, the increasing vitality and confidence of independent producers meant that S4C was not totally dependent on HTV to deliver 10 hours of programming a week, especially as it became increasingly clear that indies could be trusted to produce more programmes, squeezing the provision available for HTV to produce. Wil Aaron remembers that the independent producers were fully aware that they were being used by S4C to put pressure on HTV in the contractual negotiations between the two sides.[187]

In addition to the financial disagreement, HTV's attitude towards the new channel was considered to be the main stumbling block to the negotiations, and their stance on two specific issues that had led to the sharp disagreement on the definition of a reasonable price.[188] It was alleged that HTV believed that the Broadcasting Act placed it on a par with the BBC as the main suppliers of the new channel, and that therefore both should be treated in the same way;[189] the problem here was that S4C treated HTV as an independent producer, since it would pay directly for the programmes. HTV also wanted S4C to trust them fully and transfer all programme responsibilities so that a package of programmes could be provided with little oversight or input, thus operating a very similar pattern to that agreed with the BBC. In the same way as the BBC arrangement, HTV was also keen to retain the rights to the programmes.[190] HTV therefore sought to get the best of both worlds: securing payment for the product created on commercial terms but seeking to reap some of the benefits afforded to the public broadcaster providing content for free.

Negotiations dragged on until May 1982. By the final months, the main stumbling blocks were financial with a difference of over £5 million between what both sides thought was acceptable.[191] HTV compromised and reduced its price from £19 million to £17.5 million, but even after this, PMM believed that the cost could not be justified on commercial terms.[192] It was becoming increasingly difficult for S4C to justify any overspend on the HTV agreement politically as this would hamper the development of the independent producers that S4C had strived hard to develop into a viable sector. The development and growth of the independent production sector had received much attention for their early production successes and had contributed to S4C's positive reputation in its infancy.[193]

After all the discussion and disagreement, a contract was signed on 27 May 1982, just five months before the channel's broadcast start date.[194] The deal, which ran for eight years until the end of 1989, secured 7.75 hours of programmes a week for £34,500 an hour or £13.9 million for a whole year, until the new Culverhouse Cross facilities became operational in 1984 when the provision would increase to 9 hours for £35,790 per hour or £16.75 million per year (at 1982 prices).[195] The agreement, which is a 59-page document, is a bulky one that goes into great detail when dealing with complex issues such as the responsibilities of both parties in securing copyrights and preventing defamation, the responsibility of paying for the transfer of programmes from one centre to the other, together with details of the particular schedule of payments due to HTV. It also contains guidelines regarding where responsibility lay in the event of any dispute, whether financial, creative or procedural. HTV was successful in its attempt to retain the exploitation rights in the programmes, however HTV would have to seek the consent of the S4C Authority before selling any programme and capitalising financially.[196] It is a very pragmatic agreement since no element of S4C and HTV's relationship is left to chance, or dependent on the goodwill of any individuals who happened to work for S4C or HTV during the period of its signing.

There is a detailed specification of the number of hours in each programme category that HTV would produce. Factual, light entertainment and children's programmes would fill most of the hours.[197] In a year HTV would provide 87 hours of light entertainment programming, which would include chat shows, quizzes, folk and pop music, and sitcom. A combination of studio-produced children's programmes and dubbed films for children of all ages would fill nearly 125 hours each year, and a variety of factual programmes, such as farming programmes, 1-hour documentaries and religious series would fill 93 hours per year, with current affairs provision contributing an additional 72 hours. HTV was only scheduled to provide 26 hours per year of drama, but this would be shared evenly over the weeks ensuring that there would be an opportunity to watch half an hour a week of drama from the independent broadcaster.[198]

The agreement also sets out which programme genres the opening of Culverhouse Cross would allow HTV to develop further. As expected, there would be a doubling of mixed music programming, satirical shows, children's participatory programmes and situation comedy provision, with plans to offer two series each year rather than one.[199] The new facilities also enabled the growth of factual output produced with outside broadcast units, as the specification indicated that it was intended to introduce an additional sports programme and a series of factual features when the centre opened in 1984. Children's provision, studio programmes of all types and factual offerings would become typical of HTV's productions, and this is where it would build the expertise of its staff and make its mark.

Looking back over the contractual negotiations between HTV and S4C, one of the most problematic aspects was without a doubt coming to an agreement on the nature of 'commercial terms'. One of the main reasons for the gap between the two sides was that S4C had no other prices that could be compared with the figures provided by HTV. The BBC's analysis of its hourly programme costs was not a fair comparison as it did not take into account organisational costs. Nor could a fair comparison be made between the costs of HTV and the programme costs of the independent production companies, because their programmes were necessarily cheaper to produce because there were fewer structures to maintain, fewer full-time staff and generally fewer overheads. The phrase commercial terms was misleading, as the amount of money paid for programmes would depend entirely on how much money was available to the S4C Authority from the IBA. If the amount was much less than expected, it would have to work within those limits rather than on abstract commercial terms. This principle was publicly acknowledged by Ron Wordley in his evidence to the WASC; however, that was not sufficient to restrain him from seeking commercial terms.[200]

An integral part of the problem with commercial terms were HTV's intentions to develop new facilities at Culverhouse Cross. It was inevitable that a commercial company would include the costs of the new development when defining the prices of its programmes. HTV considered it reasonable to include costs relating to interest on loans and equipment depreciation in the prices since the construction of a new broadcast centre was seen as an investment in the future of Welsh language programming. This investment therefore heavily influenced some of the terms HTV demanded when negotiating the deal with S4C. There is room to argue that HTV's requirements were completely reasonable and that any other commercial company would have sought the same assurances in an agreement with a channel authority where there was no guarantee that it would exist in three years' time. However, it cannot be argued that HTV was taking a leap of faith by building Culverhouse Cross to meet S4C's needs, as an increase in Welsh language programming had been a constant part of the plans for the fourth channel, even before the decision to establish an independent Welsh language channel. If the channel were terminated and the government reverted to the previous two-channel plan, the number of Welsh language programmes would have to be maintained.

The blame for the protracted nature of the negotiations can be shared by HTV and S4C, due to the arrogance of the commercial company and the lack of experience or, more accurately, the lack of authority given to some S4C staff when negotiating the terms of the agreement. HTV's confidence in their integral role in the channel's plans is evidenced by their certainty of exceeding the minimum of 7 hours a week in statements such as, 'Production resources in Wales other than within the two broadcasting systems are poor, and independent producers are few.'[201] HTV dismissed the potential contribution of independent producers, and the company clearly brought that confidence into the negotiations. An example of S4C's faults in this complicated process was that the discussions went into too much detail about aspects of the relationship and tried to define it firmly and foresee every problem that might arise. This was a practice that was at odds with broadcasting management customs. Geraint Stanley Jones remembers that agreements were made in a less formal way and that the process observed between HTV and S4C were more like those seen in the civil service, which was the background of the chairman Sir Goronwy Daniel.[202]

The protracted discussions placed a strain on the relationship between S4C and HTV, but those tensions were not the only side effects. Due to the delay it was not possible for HTV to prepare or stockpile productions ready for the first few months of the channel. Besides creating frustration amongst HTV producers and creative staff, this delay offered independent producers the opportunity to demonstrate their ability and to produce far more programmes than originally expected, which would not have happened if S4C and HTV had agreed terms earlier.

News and current affairs provision

In the midst of the protracted contractual negotiations, channel officials sought to make crucial decisions about programme needs and who would provide which genres. These were decisions that would define the tone and nature of the new service. One of the key genres was the channel's news service, the cornerstone of all public service broadcasting. Deciding who should provide the news service was not easy, as both the BBC and HTV were very keen to secure the deal. Before the days of S4C there was Welsh language news provision on both channels, with the BBC broadcasting the programme *Heddiw* (1961–82) and HTV presenting *Y Dydd* (1964–82), and both attracting a loyal audience.[203] Neither understandably wanted to lose their news service. Even before the new authority was formed HTV claimed that its news department would be best equipped to provide the news: 'It is widely accepted that ITV Welsh news is hard, sharp and up to the minute. BBC news tends towards the magazine style of commentary on fewer items, but in depth.'[204]

Other organisations also had ideas about how S4C should engage with its responsibilities to provide a news service. The National Union of Journalists (NUJ) encouraged the establishment of an independent unit: they envisaged that the unit would employ the journalists who had worked on BBC and HTV Welsh language news programmes, following a similar structure to ITN, with the BBC and HTV sharing ownership.[205] The NUJ was concerned that because of the limited time to debate the various options, the BBC and HTV would dominate the negotiations.

However, it was clear that only two organisations were in the race to secure the news deal due to the significant costs of providing a completely independent news service.[206] At the start of the discussions, a plan was considered that ensured that the BBC and HTV would share the channel's most prestigious contract. The provision could be divided, with HTV broadcasting a set number of days and the BBC broadcasting the rest. This was HTVs favoured option and it confidently stated:

> We believe that the best interests of viewers in Wales would be served if ITV covered all Welsh-language news Monday to 7 pm Friday and the BBC from 7 pm to close-down on Sunday. We do not feel that BBC Wales would resist this proposal which will avoid redundancies amongst newsroom staff in both services and use the different talents of ITV and BBC news staff complementarily.[207]

HTV was clearly trying to secure the most prominent part of the news service, ensuring that its news would be most visible to the audience, offering the remaining scraps to the BBC, since weekend news coverage was negligible in comparison. Unsurprisingly, this arrangement was not acceptable to the corporation and, in fact, providing a news service following this pattern would have been difficult to implement. An inevitable consequence would have been a lack of consistency, especially if there was a big story running over the service of both broadcasters, and it would also involve the unnecessary duplication of resources by having two Welsh language newsrooms, with staff working part-time for half a week.[208]

Despite the apparent disagreement and competition to win the news service, at the beginning of 1981 Huw Davies, head of HTV programmes and Gareth Price, head of programmes at BBC Wales collaborated on a memorandum to the authority on the way forward. That memorandum concluded: 'the best, though not ideal, solution was to divide responsibility between the BBC and HTV on the basis of the news from one and current affairs from the other'.[209] When the memorandum was presented, HTV took the opportunity to deliver two pilot programmes that demonstrated what could be achieved with a 10-minute and a 25-minute programme pre-empting any submission by the BBC.[210] Both bulletins impressed the authority and they expressed admiration stating that: 'the presentation of HTV's news tapes was exceptional'.[211] Despite being impressed by the quality of the pilot programmes, the authority was shocked by the estimates for the cost of the proposed news service, which, according to HTV, would be around £9 million, with the addition of a late-night and a weekend service likely to increase the figure.[212] The authority had to consider whether it would make more financial sense for it to receive a free and high-quality BBC news service and keeping the £9 million to commission a wider range of other genres.

Two weeks later at the beginning of April 1982 a tape was presented by the BBC. The BBC's representatives at that meeting were Geraint Stanley

Jones, BBC Wales's interim controller and Richard Francis, the BBC's national director of news and current affairs.[213] *Y Cymro* believed that Richard Francis's presence showed the pressure from London to ensure that Cardiff retained its Welsh language news department.[214] At the meeting the corporation outlined that it was keen to provide the news service because it could draw on the expertise of its experienced staff and the close links that existed between BBC Wales and the rest of the corporation which had news teams around the world. The beneficial links that existed between the corporation's radio and television services were also emphasised, and the potential unity between the television and radio services for Welsh language audiences which could ensure that stories of importance were developed across both platforms. One service could also build an audience for the other because of the relationship between them. But, as noted in *Y Cymro*, this could also be considered a disadvantage since the arrangement would restrict the news sources for Welsh audiences:

> it would be much healthier for Welsh daily news to come from more than one newsroom. If the BBC are responsible for the news, then Radio Cymru programmes and S4C will originate from the same centre.
>
> Awarding the news to HTV would ensure that there would be competition in the field of Welsh language news – a key factor when you consider that there is no other competition.[215]

The BBC representatives also confirmed that the news service would be part of the free 10 hours a week. This would have appealed to the authority, especially after discussing the HTV costs which amounted to almost half the entire budget agreed with the IBA for the period to March 1983. Following talks with BBC representatives, it was decided that HTV would be invited to make a formal submission, as the company had taken advantage of a previous meeting to transfer tapes, without a formal presentation to argue its case. The authority was also keen to ask HTV for assurances that an international news service could be provided, along with local and national news, as the authority was keen to create a comprehensive news service for the Welsh language audience, not a service focused on Welsh affairs only.[216]

The meeting between S4C and HTV was held on 29 April 1981 at Tŷ Elgin, but this was not an official meeting of the authority, and therefore there are no minutes available to analyse what was discussed. However, the discussions appeared to be immaterial, because only days later, on 6 May 1981, reports appeared in the press announcing that HTV had withdrawn its application to provide the news.[217] In a statement Ron Wordley said: 'Recent policy decisions regarding the provision of ITN's facilities to organisations outside the 15 ITV companies mean that it is not now possible to provide the kind of service required by Sianel Pedwar Cymru.'[218] Without ITN's cooperation, it was impossible for HTV to provide the required comprehensive national and international news service, and as such the application had to be withdrawn. Ron Wordley's statement gives the impression that the remaining ITV network companies, which funded ITN, did not want to support S4C further through the use of their news resources, since they were already uneasy about their financial contributions to S4C.

The May issue of *Broadcast* suggested that difficulties lay elsewhere, stating that disagreements over editorial responsibilities were at the root of the troubles between ITN and HTV:

> Wells Street has told HTV that it cannot hand over to any organisation, editorial control over material produced by ITN. HTV had planned in its pilot to recast the news slant, even change the order of items to suit a Welsh-speaking audience. ITN baulked at this, as a result of which HTV was forced to pull out.[219]

ITN was not prepared to sacrifice its editorial control over the material it produced for HTV, and it is understandable why HTV therefore had to withdraw its application.[220] Constraints, such as the inability to adapt the running order of a bulletin to reflect the interests of a Welsh audience, would have been problematic and critical for the news service. Given that the channel was aiming to break new ground by presenting an international, national and local news service in one bulletin, not being able to make international events relevant to Welsh audiences would have made it much more difficult to persuade that audience of the virtues of the new news service.

Formal confirmation of HTV's inability to provide a complete news service for S4C came on 9 May 1981 and shortly afterwards it was confirmed that the BBC would provide the news service for the channel, and that HTV would provide a 'comprehensive' current affairs service.[221]

1. Members of the *Newyddion Saith* team – Deryk Williams, the editor, with presenters Beti George and Gwyn Llywelyn
(image: © BBC Photo Library)

2. *Y Byd ar Bedwar*'s production team meeting with Ramon Castro Ruz, Fidel Castro's elder brother
(image: reproduced with permission from ITV Cymru / Wales and the National Library of Wales)

Ultimately, this difficult decision was made easy for the authority. However, the decision was not without its implications: the BBC would provide the news as part of its free contribution, and therefore it could be argued that the range of the rest of the BBC's programmes would be adversely affected. S4C would therefore have to commission more expensive programmes such as drama from independent producers, in particular, since the news service made up about 3 hours a week of the proportion of the BBC's Welsh language programmes. The financial benefit was therefore not as significant as it first appeared.

Independent producers

The relationship that the channel needed to build with the new breed of independent producers was quite different from its agreements with the broadcasters. In England, having a channel where independent producers could broadcast their content was one of the main motivating factors for creating the fourth channel, but this emphasis was not there for the Welsh language fourth channel given all the other expectations placed upon it. The Broadcasting Act did not place a requirement on the fourth channel in Wales to engage with the independent producers, it merely states that the channel could do so if it wished: 'Nothing in this section shall be taken to preclude the Welsh Authority from obtaining television programmes in Welsh from sources other than the BBC and the TV programme contractor referred to in subsections (3).'[222]

There was little pressure to ensure that programmes were commissioned from independent producers in Wales, since there were so few of them in existence. Unlike the broadcasting organisations, the independent producers were relatively under-represented during the campaign to secure and establish the channel, and also during the deliberations of the WASC. The only organisation that could be said to represent the sector was the Cymdeithas Darlledwyr Cymraeg (Association of Welsh Broadcasters). A society formed to ensure a level playing field for Welsh language broadcasting in general and not just the needs of independent producers. Its membership included staff from the BBC, HTV and half a dozen independent producers. Its chief executives were Emyr Daniel of the BBC, Cenwyn Edwards of HTV and Euryn Ogwen Williams representing the independent producers. Established between September and December 1980, its purpose was to ensure that objective research was undertaken during the establishment of the channel. The intention was to ensure that, when the new authority began its work, some preparatory work had been undertaken.

The number of independent producers remained small, and Cymdeithas Darlledwyr Cymraeg estimated that only around fifteen independent producers could work through the medium of Welsh.[223] This number does not refer to fifteen companies who could work in Welsh, but fifteen individuals, each with different skills and specialisms, such as production or directing. In addition, many worked in London on productions for the BBC or ITV. The independent producers were more akin to what is regarded today as freelancers rather than the companies that are part of the current independent sector. There is no definitive list of producers, but Euryn Ogwen Williams, Wil Aaron, Gareth Wyn Williams, Colin Thomas and Norman Williams were thought to be some of the freelance directors who wished to produce programmes for the new channel. And it was thought that Wilbert Lloyd Roberts from Cwmni Theatr Cymru, Toby Freeman from Cynllun Fideo Cymunedol Blaenau Ffestiniog (Blaenau Ffestiniog Community Video Scheme) and Huw Jones from Sain planned to venture into television production, with the Bwrdd Ffilmiau Cymraeg (Welsh Film Board) also expected to contribute.

With the absence of significant numbers of independent producers, HTV, and Ron Wordley in particular, doubted the capacity within the sector to deliver programmes regularly for the channel. In his evidence to the WASC, there appears to be a judgement of these individuals and their ability to produce quality programmes:

> On the basis of the people we know to be available, who will undoubtedly grow, new talent of course will come forward, it may well be that new finance will come forward from outside sources for independent producers but I would say . . . that I find it extremely difficult to accept that independent broadcasters in Wales could regularly produce more than about two hours a week, on a regular basis[224]

It is clear that Ron Wordley's words had a significant effect on the committee with Dr Roger Thomas stating: 'I thought he was very defensive when we were discussing the independent producers, very defensive indeed, to the point that at one time I had the impression he was afraid of their contribution.'[225]

The fact of the matter was that it paid for HTV to believe that the independent producers could not consistently deliver a significant number of quality programmes for the channel. If this were the case, S4C would have to turn to HTV to produce more than the 7 hours specified in the agreement with the IBA in order to reach the target of broadcasting 22 hours of Welsh language programming a week, which, in turn, would ensure further investment in Culverhouse Cross. Lack of equipment was also a stumbling block, since independent producers only had film equipment available to them.[226] As the television industry moved towards greater use of video in the early 1980s, having to work through the medium of film alone would have been a major obstacle to the contribution and success of independent producers. But in an attempt to align themselves with the spirit of innovation found in establishing the channel, plans were made, from as early as the beginning of 1981, for a number of producers to invest in an outside broadcast unit with video equipment so that they could compete with the broadcasters in the quality of their equipment and programmes.[227]

There appeared to be proposals to create facilities back in 1980, while the exact nature of Welsh language television provision was being discussed. At a meeting between Euryn Ogwen Williams, Gwilym Owen and the IBA's Welsh committee in June 1980, to discuss the contribution of independent producers to the growth of Welsh language provision on that authority's network, Euryn Ogwen Williams noted that he had sought to purchase the BBC's old studio space in the Broadway area of Cardiff, but had not been successful.[228] Since there were no other suitable buildings in Cardiff that could be purchased without the barrier of significant additional costs for conversion for broadcasting purposes, Williams was now considering setting up an outside broadcasting unit based in Cardiff to produce on-location drama and light entertainment productions. Following the establishment of S4C, this plan was pursued in partnership with a number of other independent producers. Huw Jones recalls a meeting held over the phone in Wilbert Lloyd Roberts's office, between himself, Wil Aaron, Gareth Wyn Williams and Wilbert Lloyd Roberts with Euryn Ogwen Williams at the other end of the line.[229] The principle of establishing facilities for use by independent producers to compete against the broadcasters with their large studios was discussed, and questions were raised about who would be interested in the venture. Shortly afterwards, other independent producers were invited to join the venture, and it appeared that the original intention was that all independent companies would be involved in the developments.[230] Only four independent producers decided to invest, namely Gwilym Owen, head of Bwrdd Ffilmiau Cymraeg; Huw Jones, Sain and Teledu Tir Glas; Wil Aaron, Ffilmiau'r Nant, and Alan Clayton formerly of HTV, each investing £25,000 towards the total £500,000 needed to make the scheme a reality.[231]

The decision was made to invest in a mobile unit with video equipment and advice was sought from David Reay, HTV's head of engineering, before making a final decision on the equipment purchased. It was anticipated that the unit, named Barcud, would be operational by April 1982; in the meantime the need and potential for it was highlighted when Huw Jones and Wil Aaron hired an outside broadcasting unit by Molinaire to record the rock opera *Y Mab Darogan* performed by Cwmni Theatr Maldwyn in Newtown before the new equipment arrived. Barcud formally started operations in April 1982, under the management of Gwilym Owen, with its first week of work at Theatr Ardudwy, Harlech where several episodes of the series *Yng Nghwmni* were filmed for Teledu Tir Glas and then two or three quiz programmes produced by Gwilym Owen.[232] The significance of Barcud was that the independent producers could compete against the broadcasters, and produce programmes very reasonably for the channel: S4C estimated that one quiz show could be produced for £6,000 when using the new unit.[233] The early commitment and the willingness to take risks and invest before securing any commission was typical of the enthusiasm of the sector.

In the first meeting between S4C and the producers a contribution of 3 hours per week was discussed, with drama filling 1.5 hours of that weekly provision, light entertainment filling 1 hour and the remaining half-hour would be taken up by a 'folk' programme.[234] This shows that the independent producers were an ambitious group, not only in terms of the number of hours that they could produce, but also in terms of the genres they wanted to produce. With drama and light entertainment at the top of their list, they were keen to create popular programmes that would occupy a prominent place in the schedule.

The authority was keen to ensure that all independent producers were treated fairly, and that there was no hint of preferential treatment of some above others. Therefore, in May 1981, publicly advertised meetings were held in Caernarfon and Cardiff, to ensure that everyone who wished to create programmes received the same information and advice.[235] At that meeting Owen Edwards emphasised his hope that S4C would be a popular service, and thus ensuring that there was no confusion or misunderstanding amongst those independent producers who also wished to offer programmes to C4:

> It will be a high quality, popular, balanced service including . . . a significant proportion of popular, middle of the road content which will appeal to the majority of the population . . . There will be no room for people who want to follow their own creative whims without consideration of whether their work will fit within S4C's framework. We are here to serve the audience, not to please ourselves, but if it is possible to marry the two, that would be the best of both worlds.[236]

Similarly to Owen Edwards's first public statement at the Celtic Film and Television Festival, it was emphasised that independent producers could play a key part in the channel due to their being able to operate much more flexibly, and their work would be cheaper than the broadcasters.[237] However, their contribution was dependent on the expectation that they keep their feet on the ground, and not expect to make a fortune from their commissions.[238] Owen Edwards elaborated by confirming that there would be no quota for independent producers programmes, and their ideas would need to compete with programme ideas from HTV and their fellow independent producers in terms of appeal and price. The logic for not allocating a set number of hours to the independent producers was in case the quality of their programmes was lower than expected, and S4C would be obliged to accept low quality content due to the promised quota. Wil Aaron remembers that independent producers were not awarded contracts for long series at the outset, as the channel's officials were not entirely convinced that they could handle large budgets or produce programmes for weekly broadcast. There was concern about investing significant funds in long series before the independent producers had proved their competence.[239]

At the end of his speech, Owen Edwards set down a challenge by suggesting that the drama provision would not automatically fall into their hands: 'Of course there is the opportunity for some drama but there will have to be good reasons for it to come from the indies rather than the broadcasting organisations with their experience and resources.'[240] This statement clearly shows the channel's intentions to demand high-quality programming from the independent producers and that lack of experience would not be a valid excuse for creating second-rate shows. This statement somewhat eroded the original desire by the independent producers to produce 1.5 hours half of drama every week.

A proposed timetable was also discussed with the channel wishing to receive applications within six weeks of the meetings – at the end of June – to give staff the summer to consider before offering commissions in September. It was suggested that there would be £24,000 an hour to produce programmes, more than £10,000 less than the average HTV costs, although it was noted clearly that this figure was an average and that a large number of programmes were expected to be much cheaper. The audience at the meeting were also warned that all programmes would be expected to be produced within union regulations, and that smaller budgets should not be sought by breaching staffing rules. This was an attempt to reassure the unions, but also to make the independent producers aware that the union rules had not changed even as the broadcasting landscape had changed completely.[241]

By the middle of June 1981 Euryn Ogwen Williams, by then the channel's programme editor, had received numerous programme ideas from various producers. Amongst the ideas was a submission by London-based company Opix Films to produce two half-hour programmes following Max Boyce's travels to Dallas and Fort Worth, and a series of twelve documentaries by Wil Aaron dealing with unexpected stories from Welsh history.[242] As the commissioning process progressed, it became clear that firm guidelines were necessary on engineering and budget issues, and that there was a need for a uniform proposal form and standard contracts for their productions. S4C appeared to delay making decisions in these areas in the hope that they would gain some guidance from C4 and take advantage of the expertise there as dealing with independent producers was the main focus of their work. But S4C had to go its own way on these issues with no definitive documents published by C4 until August 1981.[243]

By mid-July 1981, the programme editor was confident that the independent sector could quite easily provide enough material to fill 3 hours a week with their programmes. It was envisaged that this could easily be increased to 3.5 hours if overseas drama, cartoons and documentaries were purchased and dubbed with Welsh actors.[244] It would appear that Williams also felt confident that by the end of the first year of S4C's existence, ten, if not more, small companies would have been formed and operating, as some individuals were starting to leave their jobs at the BBC and HTV in order to set up as independent producers.[245] This migration of individuals leaving safe jobs and venturing into a relatively uncertain terrain can be explained in many ways. For many, producing their ideas independently would give them freedom to pursue their personal production interests, freedom that they were not given within the large broadcasting organisations, where they followed the priorities of senior staff. The Cymdeithas Darlledwyr Cymraeg believed that the independent sector offered new opportunities for the older generation to broaden their horizons and utilise their skills acquired under the broadcasters' training for exciting new ventures. It was felt that this development would create opportunities for young people within the broadcasting organisations:

> there comes a point in the professional life where you feel that the scope is there to try something new. I am convinced that this is good for the industry because it is far easier for new talent to be fostered within the organisation where it can keep control, where it can teach properly, than for new talent to go immediately into the marketplace and hope that it will work: it is a cruel place. By people leaving the two organisations they are in fact creating space for this new talent to be nurtured.[246]

For HTV's creative staff there was another valid reason, namely the delay over the details of the contract with S4C that prevented them from producing programmes, while at the same time seeing the excitement of the independent sector around them.

One of the companies set up during those exciting early days, but offering production opportunities not seen within the broadcasters, was the animation company Siriol. *SuperTed* books originally published by one of HTV's subsidiary companies had proved popular, and there was a discussion between Mike Young, creator of *SuperTed*, and Chris Grace, when Grace worked for HTV, where he was persuaded that it would be a good idea to produce an animated version of the character. A series was not developed following talks with HTV due to HTV's concerns about a possible objection by DC Comics, who owned the rights to *Superman*.[247] The idea was revived after Chris Grace joined S4C, and a meeting was arranged between Chris Grace, Mike Young, Robin Lyons, an actor and screenwriter who was the ghost-writer of the *SuperTed* books, and Martin Lambie-Nairn of Robinson Lambie-Nairn who designed the channel's first logo.[248] The initial intention was that the series would be produced and animated by Robinson Lambie-Nairn in London, and Robin Lyons recalls asking, spontaneously, why a company in Wales could not be set up to do the work.[249] There was no objection from Lambie-Nairn, the idea certainly appealed to Chris Grace, and so Siriol was formed under the leadership of Mike Young, Robin Lyons and Dave Edwards, an animator working in advertising in London.[250] Robin Lyons remembers that none of them had expertise in producing animated series and a substantial budget was drawn up, sizable especially in terms of television production, but S4C's enthusiasm and unfamiliarity with animation production ensured that the budget was confirmed without difficulty.

S4C's confidence in the independent producers only grew, and by November 1981, they were confident enough in their work to implement a strategy that allowed the independent producers to develop and operate to their own strengths.[251] There is room to argue, given this statement, that independent producers' programmes were the cornerstone of S4C's service and that it was the BBC and, to a greater extent, HTV that filled the gaps around their provision. The strategy seems to have worked relatively successfully as the producers' creativity led them to produce a number of dramas, feature programmes and documentaries – exactly the kind of programmes needed in S4C's stockpile – since they required more pre-production time than many other genres.[252] Independent producers were advised to refrain from producing panel games and quizzes, pending clearer information on HTV's intentions for their programmes.[253] The independent companies were therefore gaining expertise and leaving their mark on drama, documentaries and entertainment programmes that would develop to be the highlights of the channel's schedule, possibly at the expense of similar developments in HTV. But it is significant to recall that these were individual programmes or short series, while HTV would be producing long-running series for the channel.

By February 1982, the first completed programme, of the 190 hours commissioned by the independent producers, had been delivered, *Ar Log, Ar Log* by Gerallt Jones and David Parry-Jones of Aberystwyth's Sgrin '82.[254] Other commissions included a wrestling programme, by Na-Nog from Porthmadog, a series of six children's plays on the history of Owain Glyndŵr by Platypus, a series of comedy programmes featuring comedian Gari Williams by Cwmni'r Castell, and a TV version of the rock opera *Y Mab Darogan* by Teledu Tir Glas.[255] The sector had grown beyond all expectations: 'although the independent sector was undefined and nebulous a year ago, it is now a reality and has grown to such an extent that it cannot be regarded as an annex to the main suppliers'.[256] Such was the confidence of S4C staff in the sector that they thought it was possible for them to produce 300 hours a year, quite easily.[257] If the independent producers were producing over 5 hours a week, this could mean that they would start to encroach on the minimum 7 hours per week that HTV planned to produce for the channel. For this reason, Euryn Ogwen Williams announced to the authority that any agreement with HTV must now leave room for the independent producers to make a significant contribution, allowing them to grow and develop to their full potential.[258] The above statements, arguably, were strategic, to demonstrate to HTV that the channel could no longer be forced into an unreasonable agreement and that there now existed a viable alternative for independent programming in Wales.

Although such announcements had a value in bargaining with HTV, there were a number of other benefits to the tremendous growth in the confidence of independent producers and their ability to produce a significant number of hours. The developments had fortified the channel's reputation by creating 'confidence and hope' in the venture, because they created jobs in areas where good jobs were scarce and unemployment high.[259] The independent producers had boosted the channel's public image and curtailing or limiting those developments would have been a regressive step. Producing dramas with familiar Welsh communities as their backdrop and light entertainment programmes in theatres and venues across Wales brought broadcasting closer to the viewer and shattered the historic dominance of the broadcasting centres in the capital. The independent producers, due to the flexible nature of their facilities, were fulfilling the hopes that the service would have a Welsh feel.

However, S4C's relationship with the independent producers was not entirely smooth running. With so many different independent producers, and many of them new to working independently, it meant that several needed to be offered a great deal of advice to ensure that they were able to deliver entertaining programmes on time and within budget. The various structures within these companies meant that a differing level of supervision was required depending on the size of the companies, their experience and skill in programme production. There were examples of some inexperienced producers struggling to manage a budget as well as dealing with creative issues. Some of the channel's leading productions and companies were not free from budgetary troubles; for example *SuperTed*'s budget had to be doubled. There were several reasons for that doubling: at the request of Chris Grace the episodes were doubled in length from 4 minutes to 7.75 minutes. Costs also increased as the producers and channel bought the actors' rights to make selling the series abroad easier. This shows the lack of experience of Siriol and S4C's staff as they had not foreseen all the costs involved in the production, especially when recognising the commercial potential of selling the series to other broadcasters. Additional pressure was also placed on Siriol to urgently complete two episodes for the opening night of the channel and another episode to be broadcast over Christmas 1982, in order to fulfil promises made when the channel was launched.[260] The additional cost was justified by reasoning that the series continued to offer value for money as it remained much cheaper than producing an animated series in London.[261] Not investing in this flagship production and delivering low quality animation due to a lack of investment would have damaged the channel's growing reputation. Siriol had been a catalyst to developing and nurturing a quality animation sector in Wales. Supporting a new high-profile industry bolstered the channel's reputation and contributed a great deal of the goodwill aimed at the channel. Continuing to invest and produce high-quality series was therefore essential for S4C.

There was a very similar mindset whilst the channel dealt with one of the most infamous productions in its history, *Madam Wen*. Having agreed a budget for a 90-minute film, authority minutes show that the budget tripled in a matter of weeks, and that the film grew in length to 2 hours.[262] The tremendous jump in the cost of production and the ambiguity over its duration should have been a warning to the channel's staff of the troubles that lay ahead. After the authority insisted that the film should be produced for a firm price, any concerns the staff held seemed to disappear; however, no agreement was reached between the parties as acceptable terms could not be agreed.[263] Any financial doubts were undoubtedly pushed aside as the film was intended to be broadcast as part of the 1982 Christmas offering and therefore deserving of significant investment. Furthermore, as a feature film, there was a general feeling that it was a sound investment since some of the costs could be recovered by selling it abroad. This is yet another example of the channel being willing to spend more money on a production if it was considered to have an added benefit. But, in contrast to the experience with *SuperTed*, where the investment paid off in terms of the channel's reputation and publicity, *Madam Wen* was not as successful.

Within five months of the confirmation of the commission, the staff and authority were informed that the production was in significant financial difficulty.[264] A few weeks later it was further confirmed that the overspend was significant, around £140,000, and discussions were held regarding what needed to happen next to ensure that the initiative was not entirely futile. It was decided that if the channel invested further in the film and completed it, the Bwrdd Ffilmiau Cymraeg would be expected to receive a public censure from S4C to make up for the failure and the public embarrassment derived from several negative news articles.[265] In addition, there was an intention to penalise the board further by declaring that it would not be considered for any further commissions, depriving it of a key source of income for its activities. In order to offset the overspend and to pay towards the additional investment, the board would also be expected to transfer the rights of film titles it had produced prior to the channel's existence, and the rights of the few films yet to be produced so that S4C could broadcast them free of charge.[266] Bwrdd Ffilmiau Cymraeg's reputation was ruined by this failure and Kate Woodward describes *Madam Wen* as the first nail in its coffin, stating that the film marked the beginning of the end for the board by undermining its credibility.[267]

Before deciding finally on the fate of *Madam Wen*, an external assessor was invited to look at what had been produced and to ensure whether it was appropriate to continue investing. The assessor was Muiris Mac Conghail of the Irish Film Board, who believed that investing in a 2-hour film of this nature was: '[a] significant investment in the future of independent film production in Wales'.[268] Despite the praise, there was criticism that the channel should formulate a clear policy for dealing with such productions and that the authority should appoint an executive producer on large productions to ensure that they did not go off course.[269] Mac Conghail's recommendation, therefore, was that the filming should continue and be completed. *Madam Wen* was completed, and broadcast, but hard lessons were learned by S4C staff about the need to be vigilant in commissioning.

Image, marketing and audience

The authority's decision to establish an independent broadcasting centre rather than share studio space with the other broadcasters clearly showed that it wanted to firmly declare the independence and distinctiveness of the new service.[270] The channel needed to create and develop the identity of the new service and to build a burgeoning relationship between the channel and its viewers in order to secure an enthusiastic audience for the new output. The identity of the channel was at the top of the channel's list of priorities, and Dr Glyn Tegai Hughes at the first meeting of the authority was given the responsibility, due to his links with Gregynog Press, to work on designing temporary printed materials and preparing a specification for professional designers.[271] S4C considered three different options for designing a logo and ident for use on screen and in printed materials, namely asking an external design company to come up with a design, use the BBC's or HTV's graphics department, or organising a public competition. It was suggested that commissioning a logo would cost approximately £5,000 so the authority decided to launch a competition with a prize of £500 for the winning design.[272] Spending £5,000 on a logo was considered irresponsible, especially as the authority had not yet received their formal budget notification; the authority needed to secure sufficient funding for programming before spending a significant amount on image and logo. The competition presented an opportunity for the audience to feel some ownership of the channel, and it was also part of a wider strategy and another public competition was announced at the 1981 Machynlleth National Eisteddfod to create a 'slogan for the Channel'.[273] However, by the end of 1981 the emphasis had shifted away from saving money and promoting public ownership of the channel, with the appointment of London-based Robinson Lambie-Nairn to create the logo.[274] Because the channel had now received confirmation of the allocated budget, it was able to spend money on less essential elements of its service.[275] Robinson Lambie-Nairn was also commissioned by C4 to create their logo, created with innovative computer animation techniques.[276]

There were many choices and questions facing the authority about the image it wanted to present to its audience and to the world. The main dilemma was whether an image that reflected the nature of the traditional Welsh audience should be created or an image of a more modern progressive channel. The brief presented to the design company was complex as it aimed to avoid cultural cliché and it also expressed a desire to speak to and attract a variety of different social groups to the channel. The authority stated clearly that they were not in favour of stereotypical national symbols such as the red dragon, the leek or a map of Wales; however, they were open to using the dragon as a visual gimmick. A popular, homely, warm image without reflecting an old-fashioned portrayal of the countryside was desired: the authority was happy to see images of breath-taking views, but reminded the agency of a tendency amongst Welsh people to be parochial and the logo needed to be used to attract the non-Welsh-speaking audience.[277] The designers were presented with a daunting task as they sought to navigate the fine line between acceptable and unacceptable use of Welsh images, and to find a concept that would appeal to very diverse factions amongst S4C's potential audience. From the designs submitted to the authority, the WALES4CYMRU logo was chosen by the director and chair of the authority (see front cover).

Although the selected logo, which was a play on the abbreviation S4C to incorporate the country's name in both languages, was an amusing and clever idea, it was considered by many as a compromise to try to please non-Welsh speakers, and managed to alienate many of those who had campaigned to secure the channel's existence. The fundamental problem that seemed to cause most consternation was that the word Wales appeared first. Even before it was formally launched on St David's Day 1982, Cymdeithas yr Iaith had called on the channel to reconsider: 'The Society calls upon S4C to change the logo before Monday. We fear that S4C is playing to the gallery to allay the fears of English speaking viewers.'[278] Angharad Tomos harshly criticised the logo in the Cymdeithas yr Iaith magazine *Tafod y Ddraig* by suggesting that it conveyed a wholly unsatisfactory compromise, and that it was created to allay the fears of the channel's detractors by highlighting its English-language content and declared the channel a 'mongrel'.[279]

The channel's public response to these comments was uncompromising, with Owen Edwards stating: 'We get one chance. Hopefully, we as Welsh speakers, will resist the temptation that comes so easily to us, to become disunited and quarrel. There are far more important issues than this.'[280] But, following the launch, it appears that the designers were asked to modify the logo somewhat. In order to calm the waters, it was decided that several versions should be created, so that the channel could use different forms of the logo depending on the context of its use, and thus avoid alienating parts of the audience.[281] The colours were also changed so that the emphasis was clearly on the abbreviation S4C. Despite this willingness to adapt the logo in order to alleviate tension, it was believed that there was still an advantage in using the full version to guarantee that the name became known to individuals outside Wales.[282] Articles published in the British papers about S4C during its early days show why officials were so keen for the name to become established since the press was constantly referring to the channel as SC4 in its articles. The Home Office's view of S4C's success would be crucial to the survival of the channel at the end of its trial period: it was therefore essential to secure a positive and accurate image in the British as well as the Welsh papers.

One of the other tactics used to make the channel and its message visible before it started broadcasting was to attend national and local events. Owen Edwards attended the Celtic Film and Television Festival in Harlech in April 1981 just days after taking up his post, where he gave a speech; over the following eighteen months the director visited groups as diverse as the South Wales Publicity Association, the Bankers' Institute, the National Federation of Women's Institutes and Inspectors, Headteachers and Heads of Department of Welsh Secondary Schools. The channel also secured a strong presence at the Machynlleth National Eisteddfod in 1981. A public meeting was held at Theatr Fach y Maes where Owen Edwards again gave a speech, and there was an opportunity for the public to ask questions. In addition, in partnership with the IBA, they created an exhibition about the channel. Given the significance of the National Eisteddfod to the campaign to win a Welsh language channel, the authority's presence on the festival field was essential to embed it within the culture and traditions of Welsh-speaking Wales and the lives of its people. It was also an unrivalled opportunity to gain the necessary publicity and to highlight the difference a year could make to the development of Welsh language broadcasting. The change apparent in one short year was emphasised in Owen Edwards's speech as he referred to the 'cloud of despair' ('cwmwl o anobaith') that had existed during the Lliw Valley Eisteddfod but which had now dissipated due to S4C's 'incredible' developments.[283] Despite S4C's intention to show the progress between the 1980 and 1981 eisteddfod, not everyone was happy with the developments: Cymdeithas yr Iaith called for an ongoing public dialogue between the channel and the public. Their members were concerned that more decisions were not being made in consultation with the people of Wales. Sir Goronwy Daniel rejected that principle and stated plainly: 'no business can be run in this way'.[284] However, the authority agreed to release occasional bulletins in the form of a newsletter; not on a regular basis as the society would like, but when there was important information to share.[285] Although the authority was keen to ensure that the audience felt ownership of the channel, it realised that it would not be possible to prioritise this and consult with the public on all points of principle if it was to start broadcasting in November 1982.

The launch of the channel on St David's Day 1982 was the next big event. There were various objectives, but the main aim of the launch was to correct the 'gross ignorance about S4C'.[286] The authority believed that there was apathy towards the channel and confusion about its provision amongst audience members, both Welsh and non-Welsh speakers, with some members of both groups convinced that it would be a completely Welsh language channel. They hoped to galvanise and enthuse Welsh speakers whilst at the same time persuading non-Welsh speakers that S4C would broadcast programmes of interest to them too.[287] The launch was also expected, via a live link to the IBA offices in Brompton Road, to inform the media industry and the British press that S4C was not a channel for a 'fanatical fringe of hymn singing anglophobes'.[288] The complex task, therefore, was to ensure that these various messages did not further irritate or confuse the target audience. If the success of the launch can be measured by the number of columns of press coverage, then the event was a huge success. Numerous articles appeared in local and national Welsh newspapers and magazines[289] as well as British newspapers,[290] and the industry magazine *Broadcast* devoted six pages and the cover to S4C.[291] Most of the discussion was positive, with a few exceptions that focused on the channel's inability to reach an agreement with HTV, or Leo Abse's negative statements in Parliament about S4C becoming a 'gravy train' for independent producers.[292] Many of the journalists were captivated by *SuperTed*, and the teddy bear was discussed at the expense of the wider messages about the service.[293] But the main message that was successfully promoted was that the channel would offer something for everyone, and, as a result, be as relevant to non-Welsh speakers as it would be to the Welsh speakers who had demanded its existence. Looking at the range of articles published, this particular message arguably appeared more often than the fact that the arrival of the channel was a huge step forward for Welsh language broadcasting and that the number of programmes broadcast in the language would almost double.

There was disquiet amongst S4C's target audience before it went on air, and this is evidenced by articles published by a number of individuals who had campaigned to establish it. The Rev. John Gwilym Jones described the channel in a radio interview as a 'disadvantaged baby' because of the criticism levelled at it in the months before the launch.[294] The group that was most vociferous in their criticism of the developments was Cymdeithas yr Iaith. Given that this was the group with the highest expectations for a Welsh language channel, it is not surprising that its members were vocal about any weaknesses or failure to match their ideal. Following the channel's launch on St David's Day 1982, dissatisfaction was expressed with the Englishness of the logo, but this was only one complaint amongst many, with significant discontent amongst its ranks with the channel's lack of public communication. The overriding concern was that the saga which arose from the logo would be repeated once the channel had launched and started broadcasting programmes; Angharad Tomos expressed that there was a danger that they would not be able to comment on the channel's developments until the programmes were on air, and felt that this was too late.[295] This suggests that Cymdeithas yr Iaith suspected that the channel's officers would not be able to deliver a comprehensive Welsh language service for its audience without extensive consultation on the expectations of the Welsh audience. Or was it simply that society leaders felt, having taken such a central role in the campaign to secure the channel, that they were now being ignored as the foundations of the service were laid?

> we secured it, we paid the price, and we have a right to know what is happening at the channel and to express our opinions. The broadcasting campaign isn't over. Our aim is to establish a comprehensive, quality service in Welsh and we won't give up the campaign until it is won.[296]

We must consider, in the light of the comments above, why S4C's relationship with its audience was expected to be different from that of the other broadcasters and their audiences. Parts of the Welsh-speaking audience, since they had fought to secure a Welsh language channel, felt that they were entitled to know about the development of the channel, and also to influence its evolution. Consultation and negotiation to the extent expected by Cymdeithas yr Iaith was not common amongst broadcasters. The long-established and secretive ways of the broadcasting sector were difficult to demolish, even for a channel that was breaking new ground in terms of its structure. Along with the enigmatic nature of broadcasters, audience research, as it is known today, was scarce and meant that broadcasters did not have a detailed understanding of their audiences or viewing patterns. The Broadcasters' Audience Research Board (BARB) was not established until 1981 and only occasionally had there been attempts to discover and understand audience viewing patterns and opinions, especially in Welsh. Cymdeithas yr Iaith's expectations of S4C, therefore, required a significant transformation, and it appears that it was difficult to adjust those long-established patterns.

The authority had considered in detail how to engage and consult with its audience to ensure that it received the best advice in shaping and adapting its service, a responsibility placed on the authority by the Broadcasting Act. The authority was not obliged to create new committees to exercise this responsibility, with the Act suggesting that the existing BBC and IBA systems could be used to meet its consultative needs. One of the early decisions made at the first meeting of the authority was that the channel would use the BBC and IBA systems, the Welsh committee of the IBA and the BBC Broadcasting Council for Wales, committing to review that pattern after some months.[297] Michael Brooke and Eirion Lewis, secretaries of the BBC and the IBA's consultative organisations respectively, were asked to produce a paper for the authority outlining the options available to the channel.[298] In the paper, the authors conveyed the importance of a consultative regime for the channel by stating: 'the new service is a controversial one and . . . it is breaking new broadcasting ground; it is essential that it should receive, and be seen to receive, advice on all aspects of its programme output'.[299] However, both were aware that any plan had to be logical in terms of expenditure and the administrative burden on the channel's small staff. Problems were envisaged in utilising the broadcasting council and the IBA's Welsh committee structures as these committees had specific responsibilities that could prevent them from providing independent, impartial advice to S4C on the nature of its programmes. However, it was suggested that the channel's director should meet twice a year with the broadcasting council and the IBA's Welsh committee to discuss programme issues. Because of these organisational difficulties and because S4C was established as a separate channel and authority that was directly accountable to government, the authors felt that the channel's consultative regime should reflect that.[300] It was therefore recommended that S4C should form an independent consultancy council, which would have fourteen or sixteen members, divided equally between Welsh speakers and non-Welsh speakers and that it would meet three or four times a year.[301] Despite the stated intention at the beginning of the document to try to create a manageable system, a much larger than usual committee was recommended, which, due to the number of its members, would be expensive to maintain with high travel costs and, possibly, the costs of hiring television and video equipment for each member.

The authority disagreed with the views of Michael Brooke and Eirion Lewis, stating their intention to keep any consultation plan as simple as possible, hence why they preferred not to duplicate existing provision. Another reason against forming an independent committee was that it was felt that Welsh-speaking people who had knowledge of, or were interested in, being a member of such committees had either already been members or were currently serving on the IBA's, HTV's and the BBC's committees.[302] However, the authority decided to set some money aside in case the channel was forced to establish an independent regime should the BBC or IBA be reluctant to offer assistance.[303] Despite the certainty of their conviction on this matter, the authority continued to discuss the principle of forming regional viewer panels that would provide an alternative form of representation and advice to that of the BBC and the IBA committees.[304] The idea was developed further as the authority began to realise the value of a plan that would give the audience an opportunity to respond on issues such as content, appeal and balance of the service, as well as an opportunity to express their views on the merits and shortcomings of the programmes. There were two potential benefits: it could create an image of a channel that was open and willing to listen to its audience, and it also enabled the channel to gather vital and valuable feedback that it could use and act upon. It was decided, therefore, in April 1982 to form four regional committees, at Mold, Caernarfon, Carmarthen and Cardiff, and one English-language national committee, with committee chairs forming a national advisory body.[305] They intended for the chair of each committee to suggest a cross section of suitable individuals in their area, meeting twice a year, with the national body meeting once a year. The channel intended to provide discussion topics to guide committee discussions, but there would be no link between the IBA, BBC and these committees.[306] By September, however, the decision to defer action on the issue of regional committees was minuted with the pattern reviewed after six months of broadcasting.[307] No reasons for the delay were identified, but it was undoubtedly due to the pressure and enormity of the task of launching the channel at the beginning of November 1982 that it was decided to use the existing regimes. By early 1983, the channel had received confirmation from the IBA and the broadcasting council that they were happy to meet with the S4C Authority at least twice a year to discuss the programmes that were relevant to each committee.

On the issue of obtaining specific advice on the production of educational and religious programmes, the channel decided that it was essential for it to have its own independent committees, since this was particularly emphasised in the Broadcasting Act.[308] As well as taking advantage of the broadcasting regimes that had their own committees, the authority had also considered whether existing committees, such as the Welsh Council of Churches, could be used to avoid establishing a new model.[309] Eventually, a decision was made to form independent panels that would draw on members from organisations such as the Welsh Council of Churches and the Welsh Joint Education Committee.[310] There was also a decision to set up an appeals advisory panel after the channel began broadcasting, since it considered allocating space within the schedule to conduct charitable appeals.[311] The authority therefore developed a consultative model which was a combination of establishing independent systems and drawing on established and experienced systems. However, by dropping the idea of forming regional panels, the channel was missing out because it did not have direct contact with a wide cross section of its audience, both Welsh and non-Welsh speakers, which that scheme could have provided. It was not possible to create a similar link, although attempts were made to do so, by broadcasting audience response programmes such as *Arolwg* (HTV), which invited comments on programmes, and by responding to viewers' letters only.

Although there was no direct connection with the audience the attention given to the channel in the press indicated that the expectations of lay members of the audience were high for what the new channel would achieve. Their expectations ranged from 'providing a full complement of high quality Welsh language programmes', to a channel that would appeal to Welsh speakers 'who have nothing to do with the chapel or church nor eisteddfod, people for whom a Welsh book and magazine and newspaper are anathema'; they also demanded that the programmes could 'compete with programmes such as *Crossroads*', and they expected to see 'cartoons such as *Mighty Mouse* and *Popeye* in Welsh'.[312]

The channel was expected to provide something for everyone and to the highest standard. But those efforts would be futile if there was no way to inform the audience of their existence by publishing information in the BBC and ITV programme magazines, the *Radio Times* and *TV Times*. The IBA's Welsh committee and the BBC's Broadcasting Council for Wales had considered programme publicity in early meetings as they began to prepare a complete Welsh language service across two channels. They attempted to establish the principle of cross-advertising Welsh language programmes in each other's magazines to create a sense of a single service across two channels: this according to the IBA's Welsh committee would be 'a simple gesture which would generate goodwill'.[313] Independent Television Publications (ITP), publishers of *TV Times*, agreed to include details of the BBC's Welsh language programmes as well as details of ITV's Welsh language programmes on a separate Welsh page in its Wales and the west of England edition.[314] The BBC Broadcasting Council did not share the same enthusiasm and willingness to work together, with Owen Edwards, in his role as Controller of BBC Wales, strongly opposed to the proposal for the following reason:

> CW [Controller Wales] was in no doubt that the BBC should reject the suggestion outright. The Council and the BBC had for years promoted the proposals for co-operation between the BBC and ITV in a joint service in Welsh and this had been completely undermined by ITV. He saw the suggestion as an attempt to salve their conscience.[315]

During S4C's early discussions on this issue, these factional attitudes once again reared their head as they discussed the use of the *Radio Times* and the *TV Times* to publish the schedule and details of S4C's programmes. The *Radio Times* agreed to publish details of ITV programmes, but did not want to publish editorial material to promote them.[316] It was agreed that the *Radio Times* would publish two pages of programme information on all S4C Welsh language output, but the bulk of the editorial material would focus solely on the content and merits of the programmes produced by the BBC.

The channel's discussions therefore increasingly leaned towards being part of the *TV Times* magazine, partly because the details of C4's programmes were likely to be published there. But there was a fundamental problem with the idea of using the *TV Times* for publishing details of Welsh language programmes, since there was no Wales-only edition of the magazine. In the rest of the UK regions C4 and the regional company would fill half each of the *TV Times* for that region, so in Wales and the west of England C4 and HTV would fill the magazine with details of their programmes. This did not leave adequate space for S4C programme information, with the *TV Times* insisting that only one page per week could be allocated. Giving more pages to S4C would mean losing £60,000–70,000 a year in advertising money for every page devoted to S4C.[317] But this was not sufficient for the channel's needs since it wanted to publish details of programmes produced by the BBC, HTV, the independent producers and English language output, let alone editorial material. S4C felt that the details of its programmes needed to at least appear in a box parallel to C4 programme information, but due to typographical difficulties this was considered impossible.[318] Being pragmatic, separating the Wales and the west of England edition was also not a suitable solution, as some *TV Times* customers, particularly those living close to the border, would still need C4 details rather than S4C as their TV aerials were pointing east.[319] An alternative solution was needed to enable the channel to have suitable space to promote its programmes.

The channel's staff were sceptical of the principle of producing a stand-alone magazine for S4C, as it seemed impractical and there was a desire to support Welsh language publications, rather than duplicate provision.[320] Discussions were held with *Curiad* magazine, which offered eight pages of articles per month on the channel's programmes and personalities, for an advertisement fee, turning *Curiad* into S4C's unofficial magazine.[321] Such a scheme would cost £60,000 a year, but it was difficult to warrant such expense on a small magazine and its limited appeal.[322] Similar problems arose when considering the use of other Welsh magazines too, as hardly any magazine had a circulation of more than 2,000 readers.[323] If S4C supported a number of magazines, it would have to spend an equivalent amount on each in order to communicate with a wide cross section of the audience. Such expenditure could not be justified, as the channel sought to minimise its organisational costs. Discussions were also held with *Barn* after the publication contacted the BBC, HTV and S4C to ask them to contribute financially towards a substantial and authoritative section which would discuss television and radio programmes.[324] It was acknowledged that such coverage of Welsh television and radio output was desperately needed, but it was not considered appropriate for the channel to pay for it, as it could be argued that it was purchasing good reviews.[325] A decision was made to wait and see if articles of this nature would develop naturally because of S4C's existence, without the need for investment from the broadcasting organisations. It appears that this was the case with sections such as 'Sbec ar Bedwar C' in *Y Faner*, regular articles from various commentators in *Y Cymro* and a sizable TV section published in *Barn* contributing to the increased discussion around Welsh language broadcasting.

It soon became apparent that trying to tap into the network of Welsh *papurau bro* (local newspapers) to inform viewers also posed a variety of problems since their publishing schedules were too inconsistent and irregular to rely on, and some areas of Wales had no *papur bro* at all.[326] *Y Cymro* was considered as a resource, as the paper had a wide circulation of 7,000 readers, but most of these were in north Wales (due to the paper's northern editorial focus), and therefore it was not entirely appropriate. Consideration was also given to including a page in the English language Welsh daily papers, the *Western Mail* and the *Daily Post*, but it was decided that these papers were not the most appropriate places for Welsh language material.[327] Therefore, contrary to their original intention, in order to secure the necessary space and the best possible opportunity to advertise Welsh language programming, an independent supplement or magazine would have to be produced.

As serious consideration was given to the creation of a magazine, discussions were held with ITP and the S4C Authority hoped for a better price than the original £300,000 mentioned, as it was believed that the company accepted that they had a responsibility to ensure that readers in Wales received accurate information about the programmes available to them. The authority felt that ITP had a commercial advantage in adopting a separate supplement as the company would regain valuable advertising space.[328] It was envisaged that only a 4-page supplement could be funded and produced weekly due to the workload needed. Sadly, when the final figures came from ITP, the authority was shocked by the costs of editing, printing and distributing a 4-page supplement – £382,240 – and the corresponding cost for an 8-page supplement was £565,210.[329] The authority considered alternatives, such as editing the supplement themselves, and using the *TV Times* to print and distribute the attachment. The feasibility of editing, printing and distributing a magazine entirely independent of the ITP was also considered, but this was not possible, for distribution and marketing reasons.[330] A supplement or magazine had to reach the widest possible audience, and not only Welsh language readers, in order to ensure that the profound ignorance amongst the non-Welsh-speaking audience about S4C did not continue after it began broadcasting. A completely independent magazine, and no details in other TV magazines about S4C's schedule for C4 programmes would only cause more confusion.

After weighing up all the options, S4C decided to set up its own magazine, taking full responsibility for the graphics, content, editing and printing, but using the *TV Times* for distribution as a supplement to its magazine in Wales.[331] There was also an intention to include the bare details of the names and timings of S4C programmes in the C4 sections of the *TV Times.* The best of both worlds was thus obtained. This solution meant that much less money would go into ITP's coffers as S4C only had to pay for the cost of distribution. The ITP offered a fair price and charged £15 for every 1,000 copies distributed each week, at a cost of around £100,000 a year. However, after deducting the £70,000 recouped by the *TV Times* by not including a Welsh page in the main body of the magazine, the channel would only have to pay £29,450 a year.[332] The ITP was also happy for S4C to sell its own adverts in the supplement, in an attempt to recoup some of the production costs. The working relationship was not always as straightforward: there was significant disappointment that it was not possible to ensure that the supplement was distributed with the Granada edition, which resulted in some communities in north-east Wales being deprived of comprehensive information about S4C programmes.[333]

Ann Beynon, the press officer, and her staff would produce and edit the magazine's contents, which was christened *Sbec*, and it soon grew into a 12-page publication. The channel remained concerned about the substantial expenditure on such a sizeable magazine, which was provided free of charge, and it was unlikely that they would be able to attract a high level of advertising money to fund it. However, after exploring all the possibilities in detail, producing an independent magazine was the only option that enabled the channel to promote its programmes in the most dynamic way possible.

The first issue of *Sbec* was published two weeks before the channel began broadcasting. The first issue was crucial in easing some of the ignorance that persisted amongst the non-Welsh-speaking audience. There was more English than usual in this issue in an attempt to get the message across that most of C4's entertaining programmes would still be shown on S4C. There was also an attempt not only to attract non-Welsh-speaking viewers to watch C4 programmes, but to attract them to watch some of the channel's Welsh language output, such as *Noson Lawen*, *Sgrech* and *SuperTed*. *Sbec*, therefore, aimed to create an image of a channel that would appeal to all members of society, in the hope that a respectable audience could be drawn as the channel began its three-year trial.

The activities of the S4C Authority during its period of preparation show that there was a mountain of work to be undertaken in a relatively short space of time and some key decisions were taken and actioned to create the best possible conditions for the channel to succeed during its probationary period. One of the main themes that arose was the tension between the principle of an independent channel and a channel that relied on its partners to succeed. The authority was therefore compelled to give serious consideration to when it was appropriate and necessary for the new channel to plough its own furrow and proclaim its independence, in matters such as technical facilities and programme publicity. However, on other occasions, S4C relied entirely on its broadcast partners for essential help and advice, and to fight on its behalf to secure favourable financial terms and to ensure that the technology needed to reach the widest possible audience was ready in time. S4C's relationships with its programme providers were not completely smooth running: each relationship and partnership had its own unique strains, whether in the form of disagreements on financial matters, issues of responsibility for content or the need for close oversight to ensure the production of quality programmes. Despite these pressures, it was essential that they were overcome because S4C relied entirely on its partners to fill the empty space of the fourth channel in Wales with attractive programmes and output that would appeal, attract and speak to the Welsh audience in its own language.

3

First Broadcasts and Audience Response

After decades of protest and campaigning, and after 18 months of preparation on behalf of the Welsh Fourth Channel Authority (WFCA) and its staff, the first day of November 1982 saw the culmination of all the hard work and the fulfilment of the broadcasting experiment offered to Wales. This chapter aims to discuss and analyse that long-awaited opening night, along with the first weeks and months of broadcasting on the channel. It will consider the response of the press and audience to those early broadcasts, asking how and why it changed as the early curiosity regarding a complete, dedicated service on one devoted channel dissipated. The channel's viewing and appreciation figures will be discussed along with the changes implemented by the staff in response to the new viewing patterns as they attempted to maintain the interest of the Welsh-speaking audience in the face of the appeal and quality of English language programming on other channels. S4C's staff were unable to take a breath and rest as the probationary period got underway.

Opening night

Sianel Pedwar Cymru broadcast for the first time on 1 November 1982, one day prior to the launch of Channel 4 (C4). Beginning its regular broadcasts before C4 ensured that S4C succeeded in realising one of the campaigners' original ambitions that the Welsh language channel should be launched first. But since they were launched only a day apart, there was not enough time to ensure that the channel had secured audience loyalty before C4 would start competing for viewers who lived on the border and who were able to receive both channels. S4C's launch date was the culmination of a tremendous amount of work and a colossal effort, but the hard labour was only just beginning. Authority members, except for Sir Goronwy Daniel and Gwilym Peregrine, the Independent Broadcasting Authority (IBA) representative, spent the opening night at the channel's offices in Cardiff watching the live broadcasts and sharing in the excitement.[1] Sir Goronwy and Gwilym Peregrine watched the evening from the IBA's headquarters in Brompton Road, London.[2]

Monday, 1 November 1982 did not include a full day of broadcasts, with the first programme airing at 6 o'clock at night. The first broadcast which announced the start of Welsh language broadcasting on a single dedicated channel opened with an image of the channel's offices, the logo illuminated above the entrance and the soundtrack of a fanfare, which was a mix of the electronic sounds of 1980s mixed with the harp. Owen Edwards greeted the viewer standing in the reception area of S4C's offices in Sophia Close with the words:

> A very, very warm welcome to you joining us here for the first time in the home of Sianel Pedwar Cymru. Now it is easy to kindle a fire on an old hearth as the old saying goes, but it is our intention to light a bonfire on this new hearth.[3]

Owen Edwards emphasised the word *aelwyd*, meaning household or hearth, several times in his opening remarks, the use of which gave the audience a strong impression of the channel's aim to create a warm and cosy place, where Welsh-speaking audiences would feel at home, an atmosphere which would be developed further with the channel's presentation style. Following his Welsh greeting, the non-Welsh-speaking viewer received an English greeting – not a direct translation of the Welsh, but a greeting that specifically referred to what the channel offered to them as viewers. These opening moments demonstrated the new channel's confidence in the dual nature of its existence, with its need to meet the expectations of two different audiences. With the channel rejecting the notion of translating faithfully from one language to another, we see evidence of the awareness amongst channel staff of the different needs of the two audiences and an understanding that what was important to the non-Welsh-speaking viewer was information about the English language programmes found on the channel, and not an emphasis of the growth of Welsh-medium output. This small act demonstrated the officials' awareness that these tensions had not disappeared with the birth of S4C.

As part of the welcome programme Owen Edwards and new presenters Robin Jones, Siân Thomas and Rowena Jones-Thomas presented

3. Image from the *Joni Jones* episode 'Chewing Gum' (dir. Stephen Bayly) *(image: reproduced with permission from S4C)*

a preview of the programmes that would entertain Welsh audiences over the coming weeks and months. They showed numerous clips of the various programmes *Mentro! Mentro!*, *Anturiaethau Syr Wymff a Plwmsan*, *Joni Jones*, *Gwydion*, *Y Mab Darogan*, *Ar Log – Ar Log* and *Hapnod*.[4] The first episode of the adventures of Wales's most famous bear was also shown, *SuperTed a Thrysor yr Incas* (SuperTed and the Inca Treasure), meeting the expectations that had been raised after showing clips of the series during the channel's launch on St David's Day 1982.[5] This screening on the opening night was also a means of nurturing and cultivating a wide audience of all ages for the channel, as animation, especially original animation in Welsh, was a completely new phenomenon for the audience.

The first programme was also used to inform the non-Welsh-speaking audience members of the content that would be available to entertain them on the new channel and to show clearly that they would not be deprived of C4 programmes. A Welsh greeting was given by Jeremy Isaacs, chief executive of C4, who provided a taste of the innovative C4 programmes that would fill the schedule around S4C's Welsh language programmes,[6] such as the new Liverpool-based soap opera *Brookside*, the Royal Shakespeare Company's production of *The Life and Adventures of Nicholas Nickleby*, new sports programmes focusing on British basketball tournaments and programmes on American football (bought from US broadcasters), international programmes and programmes for young people – two areas, in Jeremy Isaacs's view that were neglected by the other UK channels.[7] Given that English language programming would fill more than fifty of the channel's weekly broadcast hours, compared to the 22 hours of Welsh language content, its promotion was just as important and critical to its success.

To bring honour to the channel and reflect positively on the international support for its work greetings were broadcast from individuals such as Dr Terry James, a Kidwelly native who now lived and worked in Hollywood, and Leo Goodstadt, a native of Pembrokeshire who was a broadcaster on television in Hong Kong. Alongside these, video greetings were also received by individuals who had no obvious connection with Wales or the Welsh language, such as the tennis player Björn Borg and the winner of the Miss World competition from Venezuela.[8]

Celebrities were not the only ones who were given a chance to voice their opinions and expectations of the new channel on the first night. Two presenters, Gwenda Rees and Richard Morris Jones, were sent to Gwynedd and Dyfed to ask residents there for their views on the new development and the type of programmes that they would like to see. Several vox pops were broadcast in Welsh and English with many expressing their expectations for more Welsh language sports, pop and drama programmes, but there were also some unexpected comments amongst them. One woman from Gwynedd stated that she did not want to watch the channel as she was convinced that she would not understand the kind of Welsh used in the programmes and an interview with a non-Welsh speaker who thought the new channel would have too much English content and was not therefore a Welsh language channel.[9] These vox pops are yet another example of the channel's confident nature on its first night, with its willingness to admit that their marketing efforts had not succeeded in persuading all Welsh speakers to watch S4C or convinced them of its merits; thus showing that there remained a great deal of work facing the channel to overcome these prejudices.

While S4C launched with an informative and celebratory programme, this was not the case with C4's launch on 2 November 1982. Instead of producing a welcome programme and offering a preview of the channel's offering and well wishes for its success, they had decided to broadcast a full schedule of the programmes that could be found on the channel on any other Tuesday afternoon, starting with *Countdown* presented by Richard Whiteley.[10] The contrasting methods of presenting their opening evenings show the disparity between the attitude of S4C and C4, and the fundamental difference in the nature of their existence. S4C was aware that their viewers needed to be persuaded to take to the new pattern of broadcasting Welsh language programmes in a relatively short period of time, to achieve a favourable outcome following the Home Office review. S4C's schedule was also more complex than any other channel in that it sought to meet the needs of two distinct audiences, and so it was necessary to explain the patterns of transmission to the audience to try to avoid any adverse confusion that might result in a negative reaction from Welsh speakers and non-Welsh speakers.

The opening hour on S4C was followed by the first broadcast of *Newyddion Saith*, the first 30-minute bulletin of national and international news broadcast in Welsh; to emphasise this new international flavour to the service, there were reports from the American mid-term elections and the Pope's visit to Spain, as well as numerous local stories from Prestatyn to Cwmbran, and from Aberaeron to Cardiff. S4C and BBC officials were certain that the audience would welcome and appreciate the change of emphasis in the news; however, difficulties for the ambitious service were anticipated by *The Guardian* as its reporter James Lewis noted: 'This welcome innovation could prove difficult to maintain, if only because of the need to find fluent Welsh speakers in foreign parts.'[11] This innovation was not the focus of the articles published in the *Western Mail* on the day following the broadcast; rather, they focused, in a derogatory tone, on the amount of English heard in the report from the Confederation of British Industry (CBI) conference in Eastbourne, which was the main story of the bulletin.[12] It was surprising that the news was broadcast at all that night, due to difficulties between the National Union of Journalists (NUJ) and BBC bosses, which had threatened to derail the broadcast.[13]

The news was followed by the first episode of the series *Cerddwn Ymlaen*, with Dafydd Iwan and Ar Log presenting their most popular songs and showcasing guests and musicians from Wales and the Celtic nations.[14] Then there was a short item called *Bro* where the children of Llangadog Primary School introduced their area to the nation. Items such as these highlighted efforts to try to ensure that the Welsh language audience felt ownership of the channel; they were part of the channel's wider strategy to try to unite the audience and alleviate the alleged linguistic and social differences between the north and south, although within the first month of the channel's broadcast there were complaints that these items were too parochial.[15]

Selecting the comedy *Newydd Bob Nos* for the 8 o'clock slot on the opening night was a brave move and reflected the sense of humour of the scheduling staff as the programme portrayed a TV news programme where everything goes wrong and life behind the scenes in utter chaos.[16] Had things gone wrong during the opening night, the programme could have proven to be an unfortunate comparison. This light-hearted comedy was followed by the first episode of the *Almanac* series entitled 'Citizen Kane and Cynan', a programme that traced the relationship between the newspaper baron William Randolph Hearst and the St Donats area of the Vale of Glamorgan and with the eisteddfod. The Welsh language broadcasts came to an end with the news headlines, and the English language programmes started at 9.30 p.m. Although the Welsh language broadcasts had officially come to an end, the first English language programme had a Welsh feel to it, since S4C had selected the programme *Max Boyce Meets the Dallas Cowboys*, which chronicled the month the Welsh comedian had spent with the American football team.[17] The programme was clearly carefully selected by S4C staff in order to attract non-Welsh-speaking viewers and to show them that S4C could provide them with relevant and entertaining content. The first night broadcasts concluded with the film *Network* (1976), directed by Sidney Lumet with award-winning performances by Faye Dunaway and Peter Finch.

The troubles with the NUJ which threatened the news service were not the only union dispute that disrupted S4C's opening night. There was a significant dispute between Equity, the performers union, and the Institute of Practitioners in Advertising (IPA), because the IPA sought to change the system used to pay performers. The system at the time counted the number of broadcasts given to a particular advert, and the IPA wanted to change this to a new scheme that would allocate payments depending on the number of viewers for a particular programme or channel. Equity was unhappy with this proposed scheme as it resulted in a much lower payment to its members for adverts broadcast on C4 and S4C, compared to the ITV network. The performers' union demanded that its members be paid the same for their performances on advertisements broadcast on ITV and on the fourth channel, and until this was agreed, members were asked not to sign contracts unless they were paid a fee equal to ITV's terms.[18] As a result, the opening night of S4C did not include a full complement of adverts. HTV had managed to sell 37.5 minutes of the 40 minutes of advertising space for the opening night but, because of the dispute, only 16 minutes' worth of advertising was produced and broadcast.[19] Adverts for The Midland Bank, Llangefni Eisteddfod and Hypervalue were the only ones that managed to avoid the dispute.[20]

The response to S4C's inaugural broadcasts was generally positive, both in terms of viewing figures and the response to specific programmes. The authority in particular was very happy, and although areas for improvement were identified, the overall impression was that the opening night had been successful in introducing the nature, mood and personality of the new channel:

> Although the Authority had some critical comments on some programmes, these were small compared to the very favourable overall impression the service had made on them and the majority of their acquaintances. They praised the work of staff and programme makers in creating a professional, confident and relaxed feel to the programmes and the channel.[21]

Broadcasters' Audience Research Board's (BARB) viewing figures also confirmed that the channel had a successful first night and week as it managed to attract 12 per cent of its potential audience during peak hours, and an average of 10 per cent of the potential audience throughout the first week. These figures also compared favourably with other broadcasters' percentages, with the channel beating BBC2's peak-time audience share of around 8 per cent. But these figures, though very respectful for a new channel trying to establish itself, were far from breaking the dominance of the two main channels across peak hours, as their share of the audience remained around 36 per cent for BBC1 and 43 per cent for HTV. However, some programmes during the first week were successful in attracting significant audiences, due to the novelty value of the service and audience curiosity. S4C's welcome programme came second to *Wales Today* and *Nationwide* on the BBC, and the following evening many S4C programmes came second to HTV with *Newyddion Saith* second to *Emmerdale Farm* and *Coleg* a runner-up to *Give us a Clue*.[22]

4. The cast of *Coleg*, one of the successes of S4C's opening week *(image: reproduced with permission from ITV Cymru / Wales and the National Library of Wales)*

The viewing figures were not the only measurement available to the new channel whilst it reflected on the success of its first week. A small number of viewers' responses were received directly by telephone or letter: these indicate that the response to the service was generally favourable, but there were some elements that did not satisfy everyone. Thirty viewers praised the Welsh language service, which amounted to 94 per cent of the letters received about the Welsh elements of the service.[23] However, fifteen complaints were received about the English language service, with four of these objecting to the Welsh language content on the channel.[24] Viewers' main complaint about the English language service was the use of vulgar language and swearing, specifically in the film *Network* broadcast on the opening night, as well as the new soap opera, *Brookside*.

While the response to the service was generally favourable, there were echoes of the difficulties faced by the broadcasters during the 1960s and 1970s when a large number of non-Welsh-speaking viewers called the cable company Rediffusion in the hours before the channel began broadcasting.[25] Since William Whitelaw's second U-turn in September 1980, Rediffusion, which served large parts of the south Wales valleys, an area where historically homes were unable to receive adequate broadcast signals with a normal aerial, had sought to ensure that C4 was transmitted to its customer' homes rather than S4C.[26] This plan ignored the licence held by cable companies which insisted that only local television services should be transmitted and other services should not be broadcast at the expense of the local service. But Rediffusion believed that the rule could lead to a reduction in their customers. They believed that, since most providers had only four channels, customers would leave because they would lose the additional English language service that they were used to and paid for.[27] The number of Welsh speakers in these areas was relatively small and therefore the companies felt that it was not reasonable to insist that they should carry S4C. If these arguments were accepted, a proportion of Welsh speakers in those areas would be completely deprived of all Welsh language services, especially if they were part of the 10 per cent that could not receive a television service through a normal aerial.

The cable companies' arguments proved effective, with the Home Office persuaded to act and offer a concession, which was announced by the Home Secretary, William Whitelaw:

> If a particular cable operator seeks permission to distribute the English-language Fourth Channel rather than the Welsh-language Fourth Channel, and he is able to provide evidence that it is the wish of the majority of his subscribers, I am certainly willing to consider giving him such permission.[28]

Therefore, during 1982 Rediffusion organised a ballot of its customers in support of its bid to replace S4C with C4.[29] The poll was organised in the company's shops across south Wales and around half of customers – 53 per cent – voted, with 88 per cent demanding the English language channel, 10 per cent wishing to receive S4C and 2 per cent happy to trial S4C for six months before making a final decision.[30]

The S4C Authority was unhappy with these plans, which compromised the channel by reducing its potential audience before it had even started broadcasting. Sir Goronwy Daniel expressed his dissatisfaction with the situation: 'As a new service having to establish itself and compete for viewers with the four existing networks, S4C would not happily accept being placed in an inferior position which undermined its ability to compete on an equal footing.'[31] Whitelaw certainly listened to these arguments and at the eleventh hour, a week before S4C began broadcasting, he rejected the vote organised by Rediffusion, claiming that it was not a valid or reliable survey because the true nature of S4C's provision had not been explained to customers before they cast their votes. It was claimed that the viewers were given a choice between a 'Welsh' channel and an 'English' channel, without mention of most of C4's English language programmes being broadcast on S4C, and that there would no longer be any Welsh language programmes on the BBC channels or HTV. The vote was deemed not to have been conducted in good faith, and Whitelaw announced that he did not intend to overhaul the guidelines on the basis of unreliable and inaccurate evidence.[32]

With Rediffusion's hopes shattered, along with those of its customers, in the hours before the channel began broadcasting the company declared their dissatisfaction by announcing to the press that 'hundreds' of customers had contacted them to complain about the Home Secretary's 'diabolical' decision.[33] Moving the Welsh language programmes from the BBC and HTV services and clustering them on one channel did not alleviate the strong feelings amongst the non-Welsh-speaking audience; in their view, they were still being deprived since they lost some C4 programmes, and the programmes that were broadcast were during off-peak hours.

Audience response

Following the first week's promising viewing figures, the inevitable drop came in the second week and the channel started to analyse in more detail the viewing patterns of the audience who had been, for a short time, so enthusiastic. According to the BARB figures for the channel's second week on air, Welsh language programming was down 5 per cent, and its audience share fell by 2 per cent from 12 to 10 per cent. The change in the figures for Welsh language programmes was far less dramatic than the fall in the corresponding figures for C4 programmes broadcast on S4C. BARB figures for the same week showed that 35 per cent fewer viewers were watching the English language programmes on S4C, with the programmes at the top of the viewing charts falling from around 180,000 to 120,000 viewers, a fall that was reflected in the viewing patterns throughout Britain. C4's share of the British audience had dropped from 6 to 5 per cent, which was disappointing for its officials when they had publicly expressed their wish to attract one in ten of the potential audience.[34] Such a drop was inevitable for both channels, as the opening week figures, though encouraging, were figures that documented unique broadcasts, and were therefore unsustainable.

Opening weeks would attract viewers who would not choose to watch the channel as part of their normal viewing patterns, but who would watch opening broadcasts due to natural curiosity. It is therefore not appropriate to compare either channel's first week viewing figures with the following week's published statistics.

S4C's viewing figures fell further following the opening weeks and months. December was a disappointing month compared to the opening weeks,[35] although the channel enjoyed a very successful Christmas day with three of the most popular programmes of the week broadcast on 25 December.[36] Figures grew throughout January and February returning to a level close to the average recorded over that successful first month of viewing, and by March the average viewership of the five most popular programmes had reached 120,000.[37] The growth could be explained by the seasonal increase in winter viewing figures with the number of hours of daylight at its lowest level; or an attractive first Christmas schedule might have tempted some viewers back into the fold. Regrettably, there was a sharp drop during April to 98,000 and then a further significant drop in May to an average of 64,000 viewers for the channel's most popular programmes.[38] Following the publication of these figures there was a brutally honest discussion amongst the authority members about the reasons for the decline, with several predicting that the initial success was over. They rejected the idea that lighter summer evenings fully explained the decline, and one member attributed it, in fairly frank remarks, to a deterioration in the quality of the programmes broadcast, and that there were very few programmes that attracted him to S4C.[39] If the channel did not interest members of its own authority, then there was a significant problem facing its staff.

The fall in viewing figures clearly caused considerable concern to the authority as the chairman produced a report regarding the decline experienced across all categories of viewing figures. There was a detailed analysis of the reduction seen between viewing figures for the first five months of broadcast and the May 1983 figures, particularly the time viewers spent watching S4C programmes, which had dropped from 98 minutes a week to 60 minutes a week.[40] There had been a general fall across all the television channels, with a reduction of around 14 per cent in viewing time, a statistic that shows a lowering in overall viewing patterns at this time of year. But the fall in S4C's figures was 38 per cent, and so it was clear that the authority's instincts to dismiss seasonal patterns as the only factor effecting their viewing figures was correct.[41] In some areas, the decline was less dramatic, with the audience share of potential viewers falling from 8 to 6 per cent between March and May, a figure still higher than that of C4, which had now fallen to 4 per cent and had remained there throughout the first few months of broadcasting. But S4C's figure was now below BBC2's, which had climbed to 16 per cent in April, and dropped back to 9 per cent a month later.[42] Daily analysis of the figures showed that the channel lost out significantly on weekends, demonstrating that the channel's offering of programmes such as *Twyllo'r Teulu*, *Madam Sera*, *Antur*, *Yr Awr Fawr*, and even *SuperTed* and *Wil Cwac Cwac*, were not able to draw viewers away from the familiar and popular programmes broadcast on ITV and the BBC.[43]

The conclusion was that there were many lessons to be learned from these figures, and the programme editor indicated that there were many elements and aspects that could be adapted and changed for the future. Unfortunately for the channel, however, it was not possible to make any significant immediate changes to the schedule to respond to the poor viewing figures and to strengthen its provision by including programmes that were likely to appeal to the audience since the schedule was set firmly until the beginning of August 1983. As a result, only four weeks of the summer schedule could be modified to try to improve the viewing figures a little, before the autumn schedule, which was considered to include a strong offering, began. Here the rigid nature of television channels at the time becomes apparent, and even a relatively small channel had schedules that were inflexible: it was almost impossible to make significant changes to broadcasting plans at short notice, and the difficulty in responding to viewer trends when those came to light was tremendous.

Although S4C publicly claimed in press releases and in the annual report that the decline in viewing figures was due to the changes in viewing patterns during the summer months – thus attempting to give the decline a positive spin – internally the discussions and analysis was much more open and ruthless.[44] It was acknowledged that the April schedule had been disappointing and that the channel had lost a number of popular series when they came to an end, with no similar output to take their place, and the channel was publicly criticised for repeating programmes so early in its history.[45] Chris Grace also remembers that by spring 1983 the channel's reserve stock of Welsh language programmes had been completely exhausted: S4C had only been given just over a year of production time before the channel started broadcasting, and because of the long dispute with HTV, the stock was below where it should have been.[46] The channel's lack of confidence in its independent producers is evidenced here since it had commissioned a number of short rather than longer series, which would have maintained viewers' loyalty and would likely have achieved relatively consistent viewing figures as the months passed. S4C had also put all its finest programmes in the shop window during the early months to generate a response and to attract viewers; by spring 1983 the channel was starting to scrape the bottom of the programming barrel.

The publicity campaign had also run out of steam after the tremendous effort of the first few months, and the channel's small staff had been completely exhausted after the first winter. In contrast to the schedule, however, this situation could be rectified at short notice by investing more money and time into publicity to try to recover audience share over the summer months.[47] Euryn Ogwen Williams also suggested that the success of the early weeks had a negative rather than a positive effect on the channel's staff and viewers: 'We became over confident and assumed audience loyalty while the audience felt it no longer had an obligation to view if there was anything else that interested them.'[48] Hard lessons were learned early on in the channel's history; in particular the loyalty of any audience could not be taken for granted, and that even the most loyal Welsh-medium viewers were likely to turn to another channel if S4C's programmes did not appeal to them.

Although the viewing figures were concerning, one of the recommendations of the programming department was that the channel should not overreact or panic. There was some doubt as to whether the figures provided by BARB were reliable, a doubt that had existed since the channel's second week on air. *Y Mab Darogan* had received very low viewing figures, but had received excellent verbal feedback;[49] the perceived discrepancy had led to speculation amongst channel officials.[50] There was suspicion that the programme had been 'unlucky' by failing to attract the individuals who had BARB boxes to watch, and therefore the viewing figures could be misleadingly low.[51] These seeds of doubt in the consistency and accuracy of the figures grew, and by the end of 1983 the channel had asked another research organisation, Research and Marketing Wales and the West Limited, to investigate the 'unbelievable' figures the channel had received from BARB.[52] What prompted the channel to demand further analysis of the figures was the increasing discrepancy between the number of viewers and the number of households watching a particular programme. An example of this is in the figures received for Friday, 18 November 1983, when BARB claimed that 65,000 individuals had watched *Pobol y Cwm* in 73,000 homes, figures that were impossible to understand or explain. This statistic prompted one broadcaster to joke: 'It seems as if Welsh dogs, left alone in houses in the evening, are turning on the set for a spot of light relaxation.'[53] Receiving figures like these made S4C staff question other figures, especially since the previous year's corresponding figures showed audiences at double the number calculated for the same week and the exact time in the schedule for 1983. This scepticism was understandable, especially as the statistics for the top five programmes were published in the press, with the obvious concern that they could be used to compare the cost of the channel with its viewership. The press showed great interest in the viewing figures and cost per head, and some articles predicted the demise of the channel following low viewing figures, such as the article by Tim Jones in *The Times* who proclaimed: 'Recent celebrations of S4C's first anniversary, the Welsh language television channel, turned into something of a wake.'[54]

The inconsistency of BARB figures was partly attributed to the small sample size of households that they used to compile the statistics:[55] 220 households were part of the sample, 120 of which were homes where at least half the residents of the house spoke Welsh and the remaining 100 were non-Welsh-speaking homes or where Welsh speakers were in the minority. In order to estimate the figures for the whole of Wales these figures would be combined at a ratio of 19 to 81, as only 19 per cent of the population of Wales spoke Welsh.[56] But the problem was not the Welsh/non-Welsh language split: one of the significant difficulties with this model was that the use of a small sample to calculate a small percentage of viewers created a significant margin for error in viewing figures, especially when considering the figures for a single programme.[57] A viewing figure of 60,000 by this method of calculation could actually refer to any figure between 42,000 and 78,000, which was considered to be a very wide range. Another factor was that a more detailed analysis of the figures showed that the significant decline could be attributed almost entirely to the viewing patterns of the 100 non-Welsh-speaking homes or who had a minority of Welsh speakers. It appears therefore that many of those homes had watched the channel in its first months, but a year later those viewers were few and far between, and since the viewing patterns of these 100 homes were multiplied by 81, to represent the majority of the population of Wales, the change in figures from one year to the next was disproportionately high.[58]

5. Two of *Pobol y Cwm*'s most popular characters Jacob Ellis (Dillwyn Owen) and Harri Parri (Charles Williams) *(image: © BBC Photo Library)*

Further distrust of the viewing figures was cultivated by the picture of S4C's success that was drawn from the figures published by the Audience Appreciation Service, a service provided to BARB by the BBC's Broadcasting Research Department.[59] For S4C, this research was undertaken by surveying a sample of 720 Welsh speakers every three months to rate the programmes they had watched.[60] Compared to the BARB viewing figures, these appreciation figures had remained high, and were consistently higher than the corresponding figures collected by the Audience Appreciation Service for the other popular channels.[61] For example, if we consider the *Newyddion Saith* appreciation figures over a period of three annual reports, they began very high in the first five months of broadcasting with a score of 80, then during 1983–4 the programme received a rating of 76, before climbing back to 79 during 1984–5. A similar pattern was observed with the soap opera *Pobol y Cwm*, which started with a high score of 83 before dropping to 82 in 1983–4, and then reviving and beating the opening five-month figures in 1984–5 with 87.[62] By comparing these appreciation figures with those received by the news and current affairs programmes of the BBC, ITV and C4, it appears that they averaged 74.5 and, as previously noted, S4C's figures for its news bulletin during the same period were slightly higher.[63] In the case of series and drama serials the BBC, ITV and C4 average were around 73, while *Pobol y Cwm* in the same period received the significantly higher score of 82. The Welsh language audience's appreciation of the Welsh language programmes was therefore well above the audience appreciation of the English language programming on the other channels. There appeared to be a duality at the heart of the concept of S4C's success, namely that the programmes it broadcast succeeded in delighting its target audience, but with that satisfaction the channel had to come to terms with the fact that only a small number of viewers would actually watch the entertaining and interesting programmes televised. S4C's output was therefore proving popular but seemingly unpopular at the same time.

Due to this inconsistency, the political importance of achieving healthy viewing figures and the feeling amongst channel staff that the public and press were paying disproportionate attention to the published viewing figures, discussions were held with BARB and Audits of Great Britain (AGB), the organisation providing the audience measurement service for BARB, to see if a new system for collecting and publishing S4C data could be found.[64] The culmination of these discussions was changing the way the figures collected by BARB were published, namely by offering a more detailed analysis of the viewing patterns of the panel of Welsh-speaking homes alongside the figures.[65] The definition of a Welsh-speaking household was also strengthened to include details of the level of Welsh understanding amongst family members, to ensure that the households within the sample were able to provide a much more reliable picture for analysis. Following these changes the sample would be restricted to households in Wales that could receive S4C and where 50 per cent or more of the individuals in the home understood Welsh well enough to be able to follow a conversation either at work or between friends and relatives.[66] This new method was implemented from 9 December 1984, and within two months the director was full of praise due to the figures that were provided being much more stable, fair and relevant to the channel.[67] Because this system had not been in place for a full year, the 1984–5 annual report did not provide a detailed analysis of the figures, but it did offer a preview of the new figures which suggested a very positive picture of the loyalty towards the channel amongst Welsh audiences.[68] It was announced that 79.2 per cent of the Welsh-speaking population watched S4C every week, a figure well above the 69.3 per cent of the bilingual population of Wales who watched BBC2 every week.[69] The new figures also stated that, on average, Welsh viewers watched 4 hours and 12 minutes of S4C programmes a week compared to the less than 3 hours a week that viewers in Wales spent watching BBC2.[70] This new method of presenting information was much more beneficial to S4C, enabling the channel to display a far more positive picture of its popularity to the public and to the government – a picture that matched the appreciation figures and more accurately reflected the enthusiastic response received from the audience at public events and festivals across Wales.

Reviewing and adapting

The patterns of measuring and publishing viewing figures were not the only component of the service that was adapted to try to improve and increase the channel's popularity in the public eye and in the press. Throughout the trial period the channel changed and altered many aspects of the service in an attempt to improve and secure a respectable audience. One of the elements that was modified was the structure of the schedule or, more specifically, the location of the Welsh programmes within it. Due to a significant decline in viewing figures for Welsh language programmes during the channel's first summer in 1983, it was decided that adjusting the schedule was one way of dealing with this.

Originally Welsh language programmes were divided into three broadcasting blocks Monday to Friday, rather than being interwoven with English language programmes. This meant that programmes for young children and schools started at 2 o'clock in the afternoon for about 50 minutes with programmes such as *Ffalabalam*, *Ffenestri* and *Hwnt ac Yma* part of the provision. Subsequently *Clwb* would launch the next 40 minutes of Welsh language programming of interest to young people from approximately 4.35 p.m., before transferring to broadcast English language programmes such as *The Munsters*, *Battlestar Galactica*, *Countdown* or *Brookside* before the block of evening programming started just before

7 o'clock in the evening with *Gair yn ei Bryd*, an item for Welsh learners, followed by the nightly news. Welsh language broadcasts would continue until 9 p.m. or 9.30 p.m. on some evenings, and the later hours would be filled with English language programmes, such as *Film on Four*. The weekend pattern was slightly different with the Welsh language programmes starting in the late afternoon on Saturdays, at approximately 4.30 p.m., and continuing until 10 o'clock at night, or a little later, providing a substantial block of programmes for the Welsh-speaking household. The Sunday schedule was similar to the weekday pattern with the occasional Welsh item such as the Welsh weather for farmers and the *Sbec ar S4C* programme on S4C during the afternoon; the evening programmes would begin at 5.15 p.m. and conclude at about 9.30 p.m.[71] This original schedule proved to be very successful for the channel during its opening months, and so the pattern of Welsh language broadcast blocks continued for the channel's second winter. But for the summer of 1984 a new schedule was trialled, which would break the pattern of Welsh language programmes filling peak hours. The new schedule would see Welsh language programmes continuing to open the peak hours between 7 p.m. and 8 p.m. in the evening, but then at 8 o'clock on Monday, Tuesday, Thursday and Friday evenings it was proposed to broadcast an hour of English programmes, before returning to broadcast Welsh language output between 9 and 10 o'clock.[72] This was not the first time that the channel had broadcast English language programmes during the Welsh block in peak hours: this was done out of necessity for a few weeks during the spring of 1983 when the channel's Welsh language programme stock had been completely depleted.[73] The idea of splitting the Welsh block seemed logical, since broadcasting programmes at a later time would ensure Welsh language provision was available to the audience on their return home after spending time enjoying the summer evenings. The pattern also met the needs of some members of the audience who had corresponded to express concern about the policy of broadcasting Welsh language programmes during peak hours as the schedule would clash with numerous arts, social and religious events such as the *seiat* (fellowship meeting), the literary society and *Merched y Wawr*.[74] The authority was not completely confident in the new plan, and one member noted that he wished to see the continuous block continue, proposing that the problem could be resolved by starting it later, at 7.30 p.m. However, it was eventually concluded that this was not possible because of the channel's commitment to broadcast the news at 7 o'clock.[75]

Although the idea was logical, it could be argued that dividing the Welsh language broadcast block would bring the channel into conflict with the Broadcasting Act, which set out S4C's responsibility to allocate the vast majority of the peak hours to broadcasting Welsh language programmes: allocating one of the key peak hours to English language programming could be viewed as going against the principle and spirit of the Act. Arguably, placing English language programmes in peak hours provided a concession to non-Welsh language viewers of the channel, who had been complaining about the timing of English language programmes, but doing so at the expense of the Welsh-language provision. Most of all, the pattern set a dangerous precedent for the timing of English language programmes, potentially placing the channel on unstable ground. Close inspection of the Act reveals that: 'the programme schedules shall be drawn up so as to secure that the programmes broadcast on the Fourth Channel in Wales between the hours of 6.30 p.m. and 10.00 p.m. consist mainly of programmes in Welsh'.[76] The proposed change therefore did not breach any of the regulations, since it did not require that peak hours be completely filled by Welsh language programmes. Prior to this change the channel had been unable to completely fill peak hours with Welsh language content, since doing so would have swallowed up all the programme hours, at the expense of the schools and children's output. S4C was operating and adapting its schedule within the parameters set, seeking to find the most reasonable solution for the difficulties faced in attracting audiences during the summer. However, this change did threaten to open the door to arguments regarding better timing for English language programmes, especially given the number of complaints that the channel received directly by telephone or letter from non-Welsh-speaking viewers about the timing of C4 programmes.

Another danger posed by this strategy was the likelihood that it could reduce the audience further rather than increase it. Splitting the Welsh block could result in the loss of those viewers who would join the Welsh language programmes at 7 p.m., but switched to another channel when there was an English programme at 8 p.m., losing them to the other channels for the remainder of the evening. Despite this, the scheme was formally implemented in the summer of 1984, and no complaints were received from viewers.[77] This was an encouraging response given viewers' willingness to contact the channel to praise or complain about other issues, such as breaches in good taste and vulgar language. After initial reservations, one member of the authority suggested that the new schedule may be much more suited to encouraging viewing in multilingual homes. But another member suspected that changing the position of programmes was just a superficial adjustment, and that he was far more concerned about the quality of the programmes than their location within the schedule.[78] Since this change was made at the same time as the channel was in the process of transforming the way viewing figures were collated and published, it was not possible to quantify its success with audience data. One measure of its success is that the channel did not return to a completely continuous block of Welsh language programmes in the autumn. Instead, the pattern trialled during the summer continued on Monday and Tuesday evenings, so that Welsh language programmes more suited to late-night transmission could be broadcast on those evenings.[79]

Authority members shared their views on the channel's programmes at almost every meeting and, as has already been suggested, some were very happy to announce when they were not entirely happy with the coverage. S4C staff and the authority also occasionally had extended meetings where programme policy and commissioning would be discussed in more detail;[80] the first of these – after the channel began broadcasting – revealed that the staff were not resting on their laurels as they asked the authority to discuss whether the channel was successfully using the resources and talent available in the most effective way and to their full potential, comments that indicate good management, and demonstrate that there was a constant search for areas which could be improved and make better use of the relatively scarce resources.[81] Consideration was also given to whether the channel was successfully representing the voice of the nation. They discussed whether the fact that the channel was now regarded as a national institution had created a divide between it and its audience, that its official status in the eyes of the audience had created a sense that the channel no longer belonged to the viewers and they could not influence its activities.[82] This was problematic for the channel because of the considerable effort made to create a homely and warm atmosphere to try to attract and secure the loyalty of the Welsh-speaking audience.

The authority's response to these areas of discussion was to talk about the merits of several specific genres and the shortcomings found within the service. It was concluded that too few substantial programmes of intellectual substance had been created, and it was suggested that this aspect of the service had been neglected in an attempt to provide entertaining programmes that would attract larger audiences to the channel.[83] It was also felt that good religious programming and the talent to produce them were scarce, and it was agreed that meeting this requirement with congregational singing was not adequate, despite the popularity of those programmes. Another vital aspect of the service that was regularly discussed was the quality and style of the channel's presentation. The members of the authority were very critical, stating that 'the link between programmes is sometimes unacceptably amateurish, and the standard of English pronunciation unsatisfactory'.[84] The early difficulties encountered by the presenting team with the links between programmes were justified due to the uncertain and variable timing of C4 programmes and the lack of advertising because of the Equity dispute. These circumstances had created a difficult situation where presenters were expected to fill longer gaps than expected by resorting to unscripted and improvised conversation. This also led to the unpredictable timing of programmes, with many starting ahead of time or late, an issue that invariably irritated Welsh-speaking and non-Welsh-speaking viewers alike.[85] Since the channel had hired two young and new presenters in order to introduce new talent and faces to the screen, such inconsistencies caused initial difficulties, which the programme staff were sure would decrease as they gained more experience and confidence in their presentation skills.[86] There was also some uncertainty about the presentation style adopted by the channel: the authority was concerned that a warm and welcoming presentation might seem amateurish at times, recognising that there was a very fine line between the two.[87] The IBA's Welsh committee and the BBC's Broadcasting Council shared a similar view with one member of the broadcasting council stating that presenters needed to be very experienced and technologically sophisticated in order to appear homely on screen.[88] A very similar view was expressed in *Barn*: 'Overly affable, overly welcoming, somewhat patronising presenters. I prefer pleasant courtesy but at arm's length. S4C or not, TV is a thing, not a friendly neighbour. I demand the right to shut their mouths without feeling guilty.'[89] After all the criticism it was felt that the presenters had lost the personal touch and, as a result, by the end of 1983, there was an attempt to reinstate the close relationship with the viewer, demonstrating how difficult it was to please everyone.[90] Despite the negative comments received, the informal nature of the presentation was an unique characteristic of the channel, since there was no precedent in British broadcasting. It could be compared to the style used by breakfast television, namely *TV-am* on ITV and *Breakfast* on the BBC, which launched in the early months of 1983, but S4C was the first to adopt this style and to this extent on British television, and the channel would adhere to this pattern of presentation throughout the trial period and beyond.[91]

The news service received similar treatment. S4C was keen for the Welsh language news programme to provide a comprehensive and complete service, ensuring that Welsh-speaking viewers did not need to turn to other providers for their news. To do this, the programme would be expected to include a mix of Welsh, British and international news, ensuring that the Welsh speakers could receive all the important news of the day in their mother tongue. This strategy was agreed between the BBC and S4C, but the nation was not as enthusiastic. In January 1983 some members of the authority noted that many of their acquaintances had expressed complaints about the lack of local items on *Newyddion Saith*.[92] Dissatisfaction with the news service continued throughout 1983, with viewers and the authority concerned about the quality of the local stories.[93] The complaints focused on the imbalance between international news and Welsh news, and that the local news items were not detailed enough, and possibly less comprehensive than those found on the English regional news programmes.[94] These grievances were reiterated by a series of letters to S4C from Carmarthen Labour MP, Dr Roger Thomas, who expressed his disappointment that news provision fell between two stools and that he wished to see the news programme return to the pattern seen in the days before S4C's existence:

> criticising most severely the totally inadequate and inappropriate way in which the fourth Welsh channel is failing its viewing audience in its coverage of what is going on in Wales.
>
> The half hour programme on weekdays and fifteen minutes on a Saturday covers in a . . . less acceptable manner events of importance and interest in Wales as compared with the days when 'Y Dydd' and 'Heddiw' were in direct competition. Then of course we had a certain degree of duplication, but at least . . . events from all corners of Wales were adequately covered and presented.
>
> We need a return to that state of affairs with a half hour presentation of News of Wales in Welsh rather than News in Welsh.[95]

There was a belief that the Welsh language audience was being deprived with the news service, since non-Welsh speakers continued to receive half an hour of local material on the BBC and on HTV while the Welsh-speaking audience, who were used to receiving news and magazine programmes focusing on local events and items of interest to Wales, now received a much smaller proportion of these items.[96] Another common complaint, expressed in a letter from Dafydd Wigley to the channel, was that the channel provided its viewers with a re-hashing of images and stories transmitted on English language news without any new analysis from a Welsh perspective. These weaknesses and shortcomings were attributed to the fact that there was no longer any competition between the BBC and HTV in terms of Welsh language news, suggesting that the BBC were resting on their laurels without HTV biting at their heels.[97]

S4C responded, explaining that the duplication of visual material was an essential element of the service to ensure that the programme addressed international and national issues. It was not possible to justify sending a special camera crew to the furthest corner of the world to film material and images for *Newyddion Saith* when a crew was already there providing a service for the corporation's other news programmes. Using those made reporting on international events with a Welsh voice and a Welsh perspective possible – and cost effective. It was also noted that the allegations were not entirely accurate, as the BBC had Welsh correspondents, such as Dewi Llwyd, reporting on national events from Westminster giving a Welsh perspective to its reports. Although the response was fiercely protective of the service, Owen Edwards agreed with the MP that there was a loss after the removal of the competition between HTV and the BBC in the area of news, but that there were legitimate reasons for not resurrecting that scenario, such as the complaints that were received of the unnecessary and wasteful duplication between *Y Dydd* and *Heddiw*.[98]

Interestingly, the letters of Dafydd Wigley and Roger Thomas, in their awareness of the duplication of material between the English language news programmes and *Newyddion Saith*, highlight a viewing pattern which appears not to have been considered when devising the strategy for the Welsh language service. The possibility of Welsh language audiences continuing to turn to the English language news for their national and international news at 6 o'clock before turning to the Welsh language output was overlooked, and this resulted in viewers who were already familiar with the items from outside Wales presented on *Newyddion Saith*.[99] The Welsh-speaking audience was turning to *Newyddion Saith* for their local news, and remained faithful to the British news programmes that had established themselves in the viewing patterns of the Welsh audience for decades. S4C and the BBC therefore faced a significant battle to try to persuade the Welsh-speaking audience to transform its viewing patterns and turn to *Newyddion Saith* for all their journalistic needs.

Weighing the above comments, the BBC Broadcasting Council for Wales and S4C Authority concluded that viewers were comparing the English and Welsh language service since *Newyddion Saith* was broadcast shortly after *Wales Today*, and because the audience expected that both programmes would discuss similar material. It was thought that the Welsh language news programme was depriving its audience because local news was discussed in greater detail on *Wales Today*.[100] It was suggested, therefore, that the timing of the programme should be adjusted to either broadcast in direct competition with *Wales Today* or broadcast earlier or later the same evening. Although this was sensible, there were a number of practical reasons which determined that *Newyddion Saith* was broadcast at 7 o'clock each night; one of which was that both programmes used many of the same technical resources. In addition, S4C benefitted from having a news service that started at 7 p.m. as for most audience members it marked the beginning of Welsh language programming in the channel's schedule. Broadcasting the programme earlier would mean a larger English language gap during Welsh language provision, or the Welsh language programmes would have to end sooner. Perhaps the new channel should have considered adjusting its news strategy by ensuring more of a local news focus, especially given that dissatisfaction was beginning to lead to a reduction in viewing figures for the channel,[101] but there was a belief amongst S4C and BBC officials that the central strategy of providing a comprehensive news service was the right choice.[102] Geraint Stanley Jones, for example, stated at a joint meeting between the broadcasting council and the S4C Authority that the original concept of providing a national and international news service was 'vital to the concept of S4C';[103] because of this steadfast belief, the BBC and S4C persevered with the ethos of providing a comprehensive, multi-layered news programme. And given the news service provided on the channel today, 40 years later, the unwavering stance of the officials can be justified, since that pattern of reporting the day's events, whether local, national or international, has been established and continues to this day.

Another aspect of the service that was being criticised was the lack of provision for some groups, especially learners.[104] The channel was aware that a number of people had started learning the language because of the channel's arrival, but due to a combination of policy decisions and technical difficulties S4C had not been able to meet their needs.[105] The *Gair yn ei Bryd* programme, a short programme of just a few minutes, broadcast at the beginning of the Welsh language block before *Newyddion Saith*, was the only provision for learners.[106] S4C officials thought that it was the responsibility of HTV and the BBC to provide programmes for learners within their own schedules, and they distinguished between the linguistic ability of different learners: HTV and the BBC should provide a service for new or inexperienced learners, in their view, and S4C's role was to provide content for those learners 'crossing the bridge', who needed a little support in order to enjoy the Welsh language content on the channel.[107] They questioned the wisdom of broadcasting programmes for new learners within the 22 hours, as this would reduce the number of hours broadcast for fluent speakers. A possible compromise was to try to repeat a number of programmes with subtitles, although this did not meet the need for suitable and relevant programmes for learners.[108] This approach shows that the channel adopted a very narrow definition of Welsh speakers in its early years. Throughout the channel's preparatory period Owen Edwards, in particular, adopted the concept of 'Mrs Jones, Llanrug' as shorthand to refer to the Welsh-speaking audience to whom the channel sought to attract.[109] In one of his many addresses to societies and organisations throughout Wales during the early months of his role, the director went further by trying to define who the general Welsh person was, and therefore the target audience:

> it might be easier to try to say what he is not. He is not likely to read a Welsh language paper, apart from a *papur bro*, he is not likely to be chapel or churchgoing, and remember most of the learning to read Welsh was done in the chapel or Sunday school, he's not likely to feel strongly about the language, he is not likely to be young – a much higher proportion of the Welsh-speaking population is older than the general population – his Welsh, sadly, is probably rusty, he doesn't understand big Welsh words which would alienate him, and he is conditioned to receive his entertainment through the medium of English, and probably at least one member of his household is a non-Welsh speaker.[110]

Learners were not part of that portrayal, although non-Welsh speakers appear in the definition. There was a fundamental problem with the view that it was the responsibility of the other Welsh broadcasters to provide for entirely new learners because it did not recognise the tensions that could resurface amongst the non-Welsh-speaking audience. If HTV and the BBC were to broadcast Welsh language programmes in their schedule, even if those programmes were aimed at non-Welsh speakers, the feelings of dissatisfaction would reappear because of the expectation amongst this audience that Welsh language programmes had been removed forever from the main channels. Concerns were expressed by the IBA's Welsh committee that these programmes could revive many of the unpleasant attitudes alleviated by the establishment of S4C.[111] Learners therefore fell between two stools and three broadcasters, each claiming that it was the responsibility of the other to meet their broadcast needs. *Gair yn ei Bryd* was removed from the schedule at the beginning of 1984, with the intention of filling the space with a general calendar programme suitable for the whole audience, rather than a new offering for learners.[112] It appears that no significant discussions on the provision for learners were held until the meeting of the BBC Broadcasting Council for Wales with S4C in March 1984.[113] At the meeting there appeared to be a significant change in attitude since the BBC had been in discussions with the Welsh Joint Education Committee, and a promise was made to produce provision for Welsh learners.[114] This was a significant U-turn in S4C's approach to programmes for learners. The original policy was overturned and *Sioe Siarad*, a programme for learners, was broadcast in February and March 1985.[115] There was also a compromise from the BBC, as the programme was repeated during the same week on BBC Wales, seeking to make the provision available to a wider audience.[116] A second series of *Sioe Siarad* was broadcast in 1985–6, despite the first series not attracting a significant audience, a commitment that shows that the channel's attitude to this audience had changed completely during its years on air. This is also supported by the comments in the 1985–6 annual report where it was acknowledged that the channel, above all, was a point of contact with the Welsh language and therefore its service offered programmes for learners at different stages of their journey.[117]

Another issue pertaining to language that attracted the attention of the authority and staff from the early days of broadcasting was the use of English in Welsh language programmes.[118] Any guidelines given to producers needed to ensure that they had the editorial freedom to decide which language register would suit the programmes they were producing. However, S4C emphasised that producers should bear in mind that the essence of any programme should be Welsh, and that the use of English interviews needed to be clearly justified.[119] Some programmes were broadcast in the first month that did not adhere to this principle, and eleven complaints were received from the public about the overuse of English in *Elinor yn Ewrob* and other similar programmes such as *Now a Fi yn Nashville*.[120] The proportion of English content was relatively high in these programmes as they related to travel to foreign countries where English was the common language. The answer would be to dub in Welsh any interviews following the pattern established by the channel's opening programme, where the voices of Björn Borg and others were dubbed. One programme that provoked more negative reaction on this issue, and where dubbing would have been wholly impractical and unpleasant, was the police drama *Bowen a'i Bartner*, produced by the BBC.[121] The drama depicted the lives of police officers and criminals in the Welsh capital, and to provide a credible picture of that world a combination of English and Welsh was used in the script. There was a robust response to the programme at a public meeting in Carmarthen in March 1985 and letters were sent to S4C and the BBC by Wynfford James on behalf of Cymdeithas yr Iaith asking both organisations for their policy on the matter.[122] The response from the BBC, and confirmed by S4C, was that there were no firm rules on the use of English in Welsh language programmes, and that the organisations did not wish to impose strict rules, especially in the area of dramatic productions. It was felt that producers and scriptwriters were fully aware of the need to use as little English as possible in Welsh language productions. In the same discussion, the chairman of the S4C Authority emphasised that not all viewers of the channel were equally fluent, and that the channel was expected to appeal to a wide range of viewers in order to succeed in its responsibilities.[123] By trying to appeal to a younger and broader audience, and creating a convincing and credible portrayal of the capital city, the channel would receive a barrage of complaints from its core audience, which did not want to see the service corrupted by debased adulterated language and the overuse of English.

A few letters were also received grumbling about the standard of Welsh in various programmes such as the drama *Coleg*, slang on *Newyddion Saith* and the quality of the language and the use of English idioms by some of the channel's presenters.[124] Some viewers saw S4C's role as maintaining standards and promoting the Welsh language, rather than reflecting natural language patterns and being as inclusive as possible by using language that would be understandable to wider sections of Welsh society. Nevertheless, accuracy remained the foundation of the service, as Owen Edwards's response to a viewer's complaint about one presenter's use of the English idiom 'die out' (*marw allan*) shows, as he assured the viewer that he would insist that the use of the expression would disappear from the presentation unit scripts.[125]

After the overwhelming urgency to get the channel ready to start broadcasting in earnest on 1 November 1982, there was no time for the channel's officers, staff or authority to take a breath. Staff remember that they were completely exhausted, but the channel continued to present daily challenges for them to deal with and resolve. After all the discussion and planning, once broadcasting had started it was a chance to see if the schedule, programmes, presenters and other elements all worked. In many cases the original plans had to be modified, reconsidered and reworked; in others, the channel persevered with certain principles, even as the audience expressed its dissatisfaction, assured and confident that the audience would become accustomed with the unfamiliar and change their point of view over time. The channel could not stand still: with the Home Office review looming, it was essential that staff and the authority responded to the viewing figures and listened to audience comments as they adjusted the service for the future.

4

Financial initiatives – securing fair terms and expanding to new areas

To ensure the success and survival of S4C, the channel and its officials had to make an impact, not only on the Welsh language audience but also on politicians in Westminster, who would ultimately decide on its future. S4C had to become an indispensable component of the Welsh broadcasting landscape and an integral part of the cultural and economic landscape of Wales. S4C staff and the authority were fully aware that the channel needed to do more than commission programmes to secure its future and to that end implemented a strategy that would embed the channel deep in the fabric of Wales. To realise their ambitious plans, and to ensure that the channel could continue to deliver the core elements of its service, a fair financial settlement needed to be secured annually from the Independent Broadcasting Authority (IBA) and the ITV network. This chapter will trace and scrutinise the channel's financial dealings with the IBA and the additional economic activities undertaken that were such a significant part of its success during its probationary period.

IBA financial negotiations

In many respects the funding formula originally established for Channel 4 (C4), and modified to incorporate the additional cost of S4C, was considered highly effective and successful. It reassured both channels that money would be available for them regardless of audience figures, and confirmed that they did not have to aim for vast audiences to attract advertisers: this, therefore, gave S4C and C4 the freedom to commission and schedule programmes with their appeal to audiences at the forefront of their planning. However, the arrangement did not provide assurances that the money requested would be received each year, and to that end securing sufficient funding for the channel was a constant effort for the staff and the authority. Reasonable funding needed to be secured to maintain the high standard of service set in the early months, and to secure the necessary improvements and adaptations to the service. For the eighteen months of preparation and the first five months of broadcasting, a figure of £20 million was agreed with the IBA to start the channel on a sound footing. Although that amount was allocated for the costly activities of establishing the channel's operations and a stock of programmes, it would be necessary to guarantee equivalent, if not higher, amounts for subsequent years to continue the established commissioning pattern. Negotiations for 1983 had to begin some months before the channel went on air, and during June 1982 it became clear that S4C was not guaranteed to receive annually the amount of money requested.[1] An application for £25.7 million was sent to the IBA, but correspondence between the parties revealed that the figure was likely to be less, around £24 million.[2] S4C appealed for more money, citing that £24.5 million was the minimum amount that could be accommodated without adversely affecting the service.[3] Confirmation came in late November 1982 that £24.6 million would be allocated.[4] Of that amount, £6 million would count towards the last three months of the 1982–3 financial year and would therefore form part of the £20 million previously agreed between the two authorities.[5] As a result £18.6 million would be left to maintain the service until the end of the calendar year. The IBA acknowledged that S4C was likely to be disappointed with its income, as it did not leave much room for the channel to make any spending or commissioning mistakes. Errors that were likely considering how young the channel was and given the examples of its overspending during its first commissioning year with *Madam Wen* and *SuperTed*. Despite the disappointment it was acknowledged that it was not possible to squeeze more money from ITV's coffers, since the total of £123 million recovered from the advertising money of the independent companies was 18 per cent of their Net Advertising Revenue (NAR), the highest percentage that could be levied under the deal agreed back in 1981.[6] The total amount collected by ITV companies was £1 million less than expected, and considering the difference between S4C's bid and the amount awarded by the IBA, it could be claimed that the savings came solely from the budget of the Welsh channel, while the whole sum applied for was offered to C4. But this would go against the informal rule established at the beginning of the history of the two channels that S4C would receive 20 per cent of the money raised, with C4 receiving the remaining 80 per cent. The evidence from C4 also shows that the IBA was unable to offer it adequate funding: the management board applied for £123 million in June 1982, which would later be confirmed by the IBA as the total amount available for both C4 and S4C, and received £98.4 million, almost £25 million less than requested.[7] John Whitney in a letter to Owen Edwards justified the lack of funding thus: 'The problem was simply that, within an overall figure of £123m, Members did not feel able to squeeze Channel 4 any harder.'[8] Here we see the IBA's commitment to S4C's success, since S4C's budget was not unduly squeezed to meet C4's needs. The informal agreement was adhered to and S4C received 20 per cent of the money available even when funds were tight.

However, receiving less funding than requested had significant consequences for the channel, especially for the independent producers. Independent productions would have significantly less money to spend, with an estimate that only £7.1 million could be made available compared to £9 million in the first financial year.[9] The independent producers' budget was the only flexible element of the channel's finances due to the rigidity of the programme agreement with HTV, and the relatively small spend on S4C's operational costs.[10] As a result, some companies would lose out; it was anticipated that some of the English language companies that the channel had turned to during its first year would disappear, such as London-based Opix Films who produced Welsh programmes starring Max Boyce and one of the channel's early films, *Owain Glyndŵr*, and Jack Bellamy Productions from Bristol who produced the *Blas o'r Gorffennol* cookery programmes.[11] But the door was not completely closed to independent producers from outside Wales in 1983 and the channel continued to commission programmes from Wyvern Television of Swindon and Imago Films of Clevendon, and work with new companies from the other side of the Severn bridge with Bumper Films from Weston-Super-Mare and Red Rooster Films from London both receiving commissions.[12] Companies from across the border were not the only ones to lose out that year. The Bwrdd Ffilmiau Cymraeg received no further commissions following the troubles with *Madam Wen*, the number of Na-Nog commissions were reduced due to internal troubles and Sgrin '82 had seen their commissions reduced because their ideas had not appealed to the commissioning team. The reduction in funding was also likely to have a detrimental effect on the companies that provided services to the industry, such as Tegset who built production sets. Others, however, would be able to profit from the situation: it would encourage producers to do more with less, and the first likely change would be to switch from film to video. It was anticipated that Barcud, the outside video broadcast unit, and Eco, the audio mixing company, would benefit as more producers would want to use the video facilities offered by them.[13]

Channel staff and members of the authority feared that the following year things could get worse with HTV's new broadcast centre at Culverhouse Cross due to open and start producing programmes. The implication for S4C was that the channel would now receive 9 hours a week instead of its 7.75 hours from the broadcaster.[14] But the IBA had warned the channel during the 1983 budget negotiations that it would not be able to fund the increase in HTV hours and keep the number of hours commissioned by the independent producers constant, since that would require an increase higher than inflation.[15] However, the authority and its officials were keen not to penalise the independent producers because of the inflexible agreement drawn up between S4C and HTV. Considering that the independent producers had provided more productions than were initially expected and responded so positively to the challenge set for them, the channel wanted to be loyal to them. To that end a meeting was arranged between the chairman of S4C and the chair of the IBA, Lord Thomson, where entreaties were made for more money and special consideration given when the 1984–5 budget would be allocated: the channel's internal estimates predicted that an additional £2.5 million was needed to buy the new hours from HTV.[16] Despite S4C's earnest plea, Lord Thomson remained steadfast and noted that there was no evidence that further funding could be made available to S4C for 1984–5, especially since the predictions for commercial television advertising revenue were low. He predicted that ITV companies would wish to see their share of NAR owed to the IBA fall closer to the minimum of 14 per cent, rather than the maximum of 18 per cent recently levied, since the companies were disappointed with the share of the money they had been able to recover from the original investment in the fourth channel network.[17] They had hoped to recoup 80 per cent of the investment, but only 20 per cent had so far been recovered.[18] The outlook was not promising for S4C's 1984–5 income.

By April ITV's advertising revenue forecasts were much improved.[19] And so a bid was submitted by S4C for £29,258,563, a bid that was over £4 million more than the sum received from the IBA in 1983–4, but which included £2.4 million for the extra hour and a quarter of programmes from

HTV from July 1984 onwards with an acceptable level of inflation.[20] ITV companies submitted a forecast that there would be a 15 per cent increase in their advertising funding and therefore 18 per cent of NAR would be likely to generate £140 million of revenue for the fourth channel.[21] S4C's 20 per cent would amount to £28 million, £1.2 million less than requested, although Sir Goronwy Daniel in his correspondence with the chair of the IBA had indicated that the channel could receive £28.5 million as a bare minimum.[22] The IBA member on the S4C Authority, Gwilym Peregrine, noted that the IBA had discussed the special needs of the Welsh language channel in the coming year, noting the arrival of Culverhouse Cross, that the Welsh language hours produced by HTV would increase and the 'moral duty' to support the Welsh independent producers.[23] It is revealing that both S4C and the IBA considered providing adequate funding for the independent producers a moral responsibility, and this exemplifies the importance of this sector to the Welsh language channel. These comments demonstrate the loyalty that existed between S4C and its independent producers – and more often than not their productions showed that the channel had been correct to place their trust in them.

The independent sector was once again likely to suffer the most from the channel's probable budget deficit. A letter from Sir Goronwy Daniel was sent to Lord Thomson explaining clearly why S4C staff were reluctant to see a further reduction in the funding available to produce programmes with the independent companies. The chairman noted that the independent producers were vital because they provided high-quality, award-winning programmes which increased the channel's standing, claimed their place in the weekly chart of the five most popular programmes on S4C and received a favourable response in the audience appreciation surveys – all for less money than the programmes purchased by HTV.[24] An additional reduction in 1984–5 could be detrimental to the channel, as the strategy that had been implemented to cope with the 1983–4 budget deficit had reduced the stockpile of programmes and increased the level of programme repeats;[25] he stated explicitly that the deficit could not be absorbed again without damaging the service that was provided to the audience. If there were further financial pressures, the channel would have to cut spending on the independent producers that had provided a fair and respectable service. Sir Goronwy Daniel sought to persuade the IBA of the adverse impact of such cuts thus: 'Significant further cuts ... if made, will fall on companies who have given us good value for money and are located in Welsh rural and coal and steel industrial areas where their loss would be a serious blow.'[26] This is an attempt to appeal to the conscience of IBA members, who would be fully aware of the economic turmoil of the industrial areas where the loss of production companies would further damage those areas that had fallen victim to Thatcher's policies. The letter concludes with one last entreaty to Lord Thomson's sense of fairness, and states that depriving the channel of the opportunity to use the extra 1.25 increase in HTV provision to increase the number of Welsh language programmes would create an unfavourable comparison with C4, which had significantly increased the number of its broadcasting hours from its original aims in 1981.[27] C4 had managed to broadcast around 50 hours a week since its opening night, which was significantly higher than the 35 hours per week originally intended. By comparison S4C had broadcast an average of 22 hours a week of Welsh language programming, a number which remained below the original campaigners' requirements who had stated that 25 hours would be the minimum required for a full service in Welsh. S4C, therefore, had to capitalise on the increased provision by HTV to meet the needs and requirements of its Welsh language audience.

Although the S4C Authority focused on the adverse effect of the deficit on the independents, there is evidence that HTV would also be at a loss in such a situation. On 28 September 1983 a letter was sent to HTV, in accordance with the requirements of the programme agreement, informing the company of the likelihood that the channel would have a financial deficit, sufficiently significant to warrant a fall in the funding available for HTV to produce programmes for S4C.[28] It was anticipated that there would be a reduction of approximately £175,000 once the new Culverhouse Cross studio opened, meaning that many programmes would need to be withdrawn, including one half-hour foreign affairs programme, two 45-minute talk shows, ten 15-minute nursery-aged programmes and one half-hour episode of a serial drama and a few other programmes – which would make a total loss of 7 hours.[29] This would lead to the channel being forced once again to increase the number of repeats so that it reached its total weekly hours, further reducing new programming for audiences, which would inevitably lead to a drop, once again, in the viewing figures.

Unfortunately, the figure of £28 million was not increased when the 1984–5 budget was confirmed, although ITV companies' advertising revenue had been buoyant. The IBA decided not to insist on 18 per cent of NAR, claiming 17.5 per cent instead. It also decided not to put the entire

£146 million collected into the fourth channel coffers, claiming £7 million of that total in order to repay the ITV companies' debt to the IBA at a faster rate.[30] Although disappointing, S4C's total was higher than the normal 20 per cent, climbing slightly higher to 20.14 per cent, and leaving C4 at 79.86 per cent, or £111 million.[31] There was passionate debate among the authority's members regarding the proper method of responding to the financial offer, and they debated whether to appeal to the Home Secretary, a possible action under the Broadcasting Act.[32] It was decided that an appeal could not be justified as the difference between the offer made and the amount sought was not sufficient to argue that the income undermined the service. However, the authority did not want to quietly receive the sum, as it feared that this would give the impression that the authority was asking for more money than was actually needed, and that the channel would receive similar treatment when discussing future budgets.[33] A few quotes were fed to the Welsh press about how disappointed the channel was that the IBA had not provided the extra £500,000 for the provision.[34] These messages undoubtedly succeeded in ensuring that the channel had the sympathy of the Welsh audience. The messages also served to curb audience expectations, and possibly prepare them for more repeats and less-than-expected growth in provision.

In the autumn of 1983, the authority decided to look again at the process of working with the independent producers to see if it could be streamlined and whether more programmes could be made with the money available. The commissioning procedure formed in the first few months was relatively loose and informal, and usually if a producer presented a good idea, a commission would follow soon afterwards. This strategy led to the commissioning of programmes by forty-six different companies and individuals during the channel's first two years. Of those companies, twenty-two were commissioned in 1982–3 and 1983–4. Twelve companies that received a commission in the first year did not receive further commissions in the second year, and nine new companies were commissioned in the second year.[35] Forty-six was a significant amount for the channel's small commissioning staff to engage with, and the wide range of internal structures and administration processes amongst those companies increased the burden on S4C's staff.[36] No two companies were structured the same; however, they could be classified into three fairly distinct categories: one-man companies, self-sustaining companies and small companies where all specialist staff were brought in during production.[37] There were four measures used by S4C internally when assessing companies, and if those standards were met, the companies were on a sound footing and could be trusted to produce high-quality programmes, on time and within budget: i) creative flare and programme quality; ii) practical capability to complete the work; iii) administrative and legal organisation and iv) effective financial management. Although these are normal and expected standards, only a small number of companies met this ideal in the staff's opinion, with some producers excelling at only some.[38] The clear implication is that a high level of encouragement and assistance was offered to the remaining producers who did not reach all four.

Why did S4C's programme staff, if working with the independent producers was often arduous, continue to work with these companies? The dedication and effort of the producers, and their willingness to work in difficult circumstances to provide engaging and appealing content, ensured the channel's diligence on their part. There was a sense of loyalty between the channel's programme staff and the independent producers because of the way this new sector had responded enthusiastically to the call, even though S4C staff acknowledged that many of them would have been better off financially – and have easier lives – within the two large broadcasting institutions. The programme staff appreciated that the independent companies chose to work long hours without complaining to realise their ideas for the channel.[39]

However, due to concerns over the 1984 budget it was inevitable that staff would have to reconsider the relationship and adjust the way that they engaged with the independent producers. It was not possible to achieve the desired savings by avoiding commissioning ambitious productions and introducing measures to ensure tight financial management and preventing overspend alone.[40] A much more dramatic approach needed to be considered, and the recommendation was to offer companies different levels of support, depending on their nature and ability.[41] The channel could not provide financial support to all of the companies for a whole year. Consideration was given as to whether it would be better to decide how many companies could reasonably be supported with the funds received from the IBA and cut ties with the rest; thus substantially reducing the number of companies working with S4C. Despite the appeal of the simplicity of such a scheme, it was rejected due to the possibility that it could be detrimental to the service and damaging to the endless enthusiasm that existed amongst the independent producers. Such a decision could destroy the morale and devastate the spirit of the sector, the core elements that S4C staff admired: it would be a mistake to dampen the flame by stabilising the sector too much, when its strength was its flexibility.[42] Clearly, competition was an essential part of the spirit of the sector, and there was considerable and understandable concern that reducing competition would affect the nature of the ideas and the quality of the productions. However, there was no support for the alternative, which was to divide the money equally between everyone. Such a scheme did not consider the obvious and significant differences in capability and creativity between the companies. Instead, they decided on dividing the sector into three separate categories and offering different support and assistance depending on the category. The first category was the companies considered to be the most robust, and offering them one year support to allow the companies to develop, prepare and plan ahead, rather than live from commission to commission with no financial security. These were the backbone of the channel, not all of them were large companies, although those producers who met the four criteria set by the channel were part of this group. Consistent financial support would enable the development and employment of expertise in administrative and financial areas to ensure that those aspects encouraged rather than undermined their work.[43] But there was no guarantee that the companies would remain in this category, unless their ideas continued to gain interest and they continued to create entertaining and engaging programmes. This was an attractive proposition for the producers included on the list, and a significant reward if they continued to produce quality programmes.

The second category formed was for those companies that were considered neither bad or terribly good, and for whom S4C would offer partial support. The producers included in this category were companies where only one major production or series could be expected of them each year, and where it would be foolish to support them for the remainder of the year to keep them in business for that one series.[44] Since S4C's financial position did not enable a wider offer of support they had to be completely honest with the companies about their status within the commissioning pattern, so that they were not misled and hoping for more commissions.[45] Although this was the natural next category, it was the most problematic, as it placed companies in a difficult position. The commission they would receive from S4C was not sufficient to support them for a full year, and if it was not possible to obtain work or a commission from other broadcasters, it would be impossible for the companies to maintain an office and their administrative systems. It was acknowledged that this would lead to many companies closing their offices for part of the year when there was no work, and losing the administrative expertise built up, and that others would decide that they could not survive with such partial support.[46] Although the main objective of the review was not to reduce the number of companies, it was one of the inevitable consequences that the channel would have to come to terms with, given the financial deficit that it faced.

The third category was for companies who would produce only one programme for the channel.[47] Producers who fell into this category would not be offered any support beyond the commissioned production. However, S4C considered that this group would be very important to the flexibility and variety of its schedule: these producers would come up with a range of different ideas that would fit into the provision of the more established independent producers, such as the occasional film or specialist sports programme. This category followed a similar pattern to the way in which the independent producers were used to provide variety to the schedule in the early months of commissioning the channel.

By 1984, therefore, there were plans in place that would revolutionise the way in which commissioning staff engaged with the independent producers, imposing a firm structure to the new sector that had been relatively amorphous during its early years. The unstructured nature of the sector had ensured a wide variety of programme ideas when there were sufficient funds to commission freely and build a stockpile of programmes, but in a time of financial constraint, the variety had to be sacrificed to ensure that the channel did not live beyond its means. There were positive gains to the new scheme: initial discussions with the companies that would receive full support had indicated that S4C could receive 270 hours of programmes for the same money used to produce 221 hours when using the old, less formal pattern of negotiating and commissioning individual programmes.[48] The restructuring of the independent sector, therefore, had considerable value, although the new plan was not likely to be adopted without some consternation.

This was not the only adjustment to S4C's working relationship with the independent producers, with longer series of popular programmes now beginning to be commissioned.[49] In the early days, the staff experimented with a number of different programmes by commissioning short series of four or six episodes as they attempted to find programmes that would appeal to the audience.[50] This approach had been taken because the success of the programmes was not guaranteed since they were being produced by individuals and companies who had no background or experience in producing programmes outside the larger broadcasters. Once the programmes had proved their popularity with the audience, longer series could be commissioned, which provided better value for money, since commissioning twelve episodes is a much cheaper way of securing 6 hours of television than a combination of three or four different series. More importantly, audience viewing patterns showed that viewers enjoyed long series, and showed loyalty to established programmes that were part of the weekly schedule.[51] The financial uncertainty of 1984–5 had led to a significant shift in S4C's relationship with the independent producers.

Discussions for the financial year 1985–6 began in a similar fashion to the previous year. An application was submitted by S4C requesting £31.858 million. This was an increase of almost £4 million attributable to a whole year of HTV's additional programming, requiring the independent producers to fill the programme gaps that were not filled by the BBC and HTV, the cost of having an extra shift of technicians to cope with the increase in C4 broadcast hours, and inflation and its impact on the salaries of staff.[52] In September 1984 the budget for 1985–6 was estimated at £31 million, almost £900,000 less than requested, and the IBA stated clearly that it was not their responsibility to save the channel from its agreement with HTV.[53] One member of the S4C Authority responded that he had heard similar comments amongst some members of the IBA's national committee, who believed that the agreement with HTV was a matter for S4C and not the IBA, on the basis that S4C had agreed to it of its own volition.[54] S4C submitted a revised figure of £31.5 million and the authority requested that its staff engage in internal discussions and prepare papers considering strategies should the channel receive a lower than requested budget for the third year running.[55] These papers acknowledged that cuts would be necessary in many aspects of the service if its income was to be lower than that requested, with the provision of independent producers once again receiving the most attention.[56] Discussions also went as far as considering whether to reduce the number of Welsh hours broadcast each week to cope with the budget reduction, although this was not an option that appealed, especially given the steady increase in C4 hours.[57] To achieve budgetary cuts without completely destroying the variety of programmes available to viewers, it would be necessary to try to save drama series and documentaries, and thus reduce the number of quizzes and chat programmes. But since these were not often produced by the independent producers, the programmes that would inevitably be cut were documentaries. With documentaries being relatively reasonable to produce, several would have to be cut in order to make any worthwhile saving: removing 8 hours would achieve a saving of £200,000, a substantial dent in the broadcasting hours and in entertaining and engaging provision for the audience for a relatively measly saving in the context of the channel's funding.[58] Another option considered was abolishing plans to increase the number of hours of C4 programmes broadcast, which would save the channel approximately £180,000. By not buying the necessary equipment or employing an extra shift of technicians for the transmission of the programmes, S4C would be depriving the non-Welsh-speaking audience of nearly one-third of English language programmes broadcast on C4, which was about 24 hours a week rather than the 16 hours that they intended them to lose.[59] Such a decision would likely further annoy the non-Welsh-speaking audience based on the correspondence already received from viewers complaining that S4C was not broadcasting enough C4 programmes. There were considerable doubts amongst authority members as to whether such a move would be contrary to the Broadcasting Act and therefore may not be possible legally.[60] These discussions demonstrate that the tensions between the Welsh-speaking and non-Welsh-speaking audience continued to dominate the authority's considerations; this can undoubtedly be attributed to the imminent review of the channel's trial period. The authority did not want to revive those unpleasant feelings with only a few months to go before the review and after the channel's overwhelming success in radically reducing those tensions.

Halting the production of *Sbec* – the weekly programme magazine – was another option to consider. The authority had discussed the future of the supplement on several occasions since its launch in October 1982, since it came at a significant cost, approximately £446,031 in 1983–4. Despite the high costs, it was felt that the programme magazine made a significant contribution to the channel's success, creating a sense of confidence amongst the audience because of its professional appearance and wide-ranging discussions of the channel's programmes.[61] Research organised by BARB and questionnaires distributed on the National Eisteddfod field in 1983 showed that more than a quarter of the channel's Welsh-language viewers turned to the magazine regularly. Reading *Sbec* was directly linked to a high level of viewing of Welsh language programming, proving that the publication was of considerable value, but the magazine's lack of appeal to advertisers was worrying. However, the staff and authority decided to save the magazine, as its removal would not save the channel a meaningful amount of money in the short term.[62] There was also a more important principle to consider, more important than money, which was that if the magazine was abolished, how else would viewers find programmes to entice them, given the limited amount of information contained in the daily papers and the *Radio Times* for S4C's Welsh language programmes?[63]

All the concern and preparatory work, however, was in vain. In March 1985 the budget was confirmed to be £31.9 million, several thousand higher than the original request.[64] The channel received, for the first time since its first application to the IBA in 1981, what it considered to be sufficient funding to realise its plans. Although the amount received was appropriate and more than requested, it was a little less than the usual 20 per cent of the fourth channel pot since C4 received 80.2 per cent.[65] Despite the good news, one member of the authority was convinced that the ITCA would strengthen its case in the next round of negotiations, and that securing sufficient funding for the channel would remain a constant struggle, and to that end they decided to set aside some of the budget with the aim of reducing the effect in the event of a future shortfall.[66]

New ventures

The channel was not able to rely solely on its IBA funding to secure sufficient funding for the independent sector throughout the trial period, to alleviate this the staff had to consider and find other innovative ways to fund quality content. S4C owned the rights to the programmes produced by the independent companies, which allowed the channel to be able to sell its programmes to be shown on other channels and in other countries, thus securing an additional source of funding. To achieve this, Mentrau the subsidiary company was formed, which would operate under the auspices of S4C and, amongst other tasks, take care of this aspect of the channel's activities.[67] In the midst of the difficult discussions with the IBA regarding the 1983–4 budget, one member of staff stated ambitiously that only Mentrau could now secure adequate funding for the channel, and encouraged the channel and its staff to put serious effort into developing it as the only viable way to obtain adequate funds in the future.[68]

This scheme was not devised in response to financial deficits and difficult negotiations with the IBA, but rather a decision made at a time when the channel had received a reasonable sum in its eighteen months of preparation. A year before the channel began broadcasting, after just six months of commissioning and discussions with the independent producers, Euryn Ogwen Williams and Chris Grace had begun to consider the potential of selling the independent producers' programmes to other broadcasters and the marketing impact of such activity. It was reported in November 1981, that 'It is a cost-free way of creating awareness in Wales and abroad of the existence of the channel.'[69] These activities were considered to have significant marketing value, and there were no actual costs associated with the activity as they intended to use an agency that would receive a percentage of any sales rather than channel staff to sell the programmes. The programmes were already fully funded, and there was nothing to lose from trying to create a bit of excitement about the channel and its content on an international stage; not only would this result in spreading the name of S4C and ensure a wider awareness of the channel's existence and activities, it could also create positive impressions of a modern Wales and the Welsh language.[70] To explore this potential the channel went to Cannes in April 1982, displaying their programmes on the Trans World International (TWI) stand. TWI was the television subsidiary of International Management Group (IMG), Mark McCormack's celebrity and sports personality agency.[71] Euryn Ogwen Williams and Chris Grace had high hopes for a positive response: it would be excellent publicity if they could sell some programmes to international broadcasters before they were aired, and their confidence in the programmes commissioned was such that they considered this a distinct possibility.[72]

It was soon realised that not all programmes produced by the channel would be suitable for selling to international broadcasters. Light entertainment and music programmes were unlikely to appeal to foreign audiences as these relied on the appeal of personalities and celebrities known in the country of production for their success. On the other hand, drama and documentaries that could be produced bilingually back-to-back, dubbed or subtitled transferred well to overseas markets, depending on their themes and the quality of their production. But the one form most suited to selling in television markets was animation. Animation is an ideal product: it appeals to broadcasters since it does not date quickly, in addition dubbing into other languages can be done relatively easily and without jarring visually, which can mean that there is no limit to the number of countries that it can be sold to.[73] Animation is also a form that appeals to diverse audiences of all ages, as the productions are often full of memorable characters and fantasy which feed the imagination. Due to the considerable confidence of S4C staff in the quality of the animation being produced by Siriol and the inherent advantages of the form, Chris Grace believed that *SuperTed* could grow into a phenomenon within two years.[74]

The channel's faith and confidence in this special bear proved to be worthwhile. Although the channel promoted nineteen programmes in its Cannes sales flyer – such as *Wil Cwac Cwac*, *Hanner Dwsin*, *Yr Euog a Ffy*, *Antur*, *Dawnsionara* and *Y Bêl Hirgron* – *SuperTed* was the programme that attracted all the attention.[75] The quality of the animation was praised, and Chris Grace confidently declared to the *Western Mail*: 'The comments in Cannes were that Superted is true quality animation superior to much coming out of the United States and Japan. Those are the only countries apart from Britain, producing animation, and their cartoons look cheap.'[76] They returned to Wales with a commitment from thirty countries to buy and broadcast the cartoon, and expressions of interest from five other countries, on the back of less than 1 minute of the series.[77] This was a significant success for the channel on many levels. First, it gained widespread awareness of S4C on an international stage, almost nine months before it began broadcasting. In terms of sales *SuperTed* was successful in securing new contacts from across the globe for the channel's staff, which bode well for the sale of other programmes, and secured a new and independent income stream.[78] The considerable urgency of getting 45 seconds of *SuperTed* ready to be shown in Cannes to representatives of global broadcasters confirmed the conviction of S4C staff that this series could bring significant prestige to the channel. The interest and enthusiasm from broadcasters from all over the world, from New Zealand to Sweden and from Nigeria to Hong Kong,[79] an interest sparked by so little evidence of its content, is further testament to the appeal and the potential of the series and of Siriol's talent in animating and selecting an excellent scene to show the series' potential.[80]

During 1982 S4C began to engage in other endeavours that could bring more income to the channel. In January 1982, staff expressed their concern that around £500,000 of the channel's money was disappearing beyond the borders of Wales as independent producers used London-based video-editing units and companies to complete their programmes.[81] Because a commercial facilities company had not been formed in Wales, Euryn Ogwen Williams was motivated to submit an idea to the authority that some of the channel's £2 million underspend from 1981–2 should be invested in activities related to the television service. It was proposed to set up a company under the auspices of S4C to ensure that the production money was spent in Wales, and also to try to compete with the services available in London.[82] There was also concern that post-production facilities already established in Wales, such as the Eco dubbing theatre, were suffering because independent Welsh companies were travelling to London to complete all the post-production elements of their programmes under one roof.[83] In principle this was a genuine idea that would greatly benefit the Welsh independent production industry, as well as ensuring that the channel's spending had a positive economic impact in Wales. Arguably, however, was the channel interfering in opportunities that other commercial companies should be expected to take advantage of?[84] These considerations were expressed internally but channel staff encouraged the authority to reach an urgent decision on facilities as a different company might venture into the same area within six months.[85] The channel could be accused of acting unfairly, due to their using their position as a broadcaster, and the privileged knowledge that they therefore possessed, to pre-empt any competitors in an area that was not a top priority. Such a service created by a broadcaster would have an unfair advantage in a competitive market because of its close links with the independent sector, who would likely use their service above others. On the other hand, investing in these resources for the use of independent producers enabled the channel to build expertise and create specialist technical jobs in Wales, rather than relying on companies beyond the border. Establishing a comprehensive post-production service in Wales would also allow the channel's commissioning staff to be available to provide advice, if desired, as producers completed their projects. Because of these benefits and because there was no guarantee that an independent company would establish the necessary facilities, it was decided that post-production facilities should be one of the areas of work of the new subsidiary Mentrau. The Mentrau editing facilities centre at the Coal Exchange in Mount Stuart Square, Cardiff Bay was therefore established in September 1983 to meet the technical needs of Welsh independent producers.[86]

By March 1982 a comprehensive strategy on further activities had been developed, which clearly stated the belief amongst staff that the money invested in the independent producers' programmes could bring wider value to the Welsh economy.[87] The strategy acknowledged that there was significant value to the initial investment in that it funded content for the channel, paid the wages of independent producers' staff and provided work for a significant number of ancillary services, such as the Barcud outside broadcast unit and Tegset the set building company. There was a belief that another industry could benefit from the programmes produced, especially the animated series that had captivated international broadcasters: significant merchandising activities could be developed to accompany the series, emulating the success that *The Muppets* and *Mr. Men* series had seen during the 1970s, along with the tremendous success of Mistar Urdd products which had boosted the youth movement during the same decade.[88] Historically such merchandising production had been undertaken in counties around London, such as Kent, Buckinghamshire, Essex and Hertfordshire. But channel staff were convinced that a substantial manufacturing industry could be developed in Wales, with the help of the Welsh Development Agency and the Development Board for Rural Wales, together with the expertise of Wynne Melville Jones, originator of Mistar Urdd who had now formed a company called Strata which had received an agreement from S4C to deal with miscellaneous merchandise licences.[89] Forging links between S4C and non-broadcast industries was very beneficial to the channel: 'The aim in its wider dimension has been to integrate S4C in the affairs and social fabric of Wales.'[90] The S4C Authority and its staff saw that ensuring that S4C's activities became a fundamental part of the economic fabric of Wales was one way of safeguarding its survival; Euryn Ogwen Williams recalls that this strategy was that of the chairman's, Sir Goronwy Daniel, to ensure the channel's existence after its three-year trial period.[91]

This scheme was hugely ambitious, but some months later, after hosting seminars across Wales to draw the attention of small companies to the potential of producing goods, it began to bear fruit. By May 1982, forty jobs had been created at a Pontypool factory where *SuperTed* bears were produced, with orders arriving from around the world, including an order for 24,000 bears from Australia, providing a boost to jobs.[92] In addition to the activity in Pontypool, Gwersfa Cyf. from Newcastle Emlyn produced educational products to accompany the series, such as a *SuperTed* height chart.[93] By July 1982, thirteen companies had entered into a licence to produce *SuperTed* products, and the channel was expecting to receive prototypes of *SuperTed* and *Wil Cwac Cwac* products from twenty-nine Welsh companies.[94] By January 1984, just two years later, fifty-two British companies were producing 170 different *SuperTed*-related products, twenty

6. *SuperTed*, the major success of S4C's first visit to MIP TV in Cannes *(image: reproduced with permission from S4C)*

of them in Wales; the bear was also used to promote Wales abroad by the Tourist Board and the Welsh Development Agency.[95]

These supplementary activities had grown tremendously in a very short time, and so in September 1982 a limited subsidiary company, known as 'Mentrau Sianel 4 Cymru Cyf.', was established to manage these commercial aspects of the channel's activities.[96] The links between S4C and this subsidiary company would be very close, as Owen Edwards would be the director of the new company, and Michael Tucker, the channel secretary, would be its company secretary.[97] This close relationship was inevitable, although Mentrau's work, in principle, went beyond the core responsibilities of the channel under the Broadcasting Act, but the work could not be carried out by a completely independent organisation, since it was the responsibility of the channel to negotiate terms with individual producers – as such the work of the subsidiary company would be closely integrated with the functions of the authority.[98] Despite the enthusiasm within S4C there were some doubts among IBA officials as to whether it was appropriate to use the funding that came from the ITV companies' coffers, via the IBA, for fringe activities. The IBA's view was that the millions given to the channel annually should only be used for the production of programmes and the running costs of the channel.[99] Because of this, it was decided that it would not be appropriate to invest significant sums of money in the company before being assured that it could make a profit; as a result, the channel sought grants or loans to set it up. However, the process of securing a bank loan was complicated by the fact that the IBA did not wish to see S4C committing to guarantee the debts of Mentrau Cyf. with the annual funding from ITV companies' monies.[100] Securing the funding for the initial investment which would assist in establishing the company was proving more difficult than had been envisioned.

Despite the initial difficulties in forming Mentrau Cyf., in contrast the activities that would eventually transfer to the new company were progressing efficiently. In March 1983, Euryn Ogwen Williams and Chris Grace visited Irish broadcaster RTÉ on the first direct sales visit of Mentrau Cyf.[101] There was an encouraging response from the broadcaster, and praise for the high standard of production and acting; this was reflected in the number of programmes purchased by RTÉ, with S4C officials returning to Wales with a commitment to buy eleven programmes or series at a rate of £600 per hour, or around £10,000 in total.[102] Some of the most successful programmes of the first year were purchased, namely *Joni Jones*, *Almanac*, *Torth o Fara*, *Madam Wen*, *Owain Glyndŵr* and they also committed to buy the first and second series of *SuperTed* and *Wil Cwac Cwac*.[103] There was also a very successful second visit to Cannes, although it did raise some very difficult issues for the authority regarding the principle of selling programmes to South Africa.[104]

Shortly after the establishment of Mentrau Cyf., the company wanted to add a fourth activity to its existing pursuits, and venture into publishing. The channel had been discussing with Christopher Talfan Davies the possibility of buying the publisher Hughes a'i Fab, Wales's oldest working press, who owned the publishing rights to *Llyfr Mawr y Plant*, which contained the stories of the mischievous duck Wil Cwac Cwac along with the adventures of the fox Siôn Blewyn Coch, and an extensive music catalogue.[105] Buying a publishing company would enable the channel to take advantage of the publishing opportunities offered by some of the channel's popular programmes, and it would link neatly with the manufacturing activities.[106] Hughes a'i Fab was purchased by Mentrau Cyf. for £35,593 and it took over the reins completely from June 1983.[107] Most of its publications under the auspices of S4C in the first two years were children's books associated with the channel's popular animated series. Eight *SuperTed* books were published in addition to *Llyfr Mawr Wil Cwac Cwac*, *Hoff Straeon SuperTed* a *Llyfr Cwis Clwb S4C*.[108] Additionally books relating to the *Almanac* series and *Iesu Ddoe a Heddiw*, as well as pocket books related to *Deryn*, *Pobol y Cwm* and *Bowen a'i Bartner*, were published, which according to the channel's annual report that year brought 'an opportunity to introduce a new "house-style" for Hughes' publications and to create an exciting new image for the company'.[109] The company was forced to experiment with new styles and ideas that would attract readers as Hughes a'i Fab, despite its association with S4C, faced the same challenge as any other Welsh language publisher, namely to maintain the business and make a profit by publishing in Welsh. The company directors were disappointed that the support it had hoped to receive from the Welsh Books Council had not transpired because the organisation considered that the books should receive a substantial subsidy from the channel.[110] Because of these difficulties, the publisher had to consider again how to distribute its publications to secure a profit. It experimented with selling the *Wil Cwac Cwac* annual directly from S4C in order to reduce costs, and in 1984 and 1985 one of the *SuperTed* books was sold exclusively through Mudiad Ysgolion Meithrin (Nursery School Movement), and 4,500 copies were sold in two months.[111] These new schemes did not please everyone and many booksellers publicly expressed their dissatisfaction that they could not capitalise on the popularity of the characters by selling the books in their shops. S4C were accused of breaking the basic principle of book publishing by selling directly, and many customers were missing the opportunity to buy the books because they were not available in their local shops.[112]

SuperTed was a catalyst for many of S4C's wider activities, and it was the stimulus to the formation of a partnership that would secure the funding of the second and third series of the bear's adventures. *SuperTed*'s remarkable success in the international television market, and in the domestic market with the sale of the series to the BBC, necessitated the production of more than one series but, because the cost of producing them was high, S4C needed support to bring them to fruition.[113] The success of the series made *SuperTed* attractive to outside investors who could envisage that significant money could be made if they entered into a partnership with S4C to produce more series. One such company was the Coal Board's pension subsidiary, CIN Industrial Investments, which invested in British industries: a joint company was thus formed between S4C and CIN, called Telin.[114] CIN had experience in film production and had contributed to the budget of a number of award-winning productions such as *Chariots of Fire* (Hudson, 1981), *Ghandi* (Attenborough, 1982) and *Educating Rita* (Gilbert, 1983).[115] Telin would, therefore, produce and exploit *SuperTed* rights with Mentrau holding a 60 per cent stake in the shares and CIN claiming 40 per cent, with both organisations securing two directors each on the company's management board.[116] The authority seems to have found CIN's collaboration requirements onerous, but due to the channel's urgency to begin production of the next *SuperTed* series in order to maintain the incredible momentum behind the production, there was no time to look for other partners, especially after spending considerable time negotiating terms with CIN.[117] Although the partnership's demands were challenging for Mentrau, the benefits to S4C were considerable, since this partnership enabled the channel to purchase new Welsh language *SuperTed* series at a very reasonable price given the significant investment made in the first series.[118] S4C would buy the second and third series from Telin for a fraction of the production costs, ensuring a significant saving, and it also received a guarantee that the channel's staff would be involved in editorial decisions. The channel would have the best of both worlds.[119] Without this external investment it is unlikely that S4C would have been able to justify significant expenditure on expensive and high-quality animated series that did not fill a large number of broadcast hours, and the young Welsh animation industry could have disappeared overnight.[120] The production of more series was also key to further sales of *SuperTed* overseas.

The biggest success of *SuperTed* during this period was the sale of the first and second series by Mentrau to Disney's cable channel in America.[121] Details of the sale were announced on 12 January 1984, and there was considerable interest in the deal from the national and regional press: reports appeared in the press the following day with headlines such as 'Walt's boyo bear!', 'SuperTed Takes on America' and 'Ted's a Star'.[122] This deal was a huge accomplishment for the channel, since *SuperTed* was the first British animated series to be broadcast to the American audience by Disney's cable channel. As well as broadcasting rights, the deal with Disney meant that they could distribute the series in North America on VHS, another feat since the studio had only distributed four non-Disney films before the 1980s.[123] Not only did it attract popular press attention, but there was also an early day motion in the House of Commons by Liberal MP Geraint Howells, congratulating S4C on its success in selling *SuperTed* to Disney, and on its partnership with CIN:

> this House congratulates S4C, the Welsh fourth channel, for succeeding in selling their 'Superted' all-Welsh animation series to a television company in the United States of America, and for

> securing additional investment in the production of the series from the National Coal Board Pension Fund; believes that these gestures of confidence in the potential of Welsh language programmes will secure the future of the animation industry based in Cardiff, and will provide new business opportunities for Welsh manufacturing companies making goods linked with the series; and wishes S4C well for their future achievements.[124]

There was also a strong response from US manufacturers with the publisher Random House and toy producer Dakin entering into licences to produce related products with the same enthusiasm as Welsh and British companies, and which would ensure that *SuperTed*'s image penetrated the broad US market. Given Dakin's intention to produce 3 or 4 million bears for sale in 1985, the confidence of American companies in the product's potential was considerable.[125] Greeting card companies Hallmark and American Greetings were also competing for the rights to recreate the character's image on their cards.[126] Disney's interest had opened up a number of new markets and income streams for Telin and Mentrau, and there was hope amongst the staff of these two companies and amongst the staff in S4C that this US activity would lead to the series being broadcast on one of the major American television networks, ensuring a wider audience for the series and its characters.[127]

Despite the enthusiasm and initial attention from the British press in *SuperTed*'s sale to America, and the animators' success as the series won the silver award at the New York Film and Television Festival, there was some delay before the series appeared on screen in American homes.[128] It was a full calendar year between the announcement of the deal to sell the series to Disney and the transmission date.[129] This posed a financial problem for Telin, as the money from the sales of goods was slower arriving than originally envisaged, and prevented them from investing further or paying necessary costs.[130] These cash flow complications led to discussions with companies such as the Forward Trust and Kleinwort Benson about selling Telin's *SuperTed* rights and then leasing them back to try and release more money for the company's activities, since S4C and Mentrau were reluctant to invest further in Telin.[131] Despite these difficulties, when the series was shown on Disney's cable channel, it was enthusiastically marketed and the possibility of Disney buying the rights to the series in a number of other languages such as German, French and Dutch were also discussed.[132] The series also saw considerable success on VHS with Disney selling 26,000 copies in three months, even before re-dubbing the series with American accents.[133] By the end of the 1985–6 financial year *SuperTed* had sold to fifty countries worldwide, including ten Latin American countries, India, Dubai, New Zealand, Korea and several European countries such as Norway and France. *SuperTed*'s sale to Disney, along with all its other sales, the sales of the goods and the huge positive publicity secured *SuperTed*'s place as the channel's most valuable product. In addition, a musical entitled *SuperTed and the Comet of the Spooks* was produced, which appeared in Cardiff in the winter of 1985 and toured throughout Britain in the summer of 1986, directed by Victor Spinetti. The characters were also an integral part of many safety campaigns with the Welsh Office using them for the road safety campaign producing the short film *Stay Safe with SuperTed* and the police using them to promote the *Say No to a Stranger* slogan.[134]

A series that was undoubtedly in *SuperTed*'s shadow was *Wil Cwac Cwac*, also produced by Siriol, but it was a series which was arguably more triumphant in many respects. Although only sixteen countries purchased the animation during the trial period compared to the fifty who purchased *SuperTed*, *Wil Cwac Cwac* had its own successes.[135] Some episodes of the first series were sold to a Russian television station in 1985, a remarkable achievement given that European television programmes were not featured on the country's television sets.[136] *Wil Cwac Cwac* was also sold to an American cable channel, US Cable, but since this sale came a year after *SuperTed*'s phenomenal deal, there was no fanfare.[137] There was also much less enthusiasm from American manufacturers, adding to its lower status in public memory. However, *Wil Cwac Cwac* proved to be a significant success in Britain: the English version reached the top 100 chart of British programmes at number 90, the only programme produced for S4C to do so during the trial period.[138] Viewing figures for the series were much higher than any other programme produced by S4C and broadcast by one of the national networks, even *SuperTed*. *SuperTed* attracted around 3 million viewers, while *Wil Cwac Cwac* attracted up to 5.61 million viewers – a very high figure for children's programming and any programme broadcast in the same slot between 4.15 p.m. and 4.20 p.m. at the end of the afternoon. *Wil Cwac Cwac*'s enthusiastic viewing and audience figures could be down to the fact that ITV broadcast the series daily for almost a month in the winter of 1984. Children could therefore watch the adventures of the mischievous duck every day of the week, building an enthusiastic audience over a relatively short period of time.

7. Dafydd Hywel (Alun) and Reginald Mathias (Dick) in a scene from *Yr Alcoholig Llon* (dir. Karl Francis) *(image: reproduced with permission from S4C)*

Apart from *SuperTed*'s discernible achievements, Mentrau was not entirely successful financially in its first years. Despite all its activity, it was feared that the company had made a significant loss of £610,076 in its first year, with the production facilities' performance the biggest disappointment making much less income than expected. But the company made a relatively small profit in 1984–5 of £35,678 and then £74,558 in 1985–6.[139] Mentrau did not achieve what S4C's Authority and staff had originally hoped; namely to provide a financial safety net to the channel during dark times. Its success, however, could be defined rather in terms of the channel's international reputation. Rewarding visits to Cannes each year ensured that programmes produced in Welsh for a minority audience were broadcast worldwide, providing images of Wales in countries such as Australia, Italy, Greece and Czechoslovakia.[140] *SuperTed* was not the only success of this venture, though the relationship with Disney boosted the channel's status in the television markets, with clear evidence of this in the year the deal was announced when the so-called 'Disney Effect' was seen in the 1984 market, when £130,000 of programmes were sold. There were many other successful programmes that did not receive any press publicity, such as *Mentro! Mentro!*, which was sold to twenty-five countries including the United States by the middle of 1985.[141] S4C's programme sales were so successful that its total annual sales for 1984–5, which was £900,000, was more than the ITV network's five largest companies sales for the same year.[142] A large number of Welsh language programmes were also shown on British networks, with a total of seventy programmes sold during the trial period, such as the *Joni Jones* series on BBC2 and the animated series *Hanner Dwsin* sold to Central TV for broadcast on the ITV network on Saturday mornings.[143] C4 was also persuaded to broadcast a series of subtitled Welsh dramas with *Aderyn Papur* (Bayly, 1983), *Wil Six* (Turner, 1985), *Yr Alcoholig Llon* (Francis, 1985) and *Nid ar Redeg* (Clayton, 1984) part of that collection.[144] C4 officials appear to have had a great deal of confidence and faith in the quality and appeal of the content as it broadcast *Wil Six* on Christmas Day 1985.[145] There were therefore substantial successes from Mentrau's activities, proving to the broadcasting sector in Wales and beyond that there was value and potential for Welsh and Welsh language programmes produced by relatively small companies on an international stage, and which could compete and attract the attention of the world's leading broadcasters. Apart from enabling the channel to fund quality animation series and sustaining that burgeoning industry, this initiative failed to guarantee financial security for the independent production sector as originally hoped. Not enough profit was made to feed substantial amounts back to S4C for investment, partly because there were not enough programmes and series to sell in order to make significant profits.[146] Alternative ways of saving or raising money would therefore need to be considered to secure the prosperity of that industry.

S4C's trial period is characterised by a pattern of venturing into new territory, exploiting the output produced and turning that into assets that would secure vital publicity and a reputation for the channel – at home and on an international stage. The enterprising and innovative spirit of the channel's various staff led to new areas as the channel invested and planted its economic roots deep in the Welsh landscape. Not all enterprises were successful in the long run, but during the trial period these activities were a means of attracting a positive response from the British press and British politicians to a small channel as it promoted itself and secured a good reputation for Wales abroad. The probationary period was also characterised by a period of pressing for suitable funding from the IBA, which enabled the channel to continue with these activities and its main responsibilities of commissioning and broadcasting programmes.

5

Reviewing the Channel – Opinion Polls and the Home Office Review

S4C started its life under the public spotlight with significant expectations on what it could provide for the audience, while some members of the Welsh broadcasting sector firmly doubted whether a Welsh language channel could be sustained under the control of a new authority. Because of those expectations and doubts, its achievements were critically examined throughout the probationary period. But in late 1985 an official Home Office review was tasked with evaluating the experiment and determining whether or not the initiative was a success. The review would question whether the channel should continue to broadcast to the Welsh-speaking audience, or whether it was prudent to return to the government's original plan of broadcasting Welsh-language programming across two channels. This was not the only review that sought to evaluate the channel's successes and failures and its influence on the viewing patterns of the Welsh audience. A number of other organisations such as Cymdeithas yr Iaith, the Welsh Consumer Council (WCC) and HTV also produced or commissioned detailed reports and research. During the early years the channel also received many letters and telephone calls directly from the public which provided a partial picture of audience reaction to the output. This research and correspondence were a key component of the channel's evidence as the Home Office produced its crucial report. The aim of this chapter is therefore to track and analyse the correspondence, opinion polls and primarily the evidence sent by various organisations to the Home Office as part of the official review, to evaluate attitudes towards the fourth channel in Wales at the end of 1985.

Audience responses

The most direct and revealing way to find out if the channel was succeeding in satisfying or infuriating its audience was through the letters and phone calls the channel received. Undoubtedly, the main issue that incensed many of the viewers who corresponded with the channel was the re-scheduling of Channel 4 (C4) programmes. The fundamental freedom given to S4C to re-schedule C4 programmes at times convenient to its schedule meant that it could show the most attractive programmes, but at less convenient times, such as late at night or during the daytime. Although this was not an ideal solution, it meant that viewers in Wales could watch most C4 programmes if they so wished. The decision also had negative consequences and one of the biggest was that S4C was not able to take advantage of C4 marketing that announced the broadcast times of its programmes in the press and in the *TV Times*. Indeed, the publicity received by C4 programmes would create more confusion in Wales as viewers expected to see programmes at the advertised times; the reality was that they would have to wait a day or two before they were broadcast in Wales, if they were broadcast at all, since not all programmes broadcast by C4 could be re-scheduled. Some viewers were also furious that it was not possible to watch C4 programmes during peak hours, such as one viewer from Bala, who stated:

> You do screen some of the more important Channel 4 programmes, though unhappily at unfortunate times. I am writing to urge that you screen more of the serious programmes (i.e. not the mere entertainment items) and put them out at the time Channel 4 viewers see them, so that we keep up to date. Chanel [*sic*] Four timings seem to me more practical than yours![1]

As evidenced by this letter, it was not just the timing that was problematic. Some viewers were clearly unhappy with the selection of C4 programmes broadcast on S4C, and lamented the fact that more of the serious programmes were not part of the schedule. Selecting C4's entertainment programmes made sense to S4C, since S4C was a popular channel that aimed to appeal to the majority, rather than a channel that appealed to niche audiences, and so the more popular content, such as *Treasure Hunt*, was better suited to the wider image of the channel. However, when S4C did broadcast some of C4's bold and innovative content, the nature of the programmes caused some difficulties. The challenging tone of some of the programmes that prompted the tabloid newspapers, such as *The Sun*, to christen it 'Channel swore', elicited a strong response.[2] The following extracts from viewers' letters show the variety of responses received:

> complete and utter disgust at the film 'SEBASTIAN' [*sic*] ... If this is a sample of the sort of material you intend showing in the future I certainly will not be tuning in.
>
> S4C seems to be run by social anarchists ... If this is the contribution this vandal-run channel is going to make to Welsh culture then that culture has been put in mortal danger on that account.[3]

On occasion, therefore, S4C would decide to omit programmes that were deemed unsuitable for broadcast to the Welsh audience. Reasons of taste were not the only measure by which S4C would decide not to broadcast some C4 programmes: restrictions in the schedule would mean that some programmes could not be broadcast. The programmes which tended to be omitted were films, operas and sports, mostly because of their length.[4] Since S4C aimed to re-schedule as many of the programmes as possible to keep the non-Welsh-speaking audience happy, it was difficult to justify broadcasting a 2-hour film when two, if not four, programmes could be broadcast in the same slot.

By 1983 S4C was able to re-schedule most C4 programmes, with only 10 hours a week being omitted. But reaching these levels became increasingly difficult as C4 extended its broadcast hours. This was coupled with the fact that by 1985, S4C was able to broadcast, on average, over 24 hours of Welsh language content a week, 2 hours more than the law specified. Not only did this increase make it harder for S4C to re-schedule such a high proportion of English language programmes, thus risking the wrath of the non-Welsh-speaking audience, but it also created difficulties for the technical department. Each time C4 extended its hours, S4C would need to employ a new shift of technicians to cope with the extra hours and work.[5] This in turn would put more pressure on the channel's coffers.

The belief that S4C was depriving and neglecting the non-Welsh-speaking audience had existed since the early days of the channel, as evidenced by the vote held by the cable provider Rediffusion amongst its customers to try to ensure that C4 rather than S4C was broadcast on its systems.[6] Those sentiments intensified as the C4 service expanded and developed to include some niche programmes that attracted enthusiastic and vocal audiences. The most notable example was when C4 inherited the ITV horse racing contract and broadcast the races live on the channel from late March 1984.[7] This caused great difficulties, especially as S4C had established a pattern of broadcasting popular nursery programmes and school programmes during the afternoons, a pattern that was difficult to change at short notice without risking the loss of this important audience entirely. It was decided that S4C would join the racing programme live after the nursery programmes ended. This meant that viewers in Wales occasionally missed the first race of the programme, which prompted a relatively high level of complaints. A large number of complaints were received on 23 April 1985 when S4C failed to join the programme in time to see Princess Anne riding in a particular race. Is it clear from the minutes of the meeting that discussed this that the combination of missing the race and the opportunity to see a member of the royal family was too much for many viewers – and the dissatisfaction was directed at S4C staff and peppered with obscenities. The April 1985 report states: 'If I were a horse or a member of the royal family I would be ashamed of the obscene language and rude remarks of some of my ardent supporters!'[8] This popular addition to the C4 schedule could be a burden, as Owen Edwards professed in response to a complaint about the timing of the racing programmes on S4C in 1986: 'I must admit that placing horse racing on S4C has probably caused us more headaches than any other type of programming.'[9] These additions rekindled some of the unpleasant feelings felt in the days before S4C, as letters were received complaining about the 'inordinate amount of Welsh that is being shown on your channel'.[10] By linking the existence of S4C and C4 the government could be accused of failing to consider sufficiently what kind of programmes C4 would produce. By requiring C4 to attract the interest of advertisers, since it was expected to recoup its costs for the ITV companies which had paid for it, the government did not consider this impact on S4C.[11] Because of this, not all C4 programmes could be aimed at very small audiences, since advertisers would not be willing to pay a premium for the space. In addition to broadcasting specialist programming, C4 programmes would need to attract and engage a wider audience. This it achieved with programmes such as *Treasure Hunt*, *Brookside* and US imports *Cheers* and *Hill Street Blues*. But viewers in England and Scotland were not the only ones attracted by this content, it also appealed to audiences in Wales, and when these programmes were shown at inconvenient times outside peak hours, S4C received vociferous complaints.

Not all the letters from the channel's non-Welsh-speaking viewers were negative: viewers were watching S4C not only for the programmes provided by C4 but because they enjoyed the Welsh language provision. The concept of the inheritance factor and retaining some of the non-Welsh-speaking viewers who watched the English language programmes for the Welsh language output was somewhat effective, and lessened the concerns about Welsh language programmes being placed in a ghetto. Amongst the supportive and positive comments received were:

> I have been so impressed with the such modern and frendlie [*sic*] outlook of S4C's Welsh speaking programs [*sic*]

> writing to express my enjoyment of so much on S4C – especially undiluted Welsh.

> The series of excellent choral concerts that you have had on a Sunday evening have been wonderful, and we have enjoyed them greatly.[12]

As expected with a channel that sought to serve multiple audiences, it was not possible to please all parties, and trying to please MPs proved especially difficult. Some MPs were very happy to celebrate the successes of the Welsh language channel, by sponsoring events for the channel in the House of Commons and signing early day motions applauding S4C.[13] Some members, however, remained unconvinced by the success and contribution of the channel, such as Tom Hooson, Conservative MP for Brecon and Radnorshire. He publicly expressed his dissatisfaction with a question to the Home Secretary about the sums of money spent by the channel on lobbying to secure its annual funding.[14] S4C had clearly failed to convince him of the merits of a standalone Welsh channel; indeed, contrary to many others, his views on the matter were unwavering:

> my problem is that I am deeply convinced that a segregated channel is misconceived, and I really am not open to conversation at this point. I argued against a ghetto channel on Second Reading, and everything that has happened since has confirmed my original view.[15]

Some individuals evidently could not be persuaded, due to the strength of their feelings and belief in the merits of the two-channel system.

Opinion polls

In addition to the weekly viewing figures provided by BARB and the quarterly Audience Appreciation Service figures, one of the first surveys that asked questions about the audience response to S4C was a survey commissioned by HTV in March 1983.[16] This was not a survey focusing on the development of S4C but a general survey of the political views of the Welsh people, which asked specific questions about broadcasting. The report shows that only 22 per cent of the 994 individuals surveyed had watched Welsh language programmes over the previous seven days. But applying the linguistic filter to the figures, they showed that 65 per cent of the fluent Welsh speakers had watched Welsh language programmes in the previous week.[17] A positive figure, it could be argued, although it should be noted that the survey was conducted in the relatively prosperous early months of 1983. The survey also asked whether the individuals had watched any English language programmes on the channel. It appeared that 48 per cent of all individuals had done so, with the figure higher amongst fluent Welsh speakers at 52 per cent.[18] The survey highlighted the tendency of some fluent Welsh speakers to remain with S4C as it transitioned from Welsh to English language programmes. The channel's wider coverage seemed to appeal to the Welsh-speaking audience, and it was clear that the inheritance factor worked, but unfortunately it appeared more in favour of the English language programmes.

The survey also asked individuals for their views on the new pattern of broadcasting in Wales, following the arrival of S4C: 'Considering all four channels, do you think the reorganisation of television broadcasting in Wales has improved television, has made it worse, or has made no difference?' Taking into consideration the response of each individual, regardless of the language differences between them, 38 per cent thought that the reorganisation had improved television in Wales, 43 per cent said there was no difference after the switch and 9 per cent thought the situation was worse, and 10 per cent declared that they did not know.[19] Applying the language filters shows that there was a significant difference in the views recorded by fluent Welsh speakers, with 61 per cent believing that television in Wales had improved since the advent of S4C. However, 30 per cent believed that there had been no change, and 5 per cent thought things were worse.[20] S4C had not been able to persuade all members of the Welsh-speaking audience of the benefits of the single-channel solution, nor had it been able to effectively transfer the message about the increase in the number of Welsh hours from 15 to the 22 hours now broadcast. The small percentage of Welsh speakers who were convinced that television was worse since the advent of S4C showed that the small group of individuals who opposed the transfer of Welsh language programmes to a Welsh 'ghetto' had not changed their stance after the first months of the channel's service. It could also be argued that some viewers may have been disappointed by the channel's output having waited so long and held such high hopes, while others might have been unhappy with the strategy of producing a popular output and aiming for large audiences adopted by the channel in its trial period.

The report produced by the mass media group of Cymdeithas yr Iaith in 1984 had a different focus. Although it also asked individuals about their viewing patterns, the aim of the survey was to ask whether S4C was receiving the necessary feedback to run an effective television channel that met the needs of the people of Wales.[21] Cymdeithas yr Iaith wanted to persuade the channel to establish what the society called 'regional broadcast panels' in order to gather viewers' direct responses to the programmes it broadcast. The society believed that viewers' responses were crucial, and that they were the only way that the channel could guarantee that it gave viewers what they wanted, creating a channel the audience would want and love to watch instead of a channel that they believed they had a duty to watch.[22] Cymdeithas yr Iaith suggested that, without providing firm evidence to support the view, the channel's provision did not succeed in attracting viewers willingly but because they felt a responsibility as Welsh speakers to support a channel that they had fought so long to secure. The report also emphasised the need for the establishment of viewers' committees across Wales.[23] S4C was not the only broadcaster criticised by the society for its lack of consultation with its viewers. At the 1983 general meeting of Cymdeithas yr Iaith, BBC Radio Cymru was criticised for not seeking the advice of its listeners when devising programme policies. With the two public service broadcasters criticised, it shows that consultation was not the natural inclination of broadcasters, and that they had a long tradition of setting and defining what was considered good programming that the audience would enjoy, without the input of the audience.

Despite this criticism most of the survey findings were positive: 42 per cent responded that they watched the channel regularly, with 38 per cent stating that they watched 'fairly often', 12 per cent responded with 'very rarely' and only 8 per cent reporting that they didn't watch the channel at all;[24] 65 per cent believed that Welsh language programmes were broadcast at convenient times on the channel, with 19 per cent disagreeing with the remainder choosing not to state an opinion on the matter. Although there appeared to be confirmation that the channel's schedule suited the lives of most of its viewers, a corresponding figure of 65 per cent of those surveyed stated that not enough Welsh language programmes were broadcast.[25]

Specific questions were also included about some genres of programmes, and in response to the harsh comments expressed by viewers and politicians about the nature and content of the channel's news programme, audience views were sought on the time allocated within the programme for 'foreign', 'British' and 'Welsh' (the word used was *Cymraeg*, meaning Welsh-language rather than Welsh interest) news:[26] 54 per cent of respondents felt that coverage of foreign news was 'fine', with 15 per cent stating there was too much and 8 per cent wanting more. There was a similar response for British news, with 46 per cent feeling that coverage was sufficient, but this time the number who thought it too much was significantly higher at 28 per cent, with a very small minority of 2 per cent who wanted to see more British news. When discussing 'Welsh' news there was a slightly more ambiguous response: 34 per cent felt that coverage was satisfactory, 43 per cent wanted more, while only 8 per cent felt that too much attention was given to Welsh issues.[27] The survey therefore provided a very mixed picture. It did not corroborate the harsh criticism from MPs and others, nor did it unambiguously indicate that the audience wanted a news programme focused on Welsh issues. But it also did not fully justify the channel's strategy of providing a varied and comprehensive news programme in Welsh with less emphasis on the local. In order to fulfil the wishes of the majority of viewers surveyed, a longer programme would undoubtedly be required to ensure that there was scope to increase coverage of Welsh affairs and to maintain international and British items. Cymdeithas yr Iaith's recommendation was to report the British and foreign news with a Welsh rather than British perspective.[28] This statement ignored the fact that the programme already embraced this strategy with the reports of correspondent Dewi Llwyd from Westminster. But it showed that a similar pattern was needed for a wider range of news stories to meet the expectations of Cymdeithas yr Iaith.

Audience views were also sought on current affairs programmes, with a small majority happy with the amount shown on the channel. When considering drama series, 43 per cent wanted more, while 35 per cent thought that there were enough. But only 31 per cent thought the quality of these series was good, with 40 per cent stating that the standard was acceptable.[29] This statistic partly explains why a larger percentage of viewers did not want to see more drama series, because they did not feel that the standard was high enough to justify it. The attitude to individual films and dramas, on the other hand, was much more positive, with 65 per cent stating that they wanted to see more of them. This could be attributed to the fact that these programmes were considered to be of a high quality, with 67 per cent expressing that view. The pattern S4C had established of allocating money for large individual productions was justified, as they made a significant impression on the audience. Despite the statistical deficiencies and the unrepresentative nature of the Cymdeithas yr Iaith survey sample, the poll did confirm that the channel was generally successful in satisfying its target audience, although there was considerable room for improvement. It was also suggested that there were deficiencies in consultation and discussion with the audience in the channel's structures, an issue that would be the subject of a further study by the WCC in 1985.

S4C also commissioned research during the trial period that was conducted through Research and Marketing Wales and the West Limited. The need for additional research arose after the channel received a series of questionable figures from BARB at the end of 1983.[30] The research was given four aims, namely to discover the audience's appreciation of the channel's programmes, to analyse the temperament of the Welsh-speaking audience, to discover the reasons for the changes in audience viewing patterns, and to seek audience opinion after just over a year of broadcasting on the issue of placing Welsh language programmes on one channel rather than spreading them across two or more channels.[31] S4C hoped that this survey would identify patterns that BARB and AGB did not detect in their figures. It was also hoped that the information gathered in the report *Viewing and Listening in Wales* would be of considerable use as the channel prepared for the crucial Home Office review in late 1985. Owen Edwards justified the spend on the study to the authority by stating that it was politically important to carry out additional research, especially when they were within eighteen months of the start of the Home Office review.[32]

The survey polled 1,007 Welsh speakers who had the ability to 'follow a conversation in Welsh with friends or relatives or at work' and 526 non-Welsh speakers who answered no to the above statement.[33] The research uncovered some encouraging statistics, with more than one in two Welsh speakers, 54 per cent, saying that they watched the channel on a daily basis. That figure increased significantly when assessing how many Welsh speakers watched the channel on a weekly basis, with 91 per cent acknowledging that they did so. These were very positive figures which showed that S4C was reaching the vast majority of its target audience and that its programmes were watched weekly by the audience. This percentage placed the channel in third place in terms of popularity amongst Welsh speakers.[34] But amongst non-Welsh speakers, S4C was the channel that appealed to them the least, with only 42 per cent tuning in in any given week.[35] These figures suggest several things: perhaps C4 content did not appeal to more than half of non-Welsh-speaking viewers in Wales, or that the broadcasting times of English language programmes outside peak hours meant that they were not being watched, or that people regarded S4C as a Welsh language channel and therefore avoided it completely. This latter point is confirmed by the response to what respondents felt was the percentage of Welsh language programmes shown on the channel. Nearly half of non-Welsh-speaking respondents, 47 per cent, stated that they believed that more than half of the channel's content was in Welsh.[36] It was clear, therefore, that the message that the vast majority of C4 programmes were repeated on the fourth channel in Wales, and that English language programming dominated the schedule, was not successfully disseminated.

A clear correlation was shown between the level of language ability (or what respondents considered their language ability) and how often viewers turned to S4C. Viewers who considered themselves fluent speakers were much more likely to watch the channel on a daily basis, with 48 per cent claiming to do so. The figure fell dramatically among those who considered themselves to be relatively good speakers, with only 14 per cent stating that they watched the channel daily, falling further amongst the cohort who said that they had a smattering of Welsh to 7 per cent.[37] The figures were just as striking for the weekly viewing patterns. The channel found it difficult to attract regular and consistent viewers who were not completely confident in their Welsh language ability, reducing the likely audience significantly.[38] These figures confirm an attitude voiced on the opening night of the channel in vox pops during the welcome programme, as a resident of Gwynedd stated, in Welsh, that she did not intend to watch the channel because of her belief that she would not be able to understand it.[39] A segment of the audience believed that the channel was broadcasting programmes using a standard of Welsh that would be beyond their comprehension, impeding their enjoyment of particular programmes; although the channel tried to ensure that it used familiar and relatively informal language in its presentation, it had not succeeded in convincing significant sections of the audience of the relevance and appeal of the programmes. One can also wonder that, given this survey being held 16 months after the launch of the channel, that some of these unsuspecting viewers had tuned in to Welsh language programmes, and had been intimidated or disappointed by the nature of the language used, and therefore only tuned into the channel occasionally, if at all. Whatever the reason, and however expected these patterns were, the tendency of Welsh speakers who lacked confidence to avoid the channel was worrying and showed that S4C was struggling to find the appropriate balance between the use of standard and refined Welsh that alienated a significant section of the audience with the use of everyday informal language that could see an equally significant group turning their back on the channel. This tension could not be easily resolved, and undoubtedly is a challenge that the channel continues to grapple with.

Another insight revealed by the study was that the channel had encouraged Welsh speakers to watch more Welsh language programmes, with 34 per cent indicating that they watched more in February 1984 than a year earlier.[40] This could be attributed in part to the growth in the number of Welsh hours broadcast since the inception of the channel, which had also led to greater choice and diversity for viewers, and a significant percentage felt that the quality of the programmes had improved, which motivated the audience to watch more of the channel's output.[41] Significantly, the existence of S4C made it easier to find Welsh language programmes: with a clear and consistent pattern of broadcasting Welsh language programming during peak hours, it was no longer necessary to channel hop or study the *TV Times* or *Radio Times* in detail to find them.[42] Indeed, 67 per cent of Welsh speakers believed that it was easier to find the programmes they wanted to watch since the Welsh language output was concentrated on one channel; 54 per cent of non-Welsh speakers also agreed, making it clear that around half of the non-Welsh-speaking audience had considered the presence of Welsh language programmes on the main BBC and HTV channels problematic when trying to find specific English language programmes.

Questions were also posed about audience perceptions of specific elements of S4C's service and programmes. One surprising fact, given the early adverse response, was that 65 per cent of Welsh speakers believed that the nature of the presentation was highly professional.[43] The informal nature of the presentation seems to have become firmly established with most of the audience by 1984 and the unfamiliar pattern first used by the Welsh language channel in 1982 had now been accepted.[44]

Other statistics were not so favourable. The survey confirmed that not enough news about Wales was shown on the channel (55 per cent), with respondents over 45 years of age more likely to agree with this and obviously missing the items with a more local focus.[45] A similar response was seen about the standard of different aspects of the news service, with only 11 per cent rating news about their area as very good, 38 per cent rating it as good, 8 per cent couldn't decide if it was good or poor, 34 per cent stating that the local service was poor or even extremely poor and 10 per cent stating they did not know.[46] This was strong evidence that demonstrated that the channel had not been able to meet the Welsh audience's need or appetite for news about their communities and areas; the disquiet was not limited to one specific area who felt neglected by the national service, there was unease about this in every area which indicated that the news strategy had failed the audience in Wales as a whole.[47]

Even so, the audience continued to watch the programme regularly, with 35 per cent of the Welsh language audience watching *Newyddion Saith* four or five times a week.[48] This figure was slightly higher when considering the viewing patterns of those viewers who were over forty-five. *Newyddion Saith*'s most consistent audience were viewers aged 75 and over, with 45 per cent watching the programme four or five times a week.[49] Although the figures were lower for younger viewers, they were not as low as expected: 59 per cent of viewers aged 16 to 24 watched the Welsh language news one or more times a week, and 26 per cent of the same cohort watched the programme four or five times a week. Alongside these promising statistics, 59 per cent of those who watched the programme claimed that its content was interesting, be it 'extremely interesting' or 'very interesting'.[50] These statistics gave S4C a mixed message, as *Newyddion Saith* was appealing to the audience in its current form, but there was still a gap in the provision. After the trial period this demand was met by the channel commissioning and broadcasting magazine programmes such as *Hel Straeon*, *Heno* and *Wedi 7* that met some of the audience's appetite for local content that covered events in their villages, towns and cities.[51]

Another programme discussed in detail was the current affairs programme *Y Byd ar Bedwar*. The number of viewers for this programme were slightly lower than *Newyddion Saith*: only 28 per cent of Welsh speakers watched it weekly, and 51 per cent watched it at least once a month. However, audience satisfaction with its content was higher than *Newyddion Saith*, with 68 per cent of viewers rating the programme as 'extremely entertaining' or 'very entertaining'.[52] The channel's current affairs provision was attractive to the audience, but despite the positive nature of the figures for *Newyddion Saith* and *Y Byd ar Bedwar*, there was one programme that surpassed both – the channel's soap opera, *Pobol y Cwm*. This programme attracted the most praise from respondents as 78 per cent of those who watched the series rated it as 'extremely entertaining' or 'very entertaining'.[53] This apparent satisfaction explained the clear demand among respondents for more drama series and soap operas – this genre appeared at the top of the list of thirteen genres that viewers would like to see more of: 78 per cent of respondents were looking for more fictional content indicating that there was a significant appetite amongst the Welsh language audience for dramatic content.[54] What struck the report's authors was that very few respondents stated that they wanted more programmes with a Welsh focus, such as folk music (12 per cent), Welsh concerts (7 per cent), Welsh cultural history (4 per cent) and Welsh language musicals (3 percent). These figures highlight two possible explanations: either the channel was successful in providing enough of these programmes that met audience demand, or that the Welsh audience's appetite for programmes covering the history of Wales and the Celts and folk music was not as extensive as the producers and commissioners had thought. The matter was raised by a member of the authority during a meeting to discuss programme policy: were ordinary Welsh audience members really as interested in Celtic matters as suggested by the prevalence of these programmes on S4C?[55]

Despite the generally favourable responses, the survey warned that channel officials could not rest on their laurels. The channel's fears about *Sbec* were confirmed, as figures showed that 61 per cent of Welsh speakers said they had never read the magazine, and both Welsh and non-Welsh speakers stated that S4C should do more to support Welsh learners.[56] This survey also found that almost half of Welsh speakers, 49 per cent, believed that there was room for the channel to improve its provision. Further analysis showed that men were the most dissatisfied with the provision rather than women, with 54 per cent of men and 46 per cent of women wanting to see improvements.[57] However, there was no significant consensus on what could be implemented to improve the provision. Over twenty areas of the service were noted where improvements could be made, with more

Welsh content and a greater variety of programmes receiving the most approval.[58] In addition, less swearing, broadcasting fewer old feature films, a more professional presentation style, using a wider variety of actors and fewer regional accents were also mentioned as areas to change.[59] The lack of consensus and the considerable range of modifications proposed demonstrate how difficult it was to please all sections of the Welsh-speaking audience as there was a range of varied expectations and views regarding the channel's merits and shortcomings.

An interesting feature highlighted by the survey was that the majority of respondents, both Welsh-speaking and non-Welsh-speaking, believed that the use of the Welsh language was increasing in Wales as a whole. However, when asked about their views on its use within their areas, they felt that it was in decline.[60] Was S4C giving the impression that use of the Welsh language was increasing across Wales because of its prominence in S4C's schedules? This was misleading, however, since within the communities it was in decline. Can it be claimed, therefore, that the channel's existence created a false impression of the progress of the language, since it gave an impression that it was thriving, and that this in turn gave Welsh speakers a false sense of security, leading to efforts to save the language being thwarted? This is further evidence, arguably, that the concerns of Gwynfor Evans after the second government U-turn were being realised and that the enthusiasm of many campaigners had waned after winning the historic broadcasting campaign. Was the channel, by trying to 'save the language' through securing its place on television and creating a comprehensive service, contributing to its demise? It is impossible to prove any of these statements, as so many factors affect the growth and decline of the language, from the rise of Welsh-medium schools to the influx of non-Welsh-speaking migrants to Welsh areas. All these elements were intertwined, and as such it is difficult to place the blame or the praise on the doorstep of any organisation or any policy when trying to assess their impact on the language. A Welsh language channel was one of the many developments which sought to encourage the wider use of the language and to create a contemporary and exciting image for it.

However interesting these details and nuances in the viewing patterns of Welsh audiences, the most important finding was the attitude of Welsh speakers and non-Welsh speakers towards the pattern of Welsh language broadcasting on one channel. The research confirmed that the majority of the audience in Wales were satisfied, with 77 per cent of Welsh speakers stating that Welsh language programming should be broadcast on only one channel, and 88 per cent of non-Welsh speakers agreeing.[61] Taking the survey sample as reflective of the general audience, the vast majority of the audience in Wales was therefore in favour of the current broadcast pattern, with non-Welsh speakers much happier and convinced that they did not want to return to the old pattern of several bilingual channels. The Welsh speakers were not as unanimous, as they had been during the campaign to ensure a fair deal for the Welsh language within the British broadcasting landscape throughout the 1970s. The existence of the channel had not succeeded in convincing those who were deeply concerned about the fate of the language in a linguistic ghetto. A cluster of Welsh speakers continued to hold the same view that Welsh language programmes should be broadcast across many channels so that non-Welsh speakers come into contact with the language and that all television channels in Wales reflected the diversity and linguistic pattern of the country.

Home Office review

These polls provided useful statistics that would assist the channel in trying to persuade Home Office officials who could, in principle, signal the demise of the channel after the official review. Opening discussions between S4C and Home Office officials began in mid-1984, and by November 1984 the channel had received confirmation that the Home Office was going to maintain its promise to conduct a review of S4C with the minimum of disruption.[62] The Home Office did not want to go out of its way to try to show that the channel was failing to deliver on its original promises or hopes; instead, the picture from the S4C Authority's minutes is that Home Office officials were keen to secure a focused review that would confirm S4C's unambiguous status and position in the Welsh broadcasting landscape. This approach was confirmed in a meeting held a month later between channel officials and Quentin Thomas and Christopher Scoble of the Home Office Broadcasting Department, where Owen Edwards was given the impression that the Home Office staff regretted that there was an unavoidable commitment to conduct a review, because of the general satisfaction with the current situation.[63] Despite these positive and reassuring indications, the authority's officials were not entirely at ease with the prospect of the review: minutes show that they debated and considered whether the channel had interpreted the clause about scheduling C4 programmes around the Welsh language programmes correctly, with some concerned that the channel could be penalised if it was shown that it had not followed the requirements of the Broadcasting Act.[64]

A letter confirming the details of the review was sent by Quentin Thomas on 26 March 1985, in which he expressed the Home Office's confidence in the work of S4C. It also noted that there was no significant public demand for the channel to be terminated, a factor that could seriously threaten the survival of the channel. In his letter, Thomas said:

> In the 1980 debates, the Home Secretary also said that before reaching any decision on revision to a two-channel solution, the Government would have to be satisfied that there was widespread demand for change and that such a change would be in the interest of Wales as a whole and of the Welsh language . . . no such widespread public demand has become apparent in the past two years[65]

As there was no significant public demand for the channel to be abolished, one idea considered by the Home Office, and proposed as an option for the channel, was to conduct an internal review within the Home Office that would seek limited written evidence from the broadcasting organisations, and would avoid wider public review and consultation.[66] However attractive this suggestion was to S4C, the authority concluded that limiting the evidence to broadcasting organisations was not acceptable and that anybody wishing to comment on the channel should be offered an opportunity and an invitation to do so.[67] Undoubtedly the members of the authority considered S4C to be an organisation that belonged to the wider Welsh society and not just the broadcasting sphere. The chairman proposed that the Welsh Office could compile a list of relevant organisations that the review could contact to invite evidence; at least two members of the authority were convinced that it would not be appropriate to place such a restriction on this review, and that anyone who wished to comment should be allowed to do so. Although no comments are recorded stating the following clearly, it is obvious that authority members were concerned that the validity of any review might be called into question if it was not completely open. Had the review been restricted to supportive organisations only, the channel and the Home Office could be charged with managing the outcome of the review. The validity of this critical and legal review should not be questioned, and the channel's existence needed to be beyond reproach. The Home Office accepted the authority's wishes and understood that their role was to organise a review which was as straightforward and uncomplicated as possible, while fulfilling the promise of providing an opportunity for all who wished to express their views on the channel.[68] It was therefore announced on 23 August 1985, in a news release from the Home Office, that Giles Shaw, William Whitelaw's successor as Home Secretary, was inviting comments from broadcasting organisations and any other Welsh groups and individuals who had any comments to make on the fourth channel issue.[69]

One organisation outside the broadcasting sphere that wished to contribute to the review was the WCC, as it had devised a research project that sought to establish how accountable S4C was to its audience. The council intended to use the research to inform its evidence to the Home Office.[70] What was produced was a document called *Watching S4C: the case for consumer representation for the Fourth Channel in Wales*.[71] The introduction to the document gives the impression that WCC was not fully confident of the Home Office's intentions with the review, as it stated: 'WCC believes that it is appropriate at this time to look not only at the desirability of the single channel solution, but also to consider the operation and performance of S4C.'[72] The WCC was concerned that the review would focus on the principle of a separate Welsh language channel rather than objectively reviewing the decisions and strategies implemented by S4C. This concern was completely legitimate when considering the correspondence discussed between the Home Office and channel officials.

From the outset of the report the WCC stated that it fully supported the single channel model for Welsh language provision and that S4C should receive the government's approval to continue as a permanent institution in the Welsh broadcasting landscape. However, it was not entirely happy with the way the channel engaged with its viewers in canvassing and seeking their views since it was dependent on the BBC Broadcasting Council for Wales and the IBA's Welsh committee for this work.[73] The WCC was concerned that 'Neither of these bodies has as its primary role a concern with S4C.'[74] It was felt that the needs of S4C viewers could be neglected by this scheme, and the WCC recommended that the Welsh channel should form what they called a consumer consultative committee.[75] The committee's remit would be to consider all aspects of S4C's work, rather than just the parts of it that were relevant to the BBC or the IBA. Although the WCC admitted that no other British television authority had engaged such a committee, it was convinced that S4C should do so to protect and give voice to S4C's 'consumers'.[76] The report noted that the WCC did not seek to demonstrate that S4C viewers needed more care and protection than the viewers of other channels, but this was later countered by listing eleven reasons why it was necessary for the channel to urgently establish such a committee. One of the first reasons given for forming a consumer committee was the fact that S4C represented a monopoly in the context of Welsh language television: 'it is the only supplier of Welsh language programmes and a selection of Channel Four UK output: hence it is a monopoly'.[77] It could be contended that S4C did not hold an absolute monopoly over Welsh language broadcasting: consider, for example, the monopoly over broadcasting enjoyed by the BBC prior to the advent of ITV in 1955. In the case of S4C, its programmes were produced from many sources, and the items produced internally were very limited; it provided a platform for numerous voices, and S4C's power over the programmes produced was not absolute, especially when that output was produced within the BBC and HTV. However, it was fair to say that S4C had a monopoly over the timing of Welsh language programmes, even if it did not have the same monopoly over the content.

WCC also noted that its research showed that more could be done to meet the needs of some sections of the channel's audience, for example non-Welsh speakers and younger viewers. The council claimed that establishing a balanced consumer committee would ensure that these groups were given a voice as the channel developed and evolved in the future.[78] It also believed that general advisory committees, which were traditional to broadcasting, did not provide a voice for consumers, and that the target that should be aimed for was that which existed for the national industries, such as health. The WCC also did not consider that establishing the Broadcasting Complaints Commission for the whole industry under the Broadcasting Act 1981 had met this need either, since general advisory committees had a broader role than only dealing with specific programme complaints alone.

Another concern was that after the end of the trial period, the channel would become less open to viewers' opinions, since it would no longer be absolutely critical to respond to the comments and views of its audience. The council claimed that it was the channel's trial period that had prompted it to be as responsive as possible to the views of its viewers through the organisation of a series of public meetings, broadcasting the *Arolwg* programme and commissioning particular research projects. The council was concerned that the motive behind these activities would disappear once the channel was established as a permanent part of the broadcasting landscape and that it would be less conscientious in canvassing the views of its audience.[79] The council was of the view that the pattern of using the BBC and IBA consultative systems was not clear for the audience; it was convinced that it was not natural for the audience to consider turning to the BBC or the IBA to discuss matters relating to S4C.[80] The WCC was also persuaded that holding public meetings was not an effective means of engaging with the public or the channel's 'consumers'. Certainly, there is ample justification for this since public meetings failed to attract large or diverse audiences, even in the case of a channel that had come into being due to an unprecedented public campaign. These public meetings were unlikely to be representative, with those individuals already identified by the council as being overlooked by the channel, specifically non-Welsh speakers and young people, unlikely to attend. The council asserted that representatives of the different audience groups on a consumer committee would undoubtedly be more active and perceptive than individual users attending public meetings to push personal agendas and interests rather than the wishes of the wider audience.

WCC went on to state that establishing such a committee would not be an additional burden, but that it would be 'supportive both by helping S4C to be a popular, comprehensive and widely respected broadcasting service and increasing the effectiveness of its communications with consumers'.[81] The council believed that such a committee should, in order to gain maximum benefit, consider policy issues rather than focus on individual programme complaints. The ideal scenario set out in the report was a committee that would discuss the balance and timing of English and Welsh language programmes, the selection criteria for C4 programmes, programme production plans and production guidelines, complaints handling processes and the value for money offered by S4C.[82] Although the council stated that its suggested committee did not intend to stand on the authority's toes by duplicating its statutory responsibilities, these tasks undoubtedly were activities in which the authority had been engaged during the four years of its existence. But the biggest difference between the authority and the WCC's plans was that it would be a representative committee reflecting the variety of individuals who considered themselves viewers of S4C, both Welsh and non-Welsh speakers. During its trial period the S4C Authority was far from representative in terms of age, gender and linguistic ability, although it was relatively representative in geographical terms. The WCC had, therefore, identified one significant weakness in the authority's composition, and had produced detailed research and an in-depth report that would be difficult for S4C and the Home Office to disregard.

According to the WCC, the research showed that many organisations supported the need for S4C to do more to gather information and opinions from its audience; however the Welsh broadcasting organisations did not agree with the ideas championed in the report.[83] At a joint meeting between the BBC Broadcasting Council for Wales and the S4C Authority at the start of the WCC research project, BBC representatives questioned the value of formal advisory committees, with Gareth Price, Wales's head of programming, stridently expressing his views. The minutes report that: 'in his experience formal advisory committees were an ineffective way of achieving information about the audience; letters and phone calls were much more helpful, especially when taken together with efficient audience research'.[84] Geraint Stanley Jones believed that the pattern drawn up by S4C had shown remarkable cooperation between the broadcasting organisations in Wales, and noted that he did not fully understand the motivation and reasons of the WCC for raising this issue.[85] One member of the Broadcasting Council of Wales and a former member of the WCC, believed that the only useful recommendation that the WCC could make was to offer that the channel's complaints structures could be made clearer to the public.[86] While another believed:

> that S4C seemed to him to be under more public scrutiny proportionally than any other UK channel, to judge by the attention given to it in the Welsh press. In his opinion, there was no serious cause for concern on this issue.[87]

The IBA also gave the report an unfavourable response when it discussed the WCC consultation document in September 1985. Unlike the final report, *Watching S4C*, this consultation document set out a number of additional proposals and ideas other than the consumer consultative committee as it aimed to make the diverse voices of the audience heard by S4C. It was proposed, for example, that the BBC and the IBA could form a sub-committee that could focus only on S4C's programmes. It was also suggested that the IBA Welsh committee could be invited to provide advice to the S4C Authority on all the channel's programming, or that a new advisory committee could be formed which would advise all broadcasting organisations in Wales, the BBC, HTV and S4C.[88] Although the IBA's Welsh committee appreciated the faith shown in its committee with the proposed major role for it in the revised structures, members were convinced that none of the plans could be implemented because of the fundamental differences between the structures and remits of the IBA and BBC committees; the document also irritated the committee because of its impression that the IBA was ignoring consumer views.[89] One member of the committee, stated that the report and its position were not valid because its basic assumption – that the membership of the IBA and BBC committees was not representative and were made up with middle-class membership – was incorrect. He also believed that it was much more difficult than the WCC thought to secure fully representative committees.[90]

The detailed nature of the WCC report prompted the Home Office to seriously consider its evidence and investigate and formulate a comprehensive response to its recommendations.[91] However, there were some reservations that WCC's central concept was flawed, which was that broadcasting could be treated in the same way as any other product or service, and that they considered that the audience could not be treated solely as consumers because of public interest considerations inherent to broadcasting.[92] Neither was S4C's own response favourable to the WCC's recommendations: some members felt that many of the suggestions unnecessarily duplicated work and in their draft response to the Home Office indicated that the WCC saw S4C as a suitable test subject and an opportunity to establish a committee that would serve as a precedent for the rest of the industry.[93] Sir Goronwy Daniel was strongly opposed to the principle and, building on the views expressed by members of the IBA's Welsh committee, noted that the solution offered by the WCC was 'elite' – although the chairman acknowledged that more needed to be done to attract non-Welsh-speaking viewers to public meetings. Sir Goronwy Daniel's view was that such a committee would be less representative than the public meetings already organised by the channel. There was also a strong feeling amongst the authority members that it was not possible to justify the level of investment needed to set up and an additional administrative office to support such a committee.[94] Given the considerable opposition from the broadcast organisations and the fundamental scepticism amongst Home Office officials, it was highly unlikely that the WCC's recommendations would be realised, but the report certainly pushed the issue to the top of the agenda at the relevant organisations, and S4C drew up plans to run a series of seminars to discuss programmes with viewers, the authority and the producers.[95]

There is no direct reference to the WCC research or recommendations in the evidence produced by S4C for the Home Office; instead, the channel chronicled its achievements since its inception, focusing, as expected, on the positive and successful aspects of the work it had undertaken.[96] The evidence made significant use of viewing figures, the *Viewing and Listening in Wales* research, the tremendous international recognition for the channel in its early years and the increasingly impressive list of awards that the channel's programmes had won between 1983 and 1985.[97] The focus was on all the features that the channel had added to the Welsh broadcasting landscape, emphasising the existence of a Welsh language *service* rather than a cluster of programmes.[98] The new vitality within the Welsh production sector was emphasised, with the expansion of the numbers of independent producers, the creation of facility companies and the new staff employed by BBC Wales and HTV Wales.[99] This vigour made it impossible to state that there was no longer enough talent in Welsh-speaking Wales to sustain an independent service: 'The prophets of doom whose contention, before S4C started broadcasting, was that Wales lacked the necessary expertise and talent to sustain a high-quality programming service, have been proved embarrassingly wrong.'[100] The effort made by the channel to ensure that the money coming into its coffers was not wasted on bureaucracy and staffing was also highlighted: 90 per cent of the money went directly on purchasing programmes.[101] There is a subtle denouncement here of the WCC's proposals to establish a new consultation regime, which would have added significantly to these costs. Along with the self-congratulatory comments, there were other statements that were much more modest; the channel's officials were fully aware of the weaknesses that existed in its provision. Further developments were needed to ensure a better service for Welsh learners by providing specialist provision and increasing the subtitling service, which indicates that the channel recognised its strategy in this area had fallen wide of the mark. Reference was also made to the need for wider provision for teenagers, suggesting that, despite the existence of programmes such as *Coleg*, it had not been able to secure the loyalty of this section of the possible audience.

In summarising its evidence, the channel combined the positive with an emphasis on the complexity of the task, and a final sentence that reveals the channel's confidence in its future:

> Providing a comprehensive television service for a bilingual nation is no easy task. S4C has tackled the problem with efficiency, flair and professionalism. The greatest compliment that it could receive is that the people of Wales now take it for granted. It has become part of the fabric of Welsh society. It is now poised to meet the challenges of the next decade.[102]

The channel was confident of the outcome of the review, which was reasonable following the positive and encouraging correspondence received from the Home Office. But to realise the wishes of both organisations, positive evidence was required from a wide range of British and Welsh organisations, and from individual audience members to be absolutely certain of its continued existence.

The evidence of the IBA and the BBC Broadcasting Council for Wales was highly supportive of the channel. The BBC's evidence was relatively general, emphasising the overwhelming success of the collaboration between the BBC and ITV in forming and delivering a unified Welsh language service while continuing to compete in other areas.[103] This statement, while praising the channel's achievements, is a bit misleading as it ignores S4C's contribution to securing that cooperation between the two organisations. HTV and the BBC did not just negotiate with each other, but with S4C's staff and authority who ensured that the provision of both organisations could be interwoven to create a unified service. The heads of the three broadcasters, Owen Edwards, Geraint Stanley Jones and Ron Wordley, met regularly to discuss and plan, and had it not been for the existence of the new authority, the independent middleman, that collaboration may have been difficult to maintain.

Reference was also made in the BBC's evidence to several areas that had been challenging for the channel, but they were given a positive spin. For example, it was a notable achievement that the channel had a loyal, devoted audience that compared favourably with other British television services:

> the most popular programmes are proportionately just as successful as the most popular programmes on the main UK networks. This is a remarkable achievement when it is considered that the bulk of S4C's output is transmitted in peak hours in direct competition with the most successful programmes on the UK networks.[104]

But the backbone of the evidence received by the BBC was the significant, if not the total abatement, of complaints received by non-Welsh speakers. The BBC believed that non-Welsh-speaking audiences had begun to return to BBC1 Wales and HTV Wales rather than watching the equivalent channels in the west of England. The cable companies had also begun to remove the English channels from their services in Wales, ensuring that non-Welsh-speaking people watched local programmes about Wales, which would help restore some of the democratic deficit created when audiences turned their aerials towards England. It was warned that this change could not be explained by searching for reasons beyond S4C's existence, such as new maturity or tolerance amongst non-Welsh speakers towards the language. The unpleasant feelings continued to bubble beneath the surface and they burst into view for a short time when programmes for Welsh learners and Welsh language dramas such as *Penyberth* and *Marathon* were broadcast with English subtitles on BBC Wales during 1983 and 1984.[105] The BBC's support and commitment to the single-channel scheme was, therefore, solid, and as anticipated the corporation's evidence did not cast a critical view on S4C's decisions and activities, focusing instead on the concept of a separate Welsh channel.

Unlike the BBC, who authored one document on behalf of the corporation as a whole, separate evidence was sent by a number of organisations connected to the ITV network. Evidence was received from the IBA centrally, separate testimony from the IBA Welsh committee, evidence from HTV, a response from the ITCA, joint evidence from Scottish Television and Grampian Television, and a joint document from Thames Television and Yorkshire Television.[106] At the top of the evidence sent by the IBA centrally is an admission that, having opposed the idea of a single Welsh language channel in the years before 1981, it had changed its position, recognising that the new regime was a blessing to both language groups. The focus then shifted to what were considered to be the IBA's responsibilities in the context of S4C, namely funding, transmission, responsibilities of the Welsh contractor (HTV) and advertising management.[107] The success of the IBA engineers' efforts to ensure that 90 per cent of Welsh residents were able to receive the channel's broadcasts on its opening night was proudly reported, and the figure had now risen to an average of 96–7 per cent, matching, more or less, the reach of HTV.[108] However, the IBA was concerned about financial issues, and it was stated unambiguously that S4C was an expensive solution, in terms of broadcasting, to the social and political problems that had occurred in Wales during the 1960s and the 1970s.[109] What the IBA called a recession in advertising finance in 1985 had seen a significant impact on the profits of many ITV companies. This meant that many of them continued to contribute a portion of their advertising money towards the cost of running C4 and S4C without qualifying for the tax reduction introduced by the Conservative government in 1981 in order to reduce the additional financial pressure on ITV companies when establishing S4C.[110] There were significant and serious errors in the financial arrangements according to the IBA, since it was the smaller companies, such as Yorkshire Television, who suffered the most in this situation, and these circumstances, if they remained unchanged, would lead to further disquiet amongst ITV network companies towards S4C.[111] In addition, the IBA was concerned about S4C's reliance on C4, and how dependent that collaboration and the healthy relationship between them was on the flexibility of ITV funding. The IBA anticipated that ITV funding would not remain as healthy in the future, and that the fight for fair funding that would follow any inadequate settlement could create a rift in a relationship that had been so friendly and successful during the trial period.[112] The clear suggestion was that S4C and the one-channel solution had been successful and flourished when all the conditions were favourable, especially the financial conditions. The IBA expressed reservations that the channel would not be as successful if ITV's circumstances changed. The success of the channel and the availability of C4 programmes for transmission free of charge on the channel were entirely dependent on the fact that C4 received sufficient funding from the IBA each year: government would need to reconsider the funding pattern of the two fourth channels to ensure their continuation, as the reliance on ITV was not sustainable in the long term.

The evidence received from the ITCA also focused on this point as it discussed faults and weaknesses of the funding pattern. Foremost in the ITCA's thinking was the impact of any recommendations that the Peacock Committee would make in 1986 regarding the introduction of advertising on BBC channels.[113] The ITCA anticipated that such an action would significantly reduce the advertising income of ITV companies and would have a detrimental effect on the funding available to maintain the Welsh language channel.[114] The ITCA also believed that, even if the government did not create more competition for advertising income, the proportion of non-taxable advertising money allowed to ITV companies needed to be reconsidered, given that the costs of running S4C were much higher than anticipated when the level of financial aid was set back in 1981.[115]

Similar concerns about the channel's funding were raised in the evidence of the IBA's Welsh committee, but it also included more comments on the channel's achievements, such as: 'It has created a marriage of broadcasting skills, has successfully conserved resources and has effectively removed duplication of effort.'[116] The committee also applauded what it considered a wide range of programmes, the pattern of delivery and the overall high standard of provision. In addition, reference was made to the channel's contribution to the prosperity of the Welsh language, an issue that was ignored in the evidence of the other major broadcasting organisations. It provided a realistic analysis of the channel's contribution to the survival and growth of the language without using emotional rhetoric: 'the service . . . augments the investment made by central and local government in bi-lingual education and in other spheres and that is of considerable value and assistance to the growing number of people of all ages currently learning Welsh'.[117] It was noted that S4C's existence had created a significant impact on the Welsh job market: a number of new jobs within the broadcasting organisations had been created along with the establishment of technical facilities and independent companies in rural areas. The creation of the channel had led to the establishment of a thriving broadcasting and production sector in Wales, something that would not have happened to the same extent had Welsh language programmes not been placed on a separate channel.

The evidence submitted by HTV was far more mixed than that expressed by the other broadcasting organisations. Following the same pattern as the IBA's Welsh committee, the principle and merits of the single-channel solution were discussed and some of S4C's activities were critically considered. An attempt was made to disprove the claims that the programme contract between them was expensive for S4C and provided HTV with substantial profit.[118] The cost of HTV programmes compared favourably with those of other providers, and it was noted, were broadly equivalent to the cost of producing them, thus suggesting that the company was not making any profit at all – although the use of 'broadly' plants the seed of doubt in the reader's mind.[119] It went further by adding: 'The contract is marginally viable and the advantageous commercial terms granted to S4C for political reasons would not be acceptable to HTV in any other aspect of our business.'[120]

HTV's testimony also accuses broadcast commentators of being biased when discussing the achievements of broadcasting organisations in Wales:

> It is a popular element of broadcasting politics in Wales for the non-creators of jobs and wealth to academically exaggerate financial aspects of HTV's operation whilst nationistically [*sic*] lauding S4C exports which, like those of UK's Channel Four, are properly reflected in Report and Accounts as the reality that sales costs exceed sales income by significant margins. We find it difficult to challenge the commercial broadcasters' view that ITV funds subscribed to support a necessary bilingual broadcasting system within Wales, should be used to sustain a loss-making export public relations exercise.[121]

It is clear from this statement that two aspects of S4C's international activities had agitated HTV's managing director. It is clear that ITV companies, including HTV, were displeased that the money they contributed towards the maintenance of S4C was used for activities that they considered marginal, and that those activities, HTV believed, were not actually profitable – an anathema to commercial companies.[122] The other aspect that clearly irritated Ron Wordley was the positive publicity given to S4C because of these activities, when similar sales activities undertaken by HTV were ignored, despite these being, according to the managing director, necessary to sustaining HTV during the advertising recession that the company was facing.[123]

Following these fiery statements that derided what were commonly considered to be S4C's successes and given the company's attitude towards the idea of installing Welsh language programmes on one channel in the early 1980s, the comments on the costs of S4C's service are somewhat surprising, since they justify them. The evidence confirmed that S4C provided value for money in terms of broadcasting given its cost per head, and actively sought to disprove the common belief that only 20 per cent of the Welsh audience was served by S4C. HTV claimed that S4C provides an all-Wales service, as the fourth channel was the means by which HTV Wales and BBC Wales could meet the needs of the country's 80 per cent non-Welsh-speaking population: 'the cost of the S4C service is often mistakenly inflated by critics who ignore the size of the total viewing universe actually "serviced"'.[124] The costs of the channel per capita were compared with the same costs for the ITV network: using the principle that S4C served the 2.5 million inhabitants of Wales, the cost of the channel was stated at £13 per head, irrespective of the cost of producing BBC programmes through the licence. In comparison the national cost of the ITV network was £17 per head per person in Great Britain.[125] The HTV statement therefore set out to dispel those claims that S4C was the most expensive channel per capita in Britain, if not the world, suggesting that S4C compared very favourably with other British channels and was possibly cheaper. HTV's statement that S4C's service met the needs of the Welsh audience beyond those who spoke the language does not stretch the facts or distort the picture to create a better image for S4C. The statement is, in fact, in line with the evidence of many other organisations that praised the significant reduction in complaints from the non-Welsh-speaking audience, but it directly challenged the assumptions that existed about the channel. HTV once again, in line with its conduct during the activities of the Welsh Affairs Select Committee (WASC) when it presented realistic figures for funding a separate channel, managed to offer the channel crucial support when it was most in need of it.

HTV also referred to the unhappiness and dissatisfaction of some of the other regional broadcasting companies, notably Grampian Television, Scottish Television and Ulster Television, over the fact that 20 per cent of their contributions towards C4 went towards a broadcasting system that only served Wales.[126] Evidence to that effect was also sent directly by two of those companies, Grampian and Scottish, to the Home Office.[127] The source of contention for these regional broadcasters was that developments in the independent sector within their areas had not received the same degree of investment or development opportunities, and that the proceeds of advertising funding in Scotland were not being used to maintain and support creative and production talent there. The money that C4 and the ITV companies in Scotland spent on independent productions did not reach the same level as that being invested in Wales by S4C. To redress the imbalance and perceived unfairness it was proposed that the £1.915m that Grampian and Scottish would invest in S4C during 1985–6 could be retained, boosting the independent sector in Scotland and increasing the number of programmes made in Scotland and broadcast on C4.[128] The authors were keen to note that they were not requesting a separate channel for Scotland, as there was no obvious demand for such provision. However, they were keen to see local creative talent nurtured, and wanted to guarantee that Scotland was not left behind without its own channel. These were earnest concerns and one of the weaknesses of the system devised by the Home Office. Arguably, it was C4's responsibility to secure a suitable investment in Scotland from its production budget, but clearly this could not be achieved to the same extent as S4C's investment in Wales. Similarly, it was not possible for S4C to arbitrarily ensure that every area of Wales received its share of the production budget because of other factors such as the number of companies, the quality of ideas and so on, which influenced the distribution of funds.

In addition to the ten broadcasting organisations invited to send evidence to the Home Office, evidence was received from two local authorities (Arfon and Dwyfor) and forty-two other organisations. These other organisations ranged from Merched y Wawr branches to the University of Wales, from Plaid Cymru to the Tourist Board, and included organisations from the Welsh broadcasting world, such as Teledwyr Annibynnol Cymru (TAC) and Siriol.[129] Correspondence was also received from eighty-two individuals who wished to express their views on the channel. Evidence was therefore received from 136 organisations and individuals, of which the vast majority – 108 – were in favour of continuing with the current arrangements, and the remaining twenty-eight against. Of those against, twenty-seven were individuals, with only one organisation opposed to the broadcast pattern. The Home Office documents do not specify which organisation was in opposition.[130] The Home Office report listed the fourteen reasons expressed by the objectors to the current system. Half of the complaints related to the re-scheduling of C4 English language programmes on the channel, while the remainder called for more Welsh language programmes.[131] The familiar complaint that viewers wanted C4 programmes during peak hours and not at inconvenient times was voiced; some viewers expressed frustration that they read newspaper reviews about C4 programmes before they were broadcast in Wales, while others were frustrated by the fact that they were unable to engage in the public debate about some programmes as a result. Others complained about William Whitelaw's decision to ignore the Rediffusion customer vote in 1982, and others that they had to pay full price for a TV licence even though they believed that they were being deprived of a quarter of English language provision. Some viewers were frustrated that some genres of C4 programmes were not being broadcast on S4C, particularly the channel's unique extended news programme and current affairs provision. There were also complaints that ethnic minorities were being completely deprived of the special provision made for them on C4. By meeting the needs of one minority, other minority groups suffered. One complainant noted that other minority groups, such as the 1.5 million Muslims in Britain, did not have their own channel, and queried why Welsh-speaking people deserved special treatment.[132]

Some familiar views were expressed also, such as the complaint that S4C was a complete waste of money since Welsh speakers also understood and spoke English. But non-Welsh speakers were not the only ones who expressed dissatisfaction. There was opposition to the fact that English language advertisements were broadcast amongst Welsh language programmes, discontent about the use of the north Walian dialect that was apparently unintelligible to the inhabitants of south Wales, and also a complaint about the amateur quality of Welsh language programmes. The case for broadcasting Welsh language programmes on more than one channel was resurrected, since it was believed that it encouraged people to learn Welsh.[133] It was clear, therefore, that S4C had not succeeded in persuading everyone of its merits, of the quality of its programmes or its ability to re-schedule C4 programmes in a way that met the needs of all members of the audience. The negative opinions, however, remained in the minority, and many complainants were willing to admit that the situation was much better than it had been, and as a result the channel's case was not seriously damaged.[134]

On receipt of all the evidence a brief Home Office report was compiled in November 1985 setting out the context of the review, and reiterating the views expressed, with little additional analysis. Since no concerns not already known to the Home Office or S4C itself had been identified, it was concluded that: 'The review has demonstrated beyond doubt the continued strong level of support for S4C amongst the Welsh-speaking population in Wales and has confirmed that there is little dissatisfaction amongst either Welsh or English speakers.'[135] Recognising all the concerns expressed by various broadcast organisations about the channel's funding, it was confirmed that the Home Office would conduct an internal review into those aspects using the evidence and views expressed as a starting point.[136] It was explained that the Home Office had deliberately omitted financial matters from this review, in an attempt to avoid confusion and focus the attention of the evidence on the political issue of the future of the channel. Since the Home Office's remit was to review the arrangement of broadcasting Welsh language programmes on one channel, by 1985 the outcome of the review was a *fait accompli*: the channel had become so embedded in the

Welsh broadcasting landscape and had refuted those who had doubted the ability of the new authority and channel to establish and maintain a comprehensive service in Welsh on one channel. As such, it was unimaginable that the Home Office would reach a different conclusion given the tremendous reduction in the correspondence from non-Welsh speakers. It is accurate that the review did not analyse the channel's policies and strategies that were not directly related to that underlying principle. But since S4C had not completely failed in any aspect of its responsibilities under the Broadcasting Act – and in many areas, such as international sales, had succeeded in areas that had not been imagined back in 1980 – Home Office officials felt that they could not justify such a detailed review. A quick and expedient review was conducted that would not destabilise the broadcasting sector in Wales by creating uncertainty about the future of S4C.

On 13 December 1985 the continuation of the channel was announced before the House of Commons, with very little ceremony since it took the form of a written answer to the question posed by Robert Harvey, Conservative MP for south-west Clwyd.[137] This suggests two things: either that the existence of the channel had become accepted fully by MPs and it was now seen as an integral part of the British broadcasting landscape, or that it was a peripheral issue for most members of the House and there was not enough interest to justify a broader discussion. It was also announced that the term of the authority's chairman, Sir Goronwy Daniel, would be extended for an additional three months, until the end of March 1986. The name of the new chairman who would undertake the task of navigating the channel towards the 1990s was announced: John Howard Davies CBE, a man with a background in education as a member of the Commonwealth education service in northern Nigeria, as deputy director of education in Montgomeryshire and Flintshire, and then as Clwyd's first director of education between 1974 and 1985. He also had cultural ties as a council member of the National Library of Wales and the Arts Society of North Wales.[138] It could be anticipated that the new chairman's educational background, in contrast to his predecessor's economic background, would give the channel a new focus. Sir Goronwy Daniel had successfully navigated the channel through its formative years, and relatively smoothly through a critical review. Would the new chairman have the same opportunity to put his own stamp on the channel's activities? It was a time of change as the channel and authority moved towards its sixth year and began the second chapter in its history.

Conclusion

Having weighed up the formative years of S4C, we can state that the biggest achievement of the Welsh Fourth Channel Authority (WFCA) and its greatest contribution during the trial period was that it changed the broadcasting landscape in Wales completely. Undoubtedly, William Whitelaw's second U-turn bestowed upon the Welsh-speaking audience much more than what was expected, although not all of the protesters' demands from the 1960s and 1970s were met. The Broadcasting Act 1981 heralded the establishment of a new service which provided Wales with greater control over broadcasting by forming a completely new, independent broadcasting authority that had all the necessary statutory rights to manage and oversee its remit. That status meant that the WFCA could deal with any other organisation within the UK broadcasting landscape, in principle, on equal terms. This status was much greater than that afforded to Channel 4 (C4), since C4 was a subsidiary of the Independent Broadcasting Authority (IBA) and, as a result, their board was accountable to the broadcasting authority and at the mercy of its chief executives.[1] The relationship between them was strained, especially since C4 officials held the belief that, on certain occasions, the IBA upheld the interests of the ITV network companies at the expense of C4. By awarding it control over its own activities, the S4C Authority was spared those hostilities, and this independence meant that it could take editorial decisions and devise and implement its own priorities for the channel's output and provision.[2] This independence recognised that only a Welsh organisation with its members steeped in the culture and political complexities of Wales was capable of making sound decisions about the form and priorities of a Welsh language channel. With the establishment of the S4C Authority, there was recognition that imposing conditions upon the channel from a British or London perspective would not meet the requirements. Thus, a third broadcasting authority was introduced into the British broadcasting landscape, transforming the pattern that had existed unchanged since 1955.

S4C was part of a revolutionary change within the industry, since it offered a new operational pattern to channels. The broadcaster-publisher model used for the first time with the launch of S4C and C4 was the necessary catalyst for a new power to grow, prosper and compete with the large organisations that had dominated the British television industry. The arrival of independent producers completely changed the broadcasting sector, and the growth of this sector in Wales was the key to transforming Welsh language broadcasting. There existed very few independent producers in Wales at the beginning of 1981 when the new authority was formed, a small cluster of individuals who were interested in acting as producers only if the circumstances were favourable. By the end of the channel's trial period in 1985 the independent producers had grown into a large and strong sector, and were located across Wales, not just in the immediate vicinity of Cardiff. In the period 1981 to the end of the 1985–6 financial year, the channel had commissioned programmes from fifty-six different independent producers, with an average of thirty-six companies producing programmes for them each year.[3] Barcud's outside broadcast unit was established to serve many of those companies, enabling them to compete with the BBC and HTV by using various theatres and other buildings across Wales to film and produce programmes that would normally be produced in a Cardiff studio. Coupled with the tremendous growth in the number of independent producers, by 1984 as a sector they formed a trade association to look after their interests, Teledwyr Annibynnol Cymru (TAC) and, in 1985, discussions began to consider the training needs of the industry which would lead to the establishment of Cyfle in 1986. In four years the independent producers had grown from a nebulous group of individuals that S4C nurtured and encouraged to become a successful sector that cared for its own interests, planning for a prosperous future and providing attractive and high-quality programming for S4C.

There were many significant side effects generated by the development of this relationship between S4C and the independent producers, one of the most notable was that several producers settled in areas of high unemployment, such as areas of north-west Wales and Cardiff Bay, contributing to the economies of these vulnerable areas. Subsequently new working opportunities were offered in the Welsh-speaking heartlands; while the flow of emigration from rural areas to the cities of southern England and Wales was not halted, they showed that successful businesses could be established, and attractive and entertaining television programmes could be produced and that there were opportunities to work in an exciting industry in rural Wales. The arrival of independent producers was also a path to guaranteeing that there was room for new entrants to venture into broadcasting. S4C prompted many individuals to leave the big broadcasters and set up their own production companies; many producers and directors were urged to give up their secure jobs so as to strengthen the sector. There were two significant outcomes: first, those individuals were empowered to become involved in developing their own creative ideas, rather than realising the ideas of others and working within organisational priorities. Secondly, it created opportunities within the two main broadcasters, the BBC and HTV, for inexperienced young people to enter the industry and receive the necessary training. Due to the significant increase and the broader range of programmes that characterised the Welsh language output produced by the BBC and HTV for S4C, there was serious recruitment within both broadcasters, and an injection of new blood and energy into the television industry in Wales, and to Welsh language television in particular. This led to the success of the channel and its appeal to the audience.

New momentum was created within the industry and its output – not only because of the fresh energy provided by new staff but because of a greater variety of ideas being generated through the medium of Welsh. The arrival of independent producers was certainly a catalyst for that development, as they pitched ideas that were different from those traditionally produced by the BBC and HTV. The main difference was that their ideas were not encumbered by studio restrictions: locating their programmes in areas across Wales. The independent producers were not only closer to their audience and the Welsh community in terms of the locations of their various offices, but they also depicted those communities, both as characters within them and as locations in their productions. The activities of the independent producers contributed economically to those areas as the producers employed staff and used ancillary local services. There were therefore significant economic side effects to the work of these newcomers to Welsh language broadcasting, and these additional benefits were instrumental in bolstering the channel's reputation, since S4C not only provided extended programming through the medium of Welsh, but also invested economically in areas and communities. These economic side effects were a deliberate strategy by the S4C Authority to ensure that the channel and its activities were woven into interests beyond those of the broadcasting world, and to such an extent that it would become particularly difficult and complicated to eliminate the channel without adversely affecting many other sectors and industries in the process. This plan was exceptionally insightful, since it recognised the need to secure added value in order to justify and confirm its existence. Relying solely on viewing figures would have been irresponsible, since it was not possible to draw a fair comparison with the statistics of other UK channels, which could be used by the channel's opponents to make harsh criticisms of the cost of the service.

Due to the unique combination of programmes from the BBC, HTV and the independent producers, and the different terms that existed between the channel and its providers, S4C was first and foremost a partnership in its early years. This was evident from the outset due to the constitution of the authority, with the appointment of a representative of the BBC, the IBA and C4, and two independent members. Although the Act did not require representatives of the various broadcasting institutions on the authority, their presence meant that the authority had representatives immersed in the Welsh broadcasting landscape. The knowledge held by Alwyn Roberts, Glyn Tegai Hughes, Professor Huw Morris-Jones and Gwilym Peregrine, together with their institutional links, ensured that key decisions could be made quickly. William Whitelaw, therefore, was prudent in adhering to this principle in the face of strong opposition from many parties, since the institutional links were an indispensable tool in the short time given to the authority before the launch of the channel. In addition to the vital knowledge held by the members, their presence guaranteed that goodwill and commitment to the success of the channel were important principles to the various other broadcasting organisations. The channel was also heavily dependent on each organisation in turn when dealing with various issues; for example, they relied upon the IBA to make its first broadcasts available to as many Welsh viewers as possible on its opening night through its transmitter network, offering the channel the best possible chance of success in attracting viewers. S4C was reliant on the goodwill within the BBC towards the Welsh language channel since the corporation, because of the financial arrangement, retained editorial control over its programmes broadcast by the Welsh language channel. It was therefore necessary for S4C officials to trust the BBC and its staff to provide quality and entertaining programmes within the 10 hours provided free of charge, and without that trust, the relationship between the two sides could have soured leading to an adverse effect on the programme service. The ease of the relationship with C4 was also vital because of the agreement to provide their English language programmes free of charge, and there had been no objection to the principle that S4C officers could schedule and select those programmes as they wished. This can be attributed to the strong relationship between the two chief executives; arguably, it could also be attributed to Glyn Tegai Hughes's presence on the C4 management board and the S4C Authority, which contributed to that ease. Even though there were considerable tensions in the relationship between S4C and HTV, and the commercial company had campaigned with the rest of the ITV network to secure the fourth channel for its own use (which would have meant dividing Welsh language programmes between two channels), after the decision to establish S4C was announced HTV became instrumental in ensuring fair terms for the channel. HTV resisted the pressure to agree with the other ITV network companies that S4C should not be paid for from their coffers; instead of removing themselves from the debate, HTV promoted the need to secure sufficient funding, advocating the fact that producing quality Welsh language programming cost the same as producing English language programmes for larger audiences. After all the wrangling over money between HTV and S4C, the company executives and staff managed to bury any resentment present during contract negotiations and committed to producing some of the channel's most appealing and long-running programmes.

The support offered by the broadcasting organisations was fundamental, but the goodwill of the Conservative government and the civil service was also crucial to the success and continuation of the channel. The government had been forced to make an embarrassing U-turn, but ministers and officials did not hold a grudge against the channel following that humiliation. Following the decision to place Welsh language programmes on one channel, the channel was given every chance to succeed and sufficient financial resources at a time of financial hardship; the government remained steadfast on that issue in the face of fierce opposition from ITV network companies. Indeed, on the opening night of the channel Gwynfor Evans announced:

> they have acted honourably and I must say this, the government, ever since we secured this victory, they have been generous and willing to do everything they can to ensure that there is success for the Welsh language channel.[4]

The government's commitment to the channel's success continued throughout the trial period, and as the channel faced a review of its activities, civil servants were convinced that the continuation of the channel was the best solution for the future of Welsh language broadcasting. That attitude is evident in the decision of Whitehall officials to consult the authority and its staff on the most appropriate structure for the review, to ensure that it was comprehensive yet executed in a timely manner, which would not lead to adverse uncertainty for the channel or the broadcasting sector in Wales. Goodwill and a commitment to the channel's success from all directions was therefore crucial. It proved to be a critical factor in its success during the trial period, as S4C unquestionably proved that broadcasting Welsh language programmes on one channel was the only solution regarding meeting the needs of the Welsh-speaking audience for a comprehensive service and significantly reducing tensions between the Welsh and non-Welsh speakers of Wales.

Individuals' innovations were equally vital; although each authority and staff member made a crucial and unique contribution, the ideas and experience of some in shaping the channel's operational structures were central to its success. Owen Edwards's appointment was significant for the fledgling channel as he brought considerable experience of managing a broadcasting service in Wales, he had overseen the development and growth of the Welsh language children's television service as well as the launch of BBC Radio Cymru and BBC Radio Wales during the 1970s. The status and reputation gained from those activities at the BBC gave the new enterprise credibility, and commentators and the Welsh community were able to believe that the dream of a Welsh language channel could be realised in an effective and lasting way. That credibility came not only from his vast professional experience but also from his lineage, since he was a member of a family that had contributed greatly to the prosperity of the Welsh language, who had done much to guarantee that it remained a living language. Also, Owen Edwards's relationship with the BBC in London and with officials in the broadcasting department at the Home Office was significant: this ensured that the channel was treated with respect.

Sir Goronwy Daniel's appointment also offered credibility to the channel, being a well-known name to the Welsh community, and having spent his career dealing with politicians and policy debate he possessed considerable diplomacy skills. Sir Goronwy Daniel's awareness and experience in the field of economics and statistics was also vital: it was his foresight that gave rise to the essential strategy that firmly rooted the channel in the economic prosperity of Wales. Although Sir Goronwy Daniel was the driving force behind this strategy, the enthusiasm of the channel's staff members to implement the plans, and Chris Grace in particular, who oversaw the creation of merchandise agreements based on S4C programmes, was key to ensuring the strategy's tremendous success during the trial period. They set about creating a reaction, side effects, building a reputation and making the channel relevant to modern Wales. The channel's ancillary activities through the Mentrau subsidiary contributed to that ethos of making the channel indispensable to the Welsh economy and an integral part of the image of Wales abroad. Such a strategy tied the prosperity of specific sectors and areas to the success of the channel, making it more difficult – if not impossible – to dissolve the channel without creating a negative impact on the country's wider economy.

Another important visionary was the first programme editor, Euryn Ogwen Williams. Before anyone else, he had seen the potential of the contribution that independent producers could make to the wider Welsh language programme provision. He, above anyone else, was responsible for promoting the case of independent producers to the relevant authorities as they considered how to meet the demand for more hours of Welsh language programming. Following his appointment, he promoted that vision internally while encouraging and urging the independent sector to grow and develop so that it could compete with the BBC and HTV and offer high-quality programmes to the channel. S4C's success was therefore the result of a combination of factors, partnerships, goodwill and the visions of key individuals – and these contributions were crucial as the channel entered its probationary period.

What is difficult to comprehend when looking back at the channel's early days is that it was initially set up as a 3-year experiment. S4C was not experimental in the same sense as C4, which was tasked with trying to provide a service that offered more variety and specialist programming for British audiences. Instead S4C was expected to set up a channel that might not necessarily exist after the probationary period was over. Rather than establish a small, flexible channel that could easily be dismantled or modified at the end of that period, the authority set up something that would be increasingly difficult for the government to eradicate. The threat of abolishing the experiment, however, influenced decisions and the way in which channel officials responded to different challenges. Chris Grace recalled that the preparatory period before the channel began broadcasting was challenging because of the tremendous pressure to succeed, but also because of the lack of confidence, amongst broadcasters in particular, that the initiative would be a success.[5]

That continuous threat and concern is further evidenced by the way in which viewing figures were handled and discussed by the authority and officers. The channel needed to attract respectable audiences, and although it was acknowledged that the channel would never achieve viewing figures that were comparable with the other channels, they were nonetheless obliged to attract a reasonable percentage of the Welsh-speaking audience. These considerations influenced the policy of producing popular programmes that would appeal to the widest possible audience to achieve healthy viewing figures. This policy was a success in the early months of broadcasting, but after the initial high viewing figures, which were not necessarily a realistic picture of the channel's audience, the inevitable collapse happened. The authority's concern about the review and the fate of the channel was exposed in the way it responded to the negative viewing figures: bulky reports were produced analysing the figures and the Broadcasters' Audience Research Board (BARB) were asked to review and reconsider its methods. This response was not disproportionate, but the channel was keen to ensure that the best possible picture could be drawn from the viewing figures, since they were published in the press, and were taken to measure the success or failure of the channel. The authority knew full well that these negative stories could have an impact on public opinion and, in turn, the outcome of the review.

Coupled with the need to appeal to the widest possible audience was the need to disprove all the prophets of doom and demonstrate without doubt that a comprehensive and quality service in Welsh could be maintained. The channel therefore sought to ensure that a wide range of programmes were commissioned and that the channel and its providers developed and produced ambitious programmes and series; they were determined to show that they could broadcast programmes that moved beyond the parochial. Their news strategy, covering major events beyond the borders of Wales in addition to local news, and the pattern developed for current affairs with the programme *Y Byd ar Bedwar* (The World on Four) and its in-depth coverage of international affairs, from Cuba to Ethiopia and from Wales to Argentina, was testament to that ambition. There was real doubt during the campaign and in the early days of the channel that there were too few actors, presenters and performers in Wales to meet the increase in provision, and the channel was acutely aware of the need to make it clear that there was no shortage. The 'same old faces' complaint was not completely eradicated, but the channel did provide an impetus for many young people to venture into a career in broadcasting or performing. These activities certainly demonstrated that those concerns, of there not being enough talent in Wales to sustain a Welsh language service, were unfounded.

The channel was obliged not to deprive the non-Welsh-speaking audience of too much C4 content and to reduce the complaints that plagued the broadcasters during the 1960s and 1970s. Since there was only a day between the launch of S4C and C4, there was no time for S4C to establish itself in the broadcasting landscape and in the viewing patterns of the Welsh audience before C4 began broadcasting. As a result, there was concern that publicity surrounding the launch of C4 might mislead the non-Welsh-speaking audience to think that attractive English language provision was being with-held due to the needs of the Welsh-speaking minority audience. To meet the Home Office's main requirement – to demonstrate that there were no significant calls to return to the two-channel pattern – S4C had to ensure that it did not infuriate the non-Welsh-speaking audience. The friendly relationship that existed between S4C and C4 meant that the Welsh language channel's officials had flexibility to schedule C4's programmes around their own: this guaranteed that the audience in Wales could watch most C4 programmes, although not at the same time as they were advertised in England. Letters of complaint about the timing of English language programmes continued to be sent, and when Welsh programmes with English subtitles were broadcast on the BBC in particular, the unpleasant feelings were resurrected. These examples clearly show that S4C was a salve to those pains and to the public expression of unfavourable comments about Welsh language programmes, but the channel was not a complete cure: these issues were not eliminated but rather transferred from two popular channels to one minority channel. S4C was not a perfect solution for broadcasting in Wales, but in the early 1980s there was no surplus of channels for distribution, so splitting the fourth channel between English and Welsh content was the only possible solution. The S4C Authority and its staff considered the result of the review and the continuity of the channel to be more of a priority than meticulously following the guidelines of the Broadcasting Act and the government's original ideas. The wording of the Act, which suggested the broadcasting of C4 programmes live in the off-peak hours according to that channel's schedule, was ignored, to avoid the creation of a Welsh language channel and service that would be a regional opt-out from C4: they realised very early on in the channel's history that this would not succeed in meeting the needs of the non-Welsh-speaking viewer, so they implemented a pattern that was much more likely to reduce tensions and provide the best service for the audience in Wales. Clearly, the review, along with the expectations of the audience, were at the forefront of the minds of the officials and the authority as they interpreted the spirit of the Act rather than following it word for word.

Due to the tremendous effort that went into fulfilling these aims, the Home Office review was a formality rather than an extremely detailed review of all of the channel's activities. To that end, and in line with the promise made by the Home Office, an assessment was made as to whether there was any evidence that audience members in Wales wished to return to the principle of broadcasting Welsh language programmes across multiple channels. This decision, arguably, meant that the outcome of the review was a *fait accompli* since the channel had become completely established in the viewing patterns of a large number of Welsh and mixed-language households, and had significantly reduced the number of complaints about deprivation and scheduling in comparison with the tempestuous sentiments expressed before the channel was established. This was a fair decision, but it could be argued that the lack of critical reflection given to the channel's wider activity in 1985 set a precedent for how the channel was treated until 2010, which has led, according to many commentators, to the troubles experienced by the channel in the early part of that decade.

In late 1985, having announced the result of the Home Office survey, the channel embarked on a new chapter in its history, full of certainty about its future. There were undisputed challenges during the trial period, but as the decade progressed the channel faced entirely new demands as it sought to build on the success of its early years. The Peacock Committee's recommendations and their impact on C4's approach to selling its own advertising would lead to a revolutionary change in the channel's funding pattern. Technological advances and the growth of satellite and multi-channel television would mean increased competition for the channel's output, and further struggles to ensure that the channel and its programmes remained contemporary and appealing to the Welsh-speaking audience. The rest of the decade would also see significant changes in the channel's commissioning pattern with HTV losing more ground to the independent producers as the dynamics and power of the Welsh production sector changed. There is a rich history to the channel's developments post-1985, which merit further investigation and study so we can fully understand and appreciate how the channel has evolved.

This volume shows how little academic and analytical research has been done on S4C over the last four decades. In the years leading up to 2010 there was an overwhelming silence over many of the channel's activities due to a fear that harsh criticism could endanger its existence. There was also silence amongst the broadcast sector and producers because of concern that publicly criticising any aspect of the channel would endanger livelihoods or reduce future commissions.[6] However, in the years since the publication of the Welsh version of this monograph in 2016, further academic studies have emerged on the production of specific genres, an independent review was conducted in 2017 led by Euryn Ogwen Williams on behalf of the DCMS, and the ubiquity of social media has meant that praise and criticism from the audience and commentators has been much more visible.[7] It is hoped that this study shows that lessons can be learnt from the rich history of the channel, which will further inspire new in-depth studies of the current and historical strengths and weaknesses of the channel, and contribute to a full understanding of the service provided by the establishment of Sianel Pedwar Cymru in 1981 and which continues to evolve in today's ever-changing media landscape.

Notes

Introduction

1 Access was granted to a copy of the contract between S4C and HTV, but it was not possible to gain access to other HTV company documents.
2 See the bibliography for a full list of interviews.
3 See, for example, Nicholas Crickhowell, *Westminster, Wales and Water* (Cardiff, 1999); Geraint Talfan Davies, *At Arm's Length* (Bridgend, 2008); John Davies, *Broadcasting and the BBC in Wales* (Cardiff, 1994); John Davies, *Hanes Cymru* (Llundain, 2007); Gwynfor Evans, *Bywyd Cymro* (Caernarfon, 1982); Ifan Gwynfil Evans, '"Drunk on Hopes and Ideals": The Failure of Wales Television, 1959–1963', *Llafur*, 7/2 (1997), 81–93; Rhys Evans, *Gwynfor Evans: Portrait of a Patriot* (Talybont, 2008); Jamie Medhurst, *A History of Independent Television in Wales* (Cardiff, 2010); Rt. Hon. Lord Roberts of Conwy, *Right From the Start: The Memoirs of Sir Wyn Roberts* (Cardiff, 2006); Robert Smith, 'Broadcasting and the Welsh Language', in Geraint H. Jenkins and Mari A. Williams (eds), *Let's Do Our Best for the Ancient Tongue: The Welsh Language in the Twentieth Century* (Cardiff, 2000), pp. 311–42; William Whitelaw, *The Whitelaw Memoirs* (London, 1989).
4 Elin Haf Gruffydd Jones, 'After 35 years of S4C, shouldn't Wales have responsibility for the Welsh language channel?', *The Conversation*, 1 November 2017, *https://theconversation.com/after-35-years-of-s4c-shouldnt-wales-have-responsibility-for-the-welsh-language-channel-86629* (accessed 6 January 2022).
5 Gruffydd Jones, 'After 35 years of S4C, shouldn't Wales have responsibility for the Welsh language channel?'.
6 Unknown author, 'BBC Alba Freeview date unveiled', *BBC News*, 23 May 2011, *https://www.bbc.co.uk/news/uk-scotland-highlands-islands-13479551* (accessed 6 January 2022).
7 There was correspondence between Owen Edwards and Whatarangi Winiata of the Aotearoa Broadcasting System Inc during 1985 and 1986.
8 Gruffydd Jones, 'After 35 years of S4C, shouldn't Wales have responsibility for the Welsh language channel?'.
9 £6.851 million was the DCMS contribution to S4C's budget in 2020/1. S4C, *Annual Report and Statement of Accounts for the 12 month period to 31 March 2021* (Carmarthen, 2021), p. 139.
10 S4C, *Annual Report and Statement of Accounts for the 12 month period to 31 March 2021* p. 139. During the 2020–1 financial year the DCMS also paid £15 million as grant in aid to S4C due to changes in its VAT status. The change in VAT status allows S4C to 'recover the VAT paid on purchases used to support its non-business activity of free to air public service broadcasting', and allows it the same VAT status as the BBC. HMRC, 'Amendment to the VAT refund scheme to include the S4C television

channel', *https://www.gov.uk/government/publications/amendment-to-the-vat-refund-scheme-to-include-the-s4c-television-channel/amendment-to-the-vat-refund-scheme-to-include-the-s4c-television-channel* (accessed 5 January 2022).

11 Unknown author, 'Culture Secretary announces £7.5 million 'extra' for S4C but long term future is unclear', *Nation.Cymru*, 17 January 2022, *https://nation.cymru/news/culture-secretary-announces-7-5m-extra-for-s4c-but-long-term-future-is-unclear/* (accessed 15 February 2022). The settlement will rise with CPI inflation from 1 April 2024 to 31 March 2028. Nadine Dorries, 'Letter from Secretary of State to S4C on Final Determination of the 2022 licence fee settlement', 21 January 2022, *https://www.gov.uk/government/publications/bbc-and-s4c-final-2022-licence-fee-settlement-letters/letter-from-secretary-of-state-to-s4c-on-final-determination-of-the-2022-licence-fee-settlement* (accessed 25 July 2022).

12 Unknown author, 'Abolishing license fee 'existential threat' to the future of the Welsh language says top academic', *Nation.Cymru*, 17 January 2022, *https://nation.cymru/culture/abolishing-license-fee-existential-threat-to-the-future-of-the-welsh-language-says-academic/* (accessed 15 February 2022)

13 Unknown author, 'Abolishing license fee 'existential threat' to the future of the Welsh language says top academic'

14 S4C/BBC, *Partnership, Funding and Accountability Agreement between the BBC and S4C* (November 2017), p. 9.

15 In 2017 it was agreed between the BBC and S4C that there was a fundamental difference between the responsibilities of the BBC Trust as a non-executive regulatory body and those of a unitary board; therefore, there would not be a standing requirement for the BBC Trustee in Wales to sit on the S4C unitary board. S4C, 'S4C: Pushing the Boundaries: Multi-Platform Welsh Language Media Service', *https://www.s4c.cymru/gwthiorffiniau/index.html* (accessed 5 January 2022).

16 The pattern for C4 was different to S4C since the chief executives of three ITV network companies sat on their board.

17 Even though there was no direct representative of the ITV network on S4C's Authority, there was a representative from the IBA, but they were only one amongst many and therefore could not overly influence or push one organisation's ideas and perspective on the channel.

18 BBC/S4C, *Cytundeb Gweithredu S4C* (Caerdydd, January 2013); S4C/BBC, *Partnership, Funding and Accountability Agreement between the BBC and S4C.*

19 S4C/BBC, *Partnership, Funding and Accountability Agreement between the BBC and S4C*, p. 11; S4C, 'S4C broadcasts from Central Square', *https://www.s4c.cymru/en/press/post/41474/s4c-broadcasts-from-central-square* (accessed 5 January 2022).

20 S4C, *Annual Report and Statement of Accounts for the 12 month period to 31 March 2015* (Cardiff, 2015), p. 54; S4C, *Annual Report and Statement of Accounts for the 12 month period to 31 March 2021*, p. 75.

21 S4C, *Annual Report and Statement of Accounts for the 12 month period to 31 March 2015*, p. 54. The cost per hour of broadcast programmes also decreased 35 per cent from £16,400 to £10,800.

22 S4C, *Annual Report and Statement of Accounts for the 12 month period to 31 March 2021*, pp. 76–7, 143.

23 Elain Price, 'Llywio'r llong drwy'r dymestl', *Barn*, 630/631 (July/August 2015), 17. Robin Wilkinson, 'Will S4C be fit for the future?' *Senedd Research*, 13 April 2018, *https://research.senedd.wales/research-articles/will-s4c-be-fit-for-the-future/* (accessed 5 January 2022).
24 S4C, *Annual Report and Statement of Accounts for the 12 month period to 31 March 2021*, p. 143.
25 S4C, *Annual Report and Statement of Accounts for the 12 month period to 31 March 2021*, p. 46. The figures for 2020–1 are up from a low of 142,000 in 2019–20.
26 S4C, *Annual Report and Statement of Accounts for the 12 month period to 31 March 2021*, p. 46. The figures for 2020–1 are up from 306,000 in 2019–20.
27 S4C, *Annual Report and Statement of Accounts for the 12 month period to 31 March 2021*, p. 46. There was a significant increase between 2019–20 and 2020–1 from 396,000 to 502,000.
28 S4C, *Annual Report and Statement of Accounts for the 12 month period to 31 March 2021*, p. 48.
29 S4C, *Annual Report and Statement of Accounts for the 12 month period to 31 March 2021*, p. 48.
30 OFCOM, *Small Screen: Big Debate – Recommendations to Government on the future of Public Service Media*, 15 July 2021, https://www.smallscreenbigdebate.co.uk/__data/assets/pdf_file/0023/221954/statement-future-of-public-service-media.pdf (accessed 5 January 2022), p. 3.
31 JP Kelly and Julie Münter Lassen, '100 years on: Reinventing Public Service Media for the Streaming Age', *CST Online*, 26 November 2021, *https://cstonline.net/100-years-on-reinventing-public-service-media-for-the-streaming-age-by-jp-kelly-and-julie-muenter-lassen/* (accessed 5 January 2022).
32 Kelly and Münter Lassen, '100 years on: Reinventing Public Service Media for the Streaming Age'; OFCOM, *Small Screen: Big Debate – Recommendations to Government on the future of Public Service Media*, p. 3.
33 S4C, *Annual Report and Statement of Accounts for the 12 month period to 31 March 2021*, p. 55.
34 S4C, *Annual Report and Statement of Accounts for the 12 month period to 31 March 2021*, p. 61.

Chapter 1

1 Maggie Brown, *A Licence to be Different: The Story of Channel 4* (London, 2007), p. 10.
2 For more on this, see Simon Blanchard 'Where do new channels come from?', in S. Blanchard and D. Morley (eds), *What's this Channel Four? An alternative report* (London, 1982), p. 6, and Paul Bonner with Lesley Aston, *Independent Television in Britain: Volume 6. New Developments in Independent Television 1981–92: Channel 4, TV-am, Cable and Satellite* (Basingstoke, 2003), p. 3.
3 The groups who opposed the idea of forming ITV2 were the TV4 Campaign, which included individuals such as media critics, journalists, MPs and individuals from the advertising industry; the Association of Broadcasting Staffs (ABS), the union which represented BBC staff, and the Association of Cinematograph, Television and Allied

Technicians (ACTT), which represented the majority of technicians who worked for ITV; Blanchard, 'Where do new channels come from?', pp. 8–10.

4 Anthony Smith had been a producer of current affairs programmes at the BBC in the 1960s, then a fellow of St Antony's College, Oxford, before being appointed director of the British Film Institute and then president of Magdalen College, Oxford; Brown, *A Licence to be Different*, p. 13.

5 Brown, *A Licence to be Different*, p. 16.

6 For further discussion and analysis of Anthony Smith's ideas for a National Television Foundation, see Blanchard, 'Where do new channels come from?'; Bonner with Aston, *Independent Television in Britain: Volume 6*, pp. 3–35; Brown, *A Licence to be Different*, pp. 10–19.

7 John Davies, *Broadcasting and the BBC in Wales* (Cardiff, 1994), p. 288; Cymdeithas yr Iaith, *S4C Pwy Dalodd Amdani? Hanes Ymgyrch Ddarlledu Cymdeithas yr Iaith – Argraffiad Cyntaf* (Aberystwyth, 1985), p. 13.

8 'Ein bod yn hawlio gan y Llywodraeth sianel genedlaethol i Gymru ar gyfer rhaglenni Cymraeg ar y teledu, yn ychwanegol at y sianel ar gyfer y Cymry di-Gymraeg, a thonfedd ar gyfer rhaglenni Cymraeg ar y radio'; Cymdeithas yr Iaith, *S4C Pwy Dalodd Amdani?*, p. 13. Unless otherwise noted, translations are those of the author.

9 Cymdeithas yr Iaith, *Darlledu yng Nghymru: cyfoethogi neu ddinistrio bywyd cenedlaethol?* (Aberystwyth, 1971); Emyr Humphreys, *Diwylliant Cymru a'r Cyfryngau Torfol* (Aberystwyth, 1977); Cymdeithas yr Iaith, *Teledu Cymru i Bobl Cymru* (Aberystwyth, 1977); Emyr Humphreys, *Bwrdd Datblygu Teledu Cymraeg* (Aberystwyth, 1979).

10 Dylan Phillips, 'The History of the Welsh Language Society 1962–1998', in G. H. Jenkins and M. A. Williams (eds), *'Let's Do Our Best for the Ancient Tongue': The Welsh Language in the Twentieth Century* (Cardiff, 2000), p. 479.

11 Phillips, 'The History of the Welsh Language Society 1962–1998', p. 479. For further details about direct action undertaken by Cymdeithas yr Iaith, the reasons behind the action and who was imprisoned, see Cymdeithas yr Iaith, *S4C Pwy Dalodd Amdani?*.

12 Dylan Phillips, *Trwy ddulliau chwyldro . . .? Hanes Cymdeithas yr Iaith Gymraeg 1962–1992* (Llandysul, 1998), p. 38.

13 'Gwt dan staer y bedwaredd sianel'; *S4C yn 20 Mlwydd Oed* (prod. Vaughan Hughes, Ffilmiau'r Bont, broadcast on S4C, 31 October 2002).

14 Davies, *Broadcasting and the BBC in Wales*, p. 298.

15 Davies, *Broadcasting and the BBC in Wales*, p. 298.

16 'Pan fydda i'n gweld Mr George Thomas a Mr Leo Abse . . . yn rhuthro i gofleidio Dafydd Iwan, rwyf am awgrymu mai dim ond y mwyaf *naive* o blant dynion fyddai'n barod i gredu mai yr un yw eu cymhellion'; Davies, *Broadcasting and the BBC in Wales*, p. 293.

17 *Report of the Committee on Broadcasting Coverage. Cmnd. 5774* (London, 1974), pp. 1–2. Members of the committee were Sir Stewart Crawford (chair), James Grew, Ivor Morten, Gabrielle Pike, Ethel M. Reenie, Eifion Roberts and Professor John C. West.

18 *Report of the Committee on Broadcasting Coverage. Cmnd. 5774*, p. 39.

19 *Report of the Committee on Broadcasting Coverage. Cmnd. 5774*, p. 70.

20 *Report of the Committee on Broadcasting Coverage. Cmnd. 5774*, p. 41.
21 *Report of the Committee on Broadcasting Coverage. Cmnd. 5774*, p. 41.
22 '[N]ad oedd llawer o awydd am weithredu uniongyrchol difrifol . . . pan fod pawb o dan yr argraff fod buddugoliaeth fawr wedi'i hennill'; Alwyn D. Rees, 'Nodiadau Golygyddol', *Barn*, 145 (November/December 1974), 558–9; Cymdeithas yr Iaith, *S4C Pwy Dalodd Amdani?*, p. 45.
23 *Report of the Committee on the Future of Broadcasting. Cmnd. 6753* (London, 1977), p. 413.
24 Davies, *Broadcasting and the BBC*, p. 326.
25 Davies, *Broadcasting and the BBC*, p. 326.
26 Davies, *Broadcasting and the BBC*, p. 332.
27 *Report of the Committee on the Future of Broadcasting. Cmnd. 6753*, p. 482.
28 Davies, *Broadcasting and the BBC in Wales*, p. 335.
29 *Report of the Committee on the Future of Broadcasting. Cmnd. 6753*, p. 483; emphasis added.
30 Davies, *Broadcasting and the BBC in Wales*, p. 335.
31 '[Y]mddengys mai nod yr Adroddiad oedd dod o hyd i ddull o gadw darlledu Cymraeg a Chymreig o fewn rhigolau'r peirianwaith Prydeinig'; Cymdeithas yr Iaith, *S4C Pwy Dalodd Amdani?*, p. 60.
32 *Report of the Committee on the Future of Broadcasting. Cmnd. 6753*, p. 414.
33 Davies, *Broadcasting and the BBC in Wales*, p. 335. The Trevelyan working group is also known as the Littler working group, since Mrs S. Littler took over from Mr D. J. Trevelyan as chair in January 1978.
34 *Report of the Working Party on the Welsh Television Fourth Channel Project* (London, 1978), p. 53.
35 *Report of the Working Party on the Welsh Television Fourth Channel Project*, p. 44.
36 Davies, *Broadcasting and the BBC in Wales*, p. 338.
37 *Report of the Working Party on the Welsh Television Fourth Channel Project*, p. 40.
38 *Report of the Working Party on the Welsh Television Fourth Channel Project*, p. 18.
39 *Report of the Working Party on the Welsh Television Fourth Channel Project*, p. 16.
40 *Report of the Working Party on the Welsh Television Fourth Channel Project*, pp. 40–1; Davies, *Broadcasting and the BBC in Wales*, p. 338.
41 Davies, *Broadcasting and the BBC in Wales*, p. 339.
42 Home Office, *Broadcasting White Paper 1978, Cmnd. 7294* (London, 1978), p. 26.
43 Home Office, *Broadcasting, Cmnd. 7294*, p. 25.
44 Home Office, *Broadcasting, Cmnd. 7294*, p. 25.
45 Alwyn Roberts, 'The BBC and the Welsh Fourth Channel Debate – A Personal Note' (BBC Wales Archive, File 3573 – 'S4C 1981–7'), p. 1.
46 Roberts, 'The BBC and the Welsh Fourth Channel Debate – A Personal Note', p. 2. Unfortunately it appears that the letters of viewers have not been kept together in the BBC Wales archive, and they have more than likely been filed across the collection.
47 Davies, *Broadcasting and the BBC in Wales*, p. 327.
48 Davies, *Broadcasting and the BBC in Wales*, pp. 325–6. Not all members of the BBC Wales management team agreed with the idea of transferring Welsh programmes to a new channel. One of the most prominent members to disagree was

Gareth Price, then deputy head of programmes. Gareth Price did not air these opinions publicly, but in a private meeting; however, his comments were made public in an article in *The Guardian*.

49 Davies, *Broadcasting and the BBC in Wales*, pp. 333–4.

50 *Report of the Committee on the Future of Broadcasting. Cmnd. 6753*, p. 155.

51 *Report of the Committee on the Future of Broadcasting. Cmnd.6753*, p. 155.

52 Cymdeithas yr Iaith, *S4C Pwy Dalodd Amdani?*, p. 62.

53 Geraint Talfan Davies, *At Arms Length* (Bridgend, 2008), p. 70.

54 The opinion of the IBA's Welsh committee had been unstable since there was no consensus amongst the members. They provided evidence to the Crawford Committee in 1974 suggesting that the BBC and the IBA should share the fourth channel in order to broadcast Welsh language programmes. By the time of Annan's discussions in 1977, the Welsh committee's conviction was eroding, as its evidence indicated the intention to reconsider its support if the fourth channel was not given satisfactory terms. One of these conditions was for the fourth channel in Wales to start broadcasting two or three years ahead of the rest of the UK. Following the election of the Conservatives in 1979, it became clear to members that this condition could not be met, the plans of the OBA had fallen by the wayside, and that the fourth channel would be given to the IBA. It therefore voted at their meeting on 29 June 1979 to support the principle of broadcasting Welsh language programmes on two channels provided that the range of Welsh language programmes improved, that the programmes would be broadcast at appropriate times, that the discussions between the BBC, IBA and HTV should continue, that a commitment to promote Welsh language programming across the channels be put in place, and that the necessary resources and investment to ensure the success of a Welsh language service across two channels be established. JMPC, IBA Papers, *Minutes of the One Hundred and Thirty First Meeting of the Wales Committee*, 29 June 1979, pp. 2–5, Welsh Office, Letter from Dame Plowden to William Whitelaw, 6 July 1979, *www.walesoffice.gov.uk/2005/06/16/establishment-of-S4C-1979-81/* (accessed August 2010; by December 2010 these documents were no longer available on the Welsh Office website).

55 Rhys Evans, *Gwynfor: A Portrait of a Patriot* (Talybont, 2008), pp. 420–1.

56 'Y mae awgrymiadau'r Llywodraeth mewn cytgord a [*sic*] barn HTV Cymru, barn a fu'n rhan o bolisi'r cwmni er dechrau'r trafodaethau ar y bedwaredd sianel, er ei bod hi'n wir i ddweud fod HTV yn barod fel y dylem fod, i gydweithio i weithredu cynlluniau y Llywodraeth flaenorol sef trosglwyddo holl raglenni Cymraeg HTV a'r BBC ar un sianel. Er dweud hyn ni chredodd y cwmni erioed mai dyma fyddai'r dull gorau o weithredu. Nid yw HTV wedi 'newid ei feddwl' ynglŷn â'r mater'; HTV Cymru, *Y Bedwaredd Sianel yng Nghymru: Datganiad gan HTV Cymru* (Llandysul, 1979), p. 18.

57 Alwyn Roberts, 'Some Political Implications of S4C', *Transactions of the Honourable Society of Cymmrodorion* (1989), 219.

58 William Whitelaw, *The Whitelaw Memoirs* (London, 1989), pp. 220–1. Evidence from other authors does not support this statement. Alwyn Roberts states that these doubts started in the Home Office; Roberts, 'Some Political Implications of S4C', 224. Rhys Evans also suggests that there were many influences on the final decision,

including Dame Littler, head of the Home Office broadcasting department, who had convinced Whitelaw 'that the technical difficulties inherent in creating a new channel were insurmountable'; Evans, *Portrait of a Patriot*, p. 397. Evans also refers to the fiery correspondence between the Welsh Office and the Home Office, which shows without doubt that not all of Whitelaw's Welsh colleagues agreed with him; Evans, *Portrait of a Patriot*, p. 399. Wyn Roberts also revealed that the influence of civil servants such as Dame Littler and 'Willie Whitelaw's infinite capacity to vacillate' were the reasons behind the U-turn; Rt. Hon. Lord Roberts of Conwy, *Right From the Start: The Memoirs of Sir Wyn Roberts* (Cardiff, 2006), pp. 130–1.

59 Roberts, 'Some Political Implications of S4C', 219.

60 Lord Roberts of Conwy, *Right From the Start*, p. 131.

61 One of the most prominent actions during this period was the switching off of the Pencarreg mast by Meredydd Evans, Pennar Davies and Ned Thomas, three prominent members of the Welsh community; Evans, *Portrait of a Patriot*, pp. 403–4; Cymdeithas yr Iaith, *S4C Pwy Dalodd Amdani?*, pp. 74–84.

62 Evans, *Portrait of a Patriot*, p. 402; Cymdeithas yr Iaith, *S4C Pwy Dalodd Amdani?*, pp. 74–84.

63 Evans, *Portrait of a Patriot*, p. 405. There is detailed discussion of Plaid Cymru's efforts and the efforts of other organisations such as Cymdeithas yr Iaith to revitalise the campaign in Rhys Evans's monograph, and as such, I have not gone into the same detail here; Evans, *Portrait of a Patriot*, pp. 397–411.

64 Evans, *Portrait of a Patriot*, p. 406; Cymdeithas yr Iaith, *S4C Pwy Dalodd Amdani?*, p. 77.

65 *Hansard*, House of Commons, 24 June 1980, col. 395.

66 *Hansard*, House of Commons, 18 February 1980, col. 95.

67 *Broadcasting Bill, 2961, Part II – Provision of Second Television Service by the Authority* (London, 1980), p. i.

68 *Broadcasting Bill, 2961, Part II – Provision of Second Television Service by the Authority*, p. iv.

69 *Hansard*, House of Commons, 18 February 1980, col. 96.

70 *Hansard*, House of Commons, 18 February 1980, col. 97.

71 *Broadcasting Bill, 2961, A Bill Intitulated* (London, 1980), p. 17.

72 *Hansard*, House of Commons, 24 June 1980, col. 392.

73 Evans, *Portrait of a Patriot*, p. 396.

74 Evans, *Portrait of a Patriot*, p. 409.

75 Evans, *Portrait of a Patriot*, p. 408.

76 Evans, *Portrait of a Patriot*, pp. 412–14.

77 'Ychydig iawn o enwau oedd i lawr ar gyfer y bws o Aberystwyth i Lundain, ond y noson gynt, wedi clywed y cyhoeddiad ar y teledu, fe lanwodd y papur o enwau at y bws o fewn awr'; Cymdeithas yr Iaith, *S4C Pwy Dalodd Amdani?*, p. 87.

78 Evans, *Portrait of a Patriot*, p. 419.

79 Evans, *Portrait of a Patriot*, p. 419; Lord Roberts of Conwy, *Right from the Start*, p. 133.

80 Evans, *Portrait of a Patriot*, pp. 415–27; Lord Roberts of Conwy, *Right From the Start*, pp. 132–8; Roberts, 'Some Political Implications of S4C', 220–4.

81 Evans, *Portrait of a Patriot*, p. 418; Lord Roberts of Conwy, *Right From the Start*, p. 132.

82 Welsh Office, *Note of a Meeting – Fourth Channel/Welsh Language – Broadcasting Bill*, 10 July 1980, *www.walesoffice.gov.uk/2005/06/16/establishment-of-S4C-1979-81/* (accessed August 2010; by December 2010 these documents were no longer available on the Welsh Office website); Evans, *Portrait of a Patriot*, p. 418; Roberts, 'Some Political Implications of S4C', 220–1.

83 Welsh Office, *Note of a Meeting – Fourth Channel/Welsh Language – Broadcasting Bill*, 10 July 1980, p. 1. William Whitelaw was not completely confident that Gwynfor Evans would accept any compromise from the government; in a meeting between himself and Nicholas Edwards only three days before the meeting with the broadcasters, Whitelaw wondered: 'if there was a danger that Mr Gwynfor Evans would reject his gesture and continue with his intended fast or indeed find something else to fast about.' Welsh Office, *Secretary of State's Meeting with the Home Secretary to discuss the Fourth Channel/Welsh Language – Broadcasting Bill*, *www.walesoffice.gov.uk/2005/06/16/establishment-of-S4C-1979-81/* (accessed August 2010; by December 2010 these documents were no longer available on the Welsh Office website), p. 1.

84 Welsh Office, *Note of a Meeting – Fourth Channel/Welsh Language – Broadcasting Bill*, 10 July 1980, p. 1.

85 Welsh Office, *No Title – discussion note for meeting*, 28 May 1980, *www.walesoffice.gov.uk/2005/06/16/establishment-of-S4C-1979-81/* (accessed August 2010; by December 2010 these documents were no longer available on the Welsh Office website).

86 *Hansard*, 24 June 1980, col. 362–70.

87 Roberts, 'Some Political Implications of S4C', 221. It could be argued, following a detailed study of the internal negotiations of the Welsh Office and the Home Office on the second compromise, whether Welsh representatives were too hasty to reject the concept of a co-ordinating committee. One civil servant believed that it would be inevitable that if such a committee were established it would also have to take over English language broadcasting responsibilities in Wales. If so, given the campaigners' calls in the 1970s and the calls made today to devolve broadcasting, it could be argued that the principle was sacrificed on the altar of a separate channel. Welsh office, *Note of Meeting between Secretary of State for Wales and Home Secretary*, 7 July 1980, *www.walesoffice.gov.uk/2005/06/16/establishment-of-S4C-1979-81/* (accessed August 2010; by December 2010 these documents were no longer available on the Welsh Office website), p. 2.

88 Evans, *Portrait of a Patriot*, p. 420; NLW, Sir Goronwy Daniel, Box 3, Letter from Emyr Jenkins to Goronwy Daniel, 12 August 1980.

89 Evans, *Portrait of a Patriot*, p. 424. The Court of the National Eisteddfod was not the only organisation that discussed sending a delegation to Westminster. A letter from G. O. Williams was sent to Goronwy Daniel a week before the eisteddfod after receiving a request from Ieuan S. Jones and Noel A. Davies of the Welsh Council of Churches to arrange a delegation to see the prime minister. The names discussed to form the delegation were Goronwy Daniel, Cennydd (this is

presumed to be Cennydd Traherne, the Lord Lieutenant of Glamorganshire) and George Wright, secretary of the Transport Workers Union. NLW, Sir Goronwy Daniel Collection, Box 3, Letter from G. O. Williams to Goronwy Daniel, 24 July 1980.

90 NLW, Sir Goronwy Daniel Collection, Box 3, Letter from Cledwyn Hughes to Goronwy Daniel, 20 August 1980; Draft of a letter from Goronwy Daniel to Cledwyn Hughes, no date; Letter from Cledwyn Hughes to Goronwy Daniel, 28 August 1980; Letter from G. O. Williams to Cledwyn Hughes, 1 September 1980; Draft of a letter from Goronwy Daniel to Cledwyn Hughes, 5 September 1980. There was also correspondence between Gwynfor Evans and Goronwy Daniel, since Gwynfor was concerned that Goronwy Daniel had misunderstood his point of view on compromise. Gwynfor Evans stated clearly in his letter that he was unwilling to consider any compromise short of a separate channel; Letter from Gwynfor Evans, Islaw'r Dref, Dolgellau, to Goronwy Daniel, no date.

91 NLW, Sir Goronwy Daniel Collection, Box 3, Letter from Cledwyn Hughes to Goronwy Daniel, 28 August 1980.

92 '[R]hwymo draed a dwylo ganddo chwaith.'; Letter from Cledwyn Hughes to Goronwy Daniel, 28 August 1980.

93 Letter from Cledwyn Hughes to Goronwy Daniel, 28 August 1980; NLW, Sir Goronwy Daniel, Box 3, Letter from G. O. Williams to Cledwyn Hughes, 1 September 1980.

94 NLW, Sir Goronwy Daniel Collection, Box 3, Letter from Cledwyn Hughes to Goronwy Daniel, 28 August 1980.

95 'Nid plygu i fygythion yw'r hyn a ofynnwn gan y Llywodraeth ond cydnabod wedi pwyso holl ystyriaethau'r sefyllfa bresennol eu bod wedi gwneud camgymeriad. Ennill ac nid colli urddas y mae pwy bynnag sydd ddigon gwrol i wneud hynny'; NLW, Sir Goronwy Daniel Collection, Box 3, Letter from G. O. Williams to Cledwyn Hughes, 1 September 1980, p. 2.

96 Leopold Kohr, 'Welsh Television', *The Times*, 20 August 1980, 13.

97 NLW, Sir Goronwy Daniel Collection, Box 3, Draft of a letter from Goronwy Daniel to Cledwyn Hughes, 5 September 1980; Welsh Office, *Notes on the meeting held at the Home Office*, 10 September 1980, *www.walesoffice.gov.uk/2005/06/16/establishment-of-S4C-1979-81/* (accessed August 2010; by December 2010 these documents were no longer available on the Welsh Office website).

98 Roberts, 'Some Political Implications of S4C', 223.

99 NLW, Sir Goronwy Daniel Collection, Box 3, Home Office News Release, *Welsh Language Television*, 10 September 1980. Dafydd Jones-Williams was a solicitor by occupation, a former Merionethshire Clerk of the Peace and a former Local Administration Commissioner for Wales.

100 Roberts, 'Some Political Implications of S4C', 221; Evans, *Portrait of a Patriot*, p. 418.

101 Whitelaw, *The Whitelaw Memoirs*, p. 94.

102 BBC Wales Archive, Cardiff, Appendix by BBC Wales Management, *The Placing of Welsh Language Programmes on BBC-2*.

103 Roberts, 'Some Political Implications of S4C', 222.

104 *The Placing of Welsh Language Programmes on BBC-2*, p. 5.
105 *The Placing of Welsh Language Programmes on BBC-2*, p. 5. It is suggested in the document that children's programmes would be displaced during the cricket, golf, tennis seasons, etc.
106 *The Placing of Welsh Language Programmes on BBC-2*, p. 6.
107 Welsh Office, *No Title, re. Welsh Language Television*, 1 August 1980, *www.walesoffice.gov.uk/2005/06/16/establishment-of-S4C-1979-81/* (accessed August 2010; by December 2010 these documents were no longer available on the Welsh Office website).
108 Welsh Office, *Note of meeting between Secretary of State for Wales, PUSS Wales and Officials*, 6 August 1980, *www.walesoffice.gov.uk/2005/06/16/establishment-of-S4C-1979-81/* (accessed August 2010; by December 2010 these documents were no longer available on the Welsh Office website), p. 1.
109 Welsh Office, *Note of meeting between Secretary of State for Wales, PUSS Wales and Officials*, 6 August 1980, p. 1.
110 Welsh Office, Letter from Wyn Roberts to Nicholas Edwards, 9 August 1980; Welsh Office, *No Title re. Events in SoS's absence*, 9 August 1980, *www.walesoffice.gov.uk/2005/06/16/establishment-of-S4C-1979-81/* (accessed August 2010; by December 2010 these documents were no longer available on the Welsh Office website).
111 'Mr Whitelaw does a W-Turn', *The Times*, 18 September 1980, 15.
112 Arts Reporter, 'Welsh TV plans incorporated in Broadcasting Bill', *The Times*, 2 October 1980, 3; Home Office, *Note of a meeting re. Welsh Language Broadcasting*, 16 September 1980, *www.walesoffice.gov.uk/2005/06/16/establishment-of-S4C-1979-81/* (accessed August 2010; by December 2010 these documents were no longer available on the Welsh Office website).
113 'Hope that Welsh Television will not be expensive', *The Times*, 9 October 1980, 23.
114 *Hansard*, House of Commons, 10 November 1980, col. 53–74.
115 *Hansard*, House of Commons, 10 November 1980, col. 39.
116 *Hansard*, House of Commons, 10 November 1980, col. 39.
117 *Hansard*, House of Commons, 10 November 1980, col. 58.
118 *Hansard*, House of Commons, 10 November 1980, col. 75–8.
119 Welsh Office, *No title re. Welsh Fourth Channel Authority. Draft letter from Home Secretary*, 30 September 1980, *www.walesoffice.gov.uk/2005/06/16/establishment-of-S4C-1979-81/* (accessed August 2010; by December 2010 these documents were no longer available on the Welsh Office website).
120 *Broadcasting Act 1981, Chapter 68* (London, 1981), p. 49.
121 *Broadcasting Act 1981, Chapter 68*, pp. 13–14.
122 *Broadcasting Act 1981, Chapter 68*, pp. 13–14.
123 *Broadcasting Act 1981, Chapter 68*, p. 50.
124 *Broadcasting Act 1981, Chapter 68*, p. 50.
125 *Hansard*, House of Commons, 10 November 1980, col. 60.
126 *Broadcasting Act 1981, Chapter 68*, p. 49.
127 *Broadcasting Act 1981, Chapter 68*, p. 49.

128 *Broadcasting Act 1981, Chapter 68*, p. 49.
129 *Hansard*, House of Commons, 10 November 1980, col. 77.
130 Author's interview with Rev. Dr Alwyn Roberts, Tregarth, 24 May 2007.

Chapter 2

1 R. Gerallt Jones, 'Mawr alw am gyhoedd effro a llafar', *Y Faner*, 16 January 1981, 6.
2 Jones, 'Mawr alw am gyhoedd effro a llafar', 6
3 NLW, Sir Goronwy Daniel Collection, Box 3, Goronwy Daniel, *The Lord Mayor's Conference in Television in Wales*, 3 July 1973. Sir Goronwy Daniel had been supportive of the activists during the campaign to secure the channel: Ned Thomas remembers when he was a lecturer at the University of Wales College, Aberystwyth, that he received a supportive note from the principal the morning after the demonstration at Pencarreg mast, *Wythnos Gwilym Owen* (BBC Radio Cymru, 25 October 2010).
4 Sir Goronwy would declare his ignorance of the television sector quite openly, see the S4C Authority's evidence to the WASC, *Second Report from the Committee on Welsh Affairs: Broadcasting in the Welsh Language and the Implications for Welsh and Non-Welsh Speaking Viewers and Listeners – Volume II* (London, 1981), p. 518.
5 Meic Stephens, 'Sir Goronwy Daniel', 20 January 2003, *www.independent.co.uk/news/obituaries/sir-goronwy-daniel-602239.html* (accessed October 2008).
6 'Ar Garlam – Tomos Gee Gee', *Y Faner*, 23 January 1981, 3. The fact that Lord Hooson was part of the Hafren Consortium which applied against HTV for an ITV franchise in Wales and the west of England in 1980 may have counted against his appointment. Author's interview with the Rev. Dr Alwyn Roberts, Tregarth, 24 May 2007; author's interview with Dr Glyn Tegai Hughes, Tregynon, 31 January 2007.
7 Rhys Evans, *Gwynfor: A Portrait of a Patriot* (Talybont, 2008), p. 431.
8 Stephens, 'Sir Goronwy Daniel'.
9 *Hansard*, House of Commons, 10 November 1980, col. 39.
10 Rev. Dr. Alwyn Roberts was appointed as the BBC's governor in Wales in 1979, he was a minister with the Presbyterian Church and principal of the Extramural Studies Department at the University of Wales College, Bangor; John Davies, *Broadcasting and the BBC in Wales* (Cardiff, 1994), p. 340.
11 Professor Huw Morris-Jones was appointed the Welsh member of the IBA in 1976, he had also been a professor at the Sociology Department at the University of Wales College, Bangor until 1979; unknown author, 'Pwy ddaw i'r swydd?', *Y Cymro*, 23 February 1982.
12 As well as being a member of the C4 management board Dr Glyn Tegai Hughes was the warden of Gregynog, a University of Wales residential centre on the outskirts of Newtown. He was also Alwyn Roberts's predecessor as governor of the BBC in Wales (1971–9); Davies, *Broadcasting and the BBC in Wales*, pp. 291–2. Glyn Tegai Hughes believed that his appointment to the authority was not due to his role on the C4 management board, which was a happy coincidence. He believed that this was done in order to avoid assuming that a member of the C4 management board would have a place on the authority for years to come; author's interview with Dr Glyn Tegai Hughes, Tregynon, 31 January 2007.

13 Author's interview with the Rev. Dr Alwyn Roberts, Tregarth, 24 May 2007. The government was equally late in the day in appointing the chairman of the authority: Alwyn Roberts recalls that he contacted Sir Goronwy Daniel after his discussion with the Home Office as the officials had named him as chairman. Sir Goronwy Daniel's response was to declare that he had not yet confirmed that he would take up the post!

14 'BBC controller to be director of Wales 4th', *The Stage and Television Today*, 19 March 1981. See the appendix for a complete list of the members of the authority during the trial period.

15 *Second Report from the Committee on Welsh Affairs – Volume II*, p. 510.

16 *Second Report from the Committee on Welsh Affairs – Volume II*, p. 510.

17 *Second Report from the Committee on Welsh Affairs: Broadcasting in the Welsh Language and the Implications for Welsh and Non-Welsh Speaking Viewers and Listeners – Volume I* (London, 1981), p. xxiii.

18 *Second Report from the Committee on Welsh Affairs – Volume I*, p. xxiii. This recommendation was ignored, since in 1982 Gwilym Peregrine, Professor Huw Morris Jones's successor, was appointed to the authority.

19 Dr Jamie Medhurst Personal Collection (JMPC), IBA Papers, *Minutes of the Hundred and Forty Ninth Meeting of the Wales Advisory Committee*, 20 October 1981, p. 3.

20 *Hansard*, House of Commons, 10 November 1980, col. 58.

21 The authority was criticised by the WASC for not having a woman amongst its membership during the S4C Authority's first visit to give evidence to the committee. *Second Report from the Committee on Welsh Affairs – Volume II*, p. 511. This pattern changed in 1984 when Ken Jones retired from the authority and Eleri Wynne Jones was selected as the only female member of the authority. Professor Elan Closs Stephens would become chair of the authority (1998–2006), changing the patriarchal pattern completely.

22 '[B]arod i ymaflyd yn y swydd gydag egni a brwdfrydedd ynghyd â'r doethineb hwnnw sydd mor nodweddiadol ohono ac a fydd yn gwbl angenrheidiol yn ystod cyfnod sefydlu'r gwasanaeth'; 'Golygyddol', *Barn*, February 1981, 44. Unless otherwise noted, translations are those of the author.

23 This was not the first time the authority had met, since they had met previously at the BBC in Cardiff to record a discussion for John Morgan's *Articles* programme, which was broadcast on 30 January 1981. All members of the authority were present, except for D. Ken Jones. Everyone apart from Ken Jones knew each other well since they had been part of both the broadcasting sector and the academic sphere for many years; author's interview with the Rev. Dr Alwyn Roberts, Tregarth, 24 May 2007; *Articles* (BBC Radio Wales, 30 January 1981).

24 Dr Glyn Tegai Hughes's personal collection (GTHPC), *Cofnodion cyfarfod cyntaf Awdurdod Sianel Pedwar Cymru*, 31 January–1 February 1981, p. 1.

25 Author's interview with the Rev. Dr Alwyn Roberts, Tregarth, 24 May 2007; author's interview with Dr Glyn Tegai Hughes, Tregynon, 31 January 2007.

26 Author's interview with the Rev. Dr Alwyn Roberts, Tregarth, 24 May 2007; author's interview with Dr Glyn Tegai Hughes, Tregynon, 31 January 2007. There had been

rumours before the authority was appointed that, due to the delay, the government would install a chief executive to expedite developments without consulting the new authority. Such a decision would have been extremely damaging and problematic had the authority strongly disagreed with the government, and provided further evidence of the Conservative government's lack of understanding and respect for Wales; Jones, 'Mawr alw am gyhoedd effro a llafar'.

27 *Second Report from the Committee on Welsh Affairs – Volume II*, p. 519.

28 S4C staff shared office space with the IBA until the middle of July 1981.

29 GTHPC, *Cofnodion cyfarfod cyntaf Awdurdod Sianel Pedwar Cymru*, p. 1.

30 GTHPC, *Cofnodion cyfarfod cyntaf Awdurdod Sianel Pedwar Cymru*, p. 1. 'Once around the transmitters' is a concept where programmes broadcast in one part of the country could be shown in another area at a different time without incurring any additional costs, such as royalties. This concept was used in the context of ITV's activities because of the regional variations within its broadcast schedules.

31 These links were essential to ensure that the programmes from the BBC and HTV could be sent to S4C, and that the programmes could be transferred from S4C to the IBA for transmission over the Welsh transmitter network. The picture and sound connection lines were in Cardiff, which was also the location of the BT switching centre. GTHPC, *Cofnodion trydydd cyfarfod Awdurdod Sianel Pedwar Cymru*, 1–2 March 1981, p. 1.

32 GTHPC, *Cofnodion ail gyfarfod Awdurdod Sianel Pedwar Cymru*, 14–15 February 1981, p. 5.

33 GTHPC, *Cofnodion trydydd cyfarfod Awdurdod Sianel Pedwar Cymru*, p. 2.

34 Welsh Fourth Channel Authority, *Annual Report and Accounts, 1981–82* (Cardiff, 1982), p. 5. Chris Grace remembers the extremely difficult working environment during the building work, which added to the pressure felt by staff. Author's interview with Chris Grace, Cardiff, 29 November 2010.

35 'Doedd ganddo fo fawr ddim syniad o sut oedd pobl eraill yn teimlo a gweithio. 'Roedd o'n dod i mewn i'r swyddfa tua hanner awr wedi pump, pawb wedi bod yn gweithio trwy'r dydd, ynte'n dod i mewn a jyst mynd yn ei flaen . . . ac 'roedd Goronwy'n mynd yn ei flaen am oriau'; Author's interview with Dr Glyn Tegai Hughes, Tregynon, 31 January 2007.

36 Stephens, 'Sir Goronwy Daniel'.

37 '[D]ilyn pob sgwarnog fel oedd hi'n codi'; Author's interview with Rev. Dr Alwyn Roberts, Tregarth, 24 May 2007; author's interview with Dr Glyn Tegai Hughes, Tregynon, 31 January 2007.

38 Author's interview with Mair Owen, Rhiwbina, 19 January 2007.

39 GTHPC, *Cofnodion pedwerydd cyfarfod Awdurdod Sianel Pedwar Cymru*, 14–15 March 1981, p. 1.

40 This was not Owen Edwards's first job with the corporation. He began working for the BBC in 1961 after a brief stint at the National Library as a cataloguer, and also worked as a presenter on the Welsh language programme produced by Granada, *Dewch i Mewn*. Between 1961 and 1967 he was a presenter on the corporation's daily Welsh affairs programme *Heddiw*, before being promoted to the role of programme organiser in 1967 and then head of programmes in 1970. Meic Stephens,

Owen Edwards: Pioneering television executive and architect of S4C, 7 September 2010, *www.independent.co.uk/news/obituaries/owen-edwards-pioneering-television-executive-and-architect-of-s4c-2072091.html* (accessed September 2010).

41 'Time short for Welsh TV chief', *South Wales Echo*, 10 March 1981.

42 *A Fo Ben* (BBC Cymru, 1989).

43 Author's interview with Owen Edwards, Cardiff, 12 January 2007. Moving to London to take up a new position did not appeal to him, and he considered the post with S4C as a new challenge.

44 GTHPC, *Cofnodion pedwerydd cyfarfod Awdurdod Sianel Pedwar Cymru*, p. 1. Owen Edwards was able to begin his post less than a month after his appointment was announced, since the BBC did not insist on his giving three months' notice.

45 GTHPC, *Cofnodion pedwerydd cyfarfod Awdurdod Sianel Pedwar Cymru*, p. 3.

46 'Pwyslais ar y poblogaidd', *Y Cymro*, 19 May 1981.

47 Following the programme editor, the next post to be filled was that of finance manager and secretary to the authority with the appointment of Michael Tucker, former deputy treasurer of South Glamorgan County Council. There followed the appointment of Chris Grace, former head of HTV's Planning Department, as the channel's new head of planning and presentation; Emlyn Davies, former BBC Radio Cymru news editor as programme commissioner, and Emyr Byron Hughes, a lawyer by profession, as contracts officer. 'Fourth Channel appointment', *South Wales Evening Post*, 15 October 1981.

48 Lord Thomson, chair of the IBA (1981–8); Sir Brian Young, director general of the IBA (1970–82).

49 This idea of funding the fourth channel by imposing a tax on independent companies was not an entirely new idea; it was proposed by Jeremy Isaacs in a letter to the minister for post and telecommunications in 1973 and the same ideas were communicated in the evidence of the Association of Directors and Producers to the Annan Committee, although it was not adopted by that committee's report. Annan failed to identify any logical funding system for the fourth channel. Paul Bonner with Lesley Aston, *Independent Television in Britain: Volume 6. New Developments in Independent Television, 1981–92: Channel 4, TV-am, Cable and Satellite* (Basingstoke, 2003), pp. 7–10.

50 GTHPC, *Cofnodion ail gyfarfod Awdurdod Sianel Pedwar Cymru*, p. 1. The Broadcasting Act enabled the Home Secretary to adjust ITV tax rates given their additional responsibility to fund S4C, but the Act did not specify the level of any reduction leading to uncertainty and concern amongst ITCA members.

51 *Second Report from the Committee on Welsh Affairs – Volume II*, pp. 628–31. HTV was not involved in producing the ITCA's evidence, since the company's position was different from that of its fellow ITV franchise holders, as they were now likely to benefit financially from the prosperity of a Welsh language channel through production funding.

52 *Second Report from the Committee on Welsh Affairs – Volume II*, p. 631.

53 *Second Report from the Committee on Welsh Affairs – Volume II*, p. 630.

54 *Second Report from the Committee on Welsh Affairs – Volume II*, p. 629.

55 *Second Report from the Committee on Welsh Affairs – Volume II*, p. 632.

56 *Hansard*, House of Commons, 10 November 1980, col. 45.
57 *Hansard*, House of Commons, 10 November 1980, col. 44.
58 GTHPC, *Cofnodion ail gyfarfod Awdurdod Sianel Pedwar Cymru*, p. 1.
59 Welsh Office, *Welsh Fourth Channel Authority*, 8 June 1981, *www.walesoffice.gov.uk/2005/06/16/establishment-of-S4C-1979-81/* (accessed August 2010; by December 2010 these documents were no longer available on the website), p. 1.
60 S4CC, *Meeting with Welsh Fourth Channel Authority (Papur 9.81(9))*, p. 1; Welsh Office, *Welsh Fourth Channel Authority*, 8 June 1981, p. 4.
61 S4CC, *Meeting with Welsh Fourth Channel Authority (Papur 9.81(9))*, p. 2.
62 Welsh Office, *Welsh Fourth Channel Authority*, 8 June 1981, p. 3.
63 *Hansard*, House of Commons, 22 July 1981, col. 137. This system would initially operate for one year only, ensuring that the Home Secretary and Treasury could review the arrangement should the ITV network's financial position improve significantly.
64 *Independent Broadcasting Authority Act 1979, Chapter 35* (London, 1979).
65 JMPC, IBA Papers, *Minutes of the one hundred and twenty sixth meeting of the Welsh Committee*, 1 December 1978, p. 2. Following the publication of the bill it was noted that the IBA was confident that the necessary work could be completed to launch the channel by the original government date of 1982. JMPC, IBA Papers, *Minutes of the one hundred and twenty eighth meeting of the Welsh Committee*, 15 February 1979, p. 2.
66 JMPC, IBA Papers, *Minutes of the one hundred and thirty second meeting of the Wales Advisory Committee*, 10 August 1979, p. 3. BBC2 had begun gradually and extended its reach over a period of 10 years to 90 per cent of the British population, and had suffered in popularity because of this strategy.
67 *Minutes of the one hundred and thirty second meeting of the Wales Advisory Committee*, p. 3. UHF was launched in the UK in 1964 with BBC2 the first channel to appear on the service and the first to appear in colour in 1967. BBC1 and ITV appeared on UHF in 1969.
68 *Minutes of the one hundred and thirty second meeting of the Wales Advisory Committee*, p. 4. It can be clearly seen from these details that the IBA centrally did not recommend broadcasting Welsh language programmes over two channels for the benefit of Wales or the Welsh language, since the Welsh language areas would lose out completely with that scheme's transmitter adaptation arrangements.
69 *Minutes of the one hundred and thirty second meeting of the Wales Advisory Committee*, p. 4.
70 JMPC, IBA Papers, *Minutes of the one hundred and thirty third meeting of the Welsh Committee*, 10 October 1979, p. 2.
71 Kenneth Gosling, '£40m loan for new ITV channel', *The Times*, 13 November 1979, 6.
72 Unknown author, 'Addo S4C mor fuan ag y bo'r modd', *Y Cymro*, 23 November 1982.
73 JMPC, IBA Papers, *Minutes of the one hundred and fifty-sixth meeting of the Wales Advisory Committee*, 8 October 1982, p. 5.
74 ITA/IBA/Cable Authority Archive, Bournemouth University 3997019, RK/6/50, Letter from Eirion Lewis to Owen Edwards, 20 December 1982; these were

three-channel transmitters that were modified in 1980–1 before the government decided on the fate of the fourth channel. The other seven were Cwmamman, Abergwynfi, Broad Haven, Crucorney, Efail Fach, Kerry and Monmouth. There was also considerable concern about the Bethesda area sub-transmitter, as there were not enough UHF frequencies available to assign a particular group of channels to the area when the sub-transmitter was built in 1973. Specialist 'active deflector' technology was used instead to reuse the Llanddona signal. As it was specialist equipment used in just one other area of Britain it had been difficult for the IBA to find a supplier and it was feared that it would have to wait until late 1984 for the necessary equipment to be received. However, it was successfully adapted in 1982. ITA/IBA/Cable Authority Archive, Bournemouth University 3997019, RK/6/50, Draft of a letter from the Home Secretary William Whitelaw MP to Nicholas Edwards MP, 1982, p. 2.

75 JMPC, IBA Papers, *Minutes of the one hundred and fiftieth meeting of the Wales Advisory Committee*, 10 December 1981, p. 1; *Minutes of the one hundred and fifty first meeting of the Wales Advisory Committee*, 2 March 1982, p. 2.

76 ITA/IBA/Cable Authority Archive, Bournemouth University, 3997016, RK/6/25, Eirion Lewis, *Television Reception in Wales – Note by the Secretary*, p. 1; unknown author, 'Addo S4C mor fuan ag y bo'r modd'.

77 Unknown author, 'IBA slammed over S4C "deprivation" in north Ceredigion', *The Cambrian News*, 26 November 1982; ITA/IBA/Cable Authority Archive, Bournemouth University, 3997019, RK/6/50, Letter from the Urdd Gobaith Cymru director to Eirion Lewis, 3 December 1982.

78 ITA/IBA/Cable Authority Archive, Bournemouth University, 3997016, RK/6/25, Eirion Lewis, *Television Reception in Wales – Note by the Secretary*, p. 2.

79 *Second Report from the Committee on Welsh Affairs – Volume I*, pp. v–vi.

80 George Clark, 'Welsh TV issue to be studied by MPs', *The Times*, 18 August 1980, 2.

81 Clark, 'Welsh TV issue to be studied by MPs', 2.

82 *Second Report from the Committee on Welsh Affairs – Volume I*, p. v.

83 *Second Report from the Committee on Welsh Affairs – Volume II*, pp. 508–9.

84 *Second Report from the Committee on Welsh Affairs – Volume II*, pp. 511– 42.

85 *Second Report from the Committee on Welsh Affairs – Volume II*, p. 519.

86 *Second Report of the Committee on Welsh Affairs – Volume II*, p. 655. Owen Edwards and Sir Goronwy Daniel represented the channel at this visit.

87 S4CC, *Cofnodion seithfed cyfarfod Awdurdod Sianel Pedwar Cymru*, 9–10 May 1981, p. 2.

88 S4CC, *Cofnodion seithfed cyfarfod Awdurdod Sianel Pedwar Cymru*, p. 2.

89 *Second Report from the Committee on Welsh Affairs – Volume I*, p. xv.

90 *Second Report from the Committee on Welsh Affairs – Volume I*, pp. lxxii–lxxiii.

91 *Second Report from the Committee on Welsh Affairs – Volume II*, p. 663.

92 BBC WAC, R78/26/4, *Minutes of the 323rd Meeting of the Broadcasting Council of Wales*, 18 September 1981, p. 5.

93 *Minutes of the 323rd Meeting of the Broadcasting Council of Wales*, p. 4.

94 See Chapter 1, p. 14 for discussion.

95 It is not possible to be completely confident that C4 advertising money would make up the shortfall or if it would be the ITV regional companies' money, because ITV companies did not differentiate their sales figures between ITV advertising money and C4 advertising money – an issue that was a major source of contention between C4 and the IBA, see Edmund Dell, 'Controversies in the Early History of Channel 4', in Peter Catterall (ed.), *The Making of Channel 4* (London, 1999), p. 20.

96 Euryn Ogwen Williams, 'Owen Edwards' contribution to Welsh Broadcasting', 2 September 2010, *www.clickonwales.org /2010/09/owen-edwards-contribution-to-welsh-broadcasting/* (accessed November 2010).

97 Author's interview with Dr Glyn Tegai Hughes, Tregynon, 31 January 2007. This opinion is shared by several individuals who were part of the early history of S4C, see Williams, 'Owen Edwards' contribution to Welsh Broadcasting'; author's interview with the Rev. Dr Alwyn Roberts, Tregarth, 24 May 2007; author's interview with Euryn Ogwen Williams, Cardiff, 23 February 2007. The close relationship between them was also mentioned in the eulogy delivered by Alwyn Roberts at Owen Edwards's funeral.

98 'Alla i ddim canmol o ddigon, rêl boi gwaraidd. Fuodd Jeremy'n help mawr i ni ar y dechrau . . . yn gefn mawr i ni'; author's interview with Owen Edwards, Cardiff, 12 January 2007.

99 Jeremy Isaacs, *Storm over 4: A Personal Account* (London, 1989), p. 94.

100 *Broadcasting Act 1981, Chapter 68* (London, 1981), p. 49.

101 *Hansard*, House of Commons, 10 November 1980, col. 77.

102 *Second Report from the Committee on Welsh Affairs – Volume II*, p. 362.

103 *Hansard*, House of Commons, 10 November 1980, col. 77.

104 *Second Report from the Committee on Welsh Affairs – Volume II*, p. 362.

105 *Second Report from the Committee on Welsh Affairs – Volume II*, p. 361.

106 Isaacs, *Storm over 4*, pp. 94–5.

107 S4CC, *Cofnodion chweched cyfarfod ar hugain Awdurdod Sianel Pedwar Cymru*, 15 July 1982, p. 1; *Cofnodion seithfed cyfarfod ar hugain Awdurdod Sianel Pedwar Cymru*, 4 August 1982, p. 1.

108 S4CC, *Cofnodion Cyfarfod ar y Cyd Rhwng y Cyngor Darlledu a S4C*, 27 September 1985, p. 3.

109 S4CC, *Cofnodion cyfarfod cyntaf Awdurdod Sianel Pedwar Cymru*.

110 S4CC, *Cofnodion cyfarfod cyntaf Awdurdod Sianel Pedwar Cymru*.

111 GTHPC, *Minutes of the Meeting with HTV during the First Meeting of the Sianel Pedwar Cymru Authority*, 1 February 1981.

112 S4CC, *Cofnodion cyfarfod cyntaf Awdurdod Sianel Pedwar Cymru*, p. 2.

113 S4CC, *Cofnodion cyfarfod cyntaf Awdurdod Sianel Pedwar Cymru*, p. 3.

114 S4CC, *Cofnodion trydydd cyfarfod Awdurdod Sianel Pedwar Cymru*, p. 5.

115 *Broadcasting Act 1981*, p. 50.

116 S4CC, *Nodiadau Golygyddol Rhaglenni i'r Cyfarwyddwr, Papur Atodol i Agenda nawfed cyfarfod yr Awdurdod*, 20–1 June 1981.

117 *Nodiadau Golygyddol Rhaglenni i'r Cyfarwyddwr, Papur Atodol i Agenda nawfed cyfarfod yr Awdurdod.*

118 *Second Report from the Committee on Welsh Affairs – Volume II*, p. 671.

119 *Second Report from the Committee on Welsh Affairs – Volume II*, p. 377.
120 *Second Report from the Committee on Welsh Affairs – Volume II*, p. 262.
121 Stephen Bayly, 'The Welsh Perspective', *Sight and Sound*, 52/4 (autumn 1983), 247.
122 Clive Betts, 'Equity asks for assurances on fourth channel', *Western Mail*, 20 May 1981.
123 Betts, 'Equity asks for assurances on fourth channel'.
124 GTHPC, *Cofnodion nawfed cyfarfod Awdurdod Sianel Pedwar Cymru*, 20–1 June 1981, p. 3.
125 S4CC, *Cofnodion degfed cyfarfod Awdurdod Sianel Pedwar Cymru*, 12 July 1981, p. 4. It appears that it was an interview by one of Equity's Welsh committee members that instigated the heated comments by S4C's director.
126 Arfon Gwilym, '"Equity yn hunanol" – Pennaeth S4C', *Y Cymro*, 11 August 1981.
127 Gwilym, '"Equity yn hunanol" – Pennaeth S4C'.
128 S4CC, Euryn Ogwen's letter to Equity, *Papur Atodol i Agenda seithfed cyfarfod ar hugain Awdurdod Sianel Pedwar Cymru*, 4 August 1982.
129 S4CC, *Cofnodion wythfed cyfarfod ar hugain Awdurdod Sianel Pedwar Cymru*, 3 September 1982, p. 1. S4C also wanted to see a review of the situation in a year to ensure that Equity was accepting more members which would lead to a variety of talent for the channel.
130 S4CC, *Cofnodion unfed cyfarfod ar bymtheg ar hugain Awdurdod Sianel Pedwar Cymru*, 5–6 May 1983, pp. 1–2.
131 S4CC, *Cofnodion degfed cyfarfod Awdurdod Sianel Pedwar Cymru*.
132 S4CC, *Cofnodion degfed cyfarfod Awdurdod Sianel Pedwar Cymru*, p. 4.
133 S4CC, *The Provision of Programmes for the S4C Service, Statement of Intention by the BBC*, 30 September 1982, p. 1.
134 S4CC, *Cofnodion degfed cyfarfod Awdurdod Sianel Pedwar Cymru*, p. 4.
135 S4CC, *Cofnodion degfed cyfarfod Awdurdod Sianel Pedwar Cymru*, p. 4.
136 S4CC, *Cofnodion degfed cyfarfod Awdurdod Sianel Pedwar Cymru*, p. 4.
137 BBC Wales Archive, Cardiff, Box 3573, Memo by Michael Brooke, Broadcasting Council Secretary to the BBC Advisory Body, 4 May 1982.
138 *The Provision of Programmes for the S4C Service*.
139 *The Provision of Programmes for the S4C Service*, p. 1.
140 *The Provision of Programmes for the S4C Service*, p. 1.
141 *The Provision of Programmes for the S4C Service*, p. 3.
142 'Mae'n wir fod gennym hawl i wrthod rhaglen ond cosmetig hollol yw hyn gan nad oes cyfrifoldeb o gwbl ar y BBC i roi rhaglen yn ei lle'; S4CC, *Strategaeth Rhaglenni – Papur atodol i Agenda trydydd cyfarfod a deugain Awdurdod Sianel Pedwar Cymru*, 1–2 December 1983, p. 2.
143 *The Provision of Programmes for the S4C Service*, p. 2.
144 *The Provision of Programmes for the S4C Service*, p. 2.
145 *The Provision of Programmes for the S4C Service*, p. 2.
146 S4CC, *Cofnodion degfed cyfarfod Awdurdod Sianel Pedwar Cymru*, p. 6.
147 S4CC, *Cofnodion deuddegfed cyfarfod ar hugain Awdurdod Sianel Pedwar Cymru*, 13 January 1983, p. 1.

148 S4CC, *The Provision of Programmes for the S4C Service*, p. 3.
149 *Broadcasting Act 1980, Chapter 64* (London, 1980), p. 9.
150 *Broadcasting Act 1980, Chapter 64*, p. 8.
151 *Second Report from the Committee on Welsh Affairs – Volume II*, p. 102.
152 *Second Report from the Committee on Welsh Affairs – Volume II*, p. 103.
153 *Second Report from the Committee on Welsh Affairs – Volume II*, pp. 36, 719. The difference here can be attributed to inflation between 1979 and 1982.
154 GTHPC, *Cofnodion pumed cyfarfod Awdurdod Sianel Pedwar Cymru*, 4–5 April 1981, p. 2.
155 *Second Report from the Committee on Welsh Affairs – Volume II*, p. 720.
156 *Second Report from the Committee on Welsh Affairs – Volume II*, p. 720.
157 GTHPC, *Minutes of the Meeting with HTV during the First Meeting of the Sianel Pedwar Cymru Authority*, p. 3.
158 GTHPC, *Minutes of the Meeting with HTV during the First Meeting of the Sianel Pedwar Cymru Authority*, p. 1.
159 GTHPC, *Cofnodion ail gyfarfod Awdurdod Sianel Pedwar Cymru*, p. 2.
160 GTHPC, *Cofnodion pedwerydd cyfarfod Awdurdod Sianel Pedwar Cymru*, p. 6.
161 '[B]od HTV wedi cyflwyno tystiolaeth i'r Pwyllgor Dethol ar sail costau o £1.5m yr awr (prisiau 1979–80 a'r [*sic*] amrywiaeth presennol). Byddai 10 awr o raglenni yn costu £15m. O ychwanegu 18% chwyddiant, rhentau a chyfrandaliadau i'r IBA a newid yn yr amrywiaeth, roedd y gost yn cynyddu i £27m y flwyddyn am 10 awr – £2.7m yr awr. Roedd hyn yn gwbl gyson a'u ffigurau a'u tystiolaeth; GTHPC, *Cofnodion pedwerydd cyfarfod Awdurdod Sianel Pedwar Cymru*, p. 6.
162 GTHPC, *Cofnodion pedwerydd cyfarfod Awdurdod Sianel Pedwar Cymru*, p. 4.
163 '[B]od costau datblygu'r Cwmni yn cael eu gosod ar S4C a'r rhaglenni Cymraeg'; GTHPC, *Cofnodion pedwerydd cyfarfod Awdurdod Sianel Pedwar Cymru*, p. 5.
164 GTHPC, *Cofnodion pumed cyfarfod Awdurdod Sianel Pedwar Cymru*, p. 2.
165 GTHPC, *Cofnodion pumed cyfarfod Awdurdod Sianel Pedwar Cymru*, p. 2.
166 S4CC, Letter from Euryn Ogwen Williams to Huw Davies, 12 June 1981.
167 S4CC, Letter from Euryn Ogwen Williams to Huw Davies, 12 June 1981, p. 1. This idea was developed into the programme *Arolwg*; although it had evolved into an arts discussion programme by 1985, its original intention was to allow the audience to reflect on the channel's programmes. S4CC, *Cofnodion nawfed cyfarfod a thrigain Awdurdod Sianel Pedwar Cymru*, 12–13 December 1985, p. 4.
168 S4CC, Letter from Euryn Ogwen Williams to Huw Davies, 12 June 1981.
169 S4CC, Letter from Euryn Ogwen Williams to Huw Davies, 12 June 1981, p. 3.
170 S4CC, Letter from Euryn Ogwen Williams to Huw Davies, 12 June 1981.
171 S4CC, *Cofnodion deuddegfed cyfarfod Awdurdod Sianel Pedwar Cymru*, 4 September 1981, p. 2.
172 S4CC, *Cofnodion trydydd cyfarfod ar ddeg Awdurdod Sianel Pedwar Cymru*, 4 October 1981, p. 3.
173 S4CC, *Cofnodion pedwerydd cyfarfod ar ddeg Awdurdod Sianel Pedwar Cymru*, 15 October 1981, p. 2.
174 S4CC, *Cofnodion pymthegfed cyfarfod Awdurdod Sianel Pedwar Cymru*, 6 November 1981, p. 2.

175 S4CC, *Cofnodion pymthegfed cyfarfod Awdurdod Sianel Pedwar Cymru*, p. 3.
176 S4CC, *Cofnodion pymthegfed cyfarfod Awdurdod Sianel Pedwar Cymru*, pp. 2–3.
177 S4CC, *Cofnodion pymthegfed cyfarfod Awdurdod Sianel Pedwar Cymru*, p. 3.
178 S4CC, *Cofnodion unfed cyfarfod ar bymtheg Awdurdod Sianel Pedwar Cymru*, 4 December 1981, p. 2.
179 S4CC, *Cofnodion ail gyfarfod ar bymtheg Awdurdod Sianel Pedwar Cymru*, 8 January 1982, p. 1.
180 *Second Report from the Committee on Welsh Affairs – Volume II*, p. 349.
181 *Second Report from the Committee on Welsh Affairs – Volume II*, p. 340.
182 *Second Report from the Committee on Welsh Affairs – Volume II*, p. 340.
183 'Mae ein cynlluniau, eisoes mewn llaw, gyda miliynnau [*sic*] o bunnau wedi'u clustnodi [*sic*] ar gyfer adeiladu canolfan deledu newydd sbon yn Culverhouse Cross, ger Caerdydd'; HTV Cymru, *Y Bedwaredd Sianel yng Nghymru – Datganiad gan HTV Cymru* (Llandysul, 1979), p. 14.
184 'Gallem ennill y "frwydr" hon a cholli'r "rhyfel" am lwyddiant y sianel'; S4CC, *Cytundeb â HTV – Datblygiadau Diweddar (Papur 1.82(6)) – Papur atodol i Agenda ail gyfarfod ar bymtheg Awdurdod Sianel Pedwar Cymru*, 8 January 1982.
185 'Roedd cryn bryder am safonau rhaglenni HTV oherwydd y diffyg gwybodaeth am yr hyn oedd gan y cwmni yn yr arfaeth ac oherwydd y nifer o'u staff gorau oedd wedi troi yn gynhyrchwyr annibynnol'; S4CC, *Cofnodion ugeinfed cyfarfod Awdurdod Sianel Pedwar Cymru*, 21–2 March 1982, p. 2.
186 Euryn Ogwen Williams, 'Cynhadledd S4C: Y Chwarter Canrif Cyntaf: Sefydlu Sianel', 2 November 2007.
187 Author's interview with Wil Aaron, Llandwrog, 1 October 2010. Similar comments were made by Huw Jones; author's interview with Huw Jones, Llandwrog, 2 November 2010.
188 S4CC, *Cytundeb â HTV – Datblygiadau Diweddar (Papur 1.82(6))*, p. 1.
189 S4CC, *Cytundeb â HTV – Datblygiadau Diweddar (Papur 1.82(6))*, p. 1.
190 S4CC, *Cytundeb â HTV – Datblygiadau Diweddar (Papur 1.82(6))*, p. 4.
191 S4CC, *Cofnodion pedwerydd cyfarfod ar bymtheg Awdurdod Sianel Pedwar Cymru*, 5 March 1982, pp. 2–3. In March 1982 HTV had offered a price of £19.7 million for 9 hours, while S4C felt that £14.16 million would have been a fair price.
192 S4CC, *Cofnodion pedwerydd cyfarfod ar bymtheg Awdurdod Sianel Pedwar Cymru*, pp. 2–3.
193 S4CC, *Cofnodion pedwerydd cyfarfod ar bymtheg Awdurdod Sianel Pedwar Cymru*, pp. 2–3.
194 S4CC, *HTV Limited and The Welsh Fourth Channel Authority – Sianel Pedwar Cymru – Programme Sales Agreement*, 27 May 1982.
195 Robin Reeves, 'Harlech TV in Welsh Channel Four deal', *Financial Times*, 21 May 1982.
196 S4CC, *HTV Limited and The Welsh Fourth Channel Authority – Sianel Pedwar Cymru – Programme Sales Agreement*, p. 13. The S4C Authority could demand a refund if HTV financially exploited the programmes produced for S4C.
197 S4CC, *HTV Limited and The Welsh Fourth Channel Authority – Sianel Pedwar Cymru – Programme Sales Agreement*, Schedule 1A–1C.

198 S4CC, *HTV Limited and The Welsh Fourth Channel Authority – Sianel Pedwar Cymru – Programme Sales Agreement*, Schedule 1B.

199 S4CC, *HTV Limited and The Welsh Fourth Channel Authority – Sianel Pedwar Cymru – Programme Sales Agreement*, Schedule 1C.

200 *Second Report from the Committee on Welsh Affairs – Volume II*, p. 340.

201 *Second Report from the Committee on Welsh Affairs – Volume II*, p. 76.

202 He also remembers having a personal conversation with Ron Wordley where the latter noted that S4C could save millions if they were prepared for a slightly less formal and flexible agreement with HTV. But if they demanded an inflexible deal then Wordley would make sure that they paid for every pen, every roll of toilet paper. Author's interview with Geraint Stanley Jones, 10 November 2008, Cardiff.

203 The *Newyddion y Dydd* programme was broadcast by TWW from the outset of the service in January 1958; however, it appears that *Y Dydd* didn't start broadcasting until TWW became an all-Wales service in 1964, once they assumed the responsibilities of Teledu Cymru.

204 *Second Report from the Committee on Welsh Affairs – Volume II*, p. 83.

205 *Second Report from the Committee on Welsh Affairs – Volume II*, pp. 215–23, 234.

206 *Second Report from the Committee on Welsh Affairs – Volume II*, pp. 653–4.

207 *Second Report from the Committee on Welsh Affairs – Volume II*, p. 83.

208 *Second Report from the Committee on Welsh Affairs – Volume II*, p. 356.

209 '[M]ai'r ateb gorau, er nad delfrydol, oedd rhannu'r cyfrifoldeb rhwng BBC ac HTV ar sail y newyddion o'r un a'r materion cyfoes oddi wrth y llall'; GTHPC, *Cofnodion pedwerydd cyfarfod Awdurdod Sianel Pedwar Cymru*, p. 2.

210 GTHPC, *Cofnodion pedwerydd cyfarfod Awdurdod Sianel Pedwar Cymru*, p. 2. Geraint Talfan Davies recounts the story of HTV travelling to London and, with the help of ITN, producing both bulletins with three of the company's presenters and journalists, Elinor Jones and Alun Ffred Jones presenting the 25-minute version and Tweli Griffiths presenting the shorter bulletin. Geraint Talfan Davies, *At Arm's Length* (Bridgend, 2008), p. 72.

211 '[Y] cyflwyniad o dapiau newyddion HTV yn arbennig'; GTHPC, *Cofnodion pedwerydd cyfarfod Awdurdod Sianel Pedwar Cymru*, p. 5.

212 GTHPC, *Cofnodion pedwerydd cyfarfod Awdurdod Sianel Pedwar Cymru*, p. 5.

213 GTHPC, *Cofnodion pumed cyfarfod Awdurdod Sianel Pedwar Cymru*, p. 4.

214 Arfon Gwilym, 'Brwydr y newyddion', *Y Cymro*, 7 April 1981.

215 '[B]yddai'n beth mwy iachus o lawer i newyddion Cymraeg dyddiol ddod o fwy nag un stafell newyddion. Os mai'r BBC fydd yn gyfrifol am newyddion, bydd rhaglenni Radio Cymru yn ogystal â Sianel 4 yn deillio o'r un ganolfan.

Byddai rhoi'r newyddion i HTV yn sicrhau fod yna gystadleuaeth ym maes newyddion Cymraeg – elfen hollbwysig pan ystyrir nad oes unrhyw gystadleuwr arall mewn gwirionedd'; Gwilym, 'Brwydr y newyddion'.

216 GTHPC, *Cofnodion pumed cyfarfod Awdurdod Sianel Pedwar Cymru*, p. 4.

217 Unknown author, 'HTV pulls out of S4C news', *South Wales Evening Post*, 6 May 1981; unknown author, 'HTV say "No" on news service', *South Wales Echo*, 6 May 1981.

218 Unknown author, 'HTV pulls out of S4C news'; unknown author, 'HTV say "No" on news service'.
219 Unknown author, 'S4C's options narrowed for Welsh news', *Broadcast*, 17 May 1981.
220 Geraint Talfan Davies's recollections correspond with the remarks in *Broadcast*, citing HTV's inability to compete with the BBC's unity, Davies, *At Arm's Length*, p. 73.
221 GTHPC, *Cofnodion seithfed cyfarfod Awdurdod Sianel Pedwar Cymru*, 9-10 May 1981, p. 2; unknown author, 'News service agreed', *Daily Post*, 15 May 1981.
222 *Broadcasting Act 1980, Chapter 64*, p. 9.
223 *Second Report from the Committee on Welsh Affairs – Volume II*, p. 376.
224 *Second Report from the Committee on Welsh Affairs – Volume II*, p. 350.
225 *Second Report from the Committee on Welsh Affairs – Volume II*, p. 376.
226 *Second Report from the Committee on Welsh Affairs – Volume II*, p. 373.
227 *Second Report from the Committee on Welsh Affairs – Volume II*, p. 373.
228 JMPC, IBA Papers, *Minutes of the one hundred and thirty ninth meeting of the Welsh Advisory Committee*, 27 June 1980, p. 6.
229 Author's interview with Huw Jones, Llandwrog, 2 November 2010.
230 Author's interview with Huw Jones, Llandwrog, 2 November 2010. Not all independent producers were interested: Dennis Jones of Ffilmiau Eryri, for example, intended to set up a similar venture himself.
231 The remaining funds had to be borrowed from the Welsh Development Agency, securing a regional development grant, a financial arrangement to lease equipment and a bank loan. Huw Jones was responsible for most of this aspect of the preparatory work. Author's interview with Huw Jones, Llandwrog, 2 November 2010.
232 A dispute arose between S4C and Gwilym Owen regarding these quiz programmes, since S4C officials were convinced that they had not been commissioned, while Gwilym Owen claimed that he had received confirmation. This event was one of the reasons why Gwilym Owen left his position as managing director of Barcud, and also why his original investment was returned to him. Author's interview with Huw Jones, Llandwrog, 2 November 2010; Gwilym Owen, *Crych Dros Dro* (Caernarfon, 2003), pp. 183–9.
233 S4CC, *Adroddiad y Cyfarwyddwr i'r Awdurdod (Papur 6.82(4)) – Papur atodol i Agenda ail gyfarfod ar hugain Awdurdod Sianel Pedwar Cymru*, 7 May 1982, p. 3.
234 GTHPC, *Cofnodion cyfarfod cyntaf Awdurdod Sianel Pedwar Cymru*, p. 4.
235 GTHPC, *Cofnodion ail gyfarfod Awdurdod Sianel Pedwar Cymru*, p. 5.
236 'Felly gwasanaeth safonol, poblogaidd, cytbwys, yn cynnwys . . . [c]yfran helaeth iawn [o] ddeunydd poblogaidd, canol y ffordd, fydd yn apelio at drwch y boblogaeth . . . Fydd yna ddim lle i bobl sydd am ddilyn eu mympwyon creadigol eu hunain heb ystyried a fydd ffrwyth eu llafur yn ffitio oddimewn i fframwaith S4C. Yma i wasanaethu ein cynulleidfa yr yda ni, nid i foddhau ein hunain, ond os bo modd priodi'r ddau beth, gora i gyd'; S4CC, *Cyfarfodydd Cynhyrchwyr Annibynnol – Anerchiad y Cyfarwyddwr*, p. 1.
237 Owen Edwards spoke at the Celtic Film and Television Festival in Harlech on 11 April 1981.
238 S4CC, *Cyfarfodydd Cynhyrchwyr Annibynnol – Anerchiad y Cyfarwyddwr*, p. 2.

239 Author's interview with Wil Aaron, Llandwrog, 1 October 2010. *Hel Straeon* was the first long series commissioned from the independent producers in 1985–6.
240 'Wrth gwrs mae yna gyfle am ryw gymaint o ddrama ond bydd yn rhaid bod yna resymau da am ei dderbyn gan Annibynwyr yn hytrach na'r cyfundrefnau gyda'r profiad ac adnoddau'; S4CC, *Cyfarfodydd Cynhyrchwyr Annibynnol – Anerchiad y Cyfarwyddwr*, p. 2.
241 S4CC, *Cyfarfodydd Cynhyrchwyr Annibynnol – Anerchiad y Cyfarwyddwr*, p. 3.
242 S4CC, *Nodiadau Golygyddol Rhaglenni i'r Cyfarwyddwr – Papur Atodol i Agenda nawfed cyfarfod Awdurdod Sianel Pedwar Cymru*, 20–1 June 1981, p. 2.
243 S4CC, *Nodiadau Golygyddol Rhaglenni i'r Cyfarwyddwr – Papur Atodol i Agenda nawfed cyfarfod Awdurdod Sianel Pedwar Cymru*, p. 2.
244 S4CC, *Nodiadau'r Golygydd Rhaglenni i'r Cyfarwyddwr – Papur Atodol i Agenda degfed cyfarfod Awdurdod Sianel Pedwar Cymru*, 12 July 1981, p. 1.
245 S4CC, *Nodiadau'r Golygydd Rhaglenni i'r Cyfarwyddwr – Papur Atodol i Agenda degfed cyfarfod Awdurdod Sianel Pedwar Cymru*, p. 1. John Osmond noted in his article in *Arcade* in March 1982 that 24 HTV staff and 18 BBC staff had left their posts to form independent production companies. John Osmond, 'Fight for the Future of Television in Wales', *Arcade*, 33, 5 March 1982.
246 *Second Report from the Committee on Welsh Affairs – Volume II*, p. 376.
247 Author's interview with Chris Grace, Cardiff, 29 November 2010.
248 Author's interview with Robin Lyons, Cardiff, 15 October 2010.
249 Author's interview with Robin Lyons, Cardiff, 15 October 2010.
250 Mike Young and Robin Lyons turned to Roger Fickling for advice on how to find an animator who could work with them to create the series; he suggested that they get in touch with Dave Edwards. Author's interview with Robin Lyons, Cardiff, 15 October 2010.
251 S4CC, *Blwyddyn i Fynd (Papur 15.81(2))*, p. 1.
252 S4CC, *Blwyddyn i Fynd (Papur 15.81(2))*, p. 1.
253 S4CC, *Adroddiad y Cyfarwyddwr i'r Awdurdod – Papur Atodol i Agenda deunawfed cyfarfod Awdurdod Sianel Pedwar Cymru*, 5 February 1982, pp. 3–4.
254 S4CC, *Adroddiad y Cyfarwyddwr i'r Awdurdod – Papur Atodol i Agenda deunawfed cyfarfod Awdurdod Sianel Pedwar Cymru*, pp. 3–4.
255 S4CC, *Adroddiad y Cyfarwyddwr i'r Awdurdod – Papur Atodol i Agenda deunawfed cyfarfod Awdurdod Sianel Pedwar Cymru*, pp. 5–6.
256 '[E]r bod y sector annibynnol yn ansicr ac annelwig flwyddyn yn ôl, mae bellach yn realiti ac wedi tyfu i'r fath raddau fel nad yw'n bosibl ei hystyried fel atodiad i'r prif gyflenwyr'; S4CC, *Y Darnau'n Disgyn i'w Lle – Papur atodol i Agenda ugeinfed cyfarfod Awdurdod Sianel Pedwar Cymru*, 21–2 March 1982, p. 1.
257 S4CC, *Y Darnau'n Disgyn i'w Lle – Papur atodol i Agenda ugeinfed cyfarfod Awdurdod Sianel Pedwar Cymru*, p. 1.
258 S4CC, *Y Darnau'n Disgyn i'w Lle – Papur atodol i Agenda ugeinfed cyfarfod Awdurdod Sianel Pedwar Cymru*, p. 3.
259 'hyder a gobaith'; S4CC, *Y Darnau'n Disgyn i'w Lle – Papur atodol i Agenda ugeinfed cyfarfod Awdurdod Sianel Pedwar Cymru*, p. 3; it was estimated in 1984 that the independent production companies were employing between 500 and 750 workers, with

the biggest growth in Gwynedd and Cardiff docks: S4CC, *Nodiadau ar Wythfed Cyfarfod Pwyllgor Cymreig yr Awdurdod Darlledu Annibynnol i Drafod Rhaglenni 'Annibynnol' S4C*, 2 November 1984, p. 2.

260 S4CC, *Cofnodion degfed cyfarfod ar hugain Awdurdod Sianel Pedwar Cymru*, 5 November 1982, p. 5.

261 S4CC, *Cofnodion degfed cyfarfod ar hugain Awdurdod Sianel Pedwar Cymru*, p. 5.

262 *'Blwyddyn i Fynd' (Papur 15.81(2))*, p. 1; S4CC, *Cofnodion unfed cyfarfod ar bymtheg Awdurdod Sianel Pedwar Cymru*, p. 2.

263 S4CC, *Cofnodion unfed cyfarfod ar bymtheg Awdurdod Sianel Pedwar Cymru*, p. 2; Kate Woodward, 'Y cleddyf ym mrwydr yr iaith: Y Bwrdd Ffilmiau Cymraeg, 1970–86' (unpublished PhD thesis, University of Wales, Aberystwyth, 2009), 243, a study that has since been published as part of the Meddwl a'r Dychymyg Cymreig series: Kate Woodward, *Cleddyf ym Mrwydr yr Iaith? Y Bwrdd Ffilmiau Cymraeg* (Caerdydd, 2013).

264 S4CC, *Cofnodion ail gyfarfod ar hugain Awdurdod Sianel Pedwar Cymru*, 7 May 1982, p. 2.

265 Gerald Williams, 'Producer loses post after overspending', *Daily Post*, 1 July 1982; Western Mail reporter, 'Overspent S4C film epic may be scrapped', *Western Mail*, 1 July 1982; Paul Hoyland, 'Welsh TV spectacular costs producer his job', *The Guardian*, 2 July 1982; Glyn Evans, 'Bwch dihangol y "gravy train"?', *Y Cymro*, 6 July 1982, 5–6; unknown author, 'Dewch ar y Trên Bach', *Lol* (summer 1982), 4.

266 S4CC, *Cofnodion pumed cyfarfod ar hugain Awdurdod Sianel Pedwar Cymru*, 28–9 June 1982, p. 2; S4CC, *Adroddiad y Cyfarwyddwr (Papur 9.82(9)) – Papur Atodol i Agenda pumed cyfarfod ar hugain Awdurdod Sianel Pedwar Cymru*, 28–9 June 1982, p. 1.

267 Woodward, 'Cleddyf ym mrwydr yr iaith: Y Bwrdd Ffilmiau Cymraeg, 1970–86', 241.

268 S4CC, Letter from Muiris Mac Conghail to S4C Authority, 30 June 1982. The complimentary nature of this letter suggests that its purpose was to ensure that the channel had evidence of the film's value in the event of any public outcry over the extra money spent on it.

269 S4CC, Letter from Muiris Mac Conghail to S4C Authority, 30 June 1982.

270 GTHPC, *Cofnodion trydydd cyfarfod Awdurdod Sianel Pedwar Cymru*, p. 4.

271 GTHPC, *Cofnodion cyfarfod cyntaf Awdurdod Sianel Pedwar Cymru*, p. 1.

272 GTHPC, *Cofnodion chweched cyfarfod Awdurdod Sianel Pedwar Cymru*, 26–7 April 1981, p. 2.

273 GTHPC, *Cofnodion nawfed cyfarfod Awdurdod Sianel Pedwar Cymru*, p. 2. The winning slogan came from Phil Mostert, a gentleman from Harlech who came up with the slogan 'Dewch ar ddec S4C' ('Come up on S4C's deck'); Gwilym, '"Equity yn hunanol" – Pennaeth S4C'.

274 S4CC, *Cofnodion pymthegfed cyfarfod Awdurdod Sianel Pedwar Cymru*, p. 3.

275 *Hansard*, House of Commons, 22 July 1981, col. 137.

276 Maggie Brown, *A Licence to be Different: The Story of Channel 4* (London, 2007), p. 49. S4C was first to appoint the company, and its services were acquired at a much

cheaper rate than C4. Author's interview with Euryn Ogwen Williams, Cardiff, 26 January 2007.

277 S4CC, *Cofnodion pymthegfed cyfarfod Awdurdod Sianel Pedwar Cymru*, p. 3.

278 'English S4C logo attacked', *Western Mail*, 27 February 1982.

279 '[F]wngrel'; Angharad Tomos, 'Cadwn y Ddelfryd', *Tafod y Ddraig*, April 1982. This article also highlights another concern expressed before the channel went on air: that most of the channel's broadcast hours would be filled with English language programming.

280 'Un cyfle gawn ni. Gobeithio y byddwn ni fel Cymry Cymraeg yn ymwrthod â'r demtasiwn sy'n dod mor hawdd i ni, i ymrannu ac ymgecru. Mae 'na bethau tragwyddol bwysicach na hwn'; 'Ail-ystyried "logo" S4C', *Y Cymro*, 16 March 1982.

281 S4CC, *Cofnodion pedwerydd cyfarfod ar bymtheg Awdurdod Sianel Pedwar Cymru*, p. 1.

282 S4CC, *Cofnodion unfed cyfarfod ar hugain Awdurdod Sianel Pedwar Cymru*, 2 April 1982, p. 1.

283 Gwilym, '"Equity yn hunanol" – Pennaeth S4C'.

284 '[A]ll yr un busnes gael ei redeg fel 'na'; Gwilym, '"Equity yn hunanol" – Pennaeth S4C'.

285 A bilingual newsletter was published every two months from November 1981 onwards. S4CC, *Cofnodion pymthegfed cyfarfod Awdurdod Sianel Pedwar Cymru*, p. 1.

286 '[A]nwybodaeth affwysol ynglŷn â S4C'; S4CC, *Cyhoeddusrwydd (1.82(7)) – Papur Atodol i Agenda ail gyfarfod ar bymtheg Awdurdod Sianel Pedwar Cymru*, 8 January 1982, p. 3.

287 S4CC, *Cyhoeddusrwydd (1.82(7)) – Papur Atodol i Agenda ail gyfarfod ar bymtheg Awdurdod Sianel Pedwar Cymru*, p. 3.

288 'Double launch for S4C – levy system adjusted', *Television Today*, 29 February 1982; Patricia Williams, 'How green is the Sianel?', *Broadcast*, 1 March 1982, 16.

289 Rhydwen Williams, 'Gorau Barn . . . Gorau Chwedl', *Barn*, March 1982, 57–60; unknown author, 'St. David's day launch for Fourth Channel authority', *South Wales Argus*, 1 March 1982; Clive Betts, 'Superted and Wil can seal secure future for S4C', *Western Mail*, 2 March 1982; unknown author, 'Welsh Fourth channel is officially launched', *Daily Post*, 2 March 1982; Gerald Williams, 'Milestone for new TV channel', *Daily Post*, 2 March 1982; Gerald Williams, 'Channel launch is "language lifeboat"', *Daily Post*, 2 March 1982; unknown author, 'Bwrlwm y Sianel Newydd', *Y Cymro*, 3 March 1982.

290 Tim Jones, 'Testing time for Welsh TV channel', *The Times*, 2 March 1982; Sean Day-Lewis, 'David's Day Launch for Welsh TV', *Daily Telegraph*, 2 March 1982; 'Superted, a hero for Wales', *Daily Express*, 2 March 1982; Paul Hoyland, 'Welsh channel 4 on, but no Harlech deal', *The Guardian*, 2 March 1982; Robin Reeves, 'Channel S4C puts Welsh talents in the picture', *Financial Times*, 2 March 1982.

291 Williams, 'How green is the Sianel?', 16–19; Wynford Vaughan Thomas, 'Trwy'r Awyr', *Broadcast*, 1 March 1982, 20–1.

292 Hoyland, 'Welsh channel 4 on, but no Harlech deal'.

293 'Welsh Fourth channel is officially launched'; 'Superted, a hero for Wales'.

294 'Baban dan anfantais'; Tomos, 'Cadwn y Ddelfryd'.
295 Tomos, 'Cadwn y Ddelfryd'.
296 '[N]i a'i sicrhaodd, ni a dalodd y pris, ac y mae gennym hawl i wybod beth sydd yn digwydd iddi ac i leisio barn. Nid yw'r ymgyrch ddarlledu ar ben. Ein nôd yw sefydlu gwasanaeth cyflawn safonol yn y Gymraeg ac ni fyddwn yn rhoi'r gorau i ymgyrchu nes sicrhau hynny'; Tomos, 'Cadwn y Ddelfryd'. The 'we' referred to in the article is Cymdeithas yr Iaith and, more specifically, those who campaigned to secure the Welsh language channel.
297 GTHPC, *Cofnodion cyfarfod cyntaf Awdurdod Sianel Pedwar Cymru*, pp. 2–3.
298 BBC Wales Archive, Cardiff, M. Brooke File 3573, *Advisory Structure for Sianel Pedwar Cymru – A Preliminary Note by Eirion Lewis (IBA) and Michael Brooke (BBC)*, 19 June 1981.
299 *Advisory Structure for Sianel Pedwar Cymru – A Preliminary Note by Eirion Lewis (IBA) and Michael Brooke (BBC)*, p. 1.
300 *Advisory Structure for Sianel Pedwar Cymru – A Preliminary Note by Eirion Lewis (IBA) and Michael Brooke (BBC)*, p. 2.
301 *Advisory Structure for Sianel Pedwar Cymru – A Preliminary Note by Eirion Lewis (IBA) and Michael Brooke (BBC)*, p. 4. It was envisaged that committee meetings would be split so that the first part could deal with Welsh language matters with the Welsh-speaking members, and the afternoon session could discuss the channel's English language provision and general issues. It was thought that this plan would save some money since it wouldn't require the use of simultaneous translation equipment.
302 S4CC, *Nodyn ar Gyrff Ymgynghorol S4C (Papur 2.82(7)) – Papur Atodol i Agenda deunawfed cyfarfod Awdurdod Sianel Pedwar Cymru*, 5 February 1982, p. 1.
303 GTHPC, *Cofnodion nawfed cyfarfod Awdurdod Sianel Pedwar Cymru*, p. 3.
304 S4CC, *Cofnodion deuddegfed cyfarfod Awdurdod Sianel Pedwar Cymru*, p. 3.
305 S4CC, *Cofnodion unfed cyfarfod ar hugain Awdurdod Sianel Pedwar Cymru*, p. 1.
306 S4CC, *Cofnodion unfed cyfarfod ar hugain Awdurdod Sianel Pedwar Cymru*, p. 1.
307 S4CC, *Cofnodion wythfed cyfarfod ar hugain Awdurdod Sianel Pedwar Cymru*, p. 1.
308 S4C, *Nodyn ar Gyrff Ymgynghorol S4C (Papur 2.82(7))*, p. 1.
309 S4CC, *Cofnodion trydydd cyfarfod ar ddeg Awdurdod Sianel Pedwar Cymru*, p. 4.
310 Members of the religion panel were Rev. Hugh Rowlands (chair), The Right Rev. George Noakes, Dr Harri Pritchard-Jones, Mrs Rebecca Powell, Rev. D. R. Thomas and Dr Geraint Gruffydd. Members of the education panel were Mr John Brace (chair), Mr Edward Morus Jones, Professor I. M. Williams, Miss Rhiannon Rees (until the end of 1982) and Mr Alun Jones (from the beginning of 1983).
311 Members of the appeals panel were Dr Alun Oldfield-Davies (chair), Lady Goronwy Roberts and Rev. Herbert Hughes.
312 '[D]arparu cyflawnder amrywiol o raglenni Cymraeg o'r radd flaenaf'; 'nad oes ganddynt affliw o ddim i'w ddweud wrth gapel na eglwys nac eisteddfod, pobl y mae llyfr a chylchgrawn a phapur newydd Cymraeg yn anathema iddynt'; 'gystadlu gyda rhaglenni fel *Crossroads*'; 'cartwnau o *Mighty Mouse* a *Popeye* yn Gymraeg'; unknown author, 'Y Bedwaredd Sianel . . . Sut Sianel?', *Barn*, January 1981, 20–5.

313 JMPC, *Minutes of the one hundred and thirty fifth meeting of the Welsh Committee – ADA*, 4 January 1980, p. 3.
314 JMPC, *Mintues of the one hundred and thirty eighth meeting of the Welsh Committee – ADA*, 1 May 1980, p. 2.
315 BBC WAC, R78/26/3, *Minutes of the 309th meeting of the Broadcasting Council of Wales*, 23 May 1980, p. 3. Geraint Stanley Jones, the BBC's head of programming, stated that there was not enough space in the *Radio Times* to include details of ITV's Welsh language programmes, even if the idea was attractive.
316 GTHPC, *Cofnodion trydydd cyfarfod Awdurdod Sianel Pedwar Cymru*, p. 7.
317 S4CC, *Adroddiad y Cyfarwyddwr – Papur Atodol i Agenda nawfed cyfarfod Awdurdod Sianel Pedwar Cymru*, p. 1; S4CC, *Cyhoeddusrwydd (Papur 1.82 (7)) – Papur Atodol i Agenda ail gyfarfod ar bymtheg Awdurdod Sianel Pedwar Cymru*, p. 1.
318 S4CC, *Adroddiad y Cyfarwyddwr – Papur Atodol i Agenda nawfed cyfarfod Awdurdod Sianel Pedwar Cymru*, p. 1.
319 S4CC, *Cyhoeddusrwydd (Papur 1.82 (7))*, p. 1.
320 S4CC, *Cofnodion unfed cyfarfod ar ddeg Awdurdod Sianel Pedwar Cymru*, 6 August 1981, p. 2.
321 S4CC, *Adroddiad y Cyfarwyddwr i'r Awdurdod – Papur Atodol i Agenda unfed cyfarfod ar bymtheg Sianel Pedwar Cymru*, 4 December 1981, p. 2.
322 S4CC, *Cofnodion unfed cyfarfod ar bymtheg Sianel Pedwar Cymru*, p. 1.
323 S4CC, *Cyhoeddusrwydd (Papur 1.82 (7))*, p. 2.
324 S4CC, *Cofnodion nawfed cyfarfod ar hugain Awdurdod Sianel Pedwar Cymru*, 1 October 1982, p. 2.
325 S4CC, *Cofnodion nawfed cyfarfod ar hugain Awdurdod Sianel Pedwar Cymru*, p. 2.
326 S4CC, *Cyhoeddusrwydd (Papur 1.82 (7))*, p. 2.
327 S4CC, *Cyhoeddusrwydd (Papur 1.82 (7))*, p. 2.
328 S4CC, *Adroddiad y Cyfarwyddwr i'r Awdurdod – Papur Atodol i Agenda unfed cyfarfod ar bymtheg Sianel Pedwar Cymru*, p. 1.
329 S4CC, *Cofnodion deunawfed cyfarfod Awdurdod Sianel Pedwar Cymru*, 5 February 1981, p. 2.
330 S4CC, *Cyhoeddusrwydd (Papur 1.82 (7))*, p. 1.
331 S4CC, *Adroddiad y Cyfarwyddwr i'r Awdurdod (Papur 3.82(4)) – Papur Atodol i Agenda pedwerydd cyfarfod ar bymtheg Awdurdod Sianel Pedwar Cymru*, 5 March 1982, p. 2.
332 S4CC, *Cofnodion ugeinfed cyfarfod Awdurdod Sianel Pedwar Cymru*, p. 1.
333 S4CC, *TV Times Magazine – Papur Atodol i Agenda seithfed cyfarfod ar hugain Awdurdod Sianel Pedwar Cymru*, 4 August 1982.

Chapter 3

1 Professor Huw Morris-Jones, the IBA's original member on the authority, was invited back to watch the culmination of all the hard work.
2 A special line was provided between S4C and the IBA in London, for members of the press, individuals from the industry and MPs to watch the first broadcast. But the event evolved from a matter of courtesy and a means of attracting publicity into an official reception that required the presence of authority members, partly

because Nicholas Edwards, Secretary of State for Wales, decided to watch the opening night from London. Despite the initial inconvenience the event was judged to be a success by those who attended. S4CC, *Cofnodion nawfed cyfarfod ar hugain Awdurdod Sianel Pedwar Cymru*, 1 October 1982, p. 3; S4CC, *Cofnodion degfed cyfarfod ar hugain Awdurdod Sianel Pedwar Cymru*, 5 November 1982, p. 1; S4CC, *Adroddiad y Cyfarwyddwr i'r Awdurdod (Papur 14.82/4) – Papur Atodol i Agenda degfed cyfarfod ar hugain Awdurdod Sianel Pedwar Cymru*, 5 November 1982, p. 2; author's interview with Chris Grace, Cardiff, 29 November 2010.

3 'Croeso cynnes iawn, iawn i chi ymuno â ni yma am y tro cyntaf ar aelwyd Sianel Pedwar Cymru. Rŵan, hawdd cynnau tân ar hen aelwyd medde'r gair yntê, ond ein bwriad ni ydi cynnau coelcerth ar aelwyd newydd'; *Croeso i S4C* (internal production, S4C, 1 November 1982). A copy of the programme is available in the National Screen and Sound Archive of Wales collection. Unless otherwise noted, translations are those of the author.

4 *Croeso i S4C.*

5 *Croeso i S4C.* The *SuperTed* series was not officially scheduled to begin broadcasting until April 1983, but it was decided that it was important to include a preview of the series that had received the most attention by the press and in the promotional material. See, for example, Mario Basini, 'A Star is Born', *Western Mail – Wales Supplement*, 30 November 1982, 22.

6 Jeremy Isaacs, *Storm over 4: A Personal Account* (London, 1989), p. 48.

7 *Croeso i S4C.*

8 Their greetings were delivered in their first language and dubbed into Welsh, with Miss World pronouncing some words in Welsh at the end of her greeting. Here S4C can be seen adopting the pattern that it wished the producers to use when interviewing non-Welsh-speaking individuals, to avoid the use of English as the common language. The only likely link between S4C and Björn Borg was that the tennis player was represented by Mark McCormak's International Management Group (IMG), and IMG's subsidiary was the company that promoted S4C's programmes for sale abroad.

9 *Croeso i S4C.*

10 Clive Betts, 'Channel 4 hopes arts, films will reach one in 10', *Western Mail*, 6 October 1982, 9.

11 James Lewis, 'Superted's mission to leap TV language gap', *The Guardian*, 3 November 1982.

12 Clive Betts, 'Croeso i S4C – but not from the valleys', *Western Mail*, 2 November 1982, 1.

13 The union demanded higher remuneration for its members and insisted that all branches of BBC members held meetings during working hours on 1 November 1982 in order to disrupt newsroom activities. BBC Wales members voted not to disturb such an important event. Clive Betts, 'Pay disputes will hit tonight's S4C launch', *Western Mail*, 1 November 1982, 1; Betts, 'Croeso i S4C – but not from the valleys', 1.

14 Unknown author, '10 Channel TV Guide', *Western Mail*, 1 November 1982, 2.

15 Edward Morgan, 'Teledu Cymru', *Y Faner*, 25 November 1982.

16 S4C advertisement, *Western Mail*, 1 November 1982, 6.

17 Unknown author, '10 Channel TV Guide', 2.

18 Betts, 'Pay disputes will hit tonight's S4C launch', 1; David Hewson, 'Disputes threaten start of Channel Four', *The Times*, 7 October 1982, 1; David Hewson, 'Channel 4 dispute talks break down', *The Times*, 30 October 1982, 1.

19 Betts, 'Croeso i S4C – but not from the valleys', 1.

20 Betts, 'Pay disputes will hit tonight's S4C launch', 1; Betts, 'Croeso i S4C – but not from the valleys', 1; Lewis, 'Superted's mission to leap TV language gap'.

21 'Er bod gan yr Awdurdod rai sylwadau beirniadol ar rai rhaglenni, bach oedd y rhain o'u cymharu â'r argraff ffafriol iawn a wnaeth y gwasanaeth ar y cyfan arnyn nhw ac ar y rhelyw mawr o'u cydnabod. Buont yn canmol gwaith staff a gwneuthurwyr rhaglenni yn gosod stamp broffesiynol, hyderus, ond cartrefol ar y rhaglenni ac ar y sianel; S4CC, *Cofnodion degfed cyfarfod ar hugain Awdurdod Sianel Pedwar Cymru*, p. 3.

22 Unknown author, 'Twelve per cent watched S4C in first week', *The Free Press*, 26 November 1982.

23 Two letters were received complaining about the programme *Hapnod.*

24 S4CC, *Cofnodion degfed cyfarfod ar hugain Awdurdod Sianel Pedwar Cymru*, p. 2.

25 Betts, 'Croeso i S4C – but not from the valleys', 1.

26 In 1980 there were 170,000 homes in Wales receiving their commercial cable service, 20 per cent of Welsh homes, a figure significantly higher than the British equivalent of 8.5 per cent. By the early 1980s, it was thought that 90 per cent of these homes could receive a television service through a standard aerial, but remained loyal to the cable service due to the increased choice of channels. Many cable services could carry four services, and in the period prior to the establishment of S4C and C4 they broadcast one of the neighbouring local services from England. *Second Report from the Committee on Welsh Affairs: Broadcasting in the Welsh Language and the Implications for Welsh and Non-Welsh Speaking Viewers and Listeners, Volume I – Report and Proceedings* (London, 1981), p. lvii.

27 100,000 of the 170,000 homes receiving cable services were on four-channel systems. It was possible to extend these systems to carry more channels but this was an expensive process. *Second Report from the Committee on Welsh Affairs – Volume I*, p. lviii.

28 *Second Report from the Committee on Welsh Affairs: Broadcasting in the Welsh Language and the Implications for Welsh and Non-Welsh Speaking Viewers and Listeners, Volume II – Minutes of Evidence and Appendices* (London, 1981), p. 622.

29 Votes were organised in the following areas: Abertillery, Bargoed, south Bargoed, Deri, Merthyr Tydfil, Newbridge, Newport, Pontlottyn, Pontypool, Morriston, Swansea, Caerphilly, Llangeinor, Maesteg, Pontypridd and Rhondda. David Hughes, 'Channel 4 cable vote is vetoed by Whitelaw', *Western Mail*, 29 October 1982, 1.

30 Betts, 'Croeso i S4C – but not from the valleys', 1.

31 Clive Betts, 'Cable TV threat to S4C', *Western Mail*, 22 January 1982.

32 Hughes, 'Channel 4 cable vote is vetoed by Whitelaw', 1.

33 Betts, 'Croeso i S4C – but not from the valleys', 1.

34 Clive Betts, 'Good news and bad for S4C in ratings', *Western Mail*, 24 November 1982; Echo reporter, 'It's a big switch-off for S4C in English', *South Wales Echo*, 23 November 1982; unknown author, 'S4C drops in viewing figures', *South Wales*

Evening Post, 24 November 1982; Garry Gibbs, 'Praise for S4C – and more tune in than for BBC2', *North Wales Weekly News*, 2 December 1982.

35 James Price, 'A welcome in the hillsides for TV 4', *Daily Star*, 14 January 1982.

36 Emyr Williams, 'Ar Ddec S4C', *Cambrian News*, 31 December 1982; unknown author, 'Christmas "delight" for S4C', *South Wales Echo*, 11 January 1983; James Lewis, 'Welsh ratings beat Channel 4 and BBC 2', *The Guardian*, 17 January 1983. Iorwerth Roberts from the *Daily Post* was not as enthusiastic in his judgement of the Christmas schedules: Iorwerth Roberts, 'A poor view', *Daily Post*, 23 December 1982.

37 Jan Morris, 'A Channel 4 that works . . .', *Sunday Times*, 9 January 1982; Lewis, 'Welsh ratings beat Channel 4 and BBC2'; Brenda Maddox, 'One-up to Wales', *The Listener*, 20 January 1983; Alwyn Roberts, 'Methiant "Channel 4" – dyfodol S4C', *Y Faner*, 21 January 1983, 11.

38 Clive Betts, 'Plunge in viewing of S4C a cash threat', *Western Mail*, 15 June 1983. The figure published in the *Western Mail* for May is higher than the figure discussed by the authority when considering the deterioration of viewing figures, which was 57,000. See S4CC, *The deterioration in S4C's ratings since its initial five months of operation (Papur 7.83(5)), Papur atodol i Agenda deunawfed cyfarfod ar hugain Awdurdod Sianel Pedwar Cymru*, 1 July 1983. View further discussion on the fall in S4C's viewing figures in the following articles: unknown author, 'S4C is hit by big turn-off', *Television Weekly*, 24 June 1983; unknown author, 'Welsh TV hits sun snag', *The Guardian*, 27 June 1983; Clive Betts, 'Stale news "hits S4C figures"', *Western Mail*, 29 June 1983; Derek Hooper, 'Viewing figures shock for S4C', *South Wales Echo*, 28 June 1984.

39 S4CC, *Cofnodion ail gyfarfod ar bymtheg ar hugain Awdurdod Sianel Pedwar Cymru*, 3 June 1983, p. 3.

40 S4CC, *The deterioration in S4C's ratings since its initial five months of operation (Papur 7.83(5))*, p. 6.

41 S4CC, *The deterioration in S4C's ratings since its initial five months of operation (Papur 7.83(5))*, p. 1.

42 The tremendous growth in the BBC2 audience share can be attributed to the coverage of the world snooker championship matches at the Crucible in Sheffield during peak hours.

43 S4CC, *The deterioration in S4C's ratings since its initial five months of operation (Papur 7.83(5))*, p. 3.

44 Clive Betts, 'S4C confident despite low share of Welsh market', *Western Mail*, 12 July 1983; unknown author, 'Hyder yn nyfodol S4C', *Y Cymro*, 12 July 1983; Ivor Wynne Jones, 'S4C suffers summer switch-off', *Daily Post*, 12 July 1983.

45 During March and in early April 1983 the following series came to the end of their run: *Elinor*, *Cefn Gwlad*, *Yng Nghwmni* a *Rhaglen Hywel Gwynfryn*. Complaints about repeats were seen in Meinir Ffransis, 'Angen cyfres i'n dal a'n denu', *Y Cymro*, 3 May 1983, 2; Annes Glyn, '"Repeats" yn troi yn fwrn', *Y Faner*, 16 September 1983, 21.

46 Author's interview with Chris Grace, Cardiff, 29 November 2010. The lack of stock can also be attributed to the lower levels of production in the winter months, due to

the weather, lack of daylight, etc. which led to a lack of new material appearing on screen in the spring and early summer.

47 S4CC, *The deterioration in S4C's ratings since its initial five months of operation (Papur 7.83(5))*, p. 4.

48 S4CC, *The deterioration in S4C's ratings since its initial five months of operation (Papur 7.83(5))*, p. 4.

49 This was verbal feedback that had been communicated to authority members through their friends and acquaintances.

50 There were many other examples: there was concern about *Pobol y Cwm* figures as viewership fell by 46 per cent from 220,000 to 119,000 in three weeks, although the number of homes remained relatively constant. Clive Betts, 'S4C drop in viewers reveals muddle in ratings', *Western Mail*, 6 January 1983, 1; Echo reporter, 'Ratings probed at S4C', *South Wales Echo*, 6 January 1983; unknown author, 'S4C figures "correct"', *South Wales Evening Post*, 7 January 1983; Clive Betts, 'Battle looms on ratings', *Western Mail*, 9 January 1983.

51 Betts, 'Good news and bad for S4C in ratings'.

52 S4CC, *Adroddiad y Cyfarwyddwr i'r Awdurdod (Papur 12.83(4)) – papur atodol i Agenda trydydd cyfarfod a deugain Awdurdod Sianel Pedwar Cymru*, 1–2 December 1983, p. 2.

53 Clive Betts, 'Viewing figures puzzle for S4C', *Western Mail*, 5 December 1983.

54 Jane Harbord, 'Can even Superted save S4C?', *Television Weekly*, 22 July 1983, 7; James Tucker, 'Hidden Welsh TV bill', *Sunday Times*, 13 November 1983; DH, 'S4C "Most Costly TV in Britain"', *Broadcast*, 18 November 1983; Tim Jones, 'Will the Welsh keep their TV channel?', *The Times*, 19 November 1983; Clive Betts, 'Magazine says S4C is UK's dearest TV', *Western Mail*, 30 January 1985.

55 S4CC, *S4C's Audience – papur atodol i Agenda pumed cyfarfod a deugain Awdurdod Sianel Pedwar Cymru*, 10 February 1984.

56 WFCA, *Annual Report and Accounts, 1982–83* (Cardiff, 1983), p. 9.

57 S4CC, *S4C's Audience*, p. 1.

58 WFCA, *Annual Report and Accounts, 1983–84* (Cardiff, 1984), p. 10.

59 WFCA, *Annual Report and Accounts, 1982–83*, p. 10.

60 WFCA, *Annual Report and Accounts, 1983–84*, p. 9.

61 WFCA, *Annual Report and Accounts, 1982–83*, p. 10; WFCA, *Annual Report and Accounts, 1983–84*, p. 10; WFCA, *Annual Report and Accounts, 1984–85* (Cardiff, 1985), p. 12.

62 WFCA, *Annual Report and Accounts, 1982–83*, p. 34; WFCA, *Annual Report and Accounts, 1983–84*, p. 37; WFCA, *Annual Report and Accounts, 1984–85*, p. 40.

63 WFCA, *Annual Report and Accounts, 1983–84*, p. 37. These figures were an analysis of the audience response to several weeks in 1983.

64 S4CC, *Nodiadau ar chweched cyfarfod Pwyllgor Cymreig yr Awdurdod Darlledu Annibynnol i Drafod Rhaglenni 'Annibynnol' S4C*, 30 March 1984, p. 2; S4CC, *Cofnodion chweched cyfarfod a deugain Awdurdod Sianel Pedwar Cymru*, 9 March 1984, p. 2; Clive Betts, 'S4C bid to sort out who watches', *Western Mail*, 9 July 1984; unknown author, 'S4C solution "en-route"', *Television Weekly*, 10 August 1984.

65 S4CC, *Adroddiad y Cyfarwyddwr i'r Awdurdod – Papur atodol i Agenda cyfarfod hanner cant a saith Awdurdod Sianel Pedwar Cymru*, 7–8 February 1985, pp. 1–2; WFCA, *Annual Report and Accounts, 1984–85*, p. 11.
66 WFCA, *Annual Report and Accounts, 1984–85*, p. 11.
67 S4CC, *Adroddiad y Cyfarwyddwr i'r Awdurdod – Papur atodol i Agenda cyfarfod hanner cant a saith Awdurdod Sianel Pedwar Cymru*, pp. 1–2.
68 WFCA, *Annual Report and Accounts, 1984–85*, p. 12.
69 WFCA, *Annual Report and Accounts, 1984–85*, p. 12.
70 WFCA, *Annual Report and Accounts, 1984–85*, p. 12.
71 Unknown author, 'TV Guide', *Western Mail*, 2–6 November 1982.
72 S4CC, *Cofnodion pumed cyfarfod a deugain Awdurdod Sianel Pedwar Cymru*, 10 February 1984, p. 1. An exception was made on Wednesday evenings to allow an English feature film to be broadcast between 9 o'clock and 11 o'clock at night.
73 Author's interview with Chris Grace, Cardiff, 29 November 2010.
74 S4CC, Letter from a viewer from Llanrug to Owen Edwards, 29 May 1981.
75 S4CC, *Cofnodion pumed cyfarfod a deugain Awdurdod Sianel Pedwar Cymru*, p. 1.
76 *Broadcasting Act 1981 – Chapter 68* (London, 1981), p. 49.
77 Unknown author, 'S4C woos the viewers with reshuffle of schedules', *Western Mail*, 13 April 1984; unknown author, 'English programmes a part of Spring schedule', *Television Weekly*, 20 April 1984.
78 S4CC, *Cofnodion nawfed cyfarfod a deugain Awdurdod Sianel Pedwar Cymru*, 7–8 June 1984, p. 3.
79 S4CC, *Cofnodion cyfarfod hanner cant Awdurdod Sianel Pedwar Cymru*, 13 July 1984, p. 5.
80 More often than not these issues were discussed during meetings arranged over two days, ensuring that programme issues were treated fairly in the midst of all other matters that the authority were expected to deal with. S4CC, *Troi'r misoedd yn flynyddoedd – Papur atodol i Agenda unfed cyfarfod ar bymtheg ar hugain Awdurdod Sianel Pedwar Cymru*, 5–6 May 1983; S4CC, *Y Sector Annibynnol – pwyso a mesur (Papur 10.83(6)) – Papur atodol i Agenda unfed cyfarfod a deugain Awdurdod Sianel Pedwar Cymru*, 7 October 1983.
81 S4CC, *Troi'r misoedd yn flynyddoedd*, p. 1.
82 S4CC, *Troi'r misoedd yn flynyddoedd*, p. 2.
83 S4CC, *Cofnodion unfed cyfarfod ar bymtheg ar hugain Awdurdod Sianel Pedwar Cymru*, 5–6 May 1983, p. 3.
84 '[B]od y cysylltu rhwng rhaglenni ar brydiau yn annerbyniol o amaturaidd, a safon y llefaru Saesneg yn anfoddhaol'; S4CC, *Cofnodion deuddegfed cyfarfod ar hugain Awdurdod Sianel Pedwar Cymru*, 13 January 1983, p. 3.
85 WFCA, *Annual Report and Accounts, 1982–83*, p. 7.
86 S4CC, *Minutes of the first joint meeting between the Broadcasting Council of Wales and members of Sianel Pedwar Cymru*, 18 March 1983, p. 4; Edward Morgan, 'Teledu Cymru', *Y Faner*, 3 December 1982.
87 S4CC, *Cofnodion trydydd cyfarfod ar ddeg ar hugain Awdurdod Sianel Pedwar Cymru*, 4 February 1983, p. 2.

88 S4CC, *Nodiadau ar ail gyfarfod Pwyllgor Cymreig yr ADA i drafod rhaglenni 'annibynnol' S4C*, 11 March 1983, pp. 4–5; S4CC, *Minutes of the first joint meeting between the Broadcasting Council of Wales and members of Sianel Pedwar Cymru*, p. 4.

89 'Cyflwynwyr gor-glên, gor-groesawus, nawddoglyd braidd. Gwell gennyf gwrteisi dymunol ond hyd braich. S4C neu beidio, *peth* ydy'r teledu, nid cymydog ar yr aelwyd. Mynnaf yr hawl i gau eu ceg nhw a fo heb deimlo'n euog'; unknown author, 'Argraffiadau Cyntaf S4C – Y Da a'r Drwg', *Barn*, December 1982/January 1983.

90 S4CC, *Cofnodion trydydd cyfarfod a deugain Awdurdod Sianel Pedwar Cymru*, 1–2 December 1983, p. 3.

91 Another distinctive element of S4C's presentation was the channel's fidelity to the concept of employing young and new faces for the presenting team with Nia Ceidiog, Siân Lloyd and Gary Nicholas joining Sian Thomas and Robin Jones during the trial period. Rowena Jones-Thomas left in February 1984 to pursue a different path by working as a researcher with HTV's children's and light entertainment division; S4CC, *Adroddiad y Cyfarwyddwr i'r Awdurdod (Papur 2.84(4)) – Papur atodol i Agenda pumed cyfarfod a deugain Awdurdod Sianel Pedwar Cymru*, 10 February 1984, p. 1.

92 S4CC, *Cofnodion deuddegfed cyfarfod ar hugain Awdurdod Sianel Pedwar Cymru*, p. 3. Similar sentiments were also expressed in the press, Glyn Evans, 'Dirywiad y Gwasanaeth Newyddion Cymraeg', *Y Cymro*, 14 December 1982; unknown author, '"Dim Digon o Sylw" i Newyddion Cymru', *Y Cymro*, 4 January 1983; Clive Betts, 'S4C's news under fire from Welsh-speakers', *Western Mail*, 3 February 1983; unknown author, 'What about S4C news of Wales, asks MP', *Western Mail*, 4 February 1983.

93 S4CC, *Cofnodion trydydd cyfarfod ar ddeg ar hugain Awdurdod Sianel Pedwar Cymru*, p. 2; S4CC, *Minutes of the first joint meeting between the Broadcasting Council of Wales and members of Sianel Pedwar Cymru*, p. 4; S4CC, *Adroddiad y Cyfarwyddwr (Papur 8.83(4)) – Papur atodol i agenda pedwerydd cyfarfod ar bymtheg ar hugain Awdurdod Sianel Pedwar Cymru*, 5 August 1983, p. 1.

94 S4CC, *Cofnodion trydydd cyfarfod ar ddeg ar hugain Awdurdod Sianel Pedwar Cymru*, p. 2.

95 S4CC, Letter from Dr Roger Thomas to Owen Edwards, February 1983. See also Letter from Owen Edwards to Dr Roger Thomas, 7 February 1983 and Letter from Dr Roger Thomas to Owen Edwards, 10 February 1983.

96 A complaint was also received from Gwynedd County Council about the lack of coverage of local government on *Newyddion Saith*. See S4CC, *Adroddiad y Cyfarwyddwr i'r Awdurdod (Papur 9.83(5)) – Papur Atodol i Agenda deugeinfed cyfarfod Awdurdod Sianel Pedwar Cymru*, 9 September 1983.

97 S4CC, Letter from Dafydd Wigley MP to Owen Edwards, 6 July 1983.

98 S4CC, Letter from Owen Edwards to Dafydd Wigley MP, 8 July 1983.

99 S4CC, Letter from Dr Roger Thomas to Owen Edwards, 10 February 1983, p. 1; Eleri Rogers, 'Ysu am glecs cymdogol', *Y Cymro*, 25 January 1983.

100 S4CC, *Minutes of the first joint meeting between the Broadcasting Council of Wales and members of Sianel Pedwar Cymru*, pp. 3–4.

101 S4CC, *Cofnodion unfed cyfarfod a deugain Awdurdod Sianel Pedwar Cymru*, 7 October 1983, p. 2.

102 Some viewers agreed with the strategy despite the complaints; E. Dyfed, 'Gadewch inni drin y byd yn Gymraeg', *Y Cymro*, 1 February 1983.

103 S4CC, *Cofnodion yr ail gyfarfod ar y cyd rhwng y Cyngor ac aelodau o Sianel Pedwar Cymru*, 21 October 1983, pp. 1–4. Although there was agreement on the strategy, low viewing figures and audience dissatisfaction created tension between BBC staff and S4C. S4C demanded an improvement in the quality of the programme, but BBC officials felt defensive, as they did not agree with the criticism.

104 S4CC, *Cofnodion unfed cyfarfod ar bymtheg ar hugain Awdurdod Sianel Pedwar Cymru*, p. 3; Trefor Jones et al., 'Llythyr agored at Owen Edwards S4C', *Y Faner*, 22 May 1984.

105 S4CC, *Troi'r misoedd yn flynyddoedd*, p. 2.

106 S4CC, *Adroddiad y Cyfarwyddwr i'r Awdurdod (Papur 15.82(4)) – Papur atodol i Agenda unfed cyfarfod ar ddeg ar hugain Awdurdod Sianel Pedwar Cymru*, 3 December 1982, p. 1.

107 *Gair yn ei Bryd* was therefore appropriate for this policy; S4CC, *Nodiadau ar ail gyfarfod Pwyllgor Cymreig yr ADA i drafod rhaglenni 'annibynnol' S4C*, p. 4.

108 S4CC, *Adroddiad y Cyfarwyddwr i'r Awdurdod (Papur 15.82(4))*, p. 1.

109 Author's interview with Euryn Ogwen Williams, Cardiff, 26 January 2007.

110 '[F]alle ei bod hi'n haws ceisio dweud be na ydy' o. Dydy o ddim yn debyg i fod yn darllen papur Cymraeg, ag eithrio papur bro, dydy o ddim yn debyg i fod yn gapelwr neu eglwyswr, ac mewn capel ac Ysgol Sul yr oedd y rhan fwyaf o'r dysgu darllen Cymraeg, dydy o ddim yn debyg o fod yn teimlo'n gry' am yr iaith, dydy o ddim yn debyg o fod yn ifanc – mae cyfartaledd llawer uwch o'r boblogaeth Gymraeg yn hen nac o'r boblogaeth yn gyffredinol – mae ei Gymraeg, ysywaeth, yn debyg o fod yn fratiog, dydy o ddim yn deall geiriau mawr Cymraeg bydde'n 'i ddieithrio, ac mae o wedi'i gyflyru i dderbyn ei adloniant trwy gyfrwng y Saesneg, ac mae fwy na thebyg o leiaf un aelod o'r tŷ lle mae'n byw yn ddi-Gymraeg'; S4CC, *Anerchiad i Arolygwyr, Prifathrawon a Phenaethiaid Adrannau Ysgolion Uwchradd Cymraeg yn Aberystwyth*, 1 July 1981, p. 6.

111 S4CC, *Nodiadau ar drydydd cyfarfod Pwyllgor Cymreig yr ADA i drafod rhaglenni 'annibynnol' S4C*, 22 April 1983, pp. 5–6.

112 S4CC, *Strategaeth Rhaglenni – Papur atodol i Agenda trydydd cyfarfod a deugain Awdurdod Sianel Pedwar Cymru*, 1–2 December 1983, p. 3.

113 S4CC, *Minutes of the third joint BCW/S4C meeting*, 16 March 1984.

114 S4CC, *Minutes of the third joint BCW/S4C meeting*, p. 6. Despite this promise, doubts were expressed about the role of broadcasters in the field of learning Welsh. It was asked whether the aim of a television programme was to provide an incentive to attend courses, or to provide a complete course?

115 WFCA, *Annual Report and Accounts, 1984–85*, p. 8. *Sioe Siarad* provided much more formal Welsh lessons by illustrating everyday situations and how to use the Welsh language in them, unlike *Gair yn ei Bryd* which referred to difficult-to-understand words in that evening's output. In addition, the lessons would be accompanied by supporting materials and supplementary material in *Sbec*; S4CC, *Nodiadau ar wythfed cyfarfod Pwyllgor Cymreig Awdurdod Darlledu Annibynnol i*

drafod rhaglenni 'annibynnol' S4C, 2 November 1984, p. 4; unknown author, 'Cyfle i'r dysgwyr siarad', *Y Cymro*, 12 March 1985, 2.

116 WFCA, *Annual Report and Accounts, 1984–85*, p. 8. In addition, a videotape of the course and a booklet to accompany the broadcasts was produced by S4C's commercial arm, Mentrau, and sold to the public at a cost of £26.50; S4CC, *Draft minutes of the twenty-sixth directors' meeting of Mentrau Cyf*, 10 April 1985, p. 89.

117 WFCA, *Annual Report and Accounts, 1985–86* (Cardiff, 1986), p. 16.

118 E. Dyfed, 'Difwyno'r "dorth" gyda'r iaith fain', *Y Cymro*, 18 January 1983.

119 S4CC, *Cofnodion unfed cyfarfod ar ddeg ar hugain Awdurdod Sianel Pedwar Cymru*, 3 December 1982, p. 2. Since interviews are referred to in this discussion, the authority seems to have been referring to news, and factual programming, rather than dramas. Euryn Ogwen Williams also remembers that there were some initial difficulties in this regard with the factual programmes. Author's interview with Euryn Ogwen Williams, Cardiff, 23 February 2007.

120 S4CC, *Sylwadau ar y gwasanaeth, Tachwedd 27 1982 – Ionawr 3 1983 – Papur atodol i Agenda ail gyfarfod ar ddeg ar hugain Awdurdod Sianel Pedwar Cymru*, 13 January 1983; S4CC, *Sylwadau ar y gwasanaeth, Ebrill 5 – Mai 3 1983 – Papur atodol i Agenda unfed cyfarfod ar bymtheg ar hugain Awdurdod Sianel Pedwar Cymru*, 5–6 May 1983; Wynfford James, 'Cyfweliad Saesneg gwasaidd', *Y Faner*, 18 March 1983.

121 Not all responses to the programme were negative: Eric Wyn, 'Adloniant ysgafn Cymru yn symud gyda'r oes', *Y Faner*, 1 March 1985, 21; Glyn Môn Jones, 'In Downtown Cardiff', *Western Mail*, 2 March 1983.

122 S4CC, *Minutes of the joint meeting between the Broadcasting Council of Wales and members of Sianel Pedwar Cymru*, 15 March 1985, p. 2.

123 S4CC, *Minutes of the joint meeting between the Broadcasting Council of Wales and members of Sianel Pedwar Cymru*, 15 March 1985, p. 3.

124 S4CC, *Sylwadau ar y gwasanaeth, Ionawr 4 1983 – Ionawr 27 1983 – Papur atodol i Agenda trydydd cyfarfod ar ddeg ar hugain Awdurdod Sianel Pedwar Cymru*, 4 February 1983; S4CC, *Sylwadau ar y gwasanaeth, Mawrth 1 – Ebrill '83 – Papur Atodol i Agenda pumed cyfarfod ar ddeg ar hugain Awdurdod Sianel Pedwar Cymru*, 8 April 1983. S4CC, Letter from a viewer from Ruthin to Owen Edwards, May Day 1986; Iwan Edgar, 'Gormod o 'Mericianrwtsh Melltigedig ar y Sianel', *Y Faner*, February 1984, 12.

125 S4CC, Letter from Owen Edwards to a viewer from Ruthin, 16 May 1986.

Chapter 4

1 Sianel Pedwar Cymru Collection (S4CC), *Cofnodion pumed cyfarfod ar hugain Awdurdod Sianel Pedwar Cymru*, 28–9 June 1982, p. 3.

2 S4CC, *Cofnodion pumed cyfarfod ar hugain Awdurdod Sianel Pedwar Cymru*, p. 3. The IBA informed the channel of its likely income, before confirming the figure some months later. If the channel was unhappy with the proposed figure this process gave them opportunity to appeal to the IBA and then to the Home Secretary if the amount was unacceptably low.

3 S4CC, Letter from John Whitney to Owen Edwards, 25 November 1982, p. 1.

4 S4CC, Letter from John Whitney to Owen Edwards, 25 November 1982, p. 1; Clive Betts, 'S4C gives pledge on service as grant cut', *Western Mail*, 23 December 1982; Ivor Wynne Jones, 'Cash curb blow for growth of Welsh TV', *Daily Post*, 29 December 1982; unknown author, 'ITV to pay £98m for 4, £24m for S4C, plus £15m', *The Stage and Television Today*, 30 December 1982.

5 S4CC, Letter from John Whitney to Owen Edwards, 25 November 1982, p. 1. In the first years the patterns of calculating income for S4C and C4 were onerous. The IBA would calculate the contribution of the fifteen ITV network companies towards the fourth channel on the basis of a calendar year's worth of advertising revenue, although S4C and C4 themselves operated and prepared their accounts by financial year. This means that different income figures are referenced depending on the documents in question and the type of year referred to, creating a slightly confusing pattern. This pattern was used until 1983, moving to the fiscal year from 1984–5. Although this in principle made sense, it was a matter of concern to S4C staff because of the timetable of specifying an estimated income level in September, and then confirming the final figure in March, just weeks before the financial year was due to start; S4CC, Letter from Owen Edwards to Peter B. Rogers, 14 June 1983.

6 S4CC, Letter from John Whitney to Owen Edwards, 25 November 1982, p. 1.

7 Paul Bonner, with Lesley Aston, *Independent Television in Britain: Volume 6. New Developments in Independent Television, 1981–92: Channel 4, TV-am, Cable and Satellite* (Basingstoke, 2003), p. 96; unknown author, 'C4 snubs fixed – ITV companies liable for £123m', *Broadcast*, 13 December 1982, 5.

8 S4CC, Letter from John Whitney to Owen Edwards, 25 January 1982, p. 1.

9 S4CC, *Amcangyfrifon 1983/84 (Papur 15.82(8)) – Papur atodol i Agenda unfed cyfarfod ar ddeg ar hugain Awdurdod Sianel Pedwar Cymru*, 3 December 1982, p. 2; Clive Betts, 'S4C programme-makers face squeeze', *Western Mail*, 7 March 1983.

10 The spend on organisational costs was around 10 per cent of the whole budget (10.4 per cent in 1983–4 and 10.1 per cent in 1984–5), which meant that around 90 per cent of the budget was spent directly on programmes. The only years of the trial period to depart from this pattern was during 1981–3 when non-programme costs amounted to 19.9 per cent, due to significant expenditure on equipment, buildings and the marketing campaign before launching the service. S4CC, *S4C Income from ADA: 1981–85, Brief for Mr Peregrine for ADA meeting 7.9.83 – Papur atodol i Agenda deugeinfed cyfarfod Awdurdod Sianel Pedwar Cymru*, 9 September 1983, Appendix II.

11 S4CC, *Adroddiad i'r Awdurdod ar effaith cyllideb 1983/84 ar y Cynhyrchwyr Annibynnol – Papur atodol i Agenda ail gyfarfod ar ddeg ar hugain Awdurdod Sianel Pedwar Cymru*, 13 January 1983; Clive Betts, 'S4C to drop English firms', *Western Mail*, 2 April 1982. Even though Jack Bellamy's company disappeared from the list of independent production companies in the second and third year of production activities, he received a further commission in 1985–6.

12 Welsh Fourth Channel Authority (WFCA), *Annual Report and Accounts, 1983–4* (Cardiff, 1984), p. 34. Red Rooster was Stephen Bayly's company, he had directed *Joni Jones* for Sgrin '82.

13 S4CC, *Adroddiad i'r Awdurdod ar effaith cyllideb 1983/84 ar y Cynhyrchwyr Annibynnol.*

14 Unknown author, 'S4C needs £2–3m extra next year for HTV output', *The Stage and Television Today*, 31 March 1983.

15 S4CC, *Financial outlook for 1983–4 (Papur 15.82(7)) – Papur atodol i Agenda unfed cyfarfod ar ddeg ar hugain Awdurdod Sianel Pedwar Cymru*, 3 December 1982.

16 S4CC, Letter from Owen Edwards to Peter B. Rogers, 14 June 1983.

17 The ITV companies had invested in the fourth channel fifteen months before they were able to sell any advertising space on the channels.

18 S4CC, *Cofnodion pedwerydd cyfarfod ar ddeg ar hugain Awdurdod Sianel Pedwar Cymru*, 4 March 1983, pp. 1–2.

19 S4CC, *Cofnodion pumed cyfarfod ar ddeg ar hugain Awdurdod Sianel Pedwar Cymru*, 8 April 1983, p. 1.

20 S4CC, Letter from Owen Edwards to Peter B. Rogers, August 1983.

21 S4CC, *Cofnodion pumed cyfarfod ar ddeg ar hugain Awdurdod Sianel Pedwar Cymru*, p. 1.

22 S4CC, *Cofnodion deugeinfed cyfarfod Awdurdod Sianel Pedwar Cymru*, 9 September 1983, p. 2. There was no guarantee that ITV companies would pay 18 per cent of their NAR income to the IBA, especially given that they had not been able to recover the expected amount of their investment in the fourth channel. It was therefore likely that they could press for payment of closer to 14 per cent of NAR, the minimum accepted according to their agreement with the IBA, which would be a far worse scenario for S4C. Indeed, in August 1983 there was fiery correspondence between Owen Edwards and Paul Fox, chairman of the Independent Television Companies Association (ITCA), because what the S4C director saw as an attempt by ITV companies to lobby for withdrawal from the deal to pay for the fourth channel and their use of journalists to push their ideas and attack S4C. The allegations were vehemently denied by the ITCA; however, the nature of these letters demonstrates how sensitive this matter was to both sides. S4CC, Letter from Owen Edwards to Paul Fox, 8 August 1983; Letter from Paul Fox to Owen Edwards, 12 August 1983.

23 S4CC, *Cofnodion deugeinfed cyfarfod Awdurdod Sianel Pedwar Cymru*, p. 2.

24 S4CC, Letter from Sir Goronwy Daniel to Lord Thomson, 31 August 1983, p. 1.

25 S4CC, Letter from Sir Goronwy Daniel to Lord Thomson, 31 August 1983, p. 2.

26 S4C, Letter from Sir Goronwy Daniel to Lord Thomson, 31 August 1983, p. 2.

27 S4CC, Letter from Sir Goronwy Daniel to Lord Thomson, 31 August 1983, p. 2.

28 S4CC, *Arian o'r ADA ym 1984/85 (Papur 10.83(5)) – Papur atodol i Agenda unfed cyfarfod a deugain Awdurdod Sianel Pedwar Cymru*, 7 October 1983, p. 2.

29 S4CC, Letter from Euryn Ogwen Williams to Tim Knowles, HTV assistant managing director, 29 September 1983.

30 S4CC, Letter from John Whitney to Owen Edwards, 19 January 1984; Raymond Snoddy, 'Fourth channels to get £139m', *Financial Times*, 21 January 1984.

31 S4CC, *Adroddiad y Cyfarwyddwr i'r Awdurdod (Papur 3.85(4)) – Papur atodol i Agenda cyfarfod hanner cant a thri Awdurdod Sianel Pedwar Cymru*, 8 March 1985.

32 S4CC, *Cofnodion pumed cyfarfod a deugain Awdurdod Sianel Pedwar Cymru*, 10 February 1984, p. 4.

33 S4CC, *Amcangyfrifon 1984/5 a 1985/6, Nodyn gan y Cyfarwyddwr (Papur 2.84(6)) – Papur atodol i Agenda pumed cyfarfod a deugain Awdurdod Sianel Pedwar Cymru*, 10 February 1984.
34 Derek Hopper, 'S4C's cash bid rejected', *South Wales Echo*, 20 January 1984; Clive Betts, 'S4C to get a £28m budget', *Western Mail*, 21 January 1984; unknown author, '£28 miliwn i'r sianel', *Y Cymro*, 24 January 1984.
35 S4CC, *Y Sector Annibynnol – pwyso a mesur (Papur 10.83(6)) – Papur atodol i Agenda unfed cyfarfod a deugain Awdurdod Sianel Pedwar Cymru*, 7 October 1983, p. 1.
36 There were only four members of staff working on commissioning and overseeing productions during 1983–4, namely Euryn Ogwen Williams, programme editor, Emlyn Davies, head of programme commissioning, Dilwyn Jones, programme commissioner and one administrator. A small number of staff considering that other broadcasters had separate commissioners for each genre during the early 1980s.
37 S4CC, *Y Sector Annibynnol – pwyso a mesur*, p. 1.
38 S4CC, *Y Sector Annibynnol – pwyso a mesur*, p. 1.
39 S4CC, *Y Sector Annibynnol – pwyso a mesur*, p. 2.
40 The channel had introduced measures to ensure that independent producers were fully aware of the importance of tight financial management, by going against the industry convention of including a contingency fund for unexpected costs and expenses as part of each commission's budget. Instead, it was felt that not including this element would underline the need for tight control. The result of such a policy was that overspend would appear to be worse, and possibly much more common, as there was no contingency to cope with events and changes beyond the production team's control; S4CC, *Y Sector Annibynnol – pwyso a mesur*, p. 3.
41 S4CC, *Y Sector Annibynnol – pwyso a mesur*, pp. 3–9.
42 S4CC, *Y Sector Annibynnol – pwyso a mesur*, p. 4.
43 S4CC, *Y Sector Annibynnol – pwyso a mesur*, p. 4.
44 S4CC, *Y Sector Annibynnol – pwyso a mesur*, p. 4.
45 S4CC, *Y Sector Annibynnol – pwyso a mesur*, p. 4.
46 S4CC, *Y Sector Annibynnol – pwyso a mesur*, pp. 4–5.
47 S4CC, *Y Sector Annibynnol – pwyso a mesur*, p. 5.
48 S4CC, *Cofnodion seithfed cyfarfod a deugain Awdurdod Sianel Pedwar Cymru*, 5–6 April 1984, p. 2. That figure of 270 hours was likely to fall after the ideas discussed with the companies were fully costed; even after that process, the proposed increase remained a significant one. The channel did not appear to have been able to increase the hours of independent producers between 1984 and 1985, and 1985 and 1986 to the extent originally expected: they produced 184 hours in 1984–5, which increased to 206 hours and 30 minutes the following financial year. The cost of independent producers' programmes did not reduce on average per hour either as the cost per hour in 1984–5 was £38,459, which increased to £43,176 the following year. WFCA, *Annual Report and Accounts, 1984–85* (Cardiff, 1985), p. 6; WFCA, *Annual Report and Accounts, 1985–86* (Cardiff, 1986), p. 25.
49 S4CC, *Y Sector Annibynnol – pwyso a mesur*, p. 9.
50 S4CC, *Y Sector Annibynnol – pwyso a mesur*, p. 9.
51 S4CC, *Y Sector Annibynnol – pwyso a mesur*, p. 9.

52 S4CC, *Cofnodion cyfarfod hanner cant Awdurdod Sianel Pedwar Cymru*, 13 July 1984, p. 3.

53 S4CC, Letter from Peter B. Rogers to Owen Edwards, 20 September 1984, p. 1; Clive Betts, 'S4C's budget too low, says chief', *Western Mail*, 9 November 1984.

54 S4CC, *Cofnodion cyfarfod hanner cant a thri Awdurdod Sianel Pedwar Cymru*, 12 October 1984, p. 1.

55 S4CC, *Cofnodion cyfarfod hanner cant a phump Awdurdod Sianel Pedwar Cymru*, 6–7 December 1984, p. 4.

56 S4CC, *The effect of funding S4C below £31.857m in 1985/6 (Papur 2.85(8)) – Papur atodol i Agenda cyfarfod hanner cant a saith Awdurdod Sianel Pedwar Cymru*, 7–8 February 1985.

57 S4CC, *The effect of funding S4C below £31.857m in 1985/6.*

58 S4CC, *The effect of funding S4C below £31.857m in 1985/6.*

59 S4CC, *The effect of funding S4C below £31.857m in 1985/6*, p. 3.

60 S4CC, *Cofnodion cyfarfod hanner cant a saith Awdurdod Sianel Pedwar Cymru*, p. 5.

61 S4CC, *Dyfodol SBEC (Papur 5.84(8)) – Papur atodol i Agenda wythfed cyfarfod a deugain Awdurdod Sianel Pedwar Cymru*, 11 May 1984, p. 1.

62 There could only be a saving of £210,000 in 1984–5 should it be terminated.

63 S4CC, *The effect of funding S4C below £31.857m in 1985/6*, p. 3.

64 S4CC, *Cofnodion cyfarfod hanner cant a thri Awdurdod Sianel Pedwar Cymru*, p. 2; unknown author, 'S4C gets the cash it wants to carry out growth plans', *Western Mail*, 23 February 1985; unknown author, 'Newyddion da i S4C', *Y Cymro*, 26 February 1985.

65 S4CC, *Adroddiad y Cyfarwyddwr i'r Awdurdod (Papur 3.85(4)).*

66 S4CC, *Cofnodion cyfarfod hanner cant a thri Awdurdod Sianel Pedwar Cymru*, p. 2.

67 WFCA, *Annual Report and Accounts, 1982–83* (Cardiff, 1983), p. 8.

68 S4CC, *Amcangyfrifon 1983/84 (Papur 15.82(8))*, p. 1.

69 'Mae'n ffordd ddi-gost o greu ymwybyddiaeth yng Nghymru a thramor o fodolaeth y sianel'; S4CC, *Blwyddyn i fynd – Adroddiad yr Adran Raglenni (Papur 15.81(2)) – Papur atodol i Agenda pymthegfed cyfarfod Awdurdod Sianel Pedwar Cymru*, 6 November 1981, p. 4. Unless otherwise noted, translations are those of the author.

70 S4CC, *Adroddiad y Cyfarwyddwr i'r Awdurdod (Papur 2.82(4)) – Papur atodol i Agenda deunawfed cyfarfod Awdurdod Sianel Pedwar Cymru*, 5 February 1982, p. 2.

71 S4CC, *Adroddiad y Cyfarwyddwr i'r Awdurdod (Papur 2.82(4) – Papur atodol i Agenda deunawfed cyfarfod Awdurdod Sianel Pedwar Cymru*, p. 3; Robert Lloyd, 'Superted – S4C's bear-faced star', *South Wales Evening Post*, 19 March 1982; Unknown author, 'Gwerthu rhaglenni Cymraeg dramor', *Y Cymro*, 23 March 1982; unknown author, 'Experience to market for independents', *The Stage and Television Today*, 1 April 1982; Ann Cooper, 'Welsh Channel 4 picks teddybear for campaign', *Marketing*, 25 March 1982; unknown author, 'Gwerthu S4C i'r byd', *Herald Môn*, 30 March 1982. The programmes were promoted under the banner of 'S4C International' and three members of the channel's staff travelled to Cannes, Owen Edwards, Euryn Ogwen Williams and Chris Grace, to collaborate with Laurie Ward of TWI who would promote S4C programmes on behalf of that company.

The sale and negotiation of terms was the responsibility of TWI, and a 25 per cent commission was agreed. Using an agency to do this work made sense at this early stage, as it enabled staff to engage in more important activities, such as getting the channel ready to start broadcasting. It also allowed the channel to experiment with selling programmes without making a long-term commitment before knowing what the response would be.

72 S4CC, *Blwyddyn i fynd – Adroddiad yr Adran Raglenni (Papur 15.81(2))*, p. 4.

73 Producing in Welsh first made the process of changing voiceovers easier, as the Welsh scripts were discursive so there was enough space to change voiceovers relatively easily. Author's interview with Chris Grace, Cardiff, 29 November 2010.

74 S4CC, *Merchandising and S4C (Papur 4.82(8)) – Papur atodol i Agenda ugeinfed cyfarfod Awdurdod Sianel Pedwar Cymru*, 21–2 March 1982, p. 2.

75 S4CC, *Y Darnau'n Disgyn i'w Lle – Papur atodol i Agenda ugeinfed cyfarfod Awdurdod Sianel Pedwar Cymru*, 21–2 March 1982, Attachment 5; unknown author, 'SUPERTED YN CONCRO'R BYD!', *Y Cymro*, 4 May 1982. The other programmes promoted in addition to the six noted were *Joni Jones*, *Storïau Serch*, *Celtic Folk Club*, *Ar Log Ar Log*, *Almanac*, *Pawennau wrth y Porth*, *Y Cyswllt Cymreig*, *Max Boyce yn America*, *Madam Wen*, *O Efrog Newydd i Landdona* and *Kilimanjaro*.

76 Clive Betts, 'Superted set to make millions', *Western Mail*, 30 April 1982.

77 S4CC, *Adroddiad y Cyfarwyddwr i'r Awdurdod (Papur 6.82(4)) – Papur atodol i agenda ail gyfarfod ar hugain Awdurdod Sianel Pedwar Cymru*, 7 May 1982, p. 2.

78 S4CC, *Materion Rhaglenni i'w Trafod (Papur 8.82(9)) – Papur atodol i Agenda pedwerydd cyfarfod ar hugain Awdurdod Sianel Pedwar Cymru*, 25 May 1982, Attachment II.

79 Some of the other countries who undertook to buy the series were Australia, Kenya, Israel, France, Portugal, Finland, Chile, Columbia, Venezuela, Thailand and Malaysia. Betts, 'Superted set to make millions'; Barry Jones, 'Superted beams out on worldwide TV', *Daily Post*, 5 May 1982.

80 Robin Lyons remembers that Mike Young was a master of self-promotion, a skill that was instrumental in this context. Author's interview with Robin Lyons, Cardiff, 15 October 2010.

81 S4CC, *Datblygiadau i S4C – Papur atodol i Agenda ail gyfarfod ar bymtheg Awdurdod Sianel Pedwar Cymru*, 8 January 1982, p. 1.

82 S4CC, *Datblygiadau i S4C*, p. 1.

83 S4CC, *Mentrau S4C, Interim Report (Papur 1.83(7)) – Papur atodol i Agenda ail gyfarfod ar ddeg ar hugain Awdurdod Sianel Pedwar Cymru*, 13 January 1983.

84 This is a view now also shared by Chris Grace: he stated that in retrospect he felt this was an 'odd' activity for the channel to engage with. Author's interview with Chris Grace, Cardiff, 29 November 2010.

85 Author's interview with Chris Grace, Cardiff, 29 November 2010; S4CC, *Mentrau S4C, Interim Report (Papur 1.83(7))*.

86 Unknown author, 'Television brings new industry to the Coal Exchange in Cardiff', *Contact Cardiff*, November/December 1983.

87 S4CC, *Merchandising and S4C (Papur 4.82(8))*, p. 1.

88 S4CC, *Merchandising and S4C*, p. 1; Wynne Melville Jones, *Y Fi a Mistar Urdd a'r Cwmni Da* (Talybont, 2010); unknown author, 'Super Ted – and S4C – dream of Muppet millions', *Western Mail*, 21 April 1982; unknown author, 'Superted: big spin-off potential for Wales', *Western Mail Quarterly Ecomonic Review*, 14 July 1982.
89 Unknown author, 'Cynhyrchu nwyddau S4C', *Y Cymro*, 23 March 1982.
90 S4CC, *S4C Byd Eang – Materion Rhaglenni i'w Trafod (Papur 8.82(9))*, Attachment II.
91 Unknown author, 'Ted to the rescue of slump-hit region', *Television Weekly*, 19 January 1983; author's interview with Euryn Ogwen Williams, Cardiff, 24 April 2007.
92 Christopher Grace, 'Success story of Superted', *Western Mail*, 13 May 1982. This Australian order was estimated to be worth £100,000.
93 S4CC, *Materion Rhaglenni i'w Trafod (Papur 8.82(9))*, Attachment II; unknown author, 'Tyfu yn sgil y posteri', *Y Cymro*, 8 June 1982.
94 S4CC, *Adroddiad y Cyfarwyddwr (Papur 10.82(4)) – Papur atodol i Agenda chwechد cyfarfod ar hugain, Awdurdod Sianel Pedwar Cymru*, 15 July 1982.
95 Unknown author, 'Superted set to take U.S. by storm', *Daily Post*, 13 January 1984; WFCA, *Annual Report and Accounts, 1984–85*, p. 13.
96 Golygydd, 'S4C yn lledaenu ei hadenydd gyda "Mentrau"', *Y Faner*, 15 July 1983; Clive Betts, 'S4C Memtrau [*sic*] facility', *Broadcast*, 18 July 1983.
97 S4CC, *Cofnodion wythfed cyfarfod ar hugain Awdurdod Sianel Pedwar Cymru*, 3 September 1982, p. 1. Financially, in principle, S4C would receive instalments from Mentrau if it made enough profit to pay them. Author's interview with Chris Grace, Cardiff, 29 November 2010.
98 S4CC, *Mentrau (Papur 15.82(9)) – Papur atodol i Agenda unfed cyfarfod ar ddeg ar hugain Awdurdod Sianel Pedwar Cymru*, 3 December 1982. Despite the close relationship, Mentrau was a separate company, would have its own staff, would produce independent accounts and the company would have different tax responsibilities to S4C, to ensure that its commercial activities did not adversely affect the channel.
99 S4CC, *Cofnodion ail gyfarfod ar ddeg ar hugain Awdurdod Sianel Pedwar Cymru*, 13 January 1983, pp. 3–4.
100 S4CC, *Cofnodion pedwerydd cyfarfod ar ddeg ar hugain Awdurdod Sianel Pedwar Cymru*, p. 2; S4CC, *Cofnodion pumed cyfarfod ar ddeg ar hugain Awdurdod Sianel Pedwar Cymru*, p. 2.
101 There they visited Bob Harpur, RTÉ's acquisitions manager for both of its channels in Ireland. It was thought that the RTÉ officer's opinion of the quality of the productions was significant since he was considered one of Europe's wisest buyers.
102 Unknown author, 'Gwyddelod yn "dotio" at ein rhaglenni', *Y Cymro*, 15 March 1983; unknown author, 'S4C at MIP', *Broadcast*, 18 April 1983.
103 S4CC, *Taith Werthu Gyntaf Mentrau (Papur 4.83(11a)) – Papur atodol i Agenda pumed cyfarfod ar ddeg ar hugain Awdurdod Sianel Pedwar Cymru*, 8 April 1983.
104 S4CC, *Cofnodion unfed cyfarfod ar bymtheg ar hugain Awdurdod Sianel Pedwar Cymru*, 5–6 May 1983, p. 4; S4CC, *Cofnodion seithfed cyfarfod ar ddeg ar hugain Awdurdod Sianel Pedwar Cymru*, 3 June 1983, p. 1; S4CC, *Cofnodion wythfed cyfarfod ar ddeg ar hugain Awdurdod Sianel Pedwar Cymru*, 1 July 1983, p. 1. The

principle of selling programmes to South Africa was hotly debated for many months: the channel did not want to be seen as tolerant of the country's apartheid regime, but the chairman was anxious not to prevent the channel's officials from selling to any country. The complexity of these discussion is not reflected in the minutes, but in interviews, many channel staff and authority members remember that this was one of the main areas of disagreement during the probationary period. There was no final decision on the matter, and they decided to wait for a request to purchase a programme from a South African broadcaster before returning to the debate.

105 Jennie Thomas and J. O. Williams, *Llyfr Mawr y Plant* (Wrexham, 1931); Jennie Thomas and J. O. Williams, *Llyfr Mawr y Plant – ail argraffiad* (Wrexham, 1974).

106 WFCA, *Annual Report and Accounts, 1983–84*, p. 12.

107 WFCA, *Annual Report and Accounts, 1983–84*, p. 21; WFCA, *Annual Report and Accounts, 1984–85*, p. 14; unknown author, 'S4C publishes', *Western Mail*, 4 August 1983.

108 WFCA, *Annual Report and Accounts, 1984–85*, p. 14.

109 WFCA, *Annual Report and Accounts, 1985–86*, p. 22.

110 S4CC, *Minutes of the twenty-ninth Directors Meeting of Mentrau Cyf*, 11 July 1985, pp. 104–5.

111 WFCA, *Annual Report and Accounts, 1984–85*, p. 14.

112 Eurig Wyn, 'S4C a Hughes a'i Fab yn torri egwyddor sylfaenol cyhoeddi', *Y Faner*, 3 November 1984; Anwen Parri, 'Ergyd arall i'r Llyfrwerthwyr', *Y Faner*, 30 November 1984. Hughes a'i Fab was not the only publisher to sell directly, Gwasg Gomer had sold Moc Morgan's book through fishing clubs during the same year.

113 Unknown author, 'BBC 1 to screen English Superted', *South Wales Echo*, 2 December 1982; unknown author, 'Superted to BBC', *Broadcast*, 6 December 1982; unknown author, 'Siwpyrted yn creu jobsys', *Sulyn*, 12 December 1982; *Western Mail* reporter, 'Superted – Welsh ambassador', *Western Mail*, 27 April 1983; Roger Laing, 'Superted the star of Cannes', *Daily Post*, 28 April 1983; Phil Reiley, 'Big audience bid by Welsh bear', *South Wales Evening Post*, 23 September 1983; unknown author, 'Baddies sent packing', *Exeter Express and Echo*, 24 September 1983; Alan Road, 'The bear facts', *The Observer*, 25 September 1983.

114 It was originally intended to call the new joint company S4CIN Productions LTD but, by early 1984, as they incorporated the company it was named Telin, a combination of the words 'television' and 'investment'; S4CC, *Papur 10.83(10c) – Papur Atodol i Agenda unfed cyfarfod a deugain Awdurdod Sianel Pedwar Cymru*, 7 October 1983; S4CC, *Adroddiad y Cyfarwyddwr i'r Awdurdod (Papur 1.84(4)) – Papur atodol i Agenda pedwerydd cyfarfod a deugain Awdurdod Sianel Pedwar Cymru*, 6 January 1984, p. 1; Clive Betts, 'Miners' money helps pay for new S4C SuperTed show', *Western Mail*, 20 January 1984; Tim Jones, 'Coal fund invests in SuperTed', *The Times*, 20 January 1984; unknown author, 'Hwb i Superted gan y Glowyr', *Y Cymro*, 24 January 1984; unknown author, 'NCB PENSIONS FUND SUPERTED', *Broadcast*, 20 January 1984.

115 Diana Frampton, 'CIN backing boosts S4C and SuperTed', *Television Weekly*, 27 January 1984. CIN was the owner of the production company Acorn Productions,

which also owned 30 per cent of the Goldcrest company; S4CC, *Report: Proposed Joint Venture Company, and Funding of 'SuperTed' – Papur atodol i Agenda deugeinfed cyfarfod Awdurdod Sianel Pedwar Cymru*, 9 September 1983.

116 S4CC, *Report: Proposed Joint Venture Company, and Funding of 'SuperTed'*. Although Mentrau held the majority of the combined shares in the joint company, the two organisations shared the equity shares equally. CIN was keen to ensure that Mentrau, as the company that owned most of the shares, did not use Telin's profits to fund productions and projects that CIN was not happy with, so added various clauses that would protect CIN in the company's articles.

117 S4CC, *Report: Proposed Joint Venture Company, and Funding of 'SuperTed'*.

118 S4CC, *Cofnodion degfed cyfarfod ar hugain Awdurdod Sianel Pedwar Cymru*, 5 November 1982, p. 5.

119 S4C officials also believed that fully funding *SuperTed* through external sources supported the production of further series of *Wil Cwac Cwac* since they were produced simultaneously by the same studio, sharing the same administrative costs. S4CC, *Cofnodion degfed cyfarfod ar hugain Awdurdod Sianel Pedwar Cymru*, p. 5.

120 In 1985–6 Telin invested in the stop-motion animation series *Sam Tân/Fireman Sam* produced by Bumper, which further shows that S4C was highly dependent on outside investors to continue to commission quality animation series; WFCA, *Annual Report and Accounts, 1985–86*, p. 22.

121 The agreement with Disney gave the media giant the opportunity to also buy further series of the production. DH, 'SuperTed! Saviour of S4C?', *Broadcast*, 13 January 1984. It is assumed that Mentrau was responsible for the negotiations and the sale to Disney and not Telin, since the establishment of the joint company was not announced until late January 1984. After that, however, Telin would negotiate with broadcasters and the merchandise companies.

122 Unknown author, 'SuperTed is sold to Disney Channel', *The Stage and Television Today*, 9 January 1984; unknown author, 'Walt's boyo bear!', *The Sun*, 13 January 1984; unknown author, 'SuperTed Takes on America', *Eastern Daily Press*, 13 January 1984; unknown author, 'Ted's a Star', *Daily Star*, 13 January 1984; unknown author, 'Superted signs-up', *Greenock Telegraph*, 13 January 1984; unknown author, 'Superted joins the Disney big time', *Shropshire Star*, 13 January 1984; unknown author, 'It's . . . Superted!', *Worcester Evening News*, 13 January 1984; unknown author, 'Magic Welsh bear links-up with Mickey Mouse', *Wolverhampton Express & Star*, 13 January 1984; unknown author, 'Disney sign up "Superted"', *The Scotsman*, 13 January 1984; unknown author, 'Little Welsh bear hits big time', *South Wales Evening Post*, 13 January 1984; Clive Betts, 'Superted set to star on American TV', *Western Mail*, 13 January 1984; unknown author, 'Superted set to take U.S. by storm'; Carla Dobson, 'Welsh teddy bear scores a first in Disney deal', *The Daily Telegraph*, 13 January 1984; Paul Hoyland, 'Superted conquers world of Disney', *The Guardian*, 13 January 1984; unknown author; 'Disney buys Welsh TV cartoon', *The Times*, 13 January 1984; Robin Reeves, 'Welsh TV sells its SuperTed to Disney', *The Financial Times*, 13 January 1984; unknown author, 'SUPERTED! Saviour of S4C?', *Broadcast*, 13 January 1984; Derek Hooper, 'What a coup for Wales!', *South Wales Echo*, 14 January 1984; unknown author, 'Superted off to America',

Sheffield Morning Telegraph, 14 January 1984; unknown author, 'Disney airing for "SuperTed"', *Screen International*, 14 January 1984; unknown author, 'Superted yn Los Angeles', *Y Cymro*, 17 January 1984; unknown author, 'SuperTed is sold to Disney Channel', *The Stage*, 19 January 1984; Diana Frampton, 'Crimefighter SuperTed swooping on Stateside', *Television Weekly*, 20 January 1984.

123 Unknown author, 'Superted set to take U.S. by storm'.

124 Houses of Parliament, Order Paper – Tuesday, 24 January 1984, 408. The motion was signed by twenty-nine MPs, with seventeen representing Welsh constituencies. There was also cross-party representation as twelve Labour members, eight Conservatives, six Liberals, one SNP Member and two Plaid Cymru members signed and joined the motion to congratulate the channel. S4CC, *Adroddiad y Cyfarwyddwr i'r Awdurdod (Papur 2.84(4))*, p. 1; unknown author, 'Commons praise for Superted', *Cambrian News*, 3 February 1984.

125 S4CC, *Minutes of the fifteenth Directors' Meeting of Mentrau Cyf – Papur atodol i Agenda nawfed cyfarfod a deugain Awdurdod Sianel Pedwar Cymru*, 7–8 June 1984, p. 2.

126 S4CC, *Minutes of the sixteenth Directors' Meeting of Mentrau Cyf – Papur atodol i Agenda cyfarfod hanner cant Awdurdod Sianel Pedwar Cymru*, 13 July 1984.

127 Unknown author, 'Ted's a Star'.

128 S4CC, *Cofnodion cyfarfod hanner cant a phedwar Awdurdod Sianel Pedwar Cymru*, 9 November 1984, p. 3.

129 S4CC, *Minutes of the eighteenth Directors' Meeting of Mentrau Cyf – Papur atodol i Agenda cyfarfod hanner cant a dau Awdurdod Sianel Pedwar Cymru*, 14 September 1984; Steve Schneider, 'An Extraordinary Teddy Bear Joins the Disney Family', *The New York Times*, 3 February 1985. It appears that this delay was not out of the ordinary, because broadcasters' schedules were prepared many months in advance.

130 S4CC, *Minutes of the fourteenth Directors' Meeting of Mentrau Cyf – Papur atodol i Agenda nawfed cyfarfod a deugain Awdurdod Sianel Pedwar Cymru*, 7–8 June 1984.

131 S4CC, *Cofnodion cyfarfod hanner cant ag un Awdurdod Sianel Pedwar Cymru*, 10 August 1984.

132 S4CC, *Minutes of the twenty-fourth Directors' Meeting of Mentrau Cyf – Papur atodol i Agenda cyfarfod hanner cant ag wyth Awdurdod Sianel Pedwar Cymru*, 8 March 1985, p. 81.

133 S4CC, *Draft Minutes of the twenty-eighth Directors' Meeting of Mentrau Cyf – Papur atodol i Agenda trydydd cyfarfod a thrigain Awdurdod Sianel Pedwar Cymru*, 11–12 July 1985, p. 99; sales were just as impressive in Britain: Guild Home Video sold 2,200 VHS tapes in three weeks in 1983, which was a new record for the company, followed by 3,000 copies in two months at the end of 1984; S4CC, *Minutes of the tenth Directors' meeting of Mentrau Cyf – Papur atodol i Agenda trydydd cyfarfod a deugain Awdurdod Sianel Pedwar Cymru*, 1–2 December 1983; S4CC, *Draft Minutes of the twenty-second Directors' Meeting of Mentrau Cyf – Papur atodol i Agenda cyfarfod hanner cant a chwech Awdurdod Sianel Pedwar Cymru*, 10 January 1985.

134 WFCA, *Annual Report and Accounts, 1985–86*, p. 21.

135 S4CC, *Draft Minutes of the twenty-sixth Directors' Meeting of Mentrau Cyf*, 10 April 1985.

136 Clive Betts, 'Wil Cwac Cwac goes Muscovite', *Western Mail*, 5 March 1985.

137 S4CC, *Draft Minutes of the twenty-third Directors' Meeting of Mentrau Cyf*, 7–8 February 1985. *Wil Cwac Cwac* was also sold to the Children's Channel on the British cable network in 1985; S4CC, *Draft Minutes of the thirty-first Directors' Meeting of Mentrau Cyf – Papur atodol i agenda seithfed cyfarfod a thrigain Awdurdod Sianel Pedwar Cymru*, 7–8 November 1985.

138 S4CC, *Cofnodion cyfarfod hanner cant a chwech Awdurdod Sianel Pedwar Cymru*, 10 January 1985, p. 4.

139 WFCA, *Annual Report and Accounts, 1984–85*, p. 12; WFCA, *Annual Report and Accounts, 1985–86*, p. 19.

140 S4CC, *Adroddiad y Cyfarwyddwr i'r Awdurdod – Papur atodol i Agenda wythfed cyfarfod a deugain Awdurdod Sianel Pedwar Cymru*, 11 May 1984. By 1985 officials were beginning to worry about the suitability of many of the programmes produced for sale in overseas markets, and that the sales catalogue was not growing. To try to alleviate the problem the channel seems to have considered co-producing animated series with other broadcasters, such as Yorkshire Television, TVS and the BBC, in order to maintain their status in the television markets; S4CC, *Minutes of the twenty-ninth Directors' Meeting of Mentrau Cyf.*

141 S4CC, *Minutes of the twenty-ninth Directors' Meeting of Mentrau Cyf.* The series was renamed *Pushing the Limits* or *Risking it All* for English-medium audiences.

142 S4CC, *Minutes of the thirtieth Directors' Meeting of Mentrau Cyf – Papur atodol i Agenda chweched cyfarfod a thrigain Awdurdod Sianel Pedwar Cymru*, 10–11 October 1985. C4's sales during the same period, however, were double the amount at S4C, at £1.8 million.

143 S4CC, *Minutes of the fifteenth Directors' Meeting of Mentrau Cyf*; S4CC, *Draft Minutes of the twenty-third Directors' meeting of Mentrau Cyf – Papur atodol i Agenda cyfarfod hanner cant a saith Awdurdod Sianel Pedwar Cymru*, 7–8 February 1985.

144 S4CC, *Minutes of the twenty-ninth Directors' Meeting of Mentrau Cyf.*

145 S4CC, *Draft Minutes of the thirty-first Directors' meeting of Mentrau Cyf.*

146 Author's interview with Chris Grace, Cardiff, 29 November 2010.

Chapter 5

1 Sianel Pedwar Cymru Collection (S4CC), Letter from a viewer from Bala to the Programme Director Channel 4, 5 November 1985. This letter was sent to S4C, but the fact that the author addresses the letter to 'Channel 4' shows that a lack of understanding about the difference between the two channels persisted even at the end of the trial period.

2 Jeremy Isaacs, *Storm over 4: A Personal Account* (London, 1989), p. 51.

3 S4CC, Letter from a viewer from Swansea to Owen Edwards, 6 December 1985; S4CC, Letter from a viewer from Pontypridd to Nicholas Edwards, 25 November 1985.

4 S4CC, *Dadansoddiad Gohebiaeth Rhaglenni, Ionawr 1986 – Papur atodol i Agenda unfed cyfarfod ar ddeg a thrigain Awdurdod Sianel Pedwar Cymru*, 14 February 1986.

5 S4C, *Cofnodion Cyfarfod hanner cant a naw Awdurdod Sianel Pedwar Cymru*, 12 April 1985, p. 4.

6 The vote held by Rediffusion is discussed in Chapter 3, pp. 120–2.
7 S4CC, *Adroddiad y Cyfarwyddwr i'r Awdurdod (Papur 2.84(4)) – Papur atodol i Agenda pumed cyfarfod a deugain Awdurdod Sianel Pedwar Cymru*, 10 February 1984, p. 2.
8 'Pe bawn i'n geffyl neu'n aelod o'r teulu brenhinol buasai gennyf gywilydd o iaith anweddus ac agweddau anghwrtais rhai o'm cefnogwyr selog!'; S4CC, *Dadansoddiad Gohebiaeth Rhaglenni – Papur atodol i Agenda trigeinfed cyfarfod Awdurdod Sianel Pedwar Cymru*, 10 May 1985, p. 2. Unless otherwise noted, translations are those of the author.
9 S4CC, Letter from Owen Edwards to a viewer from Llanbradach, 19 November 1986.
10 S4CC, Letter from a viewer from Aberystwyth to Owen Edwards and Welsh Secretary of State Nicholas Edwards, 27 January 1986.
11 Stephen Lambert, *Channel Four: Television with a Difference?* (London, 1982), p. 111.
12 S4CC, Letter from a viewer from Swansea to Owen Edwards, 7 November 1985; S4CC, Letter from a viewer from Cardiff to Owen Edwards, 2 December 1985; S4CC, Letter from a viewer from Helsby to S4C, 14 July 1986.
13 Keith Best, Conservative MP for Anglesey, had sponsored a tea for House members by S4C on 4 June 1984 and an exhibition promoting the channel's activities in the Houses of Commons was organised on the 7 November 1984, which was opened by Giles Shaw, minister of state to the Home Office and the Conservative MP for Pudsey. S4CC, *Adroddiad y Cyfarwyddwr i'r Awdurdod – Papur atodol i Agenda wythfed cyfarfod a deugain Awdurdod Sianel Pedwar Cymru*, 11 May 1984, p. 1.
14 S4CC, *Cwestiwn Tom Hooson i'r Ysgrifennydd Cartref – Papur atodol i Agenda wythfed cyfarfod a deugain Awdurdod Sianel Pedwar Cymru*, 11 May 1984. According to the response drawn up by the Home Office, Tom Hooson was concerned that the channel had invited a number of MPs, and in particular many members of the Home Office and the Welsh Office, to visit the channel, and refreshments had been provided. Seven MPs visited the channel during 1983–4 and refreshments cost £6 per person. Tom Hooson's concern, it seems, was that the channel was spending scarce money on non-broadcast activities trying to persuade MPs to guarantee the channel's survival, something that he did not support.
15 S4CC, Letter from Tom Hooson to Owen Edwards, 26 April 1984; S4CC, Letter from Owen Edwards to Tom Hooson, 19 April 1984; S4CC, Letter from Glyn Tegai Hughes to Tom Hooson, 15 May 1984.
16 S4CC, *'HTV Poll, Principal Results' – Papur atodol i Agenda pedwerydd cyfarfod ar ddeg ar hugain Awdurdod Sianel Pedwar Cymru*, 4 March 1983. The field work for the survey was conducted by Research and Marketing Wales and the West Limited and the data was analysed by Denis Balsom of the Political Science Department, University of Wales, Aberystwyth.
17 *'HTV Poll, Principal Results'*, p. 5. The report does not note the number of Welsh speakers surveyed, but due to the following statement we can assume that 20 per cent of the 994 could speak the language: 'The sample is based upon interlocking quota sample derived from known population parameters of age, sex and social class.' *'HTV Poll, Principal Results'*, p. 1.

18 *'HTV Poll, Principal Results'*, p. 1.

19 *'HTV Poll, Principal Results'*, p. 1.

20 *'HTV Poll, Principal Results'*, p. 1. The remainder of respondents selected the 'don't know' column.

21 S4CC, *Adroddiad Grŵp Cyfryngau Torfol Cymdeithas yr Iaith Gymraeg ar S.4.C. – Papur atodol i Agenda cyfarfod hanner cant a dau Awdurdod Sianel Pedwar Cymru*, 14 September 1984, p. 1.

22 *Adroddiad Grŵp Cyfryngau Torfol Cymdeithas yr Iaith Gymraeg ar S.4.C.*, p. 1. The sense of duty to which Cymdeithas yr Iaith refers is now gone. The novelty, curiosity and original concern for the continuity of the channel has faded, and the Welsh language audience takes the channel for granted and thus turns to the wide range of English language provision available on other channels and streaming services.

23 *Adroddiad Grŵp Cyfryngau Torfol Cymdeithas yr Iaith Gymraeg ar S.4.C.*, p. 3. They surveyed 1,200 individuals from every county in Wales. However, the number of people in each county was not the same, 300 were surveyed in Gwynedd and Dyfed, but only 100 individuals were surveyed in West Glamorgan, South Glamorgan, Mid Glamorgan, Powys, Clwyd and Gwent. No doubt more individuals were selected in Gwynedd and Dyfed to secure an adequate sample of Welsh speakers, but the exact rationale for the sample distribution is not explained in the final report. Despite its weaknesses, it is appropriate to refer to the survey mainly since it is a record of the views of the channel's core audience, and for that purpose provides their views on the channel and its provision.

24 The categories used by Cymdeithas yr Iaith are vague, and there is no definition of what is meant by 'regularly', 'fairly often' or 'rarely'.

25 *Adroddiad Grŵp Cyfryngau Torfol Cymdeithas yr Iaith Gymraeg ar S.4.C.*, p. 2.

26 In this context it is believed that 'Cymraeg' (Welsh) refers to news about Wales and Welsh affairs, since the majority of the content on *Newyddion Saith*, with the exception of some interviews, would be in Welsh.

27 The remainder of the respondents for the questions on the news coverage did not declare an opinion.

28 S4CC, *Adroddiad Grŵp Cyfryngau Torfol Cymdeithas yr Iaith Gymraeg ar S.4.C*, p. 4.

29 The remainder of the respondents for the questions on drama series did not declare an opinion.

30 Discussion of these questionable figures can be found in Chapter 3, pp. 125–9.

31 S4CC, *Cofnodion pedwerydd cyfarfod a deugain Awdurdod Sianel Pedwar Cymru*, 6 January 1984, p. 2.

32 S4CC, *Adroddiad y Cyfarwyddwr i'r Awdurdod (Papur 1.84(4)) – Papur atodol i agenda pedwerydd cyfarfod a deugain Awdurdod Sianel Pedwar Cymru*, 6 January 1984, p. 1.

33 Research and Marketing Wales and the West Limited, 'Viewing and Listening in Wales – A survey with particular emphasis both on the appreciation of S4C (English and Welsh content) and on the use of the Welsh Language', Cardiff (June 1984), Section I.

34 BBC Wales and HTV Wales were joint first, both attracting 94 per cent of the Welsh speakers, while BBC2 attracted 88 per cent in a typical week.

35 'Viewing and Listening in Wales', Section IID3. BBC2 attracted 84 per cent; HTV Wales 79 per cent and BBC Wales 73 per cent. These figures seem peculiar as they show that BBC2 was the favourite channel of non-Welsh speakers. No doubt this picture was obtained due to the survey specifically asking who was watching HTV Wales and BBC Wales, rather than who was watching the BBC or ITV. As a result these figures exclude those viewers who lived close to the English border who watched those programmes broadcast on BBC1 West, BBC1 North, HTV West and Granada.

36 'Viewing and Listening in Wales', Section IID.10.

37 'Viewing and Listening in Wales', Section IID.7.

38 'Viewing and Listening in Wales', Section IID.7. The corresponding weekly figures were fluent speakers, 89 per cent; fairly good speakers, 64 per cent; and speakers with a little Welsh, 47 per cent. If this survey is compared to the HTV survey conducted a year earlier, then the percentage of fluent speakers who watched the channel on a weekly basis had risen from 65 per cent to 89 per cent. This increase runs counter to the pattern seen in the channel's viewing figures, which peaked in the early months of 1983, and had fallen significantly by 1984. The survey shows a pattern that was in significant contrast to BARB's viewing figures and proved the need for a more in-depth survey and that viewing figures were not a true reflection of the channel's popularity with its target audience.

39 S4CC, *Croeso i S4C* (internal production, S4C, 1 November 1982).

40 'Viewing and Listening in Wales', Section IID.14.

41 'Viewing and Listening in Wales', Section IID.15. In addition to the 34 per cent who watched more Welsh language programmes, 10 per cent of Welsh speakers claimed to watch fewer Welsh language programmes at the beginning of 1984 than the same period in 1983. The reasons for watching fewer programmes are in stark contrast to the improvement in quality reported by those watching more programmes, with 22 per cent of this cohort indicating that standards had deteriorated and a further 20 per cent stating that they believed the programmes were poor. Unfortunately the survey does not state what social class this 10 per cent belonged to, nor their age.

42 'Viewing and Listening in Wales', Section IID.9 Continued.

43 'Viewing and Listening in Wales', Section IIE.1.

44 Not all groups of Welsh-speaking viewers agreed, with individuals over the age of 55 far less likely to believe that the presentation was acceptable, demonstrating that the informal and popular nature was not appealing to everyone.

45 'Viewing and Listening in Wales', Section IIE.1.

46 'Viewing and Listening in Wales', Section IIE.3.

47 'Viewing and Listening in Wales', Section IIE.3.

48 Looking at the composite figures showing how many respondents watched one or more times during the week gives a much more promising figure of 64 per cent of Welsh speakers.

49 'Viewing and Listening in Wales', Section IIE.6.1.

50 'Viewing and Listening in Wales', Section IIE.6.1. If 'broadly entertaining' is also included, this figure would jump to 93 per cent.
51 *Hel Straeon* (1987–93); *Heno* (1993–2003; 2012–present), *Prynhawn Da* (2003–5; 2012–present), *Wedi 7* (2003–12) and *Wedi 3* (2005–12).
52 'Viewing and Listening in Wales', Section IIE.6.2. As with the figures for *Newyddion Saith*, this figure jumped to 96 per cent in the 'broadly entertaining' category in the analysis.
53 'Viewing and Listening in Wales', Section IIE.7.1.
54 'Viewing and Listening in Wales', Section IIE.9. Single dramas received 36 per cent of the vote, while comedy and documentaries came in joint second place with 26 per cent each; 16 per cent of respondents indicated that they wished to see more films on the channel. This showed a slightly different pattern to Cymdeithas yr Iaith's survey, which showed that there was no consensus on increasing the provision of drama series.
55 S4CC, *Cofnodion nawfed cyfarfod a deugain Awdurdod Sianel Pedwar Cymru*, 7–8 June 1984, p. 3.
56 'Viewing and Listening in Wales', Sections IIF and IIC.4.
57 'Viewing and Listening in Wales', Section IIE.10.
58 'Viewing and Listening in Wales', Section IIE.10; 21 per cent of respondents noted that they would like to see more Welsh programmes than English, with 20 per cent wanting more variety.
59 'Viewing and Listening in Wales', Section IIE.10, Table 10.
60 'Viewing and Listening in Wales', Section IIC.1, Table 6.
61 'Viewing and Listening in Wales', Section IID.8; 18 per cent of Welsh speakers disagreed, because they wanted to see Welsh on more than one channel, with only 9 per cent of non-Welsh speakers expressing a desire to see the same.
62 S4CC, *Cofnodion cyfarfod hanner cant a phedwar Awdurdod Sianel Pedwar Cymru*, 9 November 1984, p. 2.
63 S4CC, *Cofnodion cyfarfod hanner cant a phump Awdurdod Sianel Pedwar Cymru*, 6–7 December 1984, p. 3; equally encouraging remarks were made by the Home Secretary, Leon Brittan MP, in his address to the Cardiff Business Club on 7 January 1985, in which he noted that the comments received by him about S4C were favourable and that the channel's overseas sales were promising. S4CC, *Cofnodion cyfarfod hanner cant a chwech Awdurdod Sianel Pedwar Cymru*, 10 January 1985, p. 2.
64 S4CC, *Cofnodion cyfarfod hanner cant a chwech Awdurdod Sianel Pedwar Cymru*, p. 2.
65 S4CC, *Letter from Quentin Thomas of the Home Office to Owen Edwards, 26 March 1985 – Papur atodol i Agenda cyfarfod hanner cant a naw Awdurdod Sianel Pedwar Cymru*, 12 April 1985.
66 S4CC, *Letter from Quentin Thomas of the Home Office to Owen Edwards*. This was the plan favoured by the Broadcasting Council because it was concerned that conducting an open review could lead to bitter discussions. BBC Written Archive Centre, *Minutes of the 363rd meeting of the Council held at the University College of Wales, Aberystwyth on Friday 19th April 1985*, pp. 6–7.

67 S4CC, *Draft reply to the Home Office letter of 26 March 1985 – Papur atodol i Agenda cyfarfod hanner cant a naw Awdurdod Sianel Pedwar Cymru*, 12 April 1985, p. 1.
68 S4CC, *Cofnodion trigeinfed cyfarfod Awdurdod Sianel Pedwar Cymru*, 10 May 1985, p. 1.
69 ITA/IBA/Cable Authority archive, Bournemouth University, 3997019, RK/6/53, unknown author, *News Release – Review of the Fourth Channel in Wales*, 23 August 1985.
70 S4CC, *Cofnodion cyfarfod hanner cant a wyth Awdurdod Sianel Pedwar Cymru*, 8 March 1985, p. 2. A report on the intention of the WCC was received in this authority meeting.
71 WCC, *Watching S4C: the case for consumer representation for the Fourth Channel in Wales: The Welsh Consumer Council's evidence to the Home Office review of the Fourth Channel in Wales*, October 1985.
72 *Watching S4C*, p. 1.
73 It must be remembered that the Broadcasting Act did not require the channel to form an independent consultative regime, although particular emphasis was placed on the fields of education and religion. As such the channel had its own independent advisory committees in these areas as well as an additional committee on charitable appeals.
74 *Watching S4C*, p. 2.
75 *Watching S4C*, pp. 6–14.
76 *Watching S4C*, p. 6.
77 *Watching S4C*, p. 6.
78 *Watching S4C*, p. 7.
79 *Watching S4C*, p. 9.
80 *Watching S4C*, p. 10.
81 *Watching S4C*, p. 10.
82 *Watching S4C*, p. 12.
83 *Watching S4C*, p. 10.
84 S4CC, *Minutes of the joint meeting of the Broadcasting Council of Wales and S4C*, 15 March 1985, p. 3.
85 S4CC, *Minutes of the joint meeting of the Broadcasting Council of Wales and S4C*, p. 3.
86 S4CC, *Minutes of the joint meeting of the Broadcasting Council of Wales and S4C*, p. 3.
87 S4CC, *Minutes of the joint meeting of the Broadcasting Council of Wales and S4C*, pp. 3–4.
88 Dr Jamie Medhurst Personal Collection (JMPC), IBA Collection, *Minutes of the 175th Meeting of the Advisory Committee for Wales*, 27 September 1985, p. 5.
89 IBA Collection, *Minutes of the 175th Meeting of the Advisory Committee for Wales*, p. 5.
90 IBA Collection, *Minutes of the 175th Meeting of the Advisory Committee for Wales*, p. 5.
91 S4CC, *Llythyr oddi wrth Christopher Scoble at Owen Edwards, 20 Rhagfyr 1985 – Papur atodol i Agenda degfed cyfarfod a thrigain Awdurdod Sianel Pedwar Cymru*, 10 January 1986.
92 S4CC, *Llythyr oddi wrth Christopher Scoble at Owen Edwards.*

93 S4CC, *A Consultative Committee for the WFCA (Draft for Discussion) – Papur atodol i Agenda degfed cyfarfod a thrigain Awdurdod Sianel Pedwar Cymru*, 10 January 1986, p. 1.
94 S4CC, *Cofnodion degfed cyfarfod a thrigain Awdurdod Sianel Pedwar Cymru*, 10 January 1986, p. 3.
95 S4CC, *A Consultative Committee for the WFCA (Draft for Discussion)*, p. 3.
96 S4CC, *Adolygiad S4C, Tystiolaeth i'r Swyddfa Gartref (Drafft – Papur 11.85(2)) – Papur atodol i Agenda seithfed cyfarfod a thrigain Awdurdod Sianel Pedwar Cymru*, 7–8 November 1985.
97 S4CC, *Adolygiad S4C, Tystiolaeth i'r Swyddfa Gartref*, pp. 3–4.
98 S4CC, *Adolygiad S4C, Tystiolaeth i'r Swyddfa Gartref*, p. 1.
99 S4CC, *Adolygiad S4C, Tystiolaeth i'r Swyddfa Gartref*, pp. 1–2.
100 S4CC, *Adolygiad S4C, Tystiolaeth i'r Swyddfa Gartref*, p. 2.
101 S4CC, *Adolygiad S4C, Tystiolaeth i'r Swyddfa Gartref*, p. 5.
102 S4CC, *Adolygiad S4C, Tystiolaeth i'r Swyddfa Gartref*, p. 6.
103 S4CC, *BBC Response to the Home Office request for views on the continuation of S4C – Papur atodol i Agenda seithfed cyfarfod a thrigain Awdurdod Sianel Pedwar Cymru*, 7–8 November 1985, p. 1.
104 S4CC, *BBC Response to the Home Office request for views on the continuation of S4C*, p. 2.
105 S4CC, *BBC Response to the Home Office request for views on the continuation of S4C*, p. 3; S4CC, Llythyr Glyn Tegai Hughes at Tom Hooson, 15 May 1985.
106 S4CC, *Summary of Broadcasters' Comments (Annex C) – Papurau atodol i Agenda degfed cyfarfod a thrigain Awdurdod Sianel Pedwar Cymru*, 10 January 1986.
107 ITA/IBA/Cable Authority archive, Bournemouth University, 3997019, RK/6/28, *IBA Submission to the Home Office on the Fourth Channel in Wales*, p. 1.
108 *IBA Submission to the Home Office on the Fourth Channel in Wales*, p. 1.
109 *IBA Submission to the Home Office on the Fourth Channel in Wales*, p. 5.
110 *IBA Submission to the Home Office on the Fourth Channel in Wales*, p. 2.
111 Yorkshire Television noted in its evidence that the company had not received any compensation following its contribution of £1.5 million towards S4C's costs since the company had not made enough profit to secure a refund. S4CC, *Summary of Broadcasters' Comments (Annex C)*, p. 2.
112 *IBA Submission to the Home Office on the Fourth Channel in Wales*, p. 2.
113 S4CC, *Summary of Broadcasters' Comments (Annex C)*, p. 1.
114 This was a concern shared by S4C and C4 as demonstrated in their evidence to the Peacock Committee. S4C was convinced that radical changes to the funding patterns of the broadcasting systems in the UK would adversely affect a minority service such as S4C, which operated on the financial margins of two regimes, since only a small percentage of ITV companies' funding was given to S4C and only a small percentage of the BBC's money was used to produce Welsh language programmes. Because of its experiences with *Sbec*, the channel believed that there was not much additional advertising money available in the system, and so rather than increase advertising spend, it was thought that advertisers would shift their loyalty from one channel to another and, as a result, money would be spread thinly. Such a situation would be

very unfavourable for S4C as two of the channel's sources of funding, namely the 10 'free' hours provided by the BBC and the money from the ITV system coming through the IBA, would be under threat. S4CC, *Committee on Financing the BBC, WFCA Response to an invitation to submit evidence (draft) – Papur atodol i Agenda trydydd cyfarfod a thrigain Awdurdod Sianel Pedwar Cymru*, 11–12 July 1985.

115 S4CC, *Committee on Financing the BBC, WFCA Response to an invitation to submit evidence (draft).*

116 ITA/IBA/Cable Authority archive, Bournemouth University, 3997019, RK/6/32, unknown author, *Review of the Fourth Television Channel in Wales – The Views of the IBA's Advisory Committee for Wales*, p. 2.

117 Unknown author, *Review of the Fourth Television Channel in Wales – The Views of the IBA's Advisory Committee for Wales*, p. 3.

118 ITA/IBA/Cable Authority archive, Bournemouth University, 3997016, RK/6/38, Ron Wordley, *The Fourth Channel in Wales, Comments to the Home Office by HTV Limited*, p. 2.

119 Wordley, *The Fourth Channel in Wales, Comments to the Home Office by HTV Limited*, p. 2. It appears that S4C's 1984–5 annual report supports Ron Wordley's statement: the average cost per hour of HTV programming for that year was £38,459 and that of independent producers was £38,108 per hour. However, an analysis of the genres produced within those averages is not included in this report. WFCA, *Annual Report and Accounts, 1984–85* (Caerdydd, 1985), p. 6.

120 Wordley, *The Fourth Channel in Wales, Comments to the Home Office by HTV Limited*, p. 2.

121 Wordley, *The Fourth Channel in Wales, Comments to the Home Office by HTV Limited*, pp. 2–3.

122 There was a sharp response to this statement amongst S4C staff, and a concern that it would damage the channel's reputation. S4CC, *Cofnodion degfed cyfarfod a thrigain Awdurdod Sianel Pedwar Cymru*, 10 January 1986, p. 2.

123 Wordley, *The Fourth Channel in Wales, Comments to the Home Office by HTV Limited*, p. 3. This statement does not refer to international sales only but the programmes sold to the rest of the ITV network too.

124 Wordley, *The Fourth Channel in Wales, Comments to the Home Office by HTV Limited*, p. 4.

125 Wordley, *The Fourth Channel in Wales, Comments to the Home Office by HTV Limited*, p. 4. There is also a similar statement in S4C's evidence to the Home Office, but one of the early drafts of the document notes that the cost, when only Welsh speakers are calculated, exceeded £300 per head.

126 Wordley, *The Fourth Channel in Wales, Comments to the Home Office by HTV Limited*, p. 4.

127 ITA/IBA/Cable Authority archive, Bournemouth University, 3997016, RK/6/28, William Brown and Alex Mair, *Memorandum from Scottish Television plc and Grampian Television plc – The Fourth Channel in Wales.*

128 *Memorandum from Scottish Television plc and Grampian Television plc.*

129 The other organisations were: Trustees of the Bethesda Congregational Chapel, National Eisteddfod, Welsh Council of the CBI, Parents for Welsh Medium

Education, Dyffryn Ogwen Cultural Society, Ystalyfera Free Church Council, Mudiad Ysgolion Meithrin, Mudiad Ysgolion Meithrin's West Glamorgan Branch, Welsh Arts Council, Welsh Joint Education Committee, Carmarthen branch of Plaid Cymru, Welsh Film Board, Welsh Consumer Council, Colwyn Bay Society, Welsh Institute of Public Relations, The Association for Film and Television in the Celtic Countries, Jerusalem Welsh Presbyterian Church, National Foundation for Educational Research in England and Wales, Wern Independent Church, Interdenominational Welsh-language Committee (Arfon division), the Pwllheli, Bethesda, Abersoch, Ystalyfera, Bae Colwyn, Blaenau Ffestiniog, Chwilog, Llanfyllin, Cricieth, Waunfawr, Mynytho, Trefor and Golan branches of Merched y Wawr, Pontypool Retired Men's Society and the Welsh Office.

130 S4CC, *Review of S4C – Table of Comments Received (Annex B) – Papurau atodol i Agenda degfed cyfarfod a thrigain Awdurdod Sianel Pedwar Cymru*, 10 January 1986.

131 S4CC, *Review of arrangements for the Fourth Channel in Wales – Papurau atodol i Agenda degfed cyfarfod a thrigain Awdurdod Sianel Pedwar Cymru*, 10 January 1986, p. 2.

132 S4CC, *Summary of comments from those against present arrangements (Annex D) – Papurau atodol i Agenda degfed cyfarfod a thrigain Awdurdod Sianel Pedwar Cymru*, 10 January 1986.

133 S4CC, *Summary of comments from those against present arrangements.*

134 S4CC, *Review of arrangements for the Fourth Channel in Wales*, p. 3.

135 S4CC, *Review of arrangements for the Fourth Channel in Wales*, p. 4.

136 S4CC, *Review of arrangements for the Fourth Channel in Wales*, p. 4.

137 *Hansard*, House of Commons, 13 December 1985, col. 796–7.

138 BBC Wales Archive, Cardiff, *Mr John Howard Davies – biog*, S4C File (3835).

Conclusion

1 See chair of C4 Edmund Dell's eloquent record of the difficult relationship between the IBA and C4 and Lord Thomson, chair of the IBA's defence of the authority's activities in Peter Catterall (ed.), *The Making of Channel 4* (London, 1999), pp. 1–52.

2 This was again at odds with C4's experience, since the IBA decided on the full extent of the channel's original remit and authored and published its programme policy statement in 1980.

3 The number of independent producers commissioned were as follows, 1982–3: 33; 1983–4: 37; 1984–5: 38; 1985–6: 36.

4 '[M]aen nhw wedi ymddwyn yn gwbl anrhydeddus mae'n rhaid i mi ddweud hyn, y llywodraeth, byth ers i ni gael y fuddugoliaeth hon, maen nhw wedi bod yn hael ac yn barod i fynd bob cam o'r ffordd y gallen nhw i sicrhau bod yna lwyddiant i'r sianel Gymraeg'; NSSAW, *Newyddion Saith*, BBC Cymru Wales production, broadcast on S4C, 1 November 1982. Unless otherwise noted, translations are those of the author.

5 Author's interview with Chris Grace, Cardiff, 29 November 2010.

6 Other commentators have criticised the lack of discussion surrounding S4C in the years prior to 2010. Unknown author, '"Bloated" S4C "must think small" says leading producer', 23 November 2010, *www.bbc.co.uk/news/uk-wales-11821971* (accessed

November 2010); Geraint Talfan Davies, 'Skewering of S4C carries wider lessons (part 1)', 4 November 2010, *www.clickonwales.org/2010/11/skewering-of-s4c-carries-wider-lessons/* (accessed November 2010); Gwion Owain, 'S4C's "too big to fail" problem', 13 July 2010, *www.clickonwales.org/2010/07/s4c's-'too-big-to-fail'-problem/* (accessed November 2010).

7 Euryn Ogwen Williams, *Building an S4C for the future* (2018), *https://assets.publishing.service.gov.uk/government/uploads/system/uploads/attachment_data/file/695964/Building_an_S4C_for_the_Future_English_Accessible.pdf* (accessed 11 January 2022).

Appendix
Members of the Welsh Fourth Channel Authority (1981–1985)

Sir Goronwy Daniel *Chair*	January 1981–March 1986
Dr Glyn Tegai Hughes	January 1981–January 1987
Eleri Wynne Jones	February 1984– November 1990
Professor Huw Morris-Jones	January 1981–March 1982
D. Ken Jones	January 1981–January 1984
Gwilym Peregrine	August 1982–December 1989
Rev. Dr Alwyn Roberts	January 1981–December 1986

Bibliography

Manuscripts and collections

BBC Cymru Wales Archive (BBC Wales Record Centre), Cardiff
Fourth Channel (File 3666)
S4C (File 3835)
S4C, 1981–7 (File 3573)
Working Papers – The setting up of S4C (File 3365)

BBC Written Archive Centre, Caversham
Broadcasting Council of Wales Minutes (1979–85)

Dr Glyn Tegai Hughes Personal Collection (copies sent to the author)
Welsh Fourth Channel Authority Minutes, January–June 1981

Dr Jamie Medhurst Personal Collection (borrowed by the author)
Independent Broadcasting Authority Welsh Committee Minutes (1972–90)
Independent Television Authority Welsh Committee Minutes (1969–72)

IBA, ITA and Cable Authority Archive, Bournemouth University
Advisory Committee for Wales – S4C Minutes/Agenda (Box 3997016)
S4C – Home Office Review (Box 3997019)
The Welsh Fourth Channel Authority: Finance (Box 3997098)
Welsh Fourth Channel Finances and the Question of Levy Relief (Box 3997098)

National Archives, Kew
Conclusions of a Meeting of the Cabinet, 11 June 1980 (CAB/128/68/9)
Conclusions of a Meeting of the Cabinet, 7 August 1980 (CAB/128/67/23)

National Library of Wales
Angharad Tomos Collection – Speeches and Articles 1979–83 (A/1)
Sir Goronwy Daniel Collection – Broadcasting in Wales, 1970–85 (Box 3)

Gwynfor Evans Collection – General Correspondence (G1/134); Welsh Channel Campaign (M1/5); University of Wales Broadcasting Committee 1970–2 (M1/7); S4C (M2/10); Television and Radio (P1/80); Press and Broadcasting (P1/88); Gwynfor Evans's campaign for S4C (P1/89)

Parliamentary Archives, Westminster

Broadcasting Bill, 2961 (London, 1980)

Hansard, House of Commons (1979–85)

Hansard, House of Lords (1979–85)

Independent Broadcasting Authority Act 1979, Chapter 35 (London, 1979)

S4C Archive

Owen Edwards's speeches

Welsh Fourth Channel Authority Minutes and Papers (June 1981–January 1987)

Sir Goronwy Daniel Correspondence

Owen Edwards Correspondence

HTV Limited and The Welsh Fourth Channel Authority – Sianel 4 Cymru – Programme Sales Agreement, 27 May 1982

Interviews and correspondence

Interview with Wil Aaron, Llandwrog, 1 October 2010. Recording in author's possession

Interview with Huw Davies, Penarth, 21 July 2008. Recording in author's possession

Interview with Owen Edwards, Cardiff, 22 December 2006; 12 January 2007. Recording in author's possession

Interview with Chris Grace, Cardiff, 29 November 2010. Recording in author's possession

Interview with Dr Glyn Tegai Hughes, Tregynon, 31 January 2007. Recording in author's possession

Interview with Jeremy Isaacs, London, 3 December 2014. Recording in author's possession

Interview with Eleri Wynne Jones, Cardiff, 15 December 2014. Recording in author's possession

Interview with Geraint Stanley Jones, Cardiff, 10 November 2008. Recording in author's possession

Interview with Huw Jones, Llandwrog, 2 November 2010. Recording in author's possession

Interview with Robin Lyons, Cardiff, 15 October 2010. Recording in author's possession

Interview with Mair Owen, Cardiff, 19 January 2007. Recording in author's possession

Interview with Rev. Dr Alwyn Roberts, Tregarth, 24 May 2007. Recording in author's possession

Interview with Euryn Ogwen Williams, Cardiff, 26 January 2007; 23 February 2007; 24 April 2007. Recording in author's possession

Correspondence with Euryn Ogwen Williams, Cardiff, 9 November 2010; 3 December 2010. Copies in author's possession

Correspondence with Richard Owen, senior grants officer Welsh Books Council, 26 April 2010. Copy in author's possession

Parliamentary publications

Broadcasting Act 1980 (London, 1980)

Broadcasting Act 1981 (London, 1981)

Broadcasting Act 1990, Chapter 42 (London, 1990)

Broadcasting White Paper 1978, Cmnd. 7294 (London, 1978)

Report of the Committee on Broadcasting 1960. Cmnd. 1753 (London, 1962)

Report on the Committee on Broadcasting, 1960. Cmnd. 1819–1. Volume II, Appendix E, Memoranda submitted to the Committee (Papers 103–275) (London, 1962)

Report of the Committee on Broadcasting Coverage. Cmnd. 5774 (London, 1974)

Report of the Committee on the Future of Broadcasting – Appendices E–I: Research Papers Commissioned by the Committee, Cmnd. 6753–I (London, 1977)

Report of the Committee on the Future of Broadcasting. Cmnd. 6753 (London, 1977)

Report of the Working Party on the Welsh Fourth Channel Project (London, 1978)

Second Report from the Committee on Welsh Affairs: Broadcasting in the Welsh Language and the Implications for Welsh and Non-Welsh Speaking Viewers and Listeners, Volume I – Report and Proceedings (London, 1981)

Second Report from the Committee on Welsh Affairs: Broadcasting in the Welsh Language and the Implications for Welsh and Non-Welsh Speaking Viewers

and Listeners, Volume II – Minutes of Evidence and Appendices (London, 1981)

Second Report from the Committee on Welsh Affairs: Broadcasting in the Welsh Language and the Implications for Welsh and Non-Welsh Speaking Viewers and Listeners. Observations by the Secretary of State for the Home Department and the Secretary of State for Wales, the British Broadcasting Corporation, the Independent Broadcasting Authority and the Welsh Fourth Channel Authority. Cmnd. 8469 (London, 1981)

The Welsh Fourth Channel Authority, *Minutes of Evidence Wednesday 6 May 1981, Committee on Welsh Affairs* (London, 1981)

Official publications and reports

BBC/S4C, *Cytundeb Gweithredu S4C*, Cardiff (January 2013)

Butler, A., Bryan, J., and Roberts, A., *Effaith Economaidd S4C 2007–2010* (Cardiff, 2010)

Fuller-Love, N., *The Impact of S4C on Small Businesses in Wales* (Aberystwyth, 2001)

HTV Group, *Annual Report and Accounts 1981* (Cardiff, 1982)

HTV Group, *Annual Report and Accounts 1982* (Cardiff, 1983)

HTV Group, *Annual Report and Accounts 1983* (Cardiff, 1984)

HTV Group, *Annual Report and Accounts 1984* (Cardiff, 1985)

HTV Group, *Annual Report and Accounts 1985* (Cardiff, 1986)

OFCOM, *Small Screen: Big Debate – Recommendations to Government on the future of Public Service Media* (15 July 2021), *https://www.smallscreenbigdebate.co.uk/__data/assets/pdf_file/0023/221954/statement-future-of-public-service-media.pdf* (accessed 5 January 2022)

Research and Marketing Wales and the West Limited, 'Viewing and Listening in Wales – A survey with particular emphasis both on the appreciation of S4C (English and Welsh content) and on the use of the Welsh Language', Cardiff (June 1984)

S4C, *Annual Report and Statement of Accounts for the 12 month period to 31 March 2015* (Cardiff, 2015)

S4C, *Annual Report and Statement of Accounts for the 12 month period to 31 March 2021* (Carmarthen, 2021)

S4C/BBC, *Partnership, Funding and Accountability Agreement between the BBC and S4C* (November 2017)

Sianel Pedwar Cymru, *Sianel Pedwar Cymru: byd eang – international* (Cardiff, 1982)

Sianel Pedwar Cymru, *Memorandwm i'r Swyddfa Gartref gan Sianel Pedwar Cymru: Hydref 1985* (Cardiff, 1985)

Sianel Pedwar Cymru, *1982–87 teledu yng Nghymru – y diwydiant newydd* (Cardiff, 1987)

Sianel Pedwar Cymru, *Effaith Economaidd S4C ar Economi Cymru, 2002–2006* (Cardiff, 2007)

Welsh Consumer Council, *Watching S4C: the case for consumer representation for the Fourth Channel in Wales: The Welsh Consumer Council's evidence to the Home Office review of the Fourth Channel in Wales* (Cardiff, 1985)

Welsh Council of Labour, *Television in Wales – Report of a Labour Party Study Group* (January 1973)

Welsh Fourth Channel Authority, *Annual Report and Accounts, 1981–82* (Cardiff, 1982)

Welsh Fourth Channel Authority, *Annual Report and Accounts, 1982–83* (Cardiff, 1983)

Welsh Fourth Channel Authority, *Annual Report and Accounts,1983–84* (Cardiff, 1984)

Welsh Fourth Channel Authority, *Annual Report and Accounts, 1984–85* (Cardiff, 1985)

Welsh Fourth Channel Authority, *Annual Report and Accounts, 1985–86* (Cardiff, 1986)

Welsh Fourth Channel Authority, *Annual Report and Accounts, 1986–87* (Cardiff, 1987)

Williams, E. O., *Building an S4C for the future* (2018)

Williams, G., and Thomas, A. R., *A Feasibility Study aimed to develop techniques to study the relationship between the Welsh Language output of S4C, and any changes to the extended pattern of use, and in the linguistic characteristics of the language over time* (Bangor, 1985)

Pamphlets and lectures

Bryant, C., *Darlledu Cymru – Dyfodol Darlledu yng Nghymru* (October 2007)

Curran, Sir Charles, *The fourth television network: a question of priorities* (London, 1974)

Cymdeithas yr Iaith, *Darlledu yng Nghymru: cyfoethogi neu ddinistrio bywyd cenedlaethol?* (Aberystwyth, 1971)

Cymdeithas yr Iaith, *Teledu Cymru i Bobl Cymru* (Aberystwyth, 1977)

Cymdeithas yr Iaith, *S4C Pwy Dalodd Amdani? Hanes Ymgyrch Ddarlledu Cymdeithas yr Iaith – Argraffiad Cyntaf* (Aberystwyth, 1985)

Cymdeithas yr Iaith, *S4C Pwy Dalodd Amdani? Hanes Ymgyrch Ddarlledu Cymdeithas yr Iaith – Ail Argraffiad* (Aberystwyth, 2010)

Davies, A. T., *Darlledu a'r Genedl* (BBC Wales Annual Lecture, 1972)

Evans, G., *Byw neu Farw? Life or Death? The Struggle for the language and a Welsh T.V. Channel* (Plaid Cymru, 1980)

Evans, M., *Cloffi Rhwng Dau Feddwl; Darlledu Cymraeg Heddiw* (Cylch yr Iaith, 2004)

Evans, R., '"Softly Spoken Fanatics"? Teledu, Iaith a'r Wladwriaeth Brydeinig, 1949–1979', *Cynhadledd S4C: 25*, Aberystwyth (November 2007)

HTV Cymru, *Y Bedwaredd Sianel yng Nghymru: Datganiad gan HTV Cymru* (Llandysul, 1979)

Humphreys, E., *Diwylliant Cymru a'r Cyfryngau Torfol* (Aberystwyth, 1977)

Humphreys, E., *Bwrdd Datblygu Teledu Cymraeg* (Aberystwyth, 1979)

Isaacs, J., *Cheerio chaps, I'm off . . .* (Speech to Edinburgh Television Festival, 1987)

Lewis, S., *Tynged yr Iaith* (Darlith Flynyddol y BBC yng Nghymru, 1962)

Roberts, W., 'Teledu yng Nghymru', in *Y Chwedegau, Cyfres o Ddarlithoedd a draddodwyd ar Deledu Harlech* (Cardiff, 1970)

Williams, E. O., *Byw ynghanol chwyldro* (Darlith Cymru Heddiw, Eisteddfod Genedlaethol Bro Ogwr, 1998)

Books

Barlow, D., Mitchell, P., and O'Malley, T., *The Media in Wales: Voices of a Small Nation* (Cardiff, 2005)

Bevan, T., *Years on Air: Living with the BBC* (Talybont, 2004)

Blanchard, S. and Morley, D. (eds), *What's this Channel Four? An alternative report* (London, 1982)

Bonner, P., with Aston, L., *Independent Television in Britain: Volume 5. ITV and the IBA, 1981–92: The Old Relationship Changes* (Basingstoke, 1998)

Bonner, P., with Aston, L., *Independent Television in Britain: Volume 6. New Developments in Independent Television, 1981–92: Channel 4, TV-am, Cable and Satellite* (Basingstoke, 2003)

Brown, M., *A Licence to be Different: The Story of Channel 4* (London, 2007)

Catterall, P. (ed.), *The Making of Channel 4* (London, 1999)

Crickhowell, N., *Westminster, Wales and Water* (Cardiff, 1999)

Crisell, A., *An Introductory History of British Broadcasting*, 2nd edn (London, 1997)

Curran, J., and Seaton, J., *Power Without Responsibility: The Press and Broadcasting in Britain*, 6th edn (London, 2003)

Davies, G. T., *At Arm's Length* (Bridgend, 2008)

Davies, J., *Broadcasting and the BBC in Wales* (Cardiff, 1994)

Davies, J., *Hanes Cymru* (London, 2007)

Docherty, D., Morrison, D. E., and Tracey, M., *Keeping Faith? Channel 4 and its audience* (London, 1988)

Dunkerley, D., and Thompson, A., *Wales Today* (Cardiff, 1999)

Evans, D. G., *A history of Wales 1906–2000* (Cardiff, 2000)

Evans, G., *Bywyd Cymro* (Caernarfon, 1982)

Evans, G., *Fighting for Wales* (Talybont, 1991)

Evans, G., *The Fight for Welsh Freedom* (Talybont, 2000)

Evans, G., and Stephens, M., *For the Sake of Wales: The Memoirs of Gwynfor Evans* (Caernarfon, 1996)

Evans, J. G., *Devolution in Wales: claims and responses, 1937–1979* (Cardiff, 2006)

Evans, Rh., *Gwynfor: A Portrait of a Patriot* (Talybont, 2008)

Goodwin, P., *Television under the Tories: Broadcasting Policy 1979–1997* (London, 1997)

Hilmes, M. (gol.), *The Television History Book* (London, 2003)

Hannan, P., *Wales in Vision: the people and politics of television* (Llandysul, 1990)

Hobson, D., *Channel 4: The early years and the Jeremy Isaacs Legacy* (London, 2008)

Hume, I., and Pryce, W. T. R. (eds), *The Welsh and their Country* (Llandysul, 1986)

Isaacs, J., *Storm over 4: A Personal Account* (London, 1989)

Isaacs, J., *Look Me in the Eye* (London, 2006)

Jenkins, G., *Prif Weinidog Answyddogol Cymru: Cofiant Huw T. Edwards* (Talybont, 2007)

Jenkins, G. H., *A Concise History of Wales* (Cambridge, 2007)

Jenkins, G. H., and Williams, M. A. (eds), *'Let's Do Our Best for the Ancient Tongue': The Welsh Language in the Twentieth Century* (Cardiff, 2000)

Jones, A. G., *Press, Politics and Society: A History of Journalism in Wales* (Cardiff, 1993)

Jones, J. B., and Balsom, D. (eds), *The Road to the National Assembly for Wales* (Cardiff, 2000)

Jones, W. M., *Wyn Mel: Y Fi a Mistar Urdd a'r Cwmni Da* (Talybont, 2010)

Lambert, S., *Channel Four: Television with a Difference?* (London, 1982)
Lambie-Nairn, M., and Myerson, J., *Brand identity for television: with knobs on* (London, 1997)
Lucas, R., *The Voice of a Nation? A concise account of the BBC in Wales, 1923–1973* (Llandysul, 1981)
Medhurst, J., *A History of Independent Television in Wales* (Cardiff, 2010)
Meredith, D., *Pwy Fase'n Meddwl* (Llandysul, 2002)
Morgan, K. O., *Wales: Rebirth of a Nation, 1880–1980* (Oxford, 1981)
O'Malley, T., and Jones, J. (eds), *The Peacock Committee and UK Broadcasting Policy* (Basingstoke, 2009)
Owen, G., *Crych Dros Dro* (Caernarfon, 2003)
Phillips, D., *Trwy ddulliau chwyldro . . .? Hanes Cymdeithas yr Iaith Gymraeg 1962–1992* (Llandysul, 1998)
Potter, J., *Independent Television in Britain: Vol. 3, Politics and Control, 1968–1980* (Basingstoke, 1989)
Potter, J., *Independent Television in Britain: Vol. 4, Companies and Programmes, 1968–1980* (Basingstoke, 1990)
Roberts of Conwy, Rt. Hon. Lord, *Right from the Start: The Memoirs of Sir Wyn Roberts* (Cardiff, 2006)
Scannell, P., and Cardiff, D., *A Social History of British Broadcasting: Volume One 1922–1939, Serving the Nation* (Oxford, 1991)
Sendall, B., *Independent Television in Britain: Vol. 2, Expansion and Change, 1958–68* (Basingstoke, 1983)
Smith, A., *Television: an international history*, 2nd edn (Oxford, 1998)
Smith, D., *Wales: a question for history?* (Bridgend, 1999)
Smith, D., and Jones, G. E. (eds), *The People of Wales* (Llandysul, 1999)
Stephens, M. (ed.), *The Welsh Language Today: A New Revised Edition* (Llandysul, 1979)
Thomas, N., *The Welsh Extremist* (Talybont, 1971)
Thomas, S., *Dwy Genhedlaeth, Owen Edwards a Mari Emlyn* (Llandysul, 2003)
Tudur, G. (ed.), *Wyt Ti'n Cofio? Chwarter Canrif o Frwydr yr Iaith* (Talybont, 1989)
Whitelaw, W., *The Whitelaw Memoirs* (London, 1989)
Wigley, D., *O ddifri* (Caernarfon, 1992)
Williams, J. R., *Yr eiddoch yn gywir: atgofion* (Penygroes, 1990)
Williams, K., *Shadows and Substance: The Development of a Media Policy for Wales* (Llandysul, 1997)

Williams, K., *Get me a Murder a Day! A History of Mass Communication in Britain* (London, 1998)

Woodward, K., *Cleddyf ym Mrwydr yr Iaith? Y Bwrdd Ffilmiau Cymraeg* (Caerdydd, 2013)

Articles and essays

Bayly, S., 'The Welsh Perspective', *Sight and Sound*, 52/4 (autumn 1983), 244–7

Berry, D., 'Unearthing the Present: Television Drama in Wales', in S. Blandford (ed.), *Wales on Screen* (Bridgend, 2000), pp. 128–51

Bevan, D., 'The Mobilisation of cultural minorities: the case of Sianel Pedwar Cymru', *Media, Culture and Society*, 6 (1984), 103–17

Beynon, A., 'S4C – y misoedd cyntaf', in C. Ò Luain (ed.), *For a Celtic Future: a tribute to Alan Heusaff* (Dublin, 1983)

Briggs, Asa, 'Problems and Possibilities in the Writing of Broadcasting History', *Media, Culture and Society*, 2 (1980), 5–13

Bromley, M., and Williams, K., 'Owning the Welsh Voice', *Planet*, 135 (1999), 118–20

Comley, B., 'Heart of the Welsh Dragon', *Broadcast* (1987)

Davies, G. T., 'Broadcasting and the nation', *Planet*, 92 (1992), 16–25

Delamont, S., 'S4C and the grass roots? A review of past and future research on the mass media and the Welsh language', *Contemporary Wales*, 1 (1987)

Evans, G., 'Campaigning for Wales', *Radical Wales*, 18 (1988), 25–7

Evans, G., 'Hanes Twf Plaid Cymru 1925–1995', *Cof Cenedl 10: Ysgrifau ar Hanes Cymru* (Llandysul, 1995), pp. 153–84

Evans, I. G., '"Drunk on Hopes and Ideals": The Failure of Welsh Television, 1959–1963', *Llafur*, 7/2 (1997), 81–93

Evans, R. A., 'Brwydrau Darlledu'r Gorffennol', *Y Faner Newydd* (1999)

Howell, W. J., 'Britain's Fourth Television Channel and the Welsh Language Controversy', *Journal of Broadcasting and Electronic Media*, 25/2 (spring 1981), 123–37

Hudson, C., 'TV Film World Turned Upside Down', *Planet*, 63 (1987), 111–16

James, W., 'Frustrated Hopes', *Radical Wales*, 11 (1986), 11

Jones, H., 'Cultural Enterprise in Wales: the S4C experience', *Welsh Economic Review*, 12/2 (2000)

Lewis, E., 'Serving two cultures: Sianel Pedwar Cymru', *Airwaves* (1987–8), 20–1

Medhurst, J., 'Teledu Cymru: menter gyffrous neu breuddwyd ffôl?', *Cof Cenedl 17: Ysgrifau ar Hanes Cymru* (Llandysul, 2002), pp. 167–93

Medhurst, J., 'You say Minority, Sir, we say a Nation', *Welsh History Review*, 22/2 (2004), 302–32

Morgan, J., 'Welsh Language Television: a flowering of new talent', *The Listener* (1985)

Morris, N., 'Film and Broadcasting in Wales', *Books in Wales*, 1 (1995), 5–8

Osmond, J., 'Fight for the Future of Television in Wales', *Arcade*, 33, 5 March 1982, 4–6

Roberts, A., 'From a beleaguered city', *Planet*, 63 (1987), 9–13

Roberts, A., 'Some Political Implications of S4C', *Transactions of the Honourable Society of Cymmrodorion* (1989), 211–28

Roberts, B. M., 'Atgofion am ddyddiau cynnar teledu Cymraeg', *Y Faner Newydd*, 27 (2004)

Ryan, M., 'Blocking the Channels: TV and Film in Wales', in T. Curtis (ed.), *Wales: the imagined nation, studies in cultural and national identity* (Bridgend, 1986), pp. 183–96

Ryan, M., 'Channel No. Five?', *Radical Wales*, 11 (1986), 10–11

Smith, R., 'A mirror of Wales? Sound Broadcasting by the BBC's Welsh region 1937–1964', *Llafur*, 8/1 (2000), 131–43

Thomas, J., and Lewis, J., '"Coming out of a mid-life crisis"? The past, present and future audiences for Welsh Language Broadcasting', *Cyfrwng: Media Wales Journal*, 3 (2006), 7–40

Thomas, N., 'S4C and Europe', *Planet 66* (1987–8), 3–8

Thomas, N., 'Iaith y Sianel – Gweithredwch – angen am bolisi', *Golwg*, 3/21 (1991)

Thomas, N., 'Ten Years On: Sianel Pedwar Cymru in a comparative perspective', *Planet*, 96 (1992–3), 7–10

Thomas, N., 'Sianel Pedwar Cymru; the first years of Television in Welsh', *Briezh na Pobloù Europa* (1999), 627–34

Thomas, N., 'Tynged yr Iaith – forty years on', *Planet*, 152 (2002), 58–62

Williams, K., 'Crisis in Welsh Television', *Planet*, 96 (1992–3), 112–14

Williams, K., 'Misrepresenting Wales today: the broadcast media and the identity debate', *Planet*, 100 (1993), 40–3

Williams, K., 'Serving the nation? Deterioration in TV programming', *Planet*, 89 (1993), 111–12

Williams, K., 'And even the Welsh? The stereotyping of Wales in the Media', *Planet*, 104 (1994), 16–19

Williams, K., 'Whose life is it anyway? Representation and Welsh Television', *Planet*, 108/109 (1994–5), 16–19

Williams, K., 'Creating Myths and Writing Media History', *Planet*, 109 (1995), 12–15

Williams, K., 'Mind your language: minority language broadcasting', *Planet*, 112 (1995), 21–4

Williams, K., 'What is this Channel for? Kevin Williams discusses calls for an English-language Channel for Wales', *Planet*, 114 (1995–6), 22–5

Williams, K., 'Is there anybody out there? The audience for Welsh broadcasting', *Planet*, 118 (1996), 18–21

Williams, K., 'Sianel Pedwar Cymru – Corporate behemoth or cultural redeemer', *Planet*, 122 (1997), 59–62

Williams, K., 'An uncertain era: Welsh television, Broadcasting Policy and the National Assembly in a Multimedia world', *Contemporary Wales*, 18/1 (2006)

Williams, P., 'How green is the Sianel?', *Broadcast*, 1 March 1982, 16–20

Wright, T., and Hartley, J., 'Representations for the People? Television News, Plaid Cymru and Wales', in T. Curtis (ed.), *Wales: the imagined nation, studies in cultural and national identity* (Bridgend, 1986), pp. 201–23

Research dissertations

Black, C. E. S., 'The development of independent production in Wales and the role of S4C' (unpublished MSc Econ dissertation, University of Wales, Cardiff, 1988)

Hopkin, D. O., 'The Expectations of a Nation – Sianel Pedwar Cymru and Broadcasting in Wales' (unpublished BA dissertation, University of Wales, Cardiff, 1996)

Johnson, V. I., 'Dying for Television: the demands for and of Sianel Pedwar Cymru' (unpublished MSc Econ dissertation, University of Wales, Cardiff, 1988)

Jones, E. M., 'Astudiaeth o adwaith pobl Cymru i S4C yn ystod y cyfnod 1982–1990' (unpublished MPhil dissertation, University of Wales, Lampeter, 1995)

Jones, H. E., 'S4C: y gynulleidfa a cherddoriaeth. Astudiaeth o ddarpariaeth rhaglenni cerddorol ar gyfer cynulleidfa S4C, 1982–1996' (unpublished MA dissertation, University of Wales, Bangor, 1998)

Medhurst, J. L., 'Teledu Cymru – Teledu Mamon? Independent Television in Wales 1953–1963' (unpublished PhD dissertation, University of Wales, Aberystwyth, 2004)

Smith, S. A., 'Agweddau ar S4C: i ba raddau y bu S4C gyflawni'r disgwyliadau o safbwynt gwylwyr' (unpublished MA dissertation, University of Wales Swansea, 1999)

Williams, E. M., 'S4C: Hoff Sianel Plant Ysgol Brynhyfryd?' (unpublished MA dissertation, Prifysgol Cymru, Cardiff, 1987)

Woodward, K. E., 'Y cleddyf ym mrwydr yr iaith: Y Bwrdd Ffilmiau Cymraeg, 1970–1986' (unpublished PhD dissertation, University of Wales, Aberystwyth, 2009)

Newspapers and magazines

Arcade
Ariel
Barn
Brecon and Radnor Express
Broadcast
Caernarvon and Denbigh Herald
Cambrian News
Campaign
Carmarthen Journal
Carmarthen Times
Contact Cardiff
The County Times
Curiad
Y Cymro
Daily Express
Daily Mail
Daily Mirror
Daily Post
Daily Star
The Daily Telegraph
Eastern Daily Press
The Economist
Eco'r Wyddfa
Exeter Express and Echo
Y Faner
Film and TV Technician
The Financial Times
The Free Press
Glasgow Evening Times
Golwg
Greenock Telegraph
The Guardian
Gwent Gazette
Yr Herald Cymraeg
Herald Môn
Hereford Evening News
The Independent
The Irish Times
Kent Evening Post
Lol
The Listener
Llanelli Star
Llanw Llŷn
Lleu
Manchester Evening News
Media Week
Merthyr Express
The New York Times
North Wales Chronicle

North Wales Weekly News
The Observer
Oldham Evening Chronicle
Y Pentan
Radio Times
Rebecca
Sbec
The Scotsman
Screen International
Sheffield Morning Telegraph
Shropshire Star
Sight and Sound
South Wales Argus
South Wales Echo
South Wales Evening Post
The Stage and Television Today
Sulyn
The Sun
Sunday Mirror
The Sunday Telegraph
The Sunday Times
Television – Journal of the Television Society
Television Today
Television Weekly
Televisual
The Times
TV Times
TV World
Y Tyst
UK Press Gazettte
Video
Y Wawr
Welsh Nation
Western Daily Press
Western Mail
Wolverhampton Express and Star
Worcester Evening News
Yr Ysgub

Audio-visual material

A Fo Ben (Uned Hel Straeon Production, broadcast on S4C 1989)
Articles (BBC Radio Wales, 30 January 1981)
Y Byd ar Bedwar (ITV Wales Production, broadcast on S4C, 8 November 2010)
Croeso i S4C (internal production, S4C, 1 November 1982)
The Media Show (BBC Radio Four, 18 August 2010)
Newyddion Saith (BBC Cymru Wales Production, broadcast on S4C, 1 November 2010)
Noson Gwylwyr S4C (Tinopolis Production, broadcast on S4C, 25 October 2010)
Pethe – Rhaglen Goffa Owen Edwards (Cwmni Da Production, broadcast on S4C 28 September 2010)
Post Cyntaf (BBC Radio Cymru, 24 November 2010)
S4C yn 20 Mlwydd Oed (prod. Vaughan Hughes, Ffilmiau'r Bont, broadcast on S4C, 31 October 2002)

Teledu'r Cymry (BBC Cymru Production, broadcast on S4C, 30 October 2007 and 6 November 2007)

Wedi 7 – Rhaglen Goffa Owen Edwards (Tinopolis Production, broadcast on S4C, 31 August 2010)

Week in Week Out (BBC Wales, 26 October 2010)

Week in Week Out (BBC Wales, 30 October 2007)

Wythnos Gwilym Owen (BBC Radio Cymru, 15 March 2010)

Wythnos Gwilym Owen (BBC Radio Cymru, 25 October 2010)

Websites

www.bbc.co.uk

www.clickonwales.org

www.cymdeithas.org

www.golwg360.com

www.guardian.co.uk

www.ofcom.org.uk

www.independent.co.uk

www.nation.cymru

www.s4c.cymru

www.telegraph.co.uk

www.theconversation.com

www.walesoffice.gov.uk

www.walesonline.co.uk

Index

C